THE POLITICAL NOVEL

ITS DEVELOPMENT IN ENGLAND
AND IN AMERICA

THE RIGHT HONBLE. B. DISRAELI, M.P.
1852
from the picture by Sir Francis Grant, P.R.A.
at Hughenden

THE POLITICAL NOVEL

ITS DEVELOPMENT IN ENGLAND
AND IN AMERICA

BY

MORRIS EDMUND SPEARE

NEW YORK / RUSSELL & RUSSELL

1966

FIRST PUBLISHED IN 1924
REISSUED, 1966, BY RUSSELL & RUSSELL
A DIVISION OF ATHENEUM HOUSE, INC.
L.C. CATALOG CARD NO: 65—18834

PRINTED IN THE UNITED STATES OF AMERICA

To

MY WIFE

"Nullius boni jucunda possessio sine socio"

CONTENTS

vi CONTENTS

INTRODUCTORY REMARKS

MEN — so we have been told since the days of Plato — need not so much to be informed as to be reminded. In times like ours, when public matters have perforce been painted before the national consciousness in huge brush-strokes, it seems as necessary to revalue the significance of any literary type whose *raison-d'etre* lies altogether in the world of Anglo-Saxon political thought, as it has been essential for political historians to reconsider the status of political institutions both in England and upon the Continent because of the changes imposed by a World War. In the Representation of the People Act of 1918 England marked a great step in the transformation of her domestic government; the new status of Ireland, Egypt, India, and the Near East shows a vital modification of the old imperialistic policies. With this new revaluation has come, furthermore, a fresh curiosity. Orthodox opinions about certain Victorians have been challenged. This is observable in a definitive life of Lord Salisbury; a new emphasis is revealed by Mr. Lytton Strachey in his successful Life of Queen Victoria; reputations of English statesmen of the time of the Pitts, and Burke, and Walpole have been dissected anew; and, finally, a remarkable history of Benjamin Disraeli, Earl of Beaconsfield, has been brought to a conclusion. The "gentleman with a duster" who plied it so vigorously upon the mirrors of Downing Street in behalf of "noble polities and fair estates," must, we feel certain, have borrowed the duster from a Victorian closet. There only, could have come his old-fashioned dignity and morality.

In our own time the average man shows an almost extraordinary interest in matters political. The profound historical event which violently shattered the reputations of many living statesmen and forced sudden revaluations of nationality, has at the same time given a fresh importance to that part of literature which has dealt with public affairs. This, therefore, seems an appropriate occasion to tell the story of a literary form which was founded upon Politics, and which has never before been revealed. The Political Novel has now become definitely established as a *genre* in English letters. It has been made so not only by the importance which Benjamin Disraeli's political fortunes gave it (a relationship only now for the first time fully presented through the definitive biography of him), but also because of the number of distinguished writers both of England and America who have contributed to its development. It is a literary form which found its sources in that large parent body of English imaginative thought of an earlier century, a parent body which gave rise, in the nineteenth century, to so many diversified types of novel writing. In the twentieth century it has already challenged the attention of several of the most thoughtful English and American writers. A history of what novelists have already done must, perforce, energize the novelists of to-morrow to try their hands, in turn, at a peculiarly fascinating medium of expression, and one which is but in its first stages of development. For the critical reader a knowledge of this history will throw a new and interesting emphasis upon some of the classics of modern Anglo-Saxon literature. It will bring a fresh interpretation to George Meredith, will discover a new relationship to exist between Mr. H. G. Wells and Benjamin Disraeli, will give the works of Mrs. Humphry Ward and of George Eliot a modernity from which the most ardent exponents of the political rights of women may receive inspiration. It will shed a completely new light upon the author of *The Education of Henry Adams*, and upon the American Winston Churchill as well. It will, in short, offer a new viewpoint for the study of modern fiction.

What is a Political Novel? *It is a work of prose fiction which leans rather to "ideas" than to "emotions"; which deals rather with the machinery of law-making or with a theory about public conduct than with the merits of any given piece of legislation; and where the main purpose of the writer is party propaganda, public reform, or exposition of the lives of the personages who maintain government, or of the forces which constitute government. In this exposition the drawing-room is frequently used as a medium for presenting the inside life of politics.* This is my definition of a *genre* in English letters whose history I shall attempt to trace in the subsequent chapters.

It would be impossible to express here my thanks to the many friends, both those among English and American scholars, and among other lovers of literature who are not professional teachers, for the critical sympathy and keen interest which helped to bring this work to completion. I must not close this preface without showing a peculiar gratitude to Professor James Wilson Bright of The Johns Hopkins University. I owe much to Professor Arthur O. Lovejoy, the American philosopher, to Dr. G. Howard Maynadier of the English faculty of Harvard University, and to Professor Irving Babbitt of the same institution. My wife has by her persistent encouragement and unfailing judgement been a source of constant guidance and inspiration.

THE POLITICAL NOVEL

CHAPTER I

FIRST PRINCIPLES

THE Political Novel was born in the prismatic mind of
Benjamin Disraeli. It was a mind which unconsciously reflected peculiar legal and speculative tendencies, which seized
upon the intricacies of Chancellor of Exchequer accounts and
made him, according to the Liberal historian Herbert W. Paul,
"the best leader of the Opposition the House of Commons
ever saw," and yet one which poured itself out in amazing
kinds of romance. These romances have been called by the
poet Henley,[1] "one of the pleasantest facts in modern letters,"
by Edmund Gosse[2] the works of a minor classic, and have
caused Sir Leslie Stephen to bewail the fact that English
politics and the Prime Ministry degraded the brilliant literary
abilities of a promising English novelist.[3]

The life of Benjamin Disraeli, Earl of Beaconsfield, the man
and the statesman, has now been definitely appraised.[4] The
nature of his unique position in the history of literature still
remains unwritten. Political biography has revealed a fascinating figure of the Victorian era, — a meteor among plan-
ets. In literature, too, he now reveals himself a figure no
less unique. Anglo-Saxon neither by birth, heritage, nor by
erratic education, this strange dreamer and imperialist caught
the drift of the conventional life of Victorian society, and
transformed it, in the alembic of his imagination, into tales
which were not only like cinema pictures with gorgeous coloring, but into works which broke through established literary

I

traditions and which established a new form in English letters.
The place of Disraeli, the writer, has not yet been definitely
settled. The swing of the pendulum of literary criticism has
gone to the same extremes that praise and blame had gone, in
the years of passion and of controversy, in appraising Disraeli,
the man. While Henley thought all his novels "rare work," and
"caviare to the general," and a contemporary journal called
him "a novelist's novelist," [5] James Russell Lowell poured
vials of wrath upon Disraeli's *Young England* novels,[6] and in
recent years Viscount Bryce thought him "by literary vocation
best fitted for a journalist or a pamphleteer." [7] In time the
pendulum will find its centre, and when it does this fact will
have to be remembered, — that his works have influenced men
so far apart as George Bernard Shaw and Oscar Wilde, Mr.
Chesterton, Rudyard Kipling, and Mr. H. G. Wells. Disraeli's
verbal audacities are unquestionably reflected in the works of
Mr. Chesterton and of Bernard Shaw, the latter of whom
admits as much in the "Chemical Analysis" of *Cashel Byron's
Profession. The Picture of Dorian Gray* of Oscar Wilde owes
much to Disraeli's *Vivian Grey*, while between the youthful
Disraeli and the personality of Wilde there is revealed an
interesting comparison. Lying close to the thought of the
mature Disraeli is Mr. Wells with his Empire-building. How
much of common thought these two shared will be seen later,
in the chapter devoted to Mr. Wells's political novel. Between
Disraeli and Kipling there is, in spite of their unlike tastes and
talent, a remarkable resemblance. Both were aliens to the
English ruling classes, yet both are examples of the nineteenth
century Englishman who gave best expression to the idea of
English Imperialism. Disraeli looked to the Orient; for
Kipling, too, the voice of Great Britain was to be heard there.
Both have had the same conceptions of English greatness, and
both have revelled in great action. Both believed in a democ-
racy which was married to royalty. Both, in their utterances,

have honored the trappings of English order and English government upon the four corners of the earth. Kipling, the younger man and of the later generation, learned to express graphically the things about which Disraeli, the older man, had dreamed.

Of the place of Disraeli in establishing a definite literary *genre* there can be no differences of opinion. The importance that is his because of this fact is due to the number of distinguished novelists both of England and of America who have, since his establishment of the form, employed it. And it is altogether astonishing that, considering the great interest and importance of their total work, the fresh significance it lends and the new interpretation it offers to their literary value, as well as the rich medium this gives to the thought of the future novelist, nothing has thus far been said or written about this fascinating literary form. The Political Novel has challenged writers so far apart as Anthony Trollope and George Meredith, George Eliot, Mr. H. G. Wells, and Mrs. Humphry Ward. America eventually became aware of the existence of the *genre*, and of the two novels which the author of *The Degradation of the Democratic Dogma* wrote, the best was *Democracy*, Henry Adams's political novel. Mr. Winston Churchill then made two valuable contributions, adding thus to his fame as a writer and to his importance as an American political reformer. Others both before him and after him have appeared, but the most interesting of all of these and the most valuable has been Paul Leicester Ford's *The Honorable Peter Stirling*, inspired in large part by the life of a former president, Grover Cleveland.

What was the political novel as Benjamin Disraeli fashioned it? Out of what traditions was it born? To what social theories and political movements did it lend itself? What use have the novelists of the nineteenth century, both in England and in America, made of it? In this time of our own, and for the writer of to-morrow, what does it offer to the reading public? An

answer to some of these questions will shed not only a completely new light upon Benjamin Disraeli himself, but will
help us also to revalue the works of some of our greatest
novelists, — of George Meredith no less than of George Eliot,
of Mrs. Humphry Ward and also of Mr. Wells. A study of
the political novels of these writers will furnish us with the
means of a new interpretation of the imaginative work of Henry
Adams, and give him a new importance in the history of
American novel-writing. It will contribute an added flavor to
our appreciation of the historical romancer, Mr. Winston
Churchill, and present an unexpected and interesting relationship which he bears to Henry Adams. In a world so politically
conscious as ours is, there is the promise of a new zest and
fascination in novels otherwise well known, if we can approach
them again from a new angle, — if we can appraise them, and
their authors, not merely with principles and standards
fashioned out of a world of make-believe, but with criteria
that are of the world of reality. The political novel is a form
which challenges the ripened powers of a novelist. Mrs.
Humphry Ward, speaking in her Autobiography of the general
class into which this *genre* falls, declares that this was the most
difficult of all forms to master, and confesses that it was the
most tempting of all forms to her when she became a matured
artist.[8] When a writer of no less importance than Shakespeare
desired to portray the motive of great personal ambition he
entered the field of politics for his material, and gave us
Macbeth, and Claudius in *Hamlet*, his two greatest tragedies,
and *Julius Caesar*, his greatest historical play. The political
novel is a form which offers an unusual flexibility of treatment
of one's characters and ideas, and is at the same time one that
permits writers of widely varying qualities to express themselves by means of it. It was a vehicle for Benjamin Disraeli,
a man of no serious literary education, one who was a law
unto himself in public life, and whose complete ignoring of

'the laws of the game' in novel-writing was at all possible because he had a strong artistic sense which seized upon the things which he believed his readers would like, intuitively. It was a vehicle also for so conscious and so natural an artist, one of such sustained and careful literary expression, as George Meredith.

The one frank and deliberate attempt which has been made to discuss the political novel as a definite *genre* among the various kinds of fiction of the nineteenth century, is that of Sir A. W. Ward in the Cambridge History of English Literature, and it leads us nowhere.[9] Three pages of discussion about the religious and political truisms which mark Disraeli's life hardly do justice to one who founded a *genre* in English letters; other writers of the nineteenth century, and among these some of the greatest, who contributed a score of political novels, Dr. Ward altogether ignores.

Ours therefore must be the task of making here a new approach to a group of distinguished novelists. We are to present, for the first time, a guide to a free literary form which has tempted thus far too few brilliant writers but which must, with time and with appreciation of the significance of the *genre*, challenge many others, and those among the best on both sides of the Atlantic. A complete understanding of what the writers who used the form did in their own time with the material which lay around them, will suggest what the great political novel which has yet to be written may contain in the future.

With the single exception of Mr. Wells, all of our English political novelists were themselves Victorians, or threw into relief aspects of Victorian life. This applies with special force to Disraeli, the best exponent and the fullest of the political novel in modern letters. It is true of Anthony Trollope, and of the contributions made by George Eliot, George Meredith, and Mrs. Humphry Ward, except that the last two writers portrayed the England of Victoria's Diamond Jubilee rather than of her accession. Robert Plumer Ward's *De Vere*, which marked most completely the transition from purpose-novel to Disraeli's works, appeared a few years before Victoria became Queen of England. An age so distinguished by these writers, needs some preliminary definition and survey; its parliamentary system and its national character call for some introductory statement and speculation, if we are to grasp adequately the kind of world they portrayed and appraise fully the new tools they employed to portray it. "Every age," Bosanquet reminds us, "needs to be understood in terms of its own language."

The parliamentary system of England which existed at the accession of Queen Victoria had exhibited a stability of character which no other great European nation, either during the Napoleonic régime or in the two decades thereafter had shown. The passing of the Reform Act of 1832, though that widened considerably the right of suffrage among the middle classes, gave to several first-class cities the right to send members to Parliament, and disfranchised half a hundred boroughs, did not essentially change English political manners such as Robert Plumer Ward was familiar with in the years immediately preceding the Act. It took, as we know, the reforms of 1867 and of 1884, the Parliament Act of 1911, and the compendious measure of 1918 entitled the Representation of the People Act, before the complete character of parliamentary life was changed. The metamorphosis was completed in our own generation. The three great political novels which Disraeli wrote in the 40's describe a life which existed before the first Reform Bill was passed, and continue their stories to a period long before the second Reform Bill was devised. His last two novels still deal with a world before the seventies. His entire literary output, therefore, is not based upon anything like a

really democratized England. It was an England largely
under the old aristocratic régime, and one that was very
slowly taking its first steps in the direction of the new régime.
The fact that after 1832 government by party became more
highly developed, that the House of Lords ceased initiating
legislation and became gradually the revising and suspending
body, that government by Cabinet became increasingly important, did not decrease but rather increased the influence of
the nobility. The changes mentioned had no visible effect
upon the attitude of usual reverence with which the nobility
were held by the great mass of men; they did not diminish for
over thirty years the great influence which various peers,
through their social and economic powers, could exert upon
members of the House of Commons; they never reduced or
modified the veneration and deference which the English
masses had for their Queen, nor the belief that the Sovereign
was at the very apex of that pageant of English political life
and of society by which position she consecrated the entire
English scheme of things. To this very day the Crown is
universally popular in England; the prestige of titled classes
is no less to-day than it ever was; the House of Lords, overwhelmingly conservative, represents by that fact not only a
tremendously important class of landed gentry but proves also
that it is the guardian of a legendary sense of honor for all
classes, and that its opinions are most representative of the
Englishman's veneration for custom and his natural conservative temperament. All this, then, by way of proof that in
England there has been a greater stability of institutions, and
of the principles of government which have permitted less
variation in the tastes and habits of the English public, than
is to be found in any other nation of modern times.[10]

Here is the extraordinary fact of our nineteenth century.
An age which saw the stemming of a bloody tide in France
and the downfall of Napoleon after his power had swept over

Europe; which produced Metternich in Austria and the spread of Absolutism across almost the whole of Europe, and a consequent rebellion against it following with the break-up and the reconstruction of an untold number of nationalities amid confusion forever confounding; while civil war joined with wars of conquest in drawing nationals apart: in this age England alone, by slow but definite appeals to the constitutional processes of law, was able to meet quietly her unusual emergencies and to save uninterrupted the march of the mind. She grappled with the untold pauperism which followed upon the Napoleonic wars, she lived through the industrial and economic upheaval which was focused in the Chartist movement, she saw a transformation in scientific thought which revolutionized her industries and completely modified her public education; she met the demands for suffrage rights and political representation from enormous numbers of the working classes. These were granted, and transformed her into the greatest constitutional democracy of Europe. Without any of the violence such as characterized other nations, she was changed from a land of parochial interests to one of imperial dominion — the most widespreading in the world. All this she has accomplished by legal methods through the natural conservatism of thought and the peculiar veneration for custom which so strongly marks the English character.

With this axiom about the national psychology in mind, we may now lay down another beside it. In any general society, but in the English nation in particular, the influence of political institutions upon the ideas and customs of the people as a whole is of first rate significance. Hardly is a change in parliamentary life made before it is reflected in the ideas, the customs, the usages, of the general body politic. The government itself may change, the new law may be modified, but it is as certain as there is light which lingers for a considerable time after the sun has fallen below the horizon, that among the

masses of people the influence of the old political law, retained
as in Victorian England by the tenacity of the individual
conservatism of character and the hallowing of custom, will
stay on indefinitely in the lives of the people. This we may
call the political habit of the English nation. As the seat of
the power of government is broadened, and offers space to
more representatives of the general order, or as the dominions
over which the government forces function are widened, there
are required not only a larger number of secondary officials to
exercise the powers of the governing classes, but also a greater
number of interpreters, secondary agents, writers, by means
of whom the inspiration and the significance of the governors
may be transferred to the common mind everywhere. More
especially in early Victorian England, where the aristocratic
classes still retained the maximum governing force but where
popular agitation and economic crisis began seriously to challenge the rights of that force, champions of the landed proprietors and interpreters of the ancient customs were needed
to revive again those political habits of thought which had
been implanted in them earlier by the aristocracy, which they
had received from that aristocracy as wax receives impressions
from a sterner substance, but which, after 1832, was in danger
of becoming effaced, or at least changed to the disadvantage
of that once accepted authority. In England after 1832 two
things were essential to preserve the old régime: first, that the
people who were naturally respectful and unwilling to see
bloody violence force a change, should be made to retain as
long as possible their veneration for custom, to continue to
respect traditions even after 'the accident of 1832.' In short,
it was necessary·— from the viewpoint of the governing class
— that the old political habits of thought should not be changed,
but should rather be exercised the more vigorously in the indefinite future, in spite of the fact that the old day had gone
forever and the new day of Democracy was about to dawn.

Secondly, the nobility had to be made to see themselves as others saw them, in order that they might hasten to repair the breach before all was lost. Hence there was needed 'a mirror held up to Nature' which showed them off to themselves in their stupidities, their selfishness, their unwillingness to recognize the new and powerful industrial and social forces which had been born: a mirror which revealed a decayed church, frivolous youth possessed of no sense of their coming responsibilities, an artificial society where men and women lived under the most ignorant notions of the nature of the stirring forces abroad. These things Disraeli's novels accomplished. After that self-revelation, a vision was necessary to show the thoughtful youth what rôle might be theirs in the future, what character and strength were needed in them if they were to be in their turn the natural leaders of the whole people as their great forbears had been. This vision the political novels of Disraeli also presented.

The first half of the century found — as contribution from the Georges — the government of England in the hands of a limited number of families, who really formed by comparison with the great national body a vast aristocratic corporation wherein lay all political activity, properly so called. That number, limited we may say when compared with the vast population of England, though aristocratic by nature, by spirit, and by inheritance, was not a closed corporation. It was varied in the kinds of men who composed it, it was catholic and generous in its method of recruiting additions to its ranks, and, by comparison with other European nations which had been monarchies, it received and absorbed within its ranks men of all sorts of superiorities, with little thought given as to their origins or the avenues by which they reached their eminence. Then, as now, this open corporation, by the very fact that it was composed of many varied characters drawn from the multiform activities of life, assured an inevitable communicableness between the governing aristocracy and the great masses of the nation. It was possible then, as it is still more now,[11] to retain a firm hold upon the ideas and the conventions of the general citizenry largely through the fact that the aristocracy is so varied, represents so many interests, and is recruited from so many types of national prestige and excellence.

This nobility, in the first half of the nineteenth century, formed with the Crown the depositaries from which there sprang the political habits and customs that were generally to be found among the English people. They constituted the most important element in English parliamentary life. They represented the families whose members sat in the House of Lords, or who occupied those seats in the House of Commons which had not already been filled by members of the aristocracy with either their sons or with their hired representatives. In *Coningsby* the character of Rigby is an embodiment of this latter class. The Commons contained also, then, a considerable number of sons of titled families as well as many 'country gentlemen.' To this class of 'country gentlemen' belonged in general the so-called justices of the peace. Then the Bishops, many of whom held benefices which were equal to if not greater than the largest estates of the nobility, had also an enormous political influence. Members of the legal profession, in a country where law played so important and so honorable a part in public life, were to be found in considerable numbers in Parliament. After 1832 there was added to these several groups of the Commons already enumerated — the heirs-apparent to titles, the younger sons of the great families, the country squires, the hirelings of the nobility, and the lawyers — a considerable number of wealthy merchants and manufacturers, and eventually a small group of varied individuals who, like Disraeli himself, believed that a life of action was tantamount to a Parliamentary career, and who succeeded in convincing scattered constituencies which the Reform Bill had created, and which no member of the aristocracy still controlled, that they ought to be sent to Parliament. There were also later of course, varied 'interests' represented: such as the steamship interest, the financial interests. Outside the two houses, but with an influence upon the public which was immeasurable, were the large numbers of journalists and publicists exerting through party organs and the press generally the influence of this or of that group of men or of this or that party, upon constituencies which, as time went on, became more and more important to the ruling classes. Add to these the many thousands of public officials scattered throughout England whose livelihood was dependant upon 'standing in' with the ministers who were in power, and you see an enormous stratum lying over the whole of the nation upon which the ruling forces at the top of a pyramid were able to exert an impression on the millions of English subjects and citizens.

In a country with such stability as England showed in the 19th century, controlled at first by a single class of society which had no great concern about its pocketbook, which enjoyed much leisure, the tastes of whose members were as often gratified in Parliament as they could be at the Derby or in the hunt, there developed unique political ceremonials, a peculiar and idiomatic parliamentary language, formulae which designated the incidents of official life in a government controlled by a majority. A definite kind of oratory grew up well fitted for Parliamentary use, methods of address and even of personal appearance were encouraged, and these marked out the members of the governing bodies. These people formed a clique apart. Their common ideas developed party ties. Party ties grew tighter and more significant as competitive influences from without made themselves felt in the Chambers. Party spirit developed party discipline, which in turn had an effect upon the personal character of the repre-

sentative and even upon the members of his family. One fact
which still further distinguished the political *milieu* from every
other group of persons used by the novelists of the 19th century
was the nature of the motive which controlled all action.
Even among the journalists, the slashing-article writers, the
excise-tax gatherers, the most petty officials in the far corners
of the Empire, and those 'Tapers and Tadpoles' of politicians
among whom

> "Each soul was worth so much on 'Change,
> And marked, like sheep, with figures,"

there was an aura surrounding the political life, a thought
sometimes in them that they were a little greater, more important, than the dross of common humanity; a presumption
that because they held their places by living in the shadows
cast by the party then in power, they therefore shared in that
power, however dry and monotonous their daily tasks were.
The belief they had of their own importance — when they
were seen against the background of their neighbors, citizens
often far more valuable to the nation than they — produced
material which the novelist might use for poignant tragedy if
he had not more frequently chosen phases of this life for high
comedy, farce, and caricature. And if the expression of personal ambition in petty forms offered material to the political
novelist, of how much more importance was that motive when
seen dominating the great actors of the political stage! For
the good or for the evil of their country, ministers, chancellors,
and secretaries in high places sought in the public service the
largest and most satisfactory arena wherein they found outlet
for one of the profoundest motives in human nature — the
desire to govern others. When Shakespeare, master of all
hearts and springs of action, desired supreme expression of
great personal ambition, he entered the field of politics for his
material.

Here, then, was the kind of world which Victorian England offered to the political novelist. Benjamin Disraeli, who had travelled across every nook and corner of it during some fifty years of public service, and who could step from a desk filled with Chancellor of Exchequer accounts to weave the most glowing kind of romance, portrayed that world most perfectly. What his political novels, the product of his brilliant literary powers, did not cover in that world — a participant is not expected to report everything, and from every angle — was covered by the onlookers: Trollope, George Eliot, Mrs. Humphry Ward, and George Meredith.

Now that we have examined the stage upon which the actors were to be made to play their parts, we ought also, in order better to understand the unfolding of the plots later, to mark some of the technical difficulties which beset the political writer. There are several such difficulties. To the ordinary writer the great groups of more active participants in politics are usually too little known, to furnish him material for contemporary portraits of political manners, or of political psychology. Dickens may know his London, Hardy his Wessex, Eden Phillpotts his Dartmoor, George Eliot may know her classes of the midlands, but all these writers need to be no more than observers of these places; to be one with them in the community, or to be an active participant was not an essential. But the language of Downing Street, the jargon of Committee meetings, the interviews with the Crown, the scenes at great political dinners, the life of the great political clubs, could not even be observed; and by a layman for whom 'the political game' was a sort of higher algebra, they could not even be clearly imagined. If to the woman novelist of the Victorian era the whole of the inside life of the political arena, from the meetings at the Cosmopolitan Club or at Brooks's to the carefully guarded incidents in the official lives of the ministers of the Cabinet, was a closed door, the male professional novelist found these things no less difficult to penetrate. In the political world one had to know his material not as a reporter knows the facts which he has covered in an 'assignment,' nor even as some scholar probes and garners the fruits of his study, but rather as the fisherman knows the sea or the ploughman follows his furrow. To be able to wed politics to art and bring about a consummation where neither the first became tractarian or statistical nor the other too honey-sweet, required not only an imagination of a particularly high order, but a knowledge of material which had been gathered at first hand, with the accuracy which only a participant himself could possess. One had to be able to think in political formulae, to adorn his thoughts in the natural imagery of the political life. Then only could he interpret it intelligently and interestingly to the reader.

For every other known form of novel writing, as for the essay or narrative poem, countless experimenters had gone before and had charted the course for the newcomer. The novel in particular had many rigorous formalities left as heritage and guidance for the Victorian writer out of its historic past; to add other novels out of a newer or more modern period in history, or to garner one's material from the past and build upon that, the artist was able to revert to preceding models for his inspiration and his power. But here, in a *milieu* which no novelist before had ever penetrated, there was a form which no past practice and no predecessors could be of help to a new writer. In a completely new field, peopled by men and women who were in a class apart, and with customs and ideas which had to be interpreted carefully to the ordinary reader if he were to comprehend them, a writer had to steer his way through uncharted seas.

An outsider who attempted to apply the fruits of his study and the wealth of 'procedure' gained from working in some other literary field, to information about political life which

he had gained by chance or which he had acquired by actual
research, would inevitably betray himself. He might go too
far. He might take too many moves in the game too seriously.
He was dealing here with a class of no ordinary mortals, but
with singular human beings who were often accustomed to
consider states, parts of their own imperial kingdom, and even
nations, as if they were individuals; he had to gauge accurately
their speculations; their peculiar language of diplomacy had
to be made intelligible.   Knowing nothing about the inside
workings of party influence and party combinations, or about
the methods often adopted to spar for time or for gaining
a place of advantage, he would take every vigorous speech
upon what appeared to be a grave issue as a grave national
matter, when the man delivering it, and perhaps all on the
floor who heard it, had in mind merely an ingenious diplomatic stroke, couched in words and surrounded by sentiment
which would fall heavily upon foreign ears only.   Or he
might not take the game of politics seriously enough.   To
recognize upon the instant the evidence of a consuming ambition in the heart of a political leader for place, for great power
in a certain direction; to perceive a flame burning in the soul
of a public character for the applause of a listening and breath-
less Senate, or greater still, to know a man who is fighting for
a cause which he believes greater than himself and who would
read his own history in the eyes of his nation, is no small task
for a novelist.   The political game is played by no country
youths whose history one may read in the simple epitaphs
placed upon their tomb-stones; it is a game the most subtle,
the most varied of motive, the most complicated in effect that
is known in the range of all human activity.   It is clay not
unworthy of a potter like Shakespeare; and Shakespeare
produced no more fascinating historical figure in action than
Antony in *Julius Caesar*.
    Nor is the initiate, with a wealth of experience and insight

behind him, beset by less difficulties than the novice. The historical novel, whose form is the trunk of a tree from which this is an important offshoot, allows its writer an acknowledged purpose in his portrayals, and a range of character and of incident which is enormously vast and various, and which he may treat with extraordinary freedom. Carlyle said of the *Waverly Novels:* "These . . . have taught all men this truth, which looks like a truism and yet was as good as unknown to writers of history and others till so taught: that the bygone ages of the world were actually filled by living men, not by protocols, state-papers, controversies, and abstractions of men." We do not ask of Scott whether he depicted with absolute accuracy the personal life of Richard the Lion-hearted, or the minutiae of this or that famous battle, or whether he included all the phases of the institution of Feudalism, good, bad, and trivial. We do not require the reproduction of a past age where no single struggle — say, that between the forces of Paganism and Christianity — is given an undue importance, while other important facts are not mentioned. We ask only of the writer that the general forces of the period be placed before us; that the picture as a whole shall not violate the strictest historical sense: aside from that the historical novelist may wander how and where he pleases, provided only he stir our imagination and make some reality of men, of forces, of incidents, which we know only very vaguely or not at all. But how is it when we treat contemporary issues, events, and characters who live in the immediate present? or traditions which we inherit, or the party prejudice which we have been encouraged to share in, from our own generation? There are those among our readers who may be quite as familiar with these events as we are; their eyes then are not easily charmed nor their fancies quickly stirred by the metamorphoses which we, in the name of art, have been pleased to make. And as for the portrayal of contemporary characters, even if

we escape the charge of bad-taste by revealing those facts, or
that knowledge of the heart or the struggles of the conscience
which the intimacies of friendship and close daily contact may
permit, there is yet much that we have to falsify and weaken.
Edmond Scherer expresses a unanimous critical opinion when
he puts this objection in his own way: "L'attrait de cette
espèce de fiction devient évidemment assez vif lorsque l'ouvrage
est écrit par un homme qui a joué lui-même un rôle, et lorsque
les événements qu'il raconte et les personnages qu'il met en
scène sont contemporains . . . Le genre, en revanche, a un
inconvénient: les personnages sont trop près de nous pour
qu'il soit permis de leur conserver leurs noms ou même de les
produire d'une manière rigoureusement historique. Il est
évidemment impossible de faire parler et agir des morts tels
que Lord Melbourne ou M. Cobden, encore moins des vivants
tels que M. de Bismarck ou le cardinal Manning avec la liberté
dont usait Walter Scott à l'égard de Louis XI, de Marie Stuart
ou de Charles II. On est obligé d'atténuer leur personnalité,
de modifier leur caractère, de dénaturer leur physiognomie,
tranchons le mot, de fausser l'histoire dont on fait le cadre du
roman." [12]

The question as to how far an author may go in making use
of characters thus easily identifiable in real life is still an open
one and may, therefore, present a difficulty to any writer;
in the political novel, however, where the temptation to use
many who are of great public importance, and who may be
universally known in one degree or another, 'it becomes all
the more a truly vexing one. In English literature, since the
days of Swift and even before him, portraits of living men or
of contemporary personalities transparently employed and
boldly drawn for the purpose of caricature are not uncommon.
Writers and critics frequently cite in Victorian literature, the
practice of Charles Dickens who drew his mother in Mrs.
Nickleby, and his father who suggested to him two persons —

Mr. Micawber and William Dorrit. His own wife was presumably portrayed in Copperfield's child-wife, and Squeers was in real life one Shaw, a Yorkshire schoolmaster. He made Leigh Hunt the original of Harold Skimpole, and Walter Savage Landor the 'blustering squire' in *Bleak House.* There comes to our mind the cruel way in which Samuel Butler used members of his own family in *The Way of All Flesh.* And closer to our own time, too, there was Barrie who delineated his own mother in *Margaret Ogilvy.* Disraeli presumably filled his novels with men and women well-known, and his first publisher did not hesitate to 'puff' *Vivian Grey* on that score primarily to stir up contemporary society to buy the novel. "Everybody who is anybody is in it!" ran the advance notices. But the enigmatical author, from first work to last, denied that he had intended to portray particular persons. When the last novel of all appeared, Lord Rowton, Disraeli's secretary, relates how the queen sent a message to Disraeli requesting him that he supply her with a key to the important persons in *Endymion.* But the lady's curiosity was never satisfied: Disraeli replied that the characters were all imaginary.[13] Yet Colburn, his publisher, distributed keys to the characters of the early novels in advance of their publication, and Disraeli, in spite of all his denials, opens his famous political biography of Lord George Bentinck with a self-defensory statement justifying the practice of a writer's use of his contemporaries.[14] That fact itself is an admission from the author of the political novels published before the biography, and implies by corollary the nature of one of the difficulties the political novelist must face. Disraeli earned many enemies among his contemporaries for his use of them, not the least bitter of whom was Professor Goldwin Smith, who came from Oxford to Cornell University in America where he was a most distinguished teacher, and from whence, as late as 1905, he wrote to *The Nation* bitterly protesting against the portrait Disraeli drew of him in *Lothair* thirty-five years before.[15]   For so long can an author's act rankle!   Unfortunately, Professor Goldwin Smith had made an earlier protest, and that immediately after the appearance of the novel, and directly to Disraeli.

"In your *Lothair*," he said, "you introduce an Oxford professor, who is about to emigrate to America, and you describe him as a social parasite.   You well know that if you had ventured openly to accuse me of any social baseness, you would have had to answer for your words; but when sheltering yourself under the literary form of a work of fiction, you seek to traduce with impunity the social character of a political opponent, your expressions can touch no man's honour; they are the stingless insults of a coward."

Less than a fortnight after the publication of this letter in the English press, Longman, the publisher, wrote to Disraeli as follows:

"The Oxford professor's letter is doing its work well.   So much so that we shall print again as soon as I have your corrections." [16]

The axiomatic fact remains that great art prefers to deal not with easily identifiable personalities but with emblems, with allegories.   A work of literary art has for its end, to quote George Edward Woodberry's admirable definition, "to concentrate life and truth by the use of the imagination in examples that are finally interpreted by the mind, consciously or unconsciously, as universal symbols." [17]   A novelist who has set himself the work of embodying the national consciousness of his own time, and is thereby impelled to use living men and women for his basic characters, must needs have a singular faculty of creation and impersonation if his people, now turned into presumably fictitious heroes and heroines, are to be given importance in the mind of the reader who lives contemporaneously with the real characters.   Here, then, is a serious problem which presents itself to the political novelist who writes of his own time, and one which must be skillfully solved.

But suppose a writer by a supreme act of the imagination, softening down traits in contemporaries which do not lend themselves best to portrayal in the novel, and heightening others that help their portraiture vividly and successfully for the reader, is able to lay this particular ghost to the ground. There are others yet, no less important, that will rise up and haunt him. We deal here with a *genre* of the novel which, if excellently developed, must make its appeal to the reader not primarily as a social force but as an *intellectual* force. Dickens and Thackeray, in 19th century literature are, for example, essentially *social writers*. Their men and women, for the most part persons out of everyday life, may even be portrayed before us as monsters of caricature; as the embodiment, in what appears to be the form of a man or a woman, of some trick or trait which is extravagant and impossible to exist alone without some other qualities of mind or heart to tone them down, or to give them their proper proportion in a complete human life. Dickens filled his pages with such caricatures. Sam Weller, Dick Swiveller, Micawber, Quilp, Sairey Gamp, Captain Cuttle, Betsy Trotwood, and a host of others, are absurd enough and human enough to have appeared in the pages of *Punch*. Yet monsters as they all are, and extravagant as they seem, they live in our minds long after we have forgotten the plot in which they appeared; they seem to be creatures of flesh and blood, more true to our every-day life than are one half of our acquaintances. The *social writer* throws an air of common humanity about his creations; he deals with incidents that are not unusual to the daily lives of all of us; his streets, and homes, and schools, and interiors we have visited and have known for many years.

But the writer in the world of politics is not dealing with a common humanity. In the life of a modern nation, and particularly of the English nation with its genius for administration, everything ends, or at least is indirectly influenced by

what occurs, in the political arena. The acts of Downing
Street, put into force on the one hand by a million functionaries
who stand ready to do its bidding, and mirrored and guided
on the other hand by a horde of journalists and reviewers
whose opinions are felt in the farthest reaches of the kingdom,
pretty well encompass everything which in modern times
moulds the thought and character of a country. Mme. de
Staël uttered a vital truth when she said: "Political institutions alone can form the character of a nation." [18]   Her statement is particularly apt in its application to the English
character of the 19th century. The breaking up of the Old
Régime of the Georges, the adjustment of the New Régime,
which was created by the Reform Acts, to the Old Régime,
the introduction of science and its application to industrial
life, the transition from a parochial England to an imperialistic
Great Britain, carried in their wake stupendous changes, and
let loose influences upon the nation which gave expansion and
power to untold numbers of political characters. The game
of politics became always a more sophisticated, a more ingenious one to play, and therefore to report in a novel. By
the very reach and grasp which the *genre* of the political novel
possesses, it is the most embracing in its material of all other
novel types: it may not only record the complex machinery
of politics but, in looking out upon its world of men and
women, its writer may say with Lucretius: *Nihil humani a me
alienum puto*. Wars, industrial adventure, economic adjustment, commercial progress, diplomacy in foreign lands, social
experiences of every kind, education, art, science, discovery
and exploration, expansion and internal development — all
are grist for his mill, all may be gathered into his dragnet, if
the writer pleases to make use of them.

And yet, peculiarly enough, in spite of the fullness of representation which this material allows its writer, in spite of the
reach of the arc of life which he may include in a single work

in this *milieu*, the political novelist must, indeed, be the most selective of all novel writers. Dickens, and Thackeray, and Henry James, as social writers, deal with men and women as men and women: the variety of common human emotions they may report is endless, and the more usual and familiar they are to us the better is it for those writers. But the political novelist, if he is to be true to his craft, must be dominated, more often than not, by *ideas* rather than by *emotions*. The people who play his leading parts are above the common average of intelligence. They are endowed not with common joys and common sorrows, but are men and women sophisticated in their tastes, highly trained in the complex world of affairs and of diplomacy, dealing at first hand with problems of theology, of education, of economic barter and exchange, of philosophy. The novelist who sets characters like these in motion must be able to weave his threads into his historical pattern as easily as did Silas Marner, the untutored recluse of Raveloe and Lantern Yard, who wove his woollen cloth for the persons who lived in the shadows of the Red Inn. To keep, therefore, from scattering his forces, the writer in this *milieu* must avoid any vast panoramas (such as Scott for example could afford to treat), but must devote himself to a very particular group, to a definite compass of ideas, to a precise theory or interpretation of life much as the philosopher does in his professional treatise. This restriction of his to one class of ideas, to one peculiar attitude, to one enclosed compass of character, will leave him the freer thereafter to penetrate into the very core of his material, and to gain out of that penetration effects that are the sharper and the more successful for the purposes of the novelist's art. Is the novel to record the influence of certain ideas upon some class of society whose place, in the procession of life, has been altered by a great political reform? Is it to reveal the crises of passion and the delicacy of maneuvering which may have occurred with a change of administration? All this calls for the registering of refined emotions in the human heart, not the simple throbs of a simple humanity; the presentation of powerful forces working across large areas, of customs and forces potent in their influences upon the national life, and not the simple habits and prejudices and country-church yard epithets of an unsung humanity. That is what we mean by an *intellectual* interpretation in the novel, not a social one. When Mrs. Humphry Ward tells us, in her autobiography,[19] that the reason why it took her *three* years to write *Robert Elsmere* instead of the *one* year it should have taken her, was that she had to solve the problem common to all 'intellectual fiction,' namely, "so to suggest the argument, that both the expert and the popular consciousness might feel its force — to do this without over-stepping the bounds of fiction; without turning it into mere ratiocination, and so losing the 'simple, sensuous, passionate' element which is the true life of fiction," she is but enforcing, out of her own richly varied life, the contrast I have made here between the social writer and the writer in the political *milieu,* and is at the same time illustrating one of the greatest difficulties which besets creation of the political *genre.*

There is yet another aspect in this contrast between the political novelist and the work of the social writer. The latter, by the very nature of his material, uses scenes, passions, and moods all of which fall within the shadow of an ordinary reader's ordinary life. They may appeal, therefore, instantly to his comprehension; they lie at once within the range of his interpretation; they call forth his natural sympathies. The extent which this common, social appeal of the novelist makes upon the reader's own experiences marks often the measure of his subsequent popularity. But in the political novel the most dramatic and the most productive characters are, by their very greatness, the more removed from the ordinary world of ordinary men and women. The home of the noble lord of the Ministry, the country estate of the Prime Minister, the Cabinet meetings in Downing Street, the lives of the 'Elysians' who live in 'castles' and have great leisure and great wealth and who often guide the State in diplomacy and in executive posts out upon the far corners of the earth, are as far removed from our ordinary ken as the complicated working of party control, the news which brings tragedies and rejoicings to the groups in the political clubs, or the manipulation of the elaborate machinery of diplomacy, is from our ordinary intelligence. Though all this was much truer of the England of the Georges and then of Queen Victoria than it is of England at the close of the century, or the England of to-day, most of the political novelists we analyze deal with the England of the earlier, the less democratized or the undemocratized, periods. In some respects, indeed, as I have already shown in this study, much of what is here said still applies. When the average person, therefore, read the political novel, he was apt to feel at once the defects in his own experiences which raised obstacles for a complete comprehension of the work. His imagination had to labor imperfectly in reconstructing, his sympathies flowed inadequately in interpreting, these scenes, these passions, this caravanserai of men and matters 'of other lands not his own.' His own tastes and interests could not instantly co-operate with those of the author's. He missed the appeal that the social writer made to him, — an appeal direct, immediate, compelling!

The political novelist has, therefore, by the intellectual *milieu* in which he is at work, many difficulties to overcome before he may draw a spark and then fan it into a flame of enthusiasm in the minds and hearts of the reading class, which is everywhere a democratic class. He finds that success in this field requires that he perform adequately a two-fold task: he must not only be able to create his character, and paint his situation accurately, but he must also bring down from the heights on which they live both character and situation; he must translate both for us into our own experience and embody them in such form that we may understand them and be fascinated by them. The act of doing so may not require a greater technique than that employed by the social writer; but it is an entirely different technique. The former writes of things and in language so that he who runs may read; he does not have to educate an audience before they are able to appreciate his novel. The latter has not only to write his novel but to educate his audience as well. The first has had countless models before him which he was at liberty to study; the second has had to hew his own path, to develop his own technique.

And if he succeeds in endowing his characters and his situations with warmth, color, and vitality, and if his world of statesmen, diplomats, and all the lesser figures — man, woman, and idealized youth — are spread in an intelligible pageant before us, there is yet a philosophy of politics, so to speak, to represent in a legitimately artistic manner. In this sort of pageant men take sides on great national and international issues. Whigs, Tories, Conservatives, Liberals, Unionists, Chartists, Anti-Corn Law Leaguers, Utilitarians, Utopians of every type and color — they crowd upon your canvas and demand a hearing. To portray these diversified beings dispassionately, to let each man have his say and none the entire platform, to treat all fairly and truthfully and succeed in steering between the Scylla of partisanship and the Charybdis of tractarianism, requires the most delicate craftsmanship on the writer's part, and a scholar's knowledge of the arguments, but withal an artist's delicate fancy and power of creation, if the result is not to be a creed disguised in the garments of a novel, a political platform hidden by a mountain of decoration.

The attempt, then, to combine impersonated characters with fiction, and to add to the result some significant political or social moral, aside from acting as a check upon the genius of every writer in this field except only the greatest writer (who is still in Limbo), is fraught with endless peril. It is unfortunate indeed that in this *milieu* the critic is swift to find what may easily be termed 'propaganda' when it is actually nothing but an impassioned view of some political ideal of the novelist's. How difficult it is to draw the distinction between this 'particular' charge, and the 'art for art's sake' motive, may be seen in the endless criticisms upon the variety of treatment with which the World War was handled by novelists from Ibañez to the writers of America. It is not difficult to make out a case for the statement that in a sense all art is propaganda. By giving your own vision, by making your own interpretation of a state of things, you immediately exclude the views of others. The moment you begin to select and to emphasize you lay yourself open to the charge of preaching. And in the war the element of personal fervor was so strong in most novelists, that their works often had the appearance of propaganda when they in reality hardly meant them to have it. How far one may keep one's self out of a book where *ideas* are brought into full play, how far one may present *ideas* sharply and appealingly and yet not be accused of 'bringing firearms into an orchestra,' is a difficult question for the novelist to answer. Someone has said that one of the main tendencies in American literature since 1870 has been its use as an instrument to agitate, and to carry out investigations and reforms of various kinds. Has then all that recent literature — and particularly the novel of the last five decades — been forever damned as works of art? And even in England of our own time, the school of writers best represented by John Galsworthy has shown this fervent belief, this restless determination, in the righteousness of certain ideals and issues. Has that destroyed forever their validity as great artists?

In one form or another the arguments of critics against

what may seem the illegitimate marriage of Beauty with Use
will always be a skeleton in the novelist's closet, which he must
either destroy or disown. Most of all for the political novelist
is this skeleton a reality, and he, more than any other of his
craft, must labor to dismantle it. How far the critic will go
to shake its bones in the face of the political novelist is best
illustrated in the classic reaction of James Russell Lowell to
Disraeli's *Tancred*.

"We should not be so severe in our exactions of the novel
(i.e. *Tancred*) except that it no longer professes to amuse but
to instruct. This is the age of lectures. Even *Punch* has got
into the professor's chair and donned the doctor's cap. The
novel has become a quack advertisement in three volumes.
Formerly we could detect the political economist at a reasonable distance, and escape him by a well-contrived dodge.
Now, no sanctuary is inviolate . . . It is getting past en-
durance . . . The novelist has turned *colporteur* to some board
of political missions, and the propagandist of every philosophical soup-and-bread society assumes the disguise of a poet.
The times are well-nigh as bad as those of a century and a half
ago, when our forefathers were fain to carry their firelocks
to Meeting. Everywhere are surprisals. One cannot saunter
down what were once the green lanes or the deep withdrawn
woodpaths of literature, without being set upon by a whooping
band of savages, who knock one on the head with the balance
of trade, or tomahawk one with merciless statistics. Everywhere pure literature seems defunct. Art for the sole sake of
art is no more. Beauty is no longer 'its own excuse for being.'
It must have a certificate of membership from the Anti-
something or the Anti-everything Alliance." [20]

It has been pointed out that one of the difficulties facing the
political novelist in the early 19th century was that he could
not find, in writers of the past, models which might serve to
guide or to inspire his picturization of his own very fascinating

political era.   So far as the novel of politics was concerned
this was strictly true.   One must not forget, however, that by
the time Disraeli wrote his great trilogy of novels — *Coningsby*,
Sybil, and *Tancred* — the so-called 'novel with a purpose' was
a form already well launched in the history of English letters,
and that the relation of this 'novel with a purpose' to the
form which Disraeli perfected was as the bed of a stream to
the waters which pour through it.   From one point of view
the political novel itself was a fusion of many varied motives,
gathered to serve the interests of some single class of society,
or to advance the interests of some particular political philosophy, or to present to some person a means of best commenting
upon matters of great public import.   The 'purpose novel,'
developed by many persons and over a period which saw vast
historical changes, had resolved a heritage into a tradition by
the middle of the 19th century.   From the days when the
father of the realistic novel in England focused some of the
ethical light which was shed from the torch of John Bunyan
upon his own hero, Robinson Crusoe, across a century and a
half which brings us to Kingsley's novels preaching Christian
Socialism, and Dickens's portraits of Gradgrind and Bounderby
showing off doctrines of false political economy in *Hard Times*,
we mark the strong moral emphasis, the peculiar didacticism,
the ever-developing spirit of reform, so native to the English
novel of the last two centuries.   By the great range of English
novelists who wrote works having an underlying purpose, by
the diversity and complexity of interests within these novels,
we see how altogether unconsciously the bed was being deepened for the use of our own writer dealing in a new *milieu*.[21]

Chapter II

DISRAELI'S EXPERIMENTAL STAGE

THE unique contribution which Disraeli was to make to 19th century letters showed the form it would take in his first novel. Compared with the fully-developed political novels of his later years — particularly the novels of the trilogy — *Vivian Grey* [1] is a rehearsal rather than a performance. It is the rehearsal of a youth of twenty-one knowing next to nothing about the things of which he writes, but it shows the reader who knows Disraeli's later work that the same mental vigor which is here displayed, if applied to more worthy ends, guided by some established principles of political belief or conduct, controlled by a maturer judgment, and influenced by nobler models than those which seem to have furnished the tone of this early composition, will bring the youth into manhood and the hot-house plant into a full-blown tree. For the gloom and the sceptical philosophy of life which characterized *Childe Harold*, alternating with the wild gaiety and the cynical mockery of *Don Juan*, (both of whose influences are to be noted here), there had to be substituted the maturing intellectual discipline of a strong religious faith, and the stirring purpose of doing something to wipe out the "hungry forties." Then only could Disraeli sweep from *Vivian Grey* to *Coningsby*, *Sybil*, and *Tancred*.

It is amusing now to recall the improbability of plot and the incongruities of character in Disraeli's first novel. It made no more pretension to probability than does a nursery tale. All connection between causes and effects, as it is usually found to exist in the world, are set at defiance. Marvels — moral,

political, and physical — are heaped one upon another. The
hero moves through difficulties and dangers, unheard-of scrapes,
and accidents of a portentous character with the ease and the
coolness with which some knight of old passed through the
innocuous and unsubstantial flames that surrounded the enchanted castle of a Fairy Land. Vivian speaks a few not very
wise words, and he achieves a political revolution; arch-
duchesses sink into his arms almost at the first interview;
consumptive young ladies confess their love and expire at the
same moment; the schemes of gamblers are baffled by his
foresight and his presence of mind; tornadoes that destroy
everything in sight pass harmless by him; the hero, in short,
bears a charmed life — a talisman about him before which all
obstacles vanish. That Disraeli at twenty-one knew how
preposterous and absurd a plot he had concocted is plain from
the fact that he makes no attempt to disguise the incoherency
of his materials. He shifts his incidents and his scenes as
rapidly and with as little regard for connection that is logical,
as the moving picture operator of to-day does with the slides
announcing future performances. And yet there *was* a sort of
method in Disraeli's early madness. If the plot is improbable,
if the hero is a political intriguer and a man totally devoid of
moral principle, the particular department of literature which
Disraeli chose from among the many that he had at his hand,
was that which was best fitted for the exercise of such talents
as he then possessed. Lacking the discipline of a university
education, restless, keenly ambitious to enter into some sort of
public life but not knowing what, impatient with all restraint,
he chose a form of novel in which he could execute rapid,
dashing sketches of intrigue, incident, and character, unfettered by the needs of any close connection, or by any consistency. Here was a fairy-land of the imagination, emancipated from all the uneasy trammels of regular and systematic
composition which called for reality and probability, in which

he could disport himself to his heart's content. He himself later characterized *Vivian Grey* as a work as hot and as hurried as ever was penned. But, as he himself says, it was like its subject: for Youth itself is but an inchoate sketch, a brief hour of unsettled principles, of unrestrained passions, of unexecuted purposes. A youth of twenty-one, living in the early years of a century that was already pregnant with great and wonderful forces, just emerging from the influences which had brought about the French Revolution, eager, brilliant, and already aware that if he had a destiny it was solely in his hands to prove it and fashion it, — such a youth at such a time is not likely to make his hero, in his first novel, aim at the very noblest objects in life, nor the atmosphere with which he surrounds him illustrative of what is most refined and beautiful in chastened and civilized society.[2] He desired to produce something that was as bold, as audacious, as unstudied as he felt himself to be: something unusual in conception and execution, something provoking criticism or opposition by the heterodoxy of its opinions, something novel and startling to the reader. And he succeeded.

Upon a fashionable society novel such as Bulwer might have composed, but which Disraeli filled with the exuberance of youth, sparkling with epigram, mixed with strange romantic adventures, filled with such impossibilities as might have rivalled *The Mysteries of Udolpho*, he grafted political characters and brought into large prominence political motives. The plot is as follows. A young English adventurer, having neither great wealth nor the support of a great name, torn by great ambition to become somebody in the world, sets out to make himself a force in the game of politics by means of his wit and his intuitive knowledge of human weaknesses. Good-looking, graceful, adroit, flattering where it can gain him his ends, threatening where this can put down opposition, he gains the favor of a stupid nobleman, the Marquis of Carrabas, and under the guise of advancing his interest, forms with him a political alliance and then surrounds him with a group of narrow-minded, selfish, landed-nobles who together make the 'Carrabas Party.' To advance the interests of this party, but in reality of himself, he persuades a retired and disappointed, but withal seasoned and brilliant politician, to join the party. Cleveland has, however, his own axe to grind, and is duped neither by the Marquis of Carrabas who had been his former enemy politically, nor by the young man who is managing the business and who does so in the belief that "everything is possible . . . — if one has but the proper amount of physical and mental courage." After various political dinners and conferences, after many goings and comings of the various malcontents among both the landed proprietors and the two younger men, after alliances have been made and broken and repaired again through the wit of the young political adventurer, the latter's real motives are finally unmasked to the Marquis of Carrabas by a Mrs. Felix Lorraine, a member of the Carrabas household. The noble allies thereupon leave him in the lurch, and Cleveland grossly insults him. The first part of the book ends with the death of the treacherous lady who, after an unsuccessful attempt to poison Vivian, herself succumbs to a burst blood-vessel; with an extraordinary scene in which the Marquis wishes all sorts of evil things upon the young miscreant's head; with a duel between Vivian and Cleveland in which the latter is killed; and with the grave illness of 'the hero' after the recovery from which he takes a long tour abroad to forget and himself to be forgotten. So much for the significant half of the novel. The second part of it has to do with Vivian's travels. These are filled with elements that are grotesque, sentimental, and impossible. For the purposes of this study they have no significance.

I have said that the essential significance of part one of *Vivian Grey* lies in the fact that its principal characters are

political characters, and that the plot turns upon political
motives. The satire of those social classes which make the
mainstay of English political life in the pre-Victorian period —
Lord Carrabas, a former Undersecretary of State, and his
frivolous wife; Sir Berdmore Scrope, "a leading country gentleman who having quarreled with ministers about the corn laws
had been counted disaffected ever since: a bold man to the
world but henpecked at home"; Lord Beaconsfield, "powerful
but a dolt"; many of the props and the eminences of that
English society which alone can be influential in forming a
political cabal — from their silly wives and their languishing
daughters to their friends like 'Mrs. Million' and her toad-
eaters; from their barristers like 'Septimus Sessions' to their
diplomats like 'Mr. Metternich Scribe' and their slashing-
article writers in 'Mr. Partenopex Puff'; their scientific pedants
like 'Mr. Mackaw' to the man of genius in the Commons like
'Mr. Cleveland' whom they use and then cast aside — these
are the characters which Disraeli, at twenty-one, chooses for
his sport and his ridicule. There is scorn heaped upon the
political-dinner party of the Carrabas house. The ridiculous
hollowness of the Marquis of Carrabas's campaign speech made
at the political dinner before noble guests whose support he
desires, is equalled only by the supreme ignorance of one of
his house-guests, the young nobleman Boreall, who hearing
Goethe discussed asks naively 'And who is Gewter?' "He was
possessed," says his author, "of such a thirst for knowledge
that he never allowed an opportunity to escape him of displaying his ignorance." The ease with which new political
principles (of no particular complexion to the reader) are
developed, the sudden promises of place, power, and patronage
to the followers, the sharpness of outline with which the
character of a disappointed politician is sketched, the fluent
talk about "the common good" when men mean their own
selfish interests, the appeal to class-prejudice and to instincts

of "respectability" to gain political ends — all these, from a youth of twenty-one who must have known little or nothing of public life, are the surprising elements in the novel.

In noting these we must not lose our sense of proportion. The novel — or at least the part of it which is of importance for this study — is woven of many threads. But the most important of these, which are the binding forces in the weaving, remain always dangling and unfinished. What particular political principles this 'union' about to be formed stands for — whether Whig or Tory, whether desiring the extension of suffrage or its curtailment, their attitude toward important domestic matters or their ideas of a foreign policy (let it be anything which may draw from the reader either sympathy or repugnance) — we are never furnished. The Marquis of Carrabas is a weakly-drawn character, and the nobles who are to support him are only roughly sketched. For a man who could overturn an entire Ministry in the House of Commons, Cleveland needs more prepossessiveness than Disraeli ever gives him in this novel. But then, the novel presents only the manoeuvres of a political machine, and not the machine in action. Our interest in the novel lies here: the social *milieu* out of which came the guardians in England of parliamentary action, their toadies and their scribblers, their 'jargon' and their 'methods of combination,' their moral weaknesses and their class pride — all these, elements upon which Disraeli in the forties built up the perfected form of the *genre* in literature which he produced, are to be found in this first novel.

I have said that for the purpose here in hand there can be no value in discussing the *Sequel to Vivian Grey*, published the year following, and included in the later editions of his novels as *Part II* of the original work. The larger part of this work, almost all of which is given over to descriptions half in jest and half in earnest of the life of petty German courts and their capitals as the hero Vivian meets with them on his journeys,

Disraeli must himself have been ashamed of in his later years of discretion, for it is undoubtedly to this half of his first novel that he refers when he asks the indulgence of his readers.[3] The book is lacking in the invention, the unity of purpose or at least a semblance of it, and even the characterization, which the original production contained. It was undoubtedly produced to attract again those readers of the original volume, one which had proved so popular, partly because the book contained so many disguised characters from actual life,[4] partly for some of its own dashing merit, and partly for the puffing which the publisher gave it. Disraeli's heart was not in this second work. Yet there is one conception drawn in the *Sequel to Vivian Grey* which ought not to escape our attention. Monypenny comes to my aid here and bears a full quotation.[5]

"The most interesting character in the book is Beckendorff, the Prime Minister of Reisenberg, Disraeli's first attempt at a finished portrait of a statesman. Beckendorff is a man of plebian origin who has raised himself to power by the force of his own 'master-mind.' He is of a type that recurs more than once in Disraeli's favorite doctrines. 'Fate, destiny, Chance, particular and special Providence — idle words. Dismiss them all, Sir! A man's Fate is his own temper.' 'Man is not the creature of circumstances. Circumstances are the creatures of men. We are free agents, and man is more powerful than matter.' . . . In Beckendorff Vivian Grey sees a man with his own principles of conduct whose ambition has been crowned with success. (Monypenny here quotes a paragraph from the book to prove this statement). . . . The passage throws an illuminating flash on some of Disraeli's most cherished ideals of character, and on the significance of *Vivian Grey* in relation to those ideals."

The autobiographic element in *Vivian Grey* to which almost all biographers of Disraeli refer, and which has an interest for us because we see the thought and energy of a future parliamentarian-novelist being slowly fashioned by the moulding hand of action, becomes still more important in another of his early

works, *Contarini Fleming: A Psychological Romance.*[6] Indeed,
were not these early novels a mirror of the inner struggles and
the outer incidents in the youthful Disraeli to even a casual
reader of his actual life, Disraeli himself would prove the fact
for us. "My works," he writes in his diary, "are the embodi-
fication of my feelings. In *Vivian Grey* I have portrayed my
active and real ambition: in *Alroy* my ideal ambition: The
Psychological Romance is a development of my poetic character.
This trilogy is the secret history of my feelings — I shall write
no more about myself."[7] But it is yet an interesting fact that
in spite of the obvious and altogether successful desire to make
this a work purely of the imagination, on which score it has
received fulsome praise from all sorts of critics,[8] its author
must inject a picture of political life as the only contrast he
can possibly imagine of what is at the opposite pole to a life of
meditation. Someone has said, in speaking of Disraeli's young
heroes, that he couldn't conceive a masculine character who
didn't want to enter Parliament. The truth will not lead us
quite so far: he couldn't conceive an ambitious youth who
didn't at least do some very hard thinking before he rejected
public life (which for Disraeli almost always means Parliament), and when he did it was usually for a decidedly excellent
reason. Millman thought the larger part of the novel very
powerful, very poetical, a *Childe Harold* in prose;[9] a more
recent critic aptly calls it "the English *Wilhelm Meister.*"[10]
What stands out for us in this supremely imaginative and poetic
work of Disraeli's, — the forces which bind and guide the
poetic ambitions of the hero to become a power equal to
Goethe or Byron, the threads which tie the essentially literary
and intellectual quality of this work to the interests of the
reader — is the sober and constant desire of the hero to reflect
life not by first absorbing himself in the study of the great
masters of his imaginative art, and then showing a reaction
through the exercise of his own imagination (which is the

training we should naturally expect from one who would exhibit "the development and formation of the poetic character").[11] The interest for us is the fact that the hero chooses to engage in intense social action, to give rein to large political ambitions, to become *a master of men* in order that he may become *a master of the imagination.* This political 'posture,' an unconscious obsession (we may call it) in all of Disraeli's young heroes, has of course its autobiographical interest for one who studies the psychology of development of the youthful Disraeli. But it has its greater interest for us because it shows a determining influence in the evolution of the *fashionable novel,* the *novel of romance,* and the *purpose novel* in Disraeli's own hands, into the *genre* which is our main concern in this study. Not alone in these larger streams of literature which have already been discussed is the political novel being fashioned; in the youthful works of Disraeli himself do we see the process at work in an epitomized fashion.

I have shown how in *Vivian Grey* the interest in public affairs was the absorbing force in the hero's life. In *Contarini Fleming,* a poetic character, after many youthful escapades and adventures which lead to no purpose, taken to task by his father, a minister of state, settles down to the first concentrated plan which may lead to a career. He enters political life. For considerably more than three years he acts as a Secretary to the Cabinet, and as private counsellor and emissary to his father. That Disraeli, very characteristically for his early work, presents us here with a remarkably successful politician who enters into his duties full-fledged, provided with modern campaign methods out of nowhere, able to cut the Gordian knot of a diplomatic tangle with a brilliance and a genius which puts all the years of his father's apprenticeship to shame, made an Undersecretary of the realm when he is still, at heart, a creature of freaks and impulses who must, withal, have made countless mistakes but who never does so in the

novel, — is all part of the quixotic nature of the work in hand.
And being a quixotic character, who is, after all, only Vivian
Grey in a new attitude, Contarini must go travelling immediately upon receiving the remarkable political honors which
have fallen to his lot. He is sent off to France and England
by his father with what appears to us to be the specious excuse
that he ought to know more about the neighbors of the realm
in which he promises, eventually, to play so important a
political rôle. But he never really assumes his duties as a
Secretary of Legation at the Court of London. The wayward
youth countermands his father's orders to his servant. He
arrives in Paris, abandons his London post, gives rein to his
poetic dreams and visions, and begins that long series of
travels — through Switzerland, Italy, Spain, Constantinople,
Cyprus, Jerusalem, Damascus — which fill with their adventures the rest of the book, and which end only with the death
of his father. Then, coming into a great inheritance, Contarini
refuses a political appointment made by his sovereign, settles
down in a palace in Naples, and there closes his biography.
The last paragraphs of that biography, of a youth who forever
oscillates between a ravenous desire for power and greatness
and a life to be spent in the study and the creation of the
beautiful, leave the reader as unsatisfied as the hero must
himself have been. "Here let me pass my life. . . . Such is
my desire; but whether it will be my career is, I feel, doubtful.
My interest in the happiness of my race is too keen to permit
me for a moment to be blind to the storms that lower on the
horizon of society. Perchance also the political regeneration
of the country to which I am devoted may not be distant, and
in that great work I am resolved to participate."

This same inevitable drift toward political activity as a
means of regeneration of another hero, and this time made
the climactic salvation of an erstwhile totally frivolous and
apparently irreclaimable young nobleman, is to be seen in

another work, published a year before the *Psychological Ro-mance*, — namely *The Young Duke*.[12] By the most generous application of literary standards, this remains — from an artistic standpoint — the poorest of Disraeli's novels; all of his biographers deal summarily with it, and its author, who at least made an apology to his readers for *Vivian Grey*, ignores it completely in his years of discretion.[13] But for us, who are watching the unfolding of a mind and the evolution of a liter-ary *genre*, it has a real interest.

A young and noble profligate, ill-educated, who at twenty-three has squandered a great fortune and has made love to various women, full of affectation and conceit, a gambler because he must drift inevitably with that fast set of fashion-able youths who like him have never been disciplined into firmness of character through either 'great thoughts' or a great 'cause,' offers Disraeli, perhaps altogether unconsciously when he was writing, the means of presenting a veiled satire against the English aristocracy. In particular the author brings into relief the frivolity and the superficiality in the edu-cation which is given to the children of some of the most illustrious families in England of his time — those children who must eventually become the future legislators of the kingdom. Almost inevitably the reader is forced to draw the moral: if the English aristocracy desire to hold the direc-tion of public affairs, it is only upon condition that they be-come the guardians of the interests of the people. This only they may do by forcing their youth to appreciate that only through a high sense of public responsibility, through a close application to public duty, through a quick appreciation that idleness, ignorance, and frivolity will lead to their own de-struction, can they properly demand that allegiance which must be theirs if they are to be the liberalizing forces of the English polity. The young Duke of St. James shows his latent possibilities only when he confesses his wasting youth, when he apostrophizes his father for the traditions with which he endowed him, when he pours out in 'dithyrambs' his love for England, when he apperceives what makes for success in the House of Commons, when he soliloquizes upon his future conduct in the Parliamentary chambers.[14] The crisis in the youth's life is shown at the end. Touched finally by great love for May Dacre, who is the very prototype of Sybil, in Disraeli's later novel, the young duke determines once for all to redeem his heritage. How does he do this? He steals secretly down to the House of Lords, he takes his rightful place once for all in that distinguished Assembly, and, it being then the occasion for the discussion of certain grave injustices perpetrated upon religious beliefs in portions of England, the youth is fired and makes the great speech of the evening! Then, and then only, does he return to win the heroine for his reward, and (as the author would imply in the last paragraphs of the novel), to win also his own self-respect. He turns with "trembling and disgust from the dark terminations of un-principled careers, and their fatal evidences of the indulgence of unbridled passions"; he thanks Providence that the innate seeds of human virtue were not blighted in his own soul. Thus, so we are finally told, he finds himself, at the close of four years, the happiest and most fortunate of men. "His life is passed in the agreeable discharge of all the important duties of his exalted station, and his present career is by far a better answer to the lucubrations of young Duncan Macmorrogh than all the abstract arguments that ever yet were offered in favor of the existence of an aristocracy. . . . Parliament, and in a degree, society, invite the Duke and Duchess each year to the metropolis," and there they remain supremely happy among their worthy friends.

In recounting the early work of Disraeli one should make some mention, at least, of the three *jeux d'esprit* — slight juvenile drolleries and political satires — which have pleased many of his biographers, and which show us a side of him that he was to develop to a large degree in the writing of the full political novel. Saintsbury says of *Ixion in Heaven* [15] that "with perhaps Bedford's *Vathek* as a companion, it is the most brilliant thing of its kind in English." [16] Of *The Infernal Marriage* and *Popanilla* other critics have not been so extravagant in their praise as Saintsbury, but none of them ever pass the pieces by. And of a truth they are still worth reading for their irony, their sparkling wit and fun made at the expense of English political parties in the middle twenties, for the inimitable satire they present of the English Court and noble society, and for the scorn they show, though genially withal, for the several elements that made up the more significant English polity: the English Constitution, the English Church, the Utilitarians and the professional political economists, and the complicated artificial society which supported all the rest. *The Voyage of Captain Popanilla* was obviously written in imitation of Swift's *Gulliver's Travels* but, as has been already pointed out by Froude,[17] whereas the latter is inspired by hatred and scorn of his race, Disraeli is pleasant, laughing, and good-humored. Aimed in particular at the Benthamites it attempts to exhibit the fundamental discrepancy which lies between 'the greatest happiness of the greatest number' theory and true progress: these are combined by the Utilitarians and supposedly represent their platform.

In the city of Hubbabub (London), the capital of the island of Vraibleusia, Popanilla, born in the island of Fantaisie where life is still in a state of nature *à la Rousseau*, once an exile from his own home and now a true reformer, has opportunity to try his newly-found teachings of 'the screw-and-lever philosophy' upon those whose writings taught it to him. He finds to his sorrow, however, that 'Fruit' (the decorous Anglican Church), and 'Flummery Flum' (the professional political economist and Benthamite), and 'Skin-deep' and 'Lady

Spirituelle' do not wear as well as they look. The sketch
closes with a reflection as to whether man might not exist in
too natural a state as well as in too artificial a one. If this
first satirical sketch is a more consciously organized satire of
English laws and economic views, and suffers slightly for
being so, the two later squibs have no such weakness. Built
upon classical stories, and inspired by the work of Lucian
(whom Disraeli studied much as a youth), *Ixion* and *The
Infernal Marriage* are full of impertinence and mockery. The
scorn poured upon the follies and the artificialities of the
fashionable world (the Elysians) in a manner which never
stings but always amuses, the ingenious way in which he
contrives to make classical details the vehicle of his modern
satire upon "the splendid luxury of absolute idleness," the
"graceful, high-born beings without a duty to perform, who
are supported by the toil of a million gnomes," and the ladies
of Mayfair who surrounded the seat of the Father of the Gods
(George IV), might, with some change of names in the selection
and a detail or two, be made to apply with delightful aptness
to other, even present-day civilizations. What significance
there lies for us in these is, as I have already said, in the
chance of watching the formation of Disraeli's character and
temper by means of one of those literary methods which he
was later to employ with such vigor in the fully-developed
political novel.

It must be obvious, now, as we summarize the early work
of Disraeli, that it is not merely this slow formation of his
character, this steady movement of his mind towards an
interest in political matters, that these works exhibit. Beside
this autobiographic interest, there is for us a larger one: the
cumulative expression in him of certain principles of government and of conduct. The tide of that thought is not always
a steady one; there is an ebb and a flow in it; the ideas are
presented now through one medium and now through another,

and in one or two works not even mentioned.[18] But in the main Disraeli himself appears to be experimenting, and gaining strength for the complete enunciation of those political ideas which both experience and maturity would aid him to develop the best medium for in later years.

CHAPTER III

DISRAELI'S POLITICAL PHILOSOPHY — TORY DEMOCRACY

IT was in 1832 that Benjamin Disraeli first offered himself upon the hustings for a seat in the House of Commons. From that year until 1852, when he became leader of the House and was given his first Cabinet position as Chancellor of the Exchequer in the first Ministry of Lord Derby, we may examine the stages of progress in the active politician by noting the character of the novels which were written during these very years, and how they marked the maturing of the political novelist. All of the novels which were produced by him until he assumed a Cabinet office bear the relation to his active political career that the shadows might that are cast by the blocks of a constantly growing edifice: every increase in structure within flashed a more graphic representation outside. These novels, in short, reflect the maturing mind of a man of public affairs, his groping for a political philosophy of conduct; they are the imaginative means, adopted by a politician who is also a man of letters, of thinking his way through to a 'public attitude' and to a political program. Having asserted that 'attitude' and discovered that program, Disraeli then hurls himself into the thick of the fight, finds no further immediate need for this imaginative writing, and therefore gives himself over altogether to build up his active political fortunes. That is his history in the twenty years following the publication of the trilogy. It was only after Disraeli had succeeded in attaining the Prime Ministry, and then after he was forced to go temporarily into retirement because of the "absence of a majority" in Parliament, that the short political pause in his active career returns him to writing the political novel again. This was in 1870.

Since the relation between the novelist and the growing statesman is so close, it may be well, here, to pause for a short space merely to record the outstanding facts in the career of the rising parliamentarian to the days of his first appearance in an important Cabinet office.

Disraeli first attempted to enter Parliament from High Wycombe in 1832. He was unsuccessful that year, failed again with the same electorate two years later, and was no more fortunate a third time when, in 1835, he tried to get in from Taunton. The Taunton canvass was important largely because in the course of it he had his famous quarrel with O'Connell, a quarrel not forgotten in 1837 when, a new election taking place over England at the death of William IV, and Disraeli being finally successfully returned from Maidstone to the House of Commons, he essayed his first now famous speech before a howling, mocking, and laughing audience stirred up by the O'Connell faction, and declared defiantly that the day should come when they *would* hear him. In 1839 Disraeli married Mrs. Wyndham Lewis, the widow of his colleague from Maidstone, and the event was one of first rate importance for his immediate political prospects. Her fortune helped him to buy at once the estate at Hughenden and to take his place in England as a country gentleman; her courage and sympathy fed and inspired him to push forward to leadership. Already, in the two years preceding this event, he had taken steps ahead. He had made a brilliant and characteristic speech upon the repeal of the Corn Laws; he had made a great speech showing himself the friend of the Established Church; he spoke on Education wherein he praised the individual and the corporate methods used in England, as opposed to a centralized system of state education. It was in this speech defending

England's customary methods, and as opposed to the introduction of State education, that we hear him strike the first
note of what became later, in *Coningsby* particularly, the
program of the Young England Party.   England, he says in
these speeches, and repeats in *Coningsby* later, must be saved
by its Youth.

From the years 1839 to 1841 there arose the so-called 'condition of England question.'   Briefly, this 'condition of England
question' had, according to Disraeli in one of his speeches of
this period (and he describes the situation later in *Sybil*) come
about through the Reform Act which had brought in two new
disturbing factors into the old social order.

"On the one hand it had created a large and wealthy class of
manufacturing capitalists, who regarded with jealous eyes the
monopoly of political power that was now in the hands of the
territorial aristocracy; and on the other it had congregated in the
great towns of England a multitude of workers — men, women,
and children — the misery of whose lives was a disgrace to the
nation."

It was the condition of this multitude of workers that brought
on the Chartist Movement of the 30's, which showed Disraeli,
the author of *Sybil*, in sympathy with the Chartist demands,
and which served to help him make some palpable hits against
the Russell government.   With Disraeli the Whig measures of
the Russell government for a police force to preserve law and
order was not the solution to the difficulty; the solution lay,
so he said in his speeches and in his writings of the time, in
doing away with "a domestic oligarchy" and in reminding
English men and women of their great duties.   In short, in
1840, Disraeli began, in Parliament, to sound the trumpet for
a democratic Toryism.

In 1841 the Russell Ministry were forced to resign and the
Conservatives came in with Sir Robert Peel as Prime Minister.
Peel's failure to include Disraeli in his Cabinet led, without

doubt, to the eventual breach with him that practically forced Peel out of the party, when Disraeli had finished with his bitter attacks upon him, and it hastened the day of the reorganization of the entire Tory idea in politics. In the first years, however, Disraeli stood by Peel. But in 1843, when he found that Peel was "throwing the landed interest over" by so reducing the duty on Corn from Canada that its admission both from Canada and the United States would affect the agricultural interests of Disraeli's constituency at Shrewsbury, he voted against the Government. From the moment when this defection was sounded the 'Young England' idea began to take shape in the minds of Disraeli and his friends. In 1844, with *Coningsby*, the thing was given a local habitation and a name. In 1845, with *Sybil*, it was given a still more definite basis.

It was almost immediately after the publication of these political novels, and when the effect of Disraeli's onslaught upon Peel had begun to show, that Disraeli was generally to be considered the virtual leader of the Conservatives — though nominally the leadership was retained by Lord George Bentinck. The alliance between Disraeli and Lord Bentinck was commemorated later, upon the death of the noble lord, when Disraeli published a distinguished biography of the man whose interest in him, during his life, did so much to give to the biographer some just reward for his services to the party. The significance of this biography as expressing Disraeli's own political views has been shown elsewhere in this study. The speeches made during this critical period in European history (the years 1847–1848) by Disraeli, are mainly interesting for two facts: first, they show evidences of the famous policy of Imperialism which he was to fashion years later, and the germs of which are seen planted here, as the imaginative flowering of them are already recorded in at least one novel of this period, *Tancred;* secondly, they show his complete break with the conventional attitude of the Old Conservatives, and his struggle in Parliament to infuse new blood and ideas into the political philosophy of the landed aristocracy. In 1848 Disraeli ended his career as member from Shrewsbury, and from that year on until his elevation to the peerage the Tory chief was a member from Buckinghamshire.

The years from 1848 to 1852 he gave over, as Tory leader, to attacks upon the policy of the Government under Lord Russell; he chastised its weaknesses mainly as these were shown in the foreign policy of Lord Palmerston, and in the domestic program which relied upon the Manchester School of politicians (whom Disraeli attacked even more bitterly in the trilogy than he did upon the floor of the House of Commons), and upon the 'hopeless question of Protection.' At the same time Disraeli was successfully building up his own rejuvenated Tory Party. In 1852, as I have already indicated, the reward came to him when, Lord Russell's government being forced to resign, the Tories went into office under Lord Derby, and Disraeli received his first Cabinet office as Chancellor of the Exchequer.

In sketching briefly this outline of Disraeli's political career as it covers twenty years of his life, from his first attempts at politics to his first great attainment as a Cabinet minister, in order that we may possess some historical background for Disraeli, the writer of the trilogy, we have been obliged to run ahead a bit with our narrative of the political novelist. It must be in order, therefore, to retrace our steps, and pick up the thread of this investigation where we first left it, in the third decade of the century. This will bring us at once to the years 1844, 1845, and 1847, when Disraeli, the novelist, was busy articulating in the form of the romance what Disraeli, the statesman, was engrossed in creating out of the old landed aristocracy of England. In English statesmanship Disraeli distinguished himself for giving new vigor and power to what

appeared to be a dying party. He filled the old bottles of
Toryism with the new wine of Democracy. By the respect he
gained from the older statesmen for this contribution, and by
the younger men of noble blood that he was able to rally under
the banner of his new philosophy, lies part of the explanation
for his phenomenal success in England. To understand the
romancer one must understand, first, the political philosopher.

This naturally leads us to answer the question: What was
the political philosophy of Tory Democracy, not alone as
represented in sometimes a vague and shadowy fashion in the
three novels — *Coningsby, Sybil,* and *Tancred,* — but also, and
as more concretely exhibited, in the life-long convictions and
opinions held by its regenerator, as we look upon the full
sweep of them to-day? And vague and shadowy as they
sometimes appear in the creed of the *Young England* group of
novels, we must not leave them so in our own exposition, first,
because they seem sufficiently concrete and sharply outlined
to-day, as we examine all of Disraeli's expressed utterances,
particularly in the novels of his entire career, and also in his
speeches and his discussions of the English Constitution; and
secondly, because without expressing them in the altogether
compact and graphic manner in which we do, we shall make
the mistake that Lowell made when he focussed his eye upon
a single novel, and detached it from a great structure which
Disraeli gave his lifetime to build.[1]

Let us begin our analysis with Disraeli's own words, which
are to be found at the head of the later editions of *Coningsby.*

"*Coningsby* was published in the year 1844. The main
purpose of its writer was to vindicate the just claims of the
Tory party to be the popular political confederation of the
country; a purpose which he had, more or less, pursued from
a very early period of his life. The occasion was favorable to
the attempt. The youthful mind of England had just recovered

from the inebriation of the great Conservative triumph of 1841 and was beginning to enquire what, after all, they had conquered to preserve. It was opportune, therefore, to show that Toryism was not a phrase, but a fact; and that our political institutions were the embodiment of our popular necessities. This the writer endeavored to do without prejudice, and to treat of events and characters of which he had some personal experience, not altogether without the impartiality of the future." The proof that Toryism was a fact, and that political institutions were the embodiment of popular necessities, though first expressed in *Coningsby*, was still further developed in *Sybil*, published in the following year, 1845, and carried to full completion in *Tancred*, which appeared two years later. It will now be our purpose to disengage from the texture of historical reflections and political ideas, which forms the background of his most important political novels, that body of ideas which Disraeli moulded into the manifesto of the so-called Young England, but which — as we are at this day able to understand — also guided thereafter his political career.

Strange as it may seem to say it of one who ignored the evolutionary trend of science in his own day, and who upon more than one occasion satirized Darwinian philosophy, a philosophy which he calls, in *Tancred*, the 'Revelations of Chaos,'[2] Benjamin Disraeli assumed what might be called an Evolutionary theory of society. In his Conservative philosophy the principles of inheritance and memory were the safest and truest guiding principles. He ascribed the duration of the English Commonwealth to a deference for "reverend antiquity." He found fault with the history of the political parties in England since the Revolution of 1688 because he read in them a record of constant yielding to opportunism. Men had failed to prove themselves adequate to the great charge that the past had laid upon them. To Disraeli man's natural duties came before his 'natural rights.' He was opposed, therefore,

to the French Revolution because to him that extraordinary
event had ignored all processes of growth, all past history;
because it was based upon a false theory that man was justified
in sweeping away an entire world and all its institutions which
had been so painfully erected, and held that he might, so-to-
speak, overnight, establish a new social order.

"This respect for precedent, this clinging to prescription,
this reverence for antiquity," he says in his *Vindication of the
English Constitution*,[3] the work which contains all the principal
political ideas of his novels, "which are so often ridiculed by
conceited and superficial minds, and move the especial contempt
of the gentlemen who admire abstract principles, appear to me
to have their origin in a profound knowledge of human nature,
and in a fine observation of public affairs, and satisfactorily to
account for the permanent character of our liberties." Our
great forefathers, he continues, "knew that the foundation of
civil polity is Convention, and that everything and every person
that springs from that foundation must partake of that primary
character. They held themselves bound by the contracts of
their forefathers, because they wished their posterity to observe
their own agreements. They did not comprehend how the
perpetuity of a state could be otherwise preserved. They
looked upon the nation as a family, and upon the country as a
landed inheritance. Generation after generation was to succeed to it, with all its convenient buildings, and all its choice
cultivations, its parks and gardens, as well as its fields and
meads, its libraries and its collections of art, all its wealth,
but all its incumbrances." And elsewhere in the same brilliant
treatise on the English Constitution:[4] "In France, previous
to the great revolution, there existed all the elements of a free
Constitution, although not of the English Constitution. In its
old local divisions, indicated by nature, consecrated by custom,
in its ancient States, its Parliaments, its corporations, its
various classes of inhabitants, its landed tenure, its ecclesiasti-

cal and chivalric orders, there might have been found all that variety of interests whose balanced influences would have sustained a free and durable Constitution. The French leaders neglected these admirable materials. To secure equality they decided on indiscriminate destruction; they not only destroyed law and custom, but they destroyed their country. . . . Our forefathers, holding society to be as much an artificial creation as the fields and the cities amid which they dwelt, were of opinion that every subject was bound to respect the established Constitution of his country, because, independent of all other advantages, to that Constitution he was indebted even for his life. Had not the State been created the subject would not have existed. Man with them, therefore, was the child of the State, and born with filial duties. Our ancestors could not comprehend how this high spirit of loyalty could be more efficiently fostered and maintained than by providing that the rights, privileges, and possessions of all should rest on no better foundation than the State itself. They would permit no antagonist principle in their body politic. They would not tolerate nature struggling with art, or theory with habit. Hence their reverence for prescription, which they placed above law, and held superior to reason."

By saying that Disraeli accepted an Evolutionary theory of society we mean, then, that he conceived the state or nation as a continuous entity, made up of institutions that are rooted in national temperament, determined by the peculiarities of manners and of population, and born out of the peculiarities of the soil. These national institutions became, therefore, sacred structures, since they were built up by a laborious, age-long process of experimentation, and were directed to lofty and to permanent ends. Just as Nature has evolved a method of conduct about the biological and the physical kingdoms that are ancient, so mankind, he would have said, had evolved in England a peculiar sense of government for itself. Hence, in this conception of the state as a continuous and ever-growing entity, Disraeli emphasized — in contrast for example to Rousseau — not man's natural rights but man's natural duties. He distrusted the English liberal of his day because that politician believed in an opportunism which dealt frankly with the material needs of the hour, believed too much in human nature, and ignored the hallowed experience of the past and the obligations of the future. Disraeli satirized the utilitarian and the radical of his day because they were seduced by the belief that what man naturally desired at the moment was good for him and should be given him, whereas a sagacious mind, viewing English polity as if it were a tree made up of many branches and spreading in many directions, deeply rooted in a century-old worship, an established land-tenure, and in delicately organized institutions, would hesitate to uproot the memorial trunk, and to transplant it where many of its branches would become dwarfed and stunted, drawing the light and the warmth from its mighty arch in order that they might fall upon an untried side to foster a newer growth.

If one discovers, in these opinions expressed several decades after the events of the French Revolution had taken place, many echoes of the author of *Reflections on the Revolution in France*, it is not at all surprising, since the influence of Edmund Burke upon Disraeli's Tory philosophy is patent enough. That influence is to be seen not only in their common acceptance of constitutional government as founded upon an organic concept of the state, in their common emphasis upon the sacredness of those institutions and conventions which were the product of age-long experience and experiment, and upon the significance of national obligations and national duties as opposed to 'man's natural rights,' but also, and more intimately, in Burke's notions that the British Constitution is a balanced division of the powers of government among king, nobles, and commons, that national character is greater than national action, and in his historical attitude toward attempts at reformation. I mean his general respect for established institutions and his desire first to make certain that their true meaning has been interpreted before attempting a reform of them. Almost all of these ideas are more or less clearly expressed in the *Reflections*. They are more fully amplified and illustrated in his earlier and later addresses and essays: notably, the speech on *Conciliation with America*, in which he cried — "Turn back to your old principles. . . . Seek Freedom and follow it!" In his *Appeal from the New to the Old Whigs*, where he defends the absolute need of a Nobility, which he here considers the necessary third great pillar of the State, we find a common bond between him and Disraeli. No less do we find it in *Thoughts and Details on Scarcity* where Burke makes clear that to him the essential three pillars of the State must always be a King, a Church, and a respected Nobility. Disraeli himself pays a glowing tribute to the influence of Burke, in his opening pages of *Sybil* [5] where he characterizes Burke as having "restored the moral existence of the party."

Let us turn to Disraeli's expressed remarks. "By the Conservative Cause," he said in a speech delivered in 1838, "I mean the splendor of the Crown, the lustre of the peerage, the privileges of the Commons, the rights of the poor. I mean that harmonious union, that magnificent concord of all interests, of all classes, on which our national greatness and prosperity depends." And in *Sybil*, in 1845, ". . . in an age of political materialism, of confused purposes and perplexed intelligence, that aspires only to wealth because it has faith in no other accomplishment . . . Toryism will yet rise from the tomb over which Bolingbroke shed his last tear, to bring back strength to the Crown, liberty to the Subject, and to announce that power has only one duty: to secure the social welfare of the people." [6] Against the rival Whig political theory and practice, and against the Liberals of his day he hurled his shafts; both of them he charged with having fostered the materialism which came into England with the Utilitarian doctrines. "For him in the political cosmos," says Mony-penny,[7] summing up in two sentences Disraeli's Tory ideal of government, "there are two great realities — the Throne at the centre, and the people at the circumference; and on the maintenance of their normal and unimpeded interaction the health and balance of all depends. 'The privileges of the multitude and the prerogatives of the Sovereign had grown up together, and together they had waned'; together also they were to be redeemed from the selfish oligarchy which had usurped them, and the not less selfish and only less narrow middle class which had now taken the place of the oligarchy."

It was Disraeli's purpose to set forth in the trilogy, but more especially in the novel *Coningsby*, as he himself said in the quotation from the preface to that novel which we have referred to at the opening of this discussion, some principles of conduct whereby Young England might carry out that national redemption. So far as it is possible to sum up the hints for a political platform which Disraeli scatters through the three novels, we may now construct some such full state-ment as the following:

The principles of Young England are not to be those of a destructive party nor yet of an outworn Conservative régime. Revolution was to form no part of the policy of Young England. Changes were to be made cautiously and only with full and universal warning. "True wisdom," says Coningsby, "lies in the policy that would effect its end by the influence of opinion and yet by the means of existing forms." This full recognition of the authority of public opinion, the abolition of all specific class legislation, the restoration to the sovereign of the sov-ereign prerogatives which Parliament has gradually usurped, enlarged religious freedom, and a system of legislation adaptive and progressive, appear to be the principles of the new sect. Opinion is to be supreme in this new party. Young England do not consider parliamentary representation to be necessary for the security of the country. The country, they imply, goes on even when Parliament is not sitting, but it is always represented by the press. Parliamentary representation appears to them indeed the device of a rude age — but the representation of the press is a more complete instrument of government. Young England do not contemplate the abolition of Parliament, although they evidently regard it as by no means an impossible contingency. Coningsby contends, for example, that if we are forced into revolutions, we ought to consider the idea of "a free monarchy established on fundamental laws, itself the apex of a vast pile of municipal and local government ruling an educated people, represented by a free and an intelligent press."

In Disraeli's new perception of a Tory philosophy, which would find in the best fashion its application to the national conditions of his day, there are to be gathered some concrete ideas concerning the several elements which constitute the national polity. First, there is the NOBILITY.[8] The nobility must return again to the traditions which were characteristic of it in the Middle Ages, not alone that it may regain its own rights but also that it may recover a strong sense of its duties to its fellowmen. In the government of England a sound aristocracy is an absolute essential, but the existence of the aristocracy can be justified only by the vigor of its moral qualities and only when the people are able to see in it their natural leaders and champions. Upon this aristocracy lies the responsibility of leading the people in Parliament, of defending them against their foes from without, and of offering to them an ideal of the standards of honor, of virtue, of courage, of thrift, of refinement and manners such as characterize the birthright of every free Briton. "The Feudal System," says

Disraeli in his *General Preface to the Novels*, "may have worn out, but its main principle — that the tenure of property should be the fulfillment of duty — is the essence of good government. The divine right of kings may have been a plea for feeble tyrants, but the divine right of government is the keystone of human progress, and without it governments sink into police, and the nation is degraded into a mob." The loyalty of the people will rise again, but only when they are persuaded that it is in return for strength gained from a generous aristocracy. With the Church, which the nobility have heretofore so systematically robbed and exploited, the aristocracy of England must hereafter combine, and both bodies, now rejuvenated, must work together in the interests of the commonwealth.

What the aristocracy lacks to-day is a quickening spirit of energy and accomplishment, and this it may find in the English MIDDLE CLASSES.[9] Among these are to be found an industrial ideal based upon disciplined labor and indefatigable application, upon invention and resource, whose end is not robbery and deceit, but the upbuilding of the energies and the undeveloped wealth of a nation. In the city of Manchester, Coningsby finds what is to him a new world filled with great and stirring ideas. "He beheld," says Disraeli, "a great source of the wealth of nations which had been reserved for these times, and he perceived that this wealth was rapidly developing classes whose power was imperfectly recognized in the constitutional scheme, and whose duties in the social system seemed altogether omitted." In the elder Millbank, Coningsby finds a vigorous personification of this new spirit, and the exchange of ideas which he has with this great manufacturer becomes thereafter for him a critical chapter of a new life. Here, in the ranks of these middle-class citizens, in this "unprecedented partnership between capital and science," resides the new Spirit of Progress, whose grandeur and immensity only a philosopher could conceive. Throughout the novel *Coningsby* Disraeli paints in sharp contrast the futility and the aimlessness of the lives of many of England's nobility beside the ordered and stirring purpose of these disciples of a new age, in order that the young generation of the English aristocracy, and the resuscitated Tory party, by frankly recognizing this new factor in English economic and social life, may see the need and the responsibility of combining with the new forces and of according to them their just privileges.

With a power of realism and a strength of sympathy scarcely excelled by any other Victorian writer, and in passages which sometimes remind one of the skill of Victor Hugo's *Les Misérables*, Disraeli turns, in his *Sybil*, to a portrait of the WORKING CLASS.[10] The elements of that portrayal, wherein the author shows himself in the common stream of thought with the creator of *Chartism* and with *Past and Present*, to mention no others here, are better left for our later discussion of the literary qualities of that novel. Its political import may be summed up as follows: The end to the slavery of these masses cannot come merely through reliance upon their own powers. This he shows in the futility of their efforts to bring that consummation about. Rather must it come through the direct help and sympathy of the forces of government. These poor people must be taught that the State is not inimical to them but that it is friendly to them and desires in every way to aid them. The New Generation, the larger and finer vision of the younger aristocracy, will fashion the acts which must bring about the salvation of the proletariat, and destroy the evils which now beset them. THE ENGLISH CHURCH,[11] rejuvenated and generous, the very church whose sacred antiquity and spiritual consolations have been the mainstay of the English race, must concentrate her great powers to destroy this unnecessary struggle between the government and the people. And by making a new crusade to regain her strength from the vision on Mount

Sinai and the ascension from the Mount of Olives, she will learn again how to guide and to protect her children. And in the last paragraph of the novel Disraeli ends: "That we may live to see England once more possess a free monarchy, and a privileged and prosperous People, is my prayer; that these great consequences can only be brought about by the energy and devotion of our Youth is my persuasion. We live in an age when to be young and to be indifferent can be no longer synonymous. We must prepare for the coming hour. The claims of the Future are represented by suffering millions; and the Youth of the Nation are the trustees of Posterity."

CHAPTER IV

DISRAELI MASTERS THE ART

WITH varying degrees of strength this philosophy hangs, like the light of a rising dawn, upon the background of each of the three novels. It is strongest in *Coningsby*, where the purely political elements predominate; it becomes less so in *Sybil*, where the contrasts between aristocratic wealth and the industrial poor are emphasized; and remains only in the first half of *Tancred*, where the religious element of Toryism is illustrated. In each of the novels an aristocrat of the younger generation, urged on either by a great plan of political re-organization, or of social amelioration, or of religious zeal, goes forth armed against the frivolities and the egotism and the idleness of the privileged classes — his own people — to do battle in the new crusade. It is the light of a rising dawn, is this political creed of Young England, and never appears with the strength of full sunlight in any of the three novels. Of this fact Monypenny ingeniously remarks: "If the creed of Young England had been less vague, if the purpose of the novels had been political in any crude or narrowly partisan sense, the result must have been a failure from the viewpoint of art. But Young England was less a party than a spirit in the air, or at most a revival of Disraeli's early dream, the dream that haunts the youth of every generation, of a party truly national, rising above all factions, aims, and limitation. The wisdom of Sidonia upon Coningsby (for example) is not politics at all, or the politics of the Empyrean in its detachment, not only from party, but even from nationality and from everything of race. To this wisdom Coningsby and his friends add a

wisdom of their own. . . . Thus the politics of Young England
are so broad and disinterested as to save the novels from all
suspicion of mere party pamphleteering. From his central
viewpoint Disraeli surveys the scene with judicial impartiality,
and awards praise and blame with due discrimination." [1]

Sidonia stands in the background of the novel *Coningsby*,[2]
and, as Coningsby himself tells us, was one of the three people
(the other two were Eustace Lyle, who exemplifies Disraeli's
belief in an old religious faith, and Millbank, the epitome of
the virtues of the new industrial classes) who did most to
influence the ripening of his mind. A word about these three
important characters. Sidonia is a sort of idealized Disraeli.
He teaches Coningsby "to look for the future of England in
what is more powerful than laws and institutions — in the
national character." For his wisdom Sidonia is well equipped.
A great Hebrew who has exhausted, like Solomon, the sources
of all human knowledge, who at thirty, is acquainted with all
languages, all arts, all literatures, has travelled everywhere,
known everybody, "on all subjects his mind seemed to be
instructed, and his opinions formed. He flung out a result in
a few words; he solved with a phrase some deep problem that
men muse over for years." In spite of all this there seems to
the reader little evidence in his conversations with Coningsby
that he is an intellectual Messiah. What he says, however,
about the greatness of youth in achieving results as shown in
history, the need of mankind being governed by imagination
and not by reason, the fallacies of the Utilitarian philosophy,
the justice in asking for Jewish emancipation, the influence of
women upon the moulding of character — these are all matters
to the point for Coningsby and for us as well. If, in depicting
Sidonia, Disraeli has painted a metaphorical figure — a sort of
Hebraic Virgil leading a Coningsby Dante and advising him (a
Virgil real enough in appearance but only epitomized Reason in
speech), he was after all presenting a proper figure for the

embodiment of his idealized notions about politics, religion, and race. Anything less vague and more probable in portraiture would have destroyed the purpose which Disraeli had in hand. Furthermore, in presenting Sidonia, Disraeli was carrying out a very well known literary convention such as Byron had used when he exhibited an idealized portrait of himself in *Conrad, Don Juan,* and *Childe Harold.* In other places, in periods preceding Disraeli, there was Paul Clifford, Pelham, Maltravers, Eugene Aram, and Zanoni. Disraeli, in short, was moulding here a character in the true Romantic traditions which were still much alive at the time *Coningsby* was written, traditions which he himself, in various manner, used in many of his novels: notably in *Vivian Grey,* in *The Wondrous Tale of Alroy,* and in *Contarini Fleming,* the work of his which lay closest to the first decades of the nineteenth century. I mention this as a necessary digression because it explains to us what Sir Leslie Stephen appeared to forget when he says that "no one can ever accuse Disraeli of a want of audacity" in his drawing of "the superlative . . . the thrice miraculous Sidonia."

Eustace Lyle, the young and very generous-hearted Roman Catholic who is himself one of the Young England group, is of importance only for his reflections to Coningsby upon the evil days which had permitted the destruction of Popery in England and the consequent rise of Whiggery, and for the 'beau ideal' which he presents at his estate at St. Genvième, of an English landlord taking care of his poor by doling victuals and giving alms to them on stated days each week, — a sentimental piece of business which ought to have stirred Coningsby into some reflections about how English character, especially among the poorer classes, might be easily demoralized. For after all, a steady job to a tenant, a good home, a garden, and some investment of personal responsibility would have been a wiser boon for him. Millbank, the third influence on Coningsby, is

a more successful creation. Disraeli skilfully makes him a
realistic figure, permeated with energy and enterprise, proud
of his own class which he calls "a natural aristocracy" based
upon intelligence and worth. Disraeli furnishes him with
those opinions about the English peerage, the altogether complete superiority of the House of Commons over the House of
Lords in English administration, and the freedom of the
Saxon, that, passed on through him to Coningsby makes the
latter feel that "the Age of Ruins" had indeed passed, when
he later reflects upon his tutelage from Millbank at Manchester.

Of all the principal characters in this novel Lord Monmouth
appears to me to be one of the ablest, if not the very best,
drawn. That self-indulgent and heartless libertine, with a
pride of caste which is concealed under a surface of polished
manners that gives him a tone almost of grandeur, is a type of
the English patrician with an eighteenth century manner, dominant in political life, whom Disraeli could paint with the hand
of a master. It would be difficult indeed to point to a better
picture than this, drawn with a comprehension and a coolness
and an insight which Disraeli knew so well how to use when
he became the satirist of the weaknesses in the English nobility,
in the whole range of Victorian literature.[3] Millbank, the new
dominating influence in political life, whom Disraeli deliberately placed beside Lord Monmouth for a contrast of character for the young generation, is by comparison only a half-
finished portrait. Rigby, that political hanger-on of Lord
Monmouth's who was fashioned after Croker, the editor of
Boswell, whom Macaulay had handled so roughly in his famous
review, is drawn here in a light so contemptible and odious as
to make Macaulay's satirical portrait eulogy by comparison.
Presented mainly as an object of ridicule I cannot agree with
Monypenny that Disraeli marred his work by animus. Rigby
is inimitably drawn. A single quotation from the early part
of the novel will prove the fact.

"Mr. Rigby was member for one of Lord Monmouth's parliamentary boroughs. He was the manager of Lord Monmouth's parliamentary influence, and the auditor of his vast estates. He was more; he was Lord Monmouth's companion when in England, his correspondent when abroad; hardly his counsellor, for Lord Monmouth never required advice; but Mr. Rigby could instruct him in matters of detail, which Mr. Rigby could make amusing. Rigby was not a professional man; indeed, his origin, education, early pursuits, and studies, were equally obscure; but he had contrived in good time to squeeze himself into parliament, by means which no one could ever comprehend, and then set up to be a perfect man of business. The world took him at his word, for he was bold, acute, and voluble; with no thought, but a good deal of desultory information; and though destitute of all imagination and noble sentiment, was blessed with a vigorous mendacious fancy, fruitful in small expedients, and never happier than when devising shifts for great men's scrapes. . . . He was just the animal that Lord Monmouth wanted, for Lord Monmouth always looked upon human nature with the callous eye of a jockey. He surveyed Rigby; and he determined to buy him. He bought him with his clear head, his indefatigable industry, his audacious tongue, and his ready and unscrupulous pen; with all his dates, all his lampoons; all his private memoirs, and all his political intrigues. It was a good purchase."

The character thus firmly realized from the outset is worked out by Disraeli with a remorseless consistency. A new trait is disclosed in every chapter thereafter in which Rigby appears (and he seems to appear in most of them) until the full picture of baseness is absolutely complete. There is never any hesitation or indecision: each touch is clear, cutting, direct, and satiric. The conception deserves to stand in a Temple of Fame, not far removed from those where stand the sharply-outlined figures on which Ben Jonson expended his industrious animosity and scorn. Side by side with his master, Monmouth, whose sordid sagacity and superb selfishness are built up block upon block with no less power as the story advances, they represent Disraeli, the political satirist, at the height of his brilliance.

Next to Rigby stand the inimitable pair, Taper and Tad-pole. Subsidiary to their intellectual master, Rigby, they are like an antiphonic chorus to him. The drawing of these "political parasites" exhibits Disraeli at his greatest excellence in the use of a lightness of irony and of a Congrevian humor. Taper and Tadpole are of that class of statesmen who never despair of the Commonwealth if they receive their twelve hundred pounds annually.

"It is a peculiar class that; £1,200 per annum, paid quarterly, is their idea of political science and human nature. To receive £1,200 per annum is government; to try to receive £1,200 per annum is opposition; to wish to receive £1,200 per annum is ambition. If a man wants to get into Parliament, and does not want to get £1,200 per annum, they look upon him as daft; as a benighted being. They stare in each other's face, and ask, 'What can —— want to get into Parliament for?'"

We see them at their best at a political dinner at Mr. Orms-by's wherein Disraeli presents us with a number of varying portraits. For example, Taper and Tadpole have retired after dinner for a talk. The period was 1834, immediately after Lord Melbourne ceased to be Prime Minister and the results of Peel's audience with the King were not yet known. There was a crisis in English political life and every one is on the *qui vive* for what is about to happen.

"'And what do you put our numbers at now?' inquired Mr. Taper.
'Would you take fifty-five for our majority?' rejoined Mr. Tadpole.
'It is not so much the tail they have, as the excuse their junc-tion will be for the moderate, sensible men to come over,' said Taper. 'Our friend Sir Everard, for example; it would settle him.'
'He is a solemn imposter,' rejoined Mr. Tadpole; 'but he is a baronet and a county member, and very much looked up to by the Wesleyans. The other men, I know, have refused him a peerage.'

'And we might hold out judicious hopes,' said Taper.

'No one can do that better than you,' said Tadpole. 'I am apt to say too much about those things.'

'I make it a rule never to open my mouth on such subjects,' said Taper. 'A nod or a wink will speak volumes. An affectionate pressure of the hand will sometimes do a great deal; and I have promised many a peerage without committing myself, by an ingenious habit of deference which cannot be mistaken by the future noble.'"

The full picture of them would not be complete without a third extract from the novel.

"'Ah! Tadpole,' said Mr. Taper, getting a little maudlin; 'I often think if the time should ever come, when you and I should be joint Secretaries of the Treasury!'

'We shall see, we shall see. All we have to do is to get into Parliament, work well together, and keep other men down.'

'We will do our best,' said Taper. 'A dissolution you hold inevitable?'

'How are you and I to get into Parliament if there be not one? We must make it inevitable. I tell you what, Taper, the lists must prove a dissolution inevitable. You understand me? If the present Parliament goes on, where shall we be? We shall have new men cropping up every session.'

'True, terribly true.' said Mr. Taper. 'That we should ever live to see a Tory government again! We have reason to be very thankful.'

'Hush,' said Mr. Tadpole. 'The time has gone by for Tory governments; what the country requires is a sound Conservative government.'

'A sound Conservative government,' said Mr. Taper, musingly. 'I understand: Tory men and Whig measures.'"

If Disraeli casts his eye forward on the type of political sycophant who is with us to this day he is no less successful, by his terse and epigrammatic method, in hitting off the type of politician whom agitation for the Reform Bill of 1832 had put into power, and then thrown out of influence in many boroughs in England. One of these was Jawster Sharp, a radical shopkeeper from a manufacturing town who had hitherto been returned to Westminster as the only member from his borough.

"He had taken what is called 'a leading part' in the town in every crisis . . . one of those zealous patriots who had got up penny subscriptions for gold cups to Lord Grey; cries for the bill, the whole bill, and nothing but the bill; and public dinners where the victuals were devoured before grace was said; a worthy who makes speeches, passes resolutions, votes addresses, goes up with deputations, has at all times the necessary quantity of confidence in the necessary individual; confidence in Lord Grey; confidence in Lord Durham; confidence in Lord Melbourne: and can also, if necessary, give three cheers for the King, or three groans for the Queen."

In his day he had contrived to feather his nest pretty successfully; by which he had lost public confidence and had gained his private end. In the meantime three hungry Jawster Sharps, his hopeful sons, had all become commissioners of one thing or another.

It is not merely in the political characters that Disraeli shows his strength. For the period of time which this novel encompasses, from the passing of the Reform Act in 1832 to the victory of the Tory party in 1841, he took full advantage of painting political deputations "walking about London like mad things, eating luncheons and looking for a candidate"; he drew accounts of the contests in the newly-made boroughs; the chicaneries, the absurdities, and the comic elements of the local elections, one of which, that at Darlford, is the excellent rival of another at Eatanswill, in *Pickwick;* he reported conversations at famous political dinners where nobles sit on tip-toe, each wanting something in the general scramble and some of them not knowing what; he reflected the expectancies, the disappointments, the promises made and broken; he saw the wire-pulling, he heard the magniloquent outpour of campaign rhetoric, on the outside, and the dramatic struggles and

the hopes of the lords of the manors within. The intrigues and
the hypocrisies and the blackguardism of political life, from the
character of the slashing articles written by a Lucian Gay
"whom Nature had intended for a scholar and a wit" but
whom "necessity had made a scribbler and a buffoon" (and
who becomes the brains of Rigby, quick to catch up such a
free lance in journalism), to such methods as only Magog
Wrath and Bully Buck could employ to get votes for the
candidate who hired them, are set before us. We have vividly
portrayed the struggles for power between the new and growing industrial factor represented by Millbank and the old type
patrician like Lord Monmouth, out for Parliamentary representation. We watch the dramatic scenes between that old
pillar of "the organized hypocrisy" and his grandson Coningsby, who, he is determined, shall represent his principles in the
House of Commons; and we witness the subsequent revelation
of the clash between the young idealist and this guardian and
financial supporter of his, who is unable to understand his
revolutionary ideas because he refuses to go to Parliament
on the old man's principles. These scenes are very graphic
and humanly typical. One of them is epical: "By ——!"
exclaims Lord Monmouth, when Coningsby finally tells him
that he cannot and will not support the old Conservative
party, "by ——! some woman has got hold of him and made
him a Whig!" And in that Cimmerian darkness the old
aristocrat lives until his day of death.

In the midst of the pictures of selfish ambition in high places
and low ambition among office holders we are thrown into the
great rooms of the Carlton and the Reform Clubs. We pass
from listening to "murmuring knots of greyheaded privy-
councillors, who had held fat offices under Perceval and Liverpool, and who looked back to the Reform Act as a hideous
dream," and from "middle-aged aspirants who had lost their
seats in the convulsion, but who flattered themselves they had

done something for the party in the interval, by spending nothing except their breath in fighting hopeless boroughs, and occasionally publishing a pamphlet, which really produced less effect than chalking the walls," to the political gossip among the leaders. Here we watch the agitation and the ecstasy which every new message brings, and how a triumph is received upon election day. Then, from these varied types, and again from these institutions, seen on other days and in repose, we pass to Eton and to the great English universities and listen to the ardent and the frank discussions upon the political status of the country for all of a day and far into the night — shot through with all the theory, the generosity, and the sure certainty of judgement which only Youth is capable of, and which Disraeli loved so well to portray. And we close this volume with Disraeli's stirring appeal to them.

"They stand now on the threshold of public life. They are in the leash, but in a moment they will be slipped. What will be their fate? Will they maintain in august assemblies and high places the great truths which, in study and in solitude, they have embraced? Or will their courage exhaust itself in the struggle, their enthusiasm evaporate before hollow-hearted ridicule, their generous impulses yield with a vulgar catastrophe to the tawdry temptations of a low ambition? Will their skilled intelligence subside into being the adroit tool of a corrupt party? Will Vanity confound their fortunes, or Jealousy wither their sympathies? Or will they remain brave, single, and true; refuse to bow before shadows and worship phrases; sensible of the greatness of their position, recognize the greatness of their duties; denounce to a perplexed and disheartened world the frigid theories of a generalizing age that have destroyed the individuality of man, and restore the happiness of their country by believing in their own energies, and daring to be great? [4] "

One fact must always be remembered to the glory of Disraeli as an artist. In the *genre* of writing which he brought to greatest perfection, and contributed to the varied field of English literature and, it may be safely said, to literature in

general, he never degraded his art by the use of long parliamentary debates, elaborate political disquisitions of rivals on
the floor of the House of Commons or in the Lords, the battle-
dore and shuttle-cock play of political mechanics, such as might
have been very naturally expected in novels like these. There
is none of it in *Coningsby*. The second of the trilogy, *Sybil, or
the Two Nations*,[5] is still farther removed from the mere political
arena. It will of course be argued that Disraeli *does* introduce
lengthy discussions upon English history and English party
fortunes in his political novels. But these, at least, have as
much right to appear in his novels as long historical discussions have in the historical or romantic novel, or as pages
of psychological commentary have in the realistic novel. In
each instance an author runs the danger of impeding action
and clogging the plot by the use of these devices. But it must
also be remembered that what may impede the progress of the
novel can also serve to give a value and a cogency to the work
of art which it might not otherwise have. This is notably
illustrated in the Waverley novels of Scott, in Eliot's *Middle-
march*, and no less successfully in Disraeli's trilogy.

Sybil, published a year after *Coningsby*, is a natural continua-
tion of the ideas first propounded in that book. And of *ideas*
rather than individualities, for Disraeli appeared here more
intent on making broad and graphic outlines of the contrasting
social conditions among "two nations," i.e. the rich and the
poor of England during the period from 1837 to 1844 (in which
the story falls), and more concerned in proposing a political
philosophy which should help save the one "nation" and
discipline the virtues of the other, than he was in painting
striking persons. The sight which had been given the young
English aristocracy of Manchester, of its dynamic externals,
and of the embodiment of its enterprise in a Millbank in
Coningsby, is in this book spread out, made into a full view,
and broadened so as to include the lives of many conditions of

workers — male and female, stunted youth and children, among the agricultural class, the industrial class, the miners, — their ignorance, their extreme poverty, their serf-like obedience to their masters, their combinations into unions and their radical and lawless leaders, their dumb and animal-like pleasures. So complete is this side of the volume that its title is the name of a woman who represents the people, pity for their lot and "the hope of their redemption." Disraeli uses here the only sub-plot to be found in any of the trilogy. In the other two books most, if not all, of the characters fall into some one relation or another with the hero, and form no considerable detached or minor combinations among themselves. Here is the nation of the English Peasantry painted for itself. And through influencing eventually Young England to fight for them in Parliament, they are painted so as to educate the reader as well. In contrast with these we are shown again the English aristocracy, their gilded youth, in Lord Milford, Alfred Mountchesney, Lord Fitzheron, suffering from *ennui* at their private clubs, wasting their days and their thoughts on the race-course, ignoring alike the need of their national leadership and the dangers with which the Chartist rebellions, and the conditions of which they are the cause, threaten England. If Disraeli opens his novel with these men rather than with some scene among the poor, which the reader might naturally expect from a book which more than any other of his works shows Disraeli's humanity, it is because his main purpose is still, as he says in the climax of the work, to awaken the younger generation to a sense of their political and social duties. We see, too, in contrast with Lord Marney and the pomp and luxury of Mowbray Castle, Trafford, a model patron and a true nobleman. And finally, the English church in its rôle of helping the people, her past degradation, her present detachment from those whose natural champion she ought to be, and the immediate needs of true Christian philanthropy, are here carefully emphasized.[6]

Ostensibly written to exhibit the sufferings of the poor [7] it is the social aspect of a regenerated Tory philosophy that is here presented. Disraeli sums up in the last pages of the novel his motivating purpose. "A year ago I presumed to offer to the public some volumes that aimed at calling their attention to the state of our political parties; their origin, their history, their present position. In an age of political infidelity, of mean passions, and petty thoughts, I would have impressed upon the rising race not to despair, but to seek in a right understanding of the history of their country, and 'in the energies of heroic youth, the elements of national welfare. The present work advances another step in the same emprise. From the state of Parties it now would draw public thought to the state of the People whom those parties for two centuries have governed. The comprehension and the cure of this greater theme depend upon the same agencies as the first: it is the past alone that can explain the present, and it is youth that can alone mold the remedial future." In the selfish strife of factions many mighty forces have changed their character: Oligarchy has come to be called Liberty, an exclusive Priesthood has been christened a National Church, and Sovereignty has been named for something that has no dominion, while the real power lies in the hands of those who profess themselves to be the servants of the People. In the selfish strife of party and faction two great existences have been blotted out: the Monarchy and the Multitude. As the power of the Crown has diminished the privileges of the People have disappeared. Thus "the scepter has become a pageant and its subject has degenerated into a serf." The book, therefore, attacks the English parliamentary system; it sees little difference between the party in power and the party that is out of power: supposedly different political platforms are humbugs, and control is in the hands of a dozen or more who are unfit and uninformed, but who compose the necessary 'majority' and whose favor may be gained by the promise of a peerage, a baronetcy, or, as the influential ladies of the aristocracy think, by the invitation of their wives to a dinner or a ball. Chartists, socialists, and other radicals believe that the problems of England are to be solved by their social panaceas; they are altogether wrong. Utilitarian philosophers offer up their economic panaceas; the Utilitarians are ignorant and without imagination. When Egremont finally assumes to champion the cause of the "people" in the Commons, he persuades Sybil [8] to his conviction that the pacific method, the legal method, is the wiser method; that the natural leaders are to be found in the generous youth of England, the younger aristocracy, who, awakened to the needs of the masses, are by education, by tradition, by dignity, the proper champions of her people. The King and the People have lost their prerogatives: the two must now unite for their common weal. In a regenerated aristocracy, the germs of which lie in the rising generation, is the hope of a social renaissance. In the marriage of Sybil to Egremont, who represents Young England, Disraeli would symbolize to us, at the close of his novel, the happy consummation of his ideas, precisely as in *Coningsby* the marriage of the hero to the daughter of Millbank presents another facet of the conviction that the future of England lies in the youth of the nobility and of the middle classes.

Let us now sketch briefly the contributions which the author here makes to his world of political paraphernalia. It will be noticed, at once, that in passing from the first to the second of the trilogy we mark the maturing of their respective heroes. Coningsby is still at school when we first meet him, and he is but ready for the Parliamentary combat when the book closes: the whole course of the volume is a means of showing us the process of his education. Egremont, on the other hand, is a member of Parliament from the first, and needs only to be tutored in a great cause which the adventures in the novel furnish him, and the full responsibilities of which he assumes in the course of time, when we receive reports of his action in Parliament. Precisely as in the transition from Coningsby to Egremont we note this maturing of the 'Young England' characters, so, in passing from *Coningsby* to *Sybil* there is a development of Disraeli's political satire: in this novel it has broadened, and is made to embrace not so much persons as the conditions of which those persons are the cause. Members of the old aristocracy in this novel are Lord Marney, the brother of Egremont, and the Earl of Mowbray. These great lords are made representative of the old and despicable Whig philosophy. They are egotistical and self-sufficient, their arrogance is to be measured only by the depth of unrighteousness in their being nobles at all. Disraeli paints the sources from which the ancestors of these men attained their aristocratic station, and he does so to prove that in many instances the 'old nobility' of his own generation hold their places illegitimately: by which fact he appears to sympathize with the strong opinions held upon that point by the elder Millbank in *Coningsby*. The nobles in *Sybil* think only in terms of orthodox economics; their social sentiments are summed up in two phrases: "belief in their own rights as great proprietors," and "poor laws for the poor." The picture of Marney is a generic portrait of his class.

"The countenance of Lord Marney bespoke the character of his mind; cynical, devoid of sentiment, arrogant, literal, hard. He had no imagination, had exhausted his slight native feeling; but he was acute, disputatious, and firm even to obstinacy. He had formed his mind by Helvetius, whose system he deemed irrefutable and in whom he had faith. Armed with the principles of his great master, he believed he could pass through existence in adamantine armour, and always gave you in the business of life the idea of a man who was conscious you were trying to take him in, and rather respected you for it, but the working of whose cold, unkind eye defied you."

Within Mowbray Castle all the ceremony and the pomp with which the rich, who have never toiled for their wealth, can surround themselves stand out in the greater contrast when one steps outside the gates of the castle and visits the homes of the hand-loom weavers, learns the nature of the exactions of the millowners, Shuffle and Screw, and watches the starving and the miserable workers whose toil for a mere pittance is fostering a decrepit and stunted race for the future England. Here in Mowbray Castle we meet the Lady Marney and the Lady St. Julians, great political persons retailing little pieces of political gossip, and fancying that while they are doing so they are determining the fate of empires. There is Lady Firebrace "from whom nothing appeared to be concealed, either in the inmost mind of the Sovereign, the cabinets of the Whigs, or the clubs of the Tories." Her husband, Sir Vavasour Firebrace, believes that all will be well with the world the moment the government vindicates the order of the baronetcy, and gives him back his ancient privileges. In contrast to the conditions at Mowbray and the ruined hovels and the squalor of the agricultural laborers in the town of Marney, is the factory of Mr. Trafford. "With gentle blood in his veins, and old English feelings, he imbibed, at an early period of his career, a correct conception of the relations which should subsist between the employer and the employed. He felt that between them there should be other ties than the payment and the receipt of wages." Here are pretty village streets, beautiful children of contented workmen, pride in labor, and the contentment which alone can furnish Sybil her native home, and her father his employment.

While these broadened contrasts are presented here, first among the nobility, secondly, in the generosity of a Churchman, and thirdly, in that group of grotesque political characters which include worldly women-politicians, and gossips, and Sir Vavasour, and the inimitable Taper and Tadpole, who appear with their 'subtle' schemes for the second time in the trilogy; we are permitted to see also with these the "solemn humbug of politics" going on in Downing Street. A scene which one appreciative reader calls an Aristophanic outburst, is a dialogue between Mr. Hoaxem and 'a gentleman of the Cabinet.' To a deputation of tenant farmers Mr. Hoaxem is instructed to say that the object of the Minister has been to render protection more protective, by making it practical; to a deputation of the great manufacturers of Mowbray, complaining of the great depression of trade, and the total want of profits, he is to say exactly the reverse: show how much has been done to promote the revival of trade, by making provisions cheaper, by cutting off at one blow half the protection on corn (under conditions which make that impossible), and by keeping open the trade with the Continent in live cattle.

"Ring the changes on great measures and great experiments till it is time to go down and make a House. Your official duties, of course, must not be interfered with. They will take the hint. I have no doubt you will get through the business very well, Mr. Hoaxem, particularly if you be 'frank and explicit'; that is the right line to take when you wish to conceal your own mind and to confuse the minds of others. Good morning!"

Sybil as a work of art has fared very variously at the hands of its critics. T. E. Kebbel in his *Life of Lord Beaconsfield* calls the heroine "one of the most exquisite creations that the hand of fiction has ever drawn." [9] As late as 1903 a critic went Kebbel 'one better' by saying that the novel was one of the most marvellous productions ever written by inspired pen, and he doubted if anyone else had ever presented so catholic a picture of society in all its phases.[10] Leslie Stephen praises the novel for the fact that its creator has rivalled his literary masters in turning "blue books" into fiction,[11] which is of course but the story half told. Brandes [12] finds the strong point of the book in the series of well-drawn characters, both from the aristocratic classes and from the industrial workers. Of all of Disraeli's novels this is the one which most resembles a pamphlet on a serious topic, so that the lighter reader will pass it over with a glance; it is best not read at all if not carefully studied. This from Mr. Gosse. On the other hand it has been declared that this novel is a series of tableaux rather than a connected story, lacking therefore any organic unity. Its hero is a thing of shreds and patches with a character as little fixed as his whereabouts. Macknight,[13] a contemporary of Disraeli's, and one of his first biographers, can find no good in it whatever: its sentiment is false and lachrymose, its Chartist leaders are villains and its Chartist heroine an impossibility; the condition of the poor is exaggerated, while the plot is one of the most slender ever put together by a man of letters who takes himself seriously!

When Edmund Gosse says that of all of Disraeli's novels this is the one which most resembles a pamphlet on a serious subject, I suspect that what provoked this characterization was his unconscious dissatisfaction with a novel which was obviously written to stir the pity and the sympathy of the reader for the poor and their miseries and which should in his mind have reflected, as in a quiet body of water, only the depths and the shadows and poignant comedy of these unhappy lives (an art at which Dickens was a master); Disraeli, however, incapable of composing long periods of sustained sentiment, particularly when that sentiment has to do with the homely virtues and vices, makes a 'turbulent' thing of it all because he is so dominated by an intense intellectualism. The charge made against Disraeli that he was incapable of touching the depths of the human heart is ridiculous. But this fact is true, and it is an anomaly as well. The novelist Disraeli could present the tragic story of a hand-loom weaver. That weaver worked twelve hours a day for a penny an hour. He lived in one room with five human beings who were dependent upon him; all of them being accustomed, on cold days, to lie in a couple of wretched beds because they had no clothes, and so got what warmth they could from their huddled bodies.   That room was without food, fuel, or furniture.   His oldest daughter, Harriet, who epitomized the young women working for their daily bread, was seldom at home, spending her evenings in some 'Temple of the Muses' whose hectic and immoral pleasures alone offered her young and buoyant nature some relief from the humdrum and machine-like life of daily toil; the weaver was an artist in his day at his loom, who loved it, and who now, in his old age, is unable to compete with the great machinery of the textile mills and is unable to learn.   Disraeli could paint so poignant and moving a picture as this and then, on the very next page, in a flash and without warning to the reader, could take him as suddenly into a disquisition upon the integral weaknesses of Utilitarian economics, and the historical lapses of the English Church!

This is the method of a writer who attends little or not at all to the working of the average reader's mental processes. A great master of the human soul like Shakespeare, the wiser psychologist, invariably relieved the movement of the story, after an unusually stirring or harrowing scene in his plays, by a bit of comedy or by a farcical situation, — just long enough 'to let the reader down'; and then only did he resume the story.   Disraeli, egotistical, subjective, yet with a mind that played nimbly and worked swiftly upon a wide range of human emotions and ideas, saw no reason why the reader should not be equally well equipped.   But even the best among readers of literature cannot follow this method.   They can understand a humanitarian Dickens, because he aims primarily to inculcate the ideals of Christlike good will and forgiveness among men, and so expatiates lengthily upon his noble lessons.   Dickens does not cross his palm with too many purposes.   For that reason people trust him: they call him

kind, good, gentle, and above all, honest. But Disraeli is an
enigma. And few persons have interest enough to stop and
analyze the processes of a writer's peculiar mental structure.
If he does not fall in with the ordinary conventions and expectations they go on to new fields and pastures, where the
growth is deep and the emotion is luxuriant.

One fact is certain. Lord Morley's belief [14] that Disraeli
showed in Sybil an unusually able grasp of the problem which
"the hungry forties" presented, is that of the most considerable critics of Disraeli's novels. Whether the remedy he
offered was, however, a definite one, or whether, in the work of
art, Disraeli was able to sustain plot and character as a great
writer might have done with the material which was offered
him, are matters which must be more properly left for discussion elsewhere.

We turn now to the last of the trilogy.

To the uninitiated, *Tancred or the New Crusade* (1847) will
always remain a mosaic of brilliant extravagances and theo-
logic discussions, inciting the critics to opinions no less astonishing than is the book itself. Upon its publication James Russell Lowell said: [15] "It is as dumb as the poor choked hunch-
back in the Arabian Nights, when we ask what its business is.
There are no characters in it. There is no dramatic interest,
none of plot or incident. . . . An epigram in three volumes
post octavo is out of the question. The catastrophe has no
moral or aesthetic fitness. Indeed, there is no principle of
cohesion about the book, if we except the covers." And
Walter Frewen Lord, on the other hand, in his *Lord Beaconsfield's Novels:* "There remains a book that is rarely mentioned,
but one that should take rank immediately after, if it does not
take rank side by side, with the masterpiece of *Henry Esmond.*
That book is *Tancred.* The work opens with scenes of rich
comedy . . . some of them the highest form of comedy. . . .
It is filled with galleries of portraits, much bright talk, lofty

scenes, lofty objects . . . and is as different from the curate-
and-tea novel as a book can possibly be. . . . There is a cabbage
by Mieris, and it is very precious; there is also a feast painted
by Veronese. The one art is soothing; the other is noble.
The nobler art is Disraeli's." [16] In considering the place of
this novel in his political trilogy we should do well, first, to
recall the author's own expression of purpose with regard
to it.[17] That purpose, translated in a single sentence from his
system of Tory philosophy as we have already analyzed it,
said, that to bring about the much-desired and necessary
consummation of an alliance between the Crown, the Church,
and the People, faith and faith alone was needed. But that
faith was not to be found in the corrupted church of the day.
A spiritual renaissance was necessary for England; a new
crusade had to be undertaken, the Asian mystery had to be
again discovered before English character, chastened and made
intelligent by a visit to the Holy Land, might rear a great
empire. This program, wedded to the stirring desire of Disraeli to vindicate once for all before England the glories and
the rights of the Jewish race, necessarily gave to *Tancred* less
the quality of a book with a narrow political purpose than of
one in which mere party platforms and interpretations of
English history were crowded out by a supreme religious
motive. And if we consider the fact that in the East, to which
two-thirds of this novel transports us, Disraeli found an outlet
for all that mysticism, that extravagance, those Oriental
flights of fancy which were so peculiar to his character and
which color so much of his literary work, we can better understand why this was an extraordinary novel and was, even
among his own work, *sui generis*. When Mr. Saintsbury says
that one or another of Disraeli's novels stands pretty much
alone, that in each there is something more or less political,
more or less 'society,' more or less fantastic, — that "the
whole is inorganic somehow, and more than somehow unreal,

without attaining that obviously unreal but persuasive phantas-
magoria which some great writers of fiction have managed to put
into existence and motion," [18] he must have in mind, I think,
more than all others of Disraeli's novels — the best of which he
praises in his other writings [19] so splendidly—the novel *Tancred*.

The book begins in the light of common day among London
society, and offers Disraeli material for perhaps more bitter
satire of high society in England' than is to be found in either
of the other two novels. There is the Puritan Duchess of
Bellamont, who thinks she can solve the mystery of a son
brooding over eternal verities and the decay of faith, by appealing to her favorite Bishop; the Bishop, a man with great
talent for action but with very limited powers of thought, is a
leader who was never a guide, only a bustling intermeddler
who enunciated second-hand, and with characteristic precipita-
tion, some big principle already in vogue, and a man who was
never able to supply society with a single solution for its perplexities. The man of the world, Lord Eskdale, urges the
allurements of female society to dissuade Tancred from going
to Jerusalem, and consoles the parents with the thought that
Tancred's resolve to travel to the Holy Land was "better than
going to the Jews, which most men do at his time of life";
the Lady Constance Rawleigh is here, she who admired intellect and found in *The Revelations of Chaos* the 'explanation of
everything'; Lady Bertie and Bellair, though not like Lady
Rawleigh "a distinguished beauty of two seasons, fresh but
adroit," proves to be not the beautiful prophetess Tancred
thinks her, sharing only as a noble spirit can his divine enthusiasms, — but, the most inveterate gambler in Europe!
All these and many others, in amusing dialogue and by occasional dramatic situation, explaining themselves to the reader
by their notions about history, finance, religion, evolution, by
their adroit maneuverings in London society, by their country-
houses, their cooks, and their ailments, — all these are admir-

ably depicted. In an epigrammatic phrase, in a short paragraph which reveals character, Disraeli links himself, through
the first third of this book, with Congreve and with Sheridan.

"There was Lady Hampshire, a character always familiar in
society. . . . She was an invalid; but her ailment was one of
those mysteries which still remained insoluble, although, in the
most liberal manner, she delighted to afford her friends all the
information in her power." . . . "A great nobleman met Mrs.
Guy Flouncey at a country house, and was fairly captivated by
her. Her pretty looks, her coquettish manner, her vivacity, her
charming costume, above all, perhaps, her imperturbable good
temper, pierced him to the heart. The great nobleman's wife had
the weakness to be annoyed. Mrs. Guy Flouncey saw her opportunity. She threw over the Earl, and became the friend of the
countess, who could never sufficiently evince her gratitude to the
woman who would not make love to her husband. This friendship
was the incident for which Mrs. Guy Flouncey had been cruising
for years."

But, says the reader, this social satire is all of a piece in the
trilogy; one finds nothing astonishing here, nor is anything
added to Disraeli's political background! True enough, until
the author turns the screw at the close of the first third of the
book, and sends us off, dressed in seven-league boots of adventure, with his hero to the Orient, on a new crusade to the Holy
Land. No cinematograph producer of this present year of
ours will ever find more grist for his insatiable mill, wherewith
to serve 'the material' and 'the emotional appeal' of a combined performance of adventure for, say, the American 'Bill'
Hart and Douglas Fairbanks, than did Tancred in the Holy
Land in 1845–1847 in his search for "the great Asian mystery."

It all begins in a beautiful garden in Bethany, where, overpowered by the heat of the sun, Tancred falls asleep. He
awakes to find himself in the presence of a lady, exceedingly
beautiful, clothed in rich Syrian costume: amber vest of silk
embroidered with gold and fastened with buttons of precious
stones; huge Mameluke trousers tied with clasps of rubies;

an embroidered pelisse of violet silk, out of whose long, loose sleeves showed occasionally an arm encrusted with more precious jewels; cap, hair, oval countenance of brilliant complexion; large dark eyes whose irresistible power is modified by ineffable tenderness; delicately-moulded chin, neatly-turned ankle, — each and all fashioned with the rest. This is Eva, the Jewess, called the Rose of Sharon, who is also the daughter of the Croesus of Syria, a noble and wealthy Besso to whom Tancred carried letters from his friend Sidonia. Eva stands for the genius of Judaism. From the very moment of her meeting with Tancred and her speech with him we are convinced that her mind must be as marvellous as her many jewels are rare, dazzling, and beautiful. Before the close of the story, after she has rescued him from a powerful Bedouin chief, the sheikh of sheikhs, Amalek, who had captured Tancred and his followers in a great and terrible wilderness of a defile not far from the tomb of Rachel, and was holding him for ransom; after she had nursed him during a dangerous illness and had saved his life with native herbs; after she has initiated him in the festivals of the Hebrew faith, and still more profoundly affected him by her ethnological lore and the inexorable logic of her arguments that the Semitic race is the most consequential of all races, historically, and that the Jews were the greatest of the Semites, — after all this we are not only convinced but we are certain that if ever the hero finds the great Asian mystery it will have something to do with this Lady of Bethany. And so it evidently must, for the novel closes with a love-scene in a kiosk on the margin of a fountain in the road to Bethany, in which Tancred says he is ready to trample to the dust all other ties that bind him to this world if Eva is ready to unite her destiny with his; and Eva lets her head fall upon his shoulder.

Tancred visits the Convent of Terra Santa, and spends his first night in the Holy Land kneeling before the tomb of a

descendant of the kings of Israel and is thus ready thereafter
to pour forth his perplexities on the tomb of the Redeemer.
He descends Mount Sion, crosses Kedron, and enters the sacred
grove where he spends hours in pious ecstasy.   He mounts the
road to Bethany and looks over rocks, and groves, valleys and
mountains, where every spot, every visible tree, is on conse-
crated and hallowed ground.   Before him lies the city which
Mahomet sighed to rule, and over which the Creator of
Christendom poured forth the full measure of his divine sorrow.
Here he meets Fakredeen, a young emir of brilliant and ingenious political stratagems, who is now concerned in obtaining
sovereignty over Syria, now impatient with merely petty
mountain intrigues, and now ambitious to startle the powers
of all Europe by a magnificent scheme or plot whereby,
with the help of Tancred and the fleets of the English queen,
a new social system was to be established for the world, under
the sanction and the superintendence of the God of Sinai and
of Calvary.   Here is one of Fakredeen's political phantasies.
"You Englishmen," he says, speaking to Tancred, "must
perform the Portuguese scheme on a grand scale; quit a petty
and exhausted position for a vast and prolific empire.   Let the
Queen of England collect a great fleet, let her stow away all
her treasure, bullion, gold plate, and precious arms; be accompanied by all her court and chief people, and transfer the seat
of her empire from London to Delhi.   There she will find an
immense empire ready made, a first rate army, and a large
revenue. . . . I will take care of Syria and Asia Minor.   The
only way to manage the Afghans is by Persia and by the
Arabs.   We will acknowledge the Empress of India as our
suzerain, and secure for her the Levantine coast.   If she like,
she shall have Alexandria, as she now has Malta; it could be
arranged.   Your Queen is young; she has an *avenir*.   Aberdeen
and Sir Peel will never give her this advice; their habits are
formed.   They are too old, too *rusés*.   But, you see!   It will

be the greatest Empire that ever existed; besides which she gets rid of the embarrassment of her Chambers! And quite practicable; for the only difficult part, the conquest of India, which baffled Alexander, is all done." Tancred, perhaps somewhat naturally, does not here fall in with this marvellous plan of high statesmanship!

But let us go on. After a week of solitude and of fasting Tancred kneels at the sepulchre of Christ but he receives no message from Heaven. He is determined now to go to Sinai. But on his way across a fearful wilderness of a desert, he and his little force are overpowered by a large number of Arabs, and they are taken to the Great Sheikh. Here, on the supposition that he is the brother of the Queen of England, Tancred is held for an enormous ransom. The machinations which Fakredeen unfolds to Tancred in conversations here, the visit Tancred makes to Sinai and the vision that he finally sees there alone and the message the Angel of Arabia brings him, how he suddenly falls ill and how he is nursed back to life by Eva who has come from Jerusalem, his subsequent desire for great political combinations, — are all matters which can hardly be treated in this survey. Of subsequent adventures, one must not pass over his visit to the mysterious and isolated tribe, in the northern fastnesses of Syria, called the Tribe of Ansarey, whose queen, Astarte, is of a religion that is not of Sinai, nor of Calvary, but rather of Mount Olympus. Her tribe, we are told, are Hellenes who still worship the Greek deities. The visit to this queen having been made from Canobia, the mountain fastness of Fakredeen, after the latter had surrounded himself with Maronites and Druses who felt that they needed still more support through the army which the Queen of the Ansarey might add, the two young men apparently win her favor, since she presumably falls in with their ambitious schemes of conquest. Let us pause here for a moment to reproduce a dialogue between a character named

Keferinis, a Polonius-like Prime Minister to the Queen, and a Consul in the Court, while these discuss high finance and world-politics.

"'Palmerston,' said Barizy of the Tower, 'will never rest till he gets Jerusalem.'

'The English must have markets,' said the Consul Pasqualigo.

'Very just,' said Barizy of the Tower. 'There will be a great opening here.'

'I think of doing a little myself in cottons; but the house of Besso will monopolize everything.'

'I don't think the English can do much here,' said the Consul, shaking his head. 'What have we to give them in exchange? The people here had better look to Austria, if they wish to thrive. The Austrians also have cottons, and they are Christians. They will give you their cottons and take your crucifixes.'

'I don't think I can deal in crucifixes,' said Barizy of the Tower.

'I tell you what, if you won't, your cousin Barizy of the Gate will. I know he has given a great order to Bethlehem.'

'The traitor!' exclaimed Barizy of the Tower. 'Well, if people will purchase crucifixes and nothing else, they must be supplied. Commerce civilizes man.'"

If Disraeli is not above satire of politics and insincere faith as he finds them in the Holy Land, neither is he averse to painting in graphic form, as if to counteract the merely Jewish influences in Palestine, the profound faith of the Greeks as represented in the person of the attractive Queen.[20] As a matter of fact this lady falls madly in love with Tancred; is induced to make a distinct offer to him of her throne and her kingdom, and gives him the troops with which he battles against the Turks. But Tancred's tastes, we soon find, really lie in other directions. Once his love for the Jewess is discovered by the Greek lady, she plans a revenge by scheming to put

both Eva and Tancred to death. The first, however, escapes
through the machinations of Fakredeen; the second (now
that his author must hasten to bring the story to a conclusion pleasing to his readers) himself escapes, both from the
affections and the wrath of the beautiful Astarte, to fly to
the arms of Eva, the Lady of Bethany. With her in the hour
of twilight in enchanted gardens the author winds up his story.

The book is a riot of incident, of extraordinary adventure,
of the incongruities of Eastern life with its squalor and its
splendor made the more memorable by the pilgrimage of the
hero; it is full of the sparkle, the zest, and the fascination of
political intrigue of the Orient, all limned against the picturesque and romantic coloring of the Holy Land, all of it the more
graphic and fascinating to the reader because the author talks
with an eloquence, with a vivacity, paints his descriptions
with a magic of style, which prove that we are sounding the
very depths of him. — There is, indeed, something here, in
this novel (bizarre and incoherent and inorganic as the entire
work afterwards seems to us) which says: this man is talking
with his very soul; the belief he holds is of a sincerity, of an
intensity of conviction, of a terrible earnestness, which will
not let us take him otherwise than seriously. Monypenny
quotes Jowett as saying, that thirty years after its publication, Disraeli told him that he still liked *Tancred* the best of
his novels. One who understands the many-sided Disraeli can
easily see why.

If we attempt to sum up the political message which Disraeli
enfolds within the plot of this volume, we must turn first to
the character of Fakredeen. In spite of the Raisuli-like type
which Disraeli makes of him, one may gather, from the brilliant imagination he exhibits in his talks with Tancred and in
the loyalty which he later shows for his views, that these two
young men serve a purpose in Disraeli's mind. If Tancred is
representative of Young England, Fakredeen, who is really a

copy of Francis of Kazin, is intended to represent Young
Syria. Both men, after full acquaintance, find themselves
suffering from the same religious and political "prostration."
We gather from their many exchanges of views some common
grievances. The land of each of them maintains a certain
order of things, but in neither is there to be found an enduring
principle of conduct. Both complain that in their respective
countries, there is no such thing as a paramount political
right, or a paramount religious truth, or an assurance that
social property is either safe or secure. If truth is in the established church of their respective countries, why, they ask, does
the government support dissent? If the monarch has the
right to govern, why is he robbed of his prerogatives? If the
people really constitute the state, why are they not properly
educated? No, money, capital, profits are the measure of all
worth in these countries. Men's welfare is tested by the
amount of their wages. The least ennobling of all human
impulses, the utilitarian impulse, appears to be the sole and
enduring principle of conduct. In nothing, therefore, whether
it be religion, government, manners, sacred or political or
social life, do they find Faith paramount over Mammon. And,
if there is no Faith, if there is no leading or divine principle of
conduct, how can there be a conception of Duty? So much
for their common philosophy.

In the second place, there emerges out of this volume, if we
look upon it in the light of the political program which Disraeli
evolved for England thirty years after its publication, a
serious group of ideas which were *the very seeds of his foreign
policy* when he came into full political power in the seventies.
"Let the Queen of the English transfer the seat of the Empire
from London to Delhi. . . . We will acknowledge the Empress
of India as our suzerain. . . . The Eastern question is who
shall govern the Mediterranean. . . ." With these sentences of
the year 1847 in our minds look at the events of the seventies.

England was then defined by Lord Beaconsfield as an Asiatic power. If he did not remove the seat of government to India, he had emphatically proved that "the centre of gravity" of British power lay in that colony. He made his Queen the Empress of India, and he sent the Prince of Wales there furnished with "treasure, bullion, and precious arms" and accompanied by all the trappings which would have satisfied even Fakredeen who talked of them in 1847. Fakredeen's vision of an Empress of India holding sway over Asia Minor became the reality in later years of Lord Beaconsfield. He bought the Suez Canal shares to secure an assured way for England to the East, he took Cyprus, and the British Crown eventually got Alexandria. The very writer of an "Arabian Nights' tale" (as the critics like Leslie Stephen have called *Tancred*) showed in that volume, in his knowledge of the political parties of Syria and the entire East, in his pictures of the then Ibrahim Pasha, in his intimate appreciation of the character of Oriental people for whom England had no interest until he, as Lord Beaconsfield awakened it, — he showed there the very heart of his foreign policy when he became Prime Minister of England. It is not too much to say, therefore, that the whole policy of British Imperialism as it was born in the mind of Disraeli, and first put into effect by him as Lord Beaconsfield, Prime Minister, is to be found in its inception in this extraordinary and picturesque romance entitled *Tancred*, published in 1847. During the years 1874 to 1880 the author of *Tancred* and the creator of *Sybil*, realized not only many of the measures of amelioration which he discusses in the last-named work, but almost all of the measures of imperial expansion which saw its germs in the other.

Here is one reason, I think, why Disraeli liked *Tancred* better than any other of his novels so many years after he wrote it. It was the repository for him of those ideas which he, as a statesman, put into practice and brought to full fruitage, and made as his special contribution to the history of Great Britain. The other reason why he liked this best of all his books was because it encompassed his sincere and profound convictions about the Jewish race and the religion of the Old Testament. The ideas about these things were first outlined in *Coningsby*, they were added to in *Sybil*, but they came to their full fruition in *Tancred*.[21] How much, on this particular score, this novel lay close to Disraeli's heart is to be seen in the great poetry and the great beauty with which Disraeli, looking out in imagination upon a land which he loved as if he himself were upon a new crusade, portrays the many scenes of mountain, vale, and stream, that flash before the eyes of the impressionable and poetic youth who carried, as it were, Disraeli's own soul with him in his travels to the Holy Land. After the publication of the *Biography of Lord George Bentinck*, in 1851, in which Disraeli set forth in that prose essay his notions about race, and the importance to the world of the Semitic principle, we find in no other novel thereafter a recurrence to this idea. As Disraeli became constantly more absorbed in matters of state, and as England was forced to recognize his abilities in spite of his personal and racial idiosyncrasies, these matters naturally fell into abeyance with him. But in the forties, when he suffered his great disappointment from Peel, when he was out of office and had time to reflect upon some of the possible obstacles which continued thwarting his insatiable ambition to get ahead, he let his mind dwell upon certain historical facts, and he became convinced that he had hit upon one great obstacle anyway, — that of race. While hundreds of Jewish statesmen, writers, and men of affairs, in 19th century Europe, had preferred to 'let well enough alone,' and were the last to exploit their ancestral origins, Disraeli began now to emphasize them. "The Jews," he cries, "represent the Semitic principle! — all that is spiritual in our nature. They are the trustees of tradition, and the conservators of the religious element. . . . Christianity is the completion of Judaism. . . . Vast as the obligations of the whole human family are to the Hebrew race, there is no portion of the modern populations so much indebted to them, as the British people. It was 'the sword of the Lord and of Gideon' that won the boasted liberties of England; chanting the same canticles that cheered the heart of Judah, amid their glens, the Scotch upon their hillsides, achieved their religious freedom."

Benjamin Disraeli's almost aggressive exploitation of Judaism was, to my mind, evidence in him of a sort of religious conversion. When one considers the fact of his baptism at a very early age, and the altogether cosmopolitan character of his father's literary surroundings and Benjamin's home, one is driven to that conclusion after noting in *Coningsby*, and to a much larger degree in *Sybil* and in *Tancred*, how far the author goes to prove Judaism the noblest of religions and the House of Israel a superior race. That religious conversion was the product of what William James would have entitled, in his *Varieties of Religious Experience*, "the subconscious 'incubation' of motives deposited by a growing experience." A man so profoundly imaginative and egotistical as Disraeli was, persistently impelled by a daemonic ambition to rise, yet lacking those several advantages in the form of family connections and of wealth which might have opened doors for him as they did for less brilliant men, felt the more keenly the persecutions, the reproach, and the isolation with which his political enemies and antagonists surrounded him — a reproach and an isolation due as much to his Jewish ancestry as to any other reason.

His father had cut himself completely off from his synagogue during Benjamin's infancy, his grand-mother was always ashamed of her Jewish ancestry, and Benjamin himself had been baptized at the parish church of St. Andrew, Holborn, when he was thirteen. Yet in spite of all this we learn from Disraeli's *Vivian Grey*, and his *Contarini Fleming*, the two early novels which all critics agree contain the most unmistakable elements of autobiography, that the early period of Disraeli's life abounded in humiliations at least equal to its triumphs, and this was largely on the score of his being an alien, "a stranger." Vivian Grey is a popular hero, an acknowledged leader among his school-fellows for his boldness, his originality, and his mental talents, and yet around him there seems always concealed the possibility of general hatred; nor is it the hatred born of envy, or the ill-will due to success, but it is something more deeply imbedded, something ancestral, something impersonal. When the usher at school first expresses his dislike for Vivian he calls him "a seditious stranger," and some of the boys in defence of their fallen favorite murmur, "No stranger! No stranger!" This appellation, by no stretch of the reader's imagination, can be accounted for in the book as applying to the schoolboy, since of all the youths at the Burnsley school the word "stranger" was least fitted to Vivian. We must interpret this as a passage which obviously enough crept into the novel from some reminiscence of the author's own childhood. To any person familiar with the social life of the private school in the twenties of the past century — and the fact is unfortunately no less true of the twenties of the present — such evidence of boyish intolerance and persecution is altogether probable. "Stranger" was, undoubtedly, not the word actually used against Disraeli, but one decidedly more suggestive of a foreign 'nationality,' expressed with contemptuousness, and therefore felt all the more poignantly by the sensitive youth.

The young Contarini, having a southern appearance and of Italian descent, also emphasizes his unhappiness when he describes his life among his fair half-brothers in the North. "They were called my brothers," he says, "but nature gave the lie to the reiterated assertion. There was no similitude between us. Their blue eyes, their flaxen hair, and their white visages, claimed no kindred with my Venetian countenance. Wherever I moved I looked around me, and beheld a race different from myself. There was no sympathy between my frame and the rigid clime whither I had been brought to live."

Into a character of such intensity, of such passion, and of such aristocratic pride as Disraeli's, these whips and scorns of a cruel prejudice, all the greater to him since his father's home and its literary atmosphere in some respects out-Englished the English homes of many of his youthful acquaintances, would have bit all the more deeply. And in a nature so sensitive as his the resentment would be all the greater, and would hardly be effaced with growing manhood when he took his place on the hustings and in Parliament. There was Daniel O'Connell,[22] the cartoonists in Punch,[23] and that congerie of barking and snapping dogs who, by invective which took the form of verse and of prose, were always at his heels. Disraeli's first candidature at the polls was greeted with a poem of several cantos entitled *Jew-de-Brass*, a violent and bitter attack upon his personal character. In *The Fall of Benjamin*, and in *The Second Book of Benjamin* we find two twenty-five page pamphlets, part of Watt's Political Series which were widely circulated in England, in which Disraeli is described as "a stranger to the feelings and an enemy of the aspirations of the Anglo-Saxon race." Disraeli's later political fortunes were celebrated in various satires, a few of the most interesting of which — typical of so many others printed at the time — may be understood from their titles: *The Blot on the Queen's Head, or How little Ben, the head waiter, changed the sign of the "Queen's Inn" to "Empress Hotel, limited," and the consequences thereof; Ben changes the motto: a Sequel to The Blot on the Queen's Head; Benjamin D—— his little dinner, illustrated by 'Whew.'* One of the cleverest of verse satires, bitterly attacking every known fact in his personal life, and all the events of his political career, was a long poem written in musical-comedy style, entitled

Dizzi-Ben-Dizzi: or, the Orphan of Bagdad.

The 'comedy' of genii, dark caverns, witches, harems, harridans, and other 'Persian' clap-trap, closes with the death of Dizzi-Ben-Dizzi, and the lines

> "Such be the fate of all who do aspire,
> Not with their state content, to reach a higher,
> And who, with pride of place and power imbued,
> Prefer their own ends to the nation's good!"

For a masterpiece of invective, race-prejudice, and distortion of fact, it would be difficult to find another biography to match Thomas Macknight's *The Right Honourable Benjamin Disraeli*, of 646 pages, published in 1854. On the side of his literary work Disraeli's critics were no less severe. Thackeray's satire on *Coningsby* which he entitled *Codlingsby*, one of his "Novels by Eminent Hands," was one of the kindest; and yet Thackeray takes special pleasure in making ridiculous his character of 'Sidonia,' who is here a London Shylock and an old clothes man.

Disraeli had more than a usual share of public criticism to face in the course of his life, and because he sometimes used the bizarre and the unconventional while in the public eye, he no doubt earned more than the usual share of abuse. An appeal to racial prejudice in England in the thirties and forties was apt to be more effective then than it would be now: no doubt, in many instances, it played heavily against Disraeli's popularity. If, then, as Disraeli became a more important public figure, these attacks became more bitter, and continued to remind him of the race in which he was born, can there be anything surprising in the theory that an emotional experience which had been born, and had developed, in impressionable youth, should have become rationalized in his manhood, and, as the psychologist Freud would say in modern terms, exhibit itself then as a *defense reaction* in his writings? Out of his subliminal self, quite unconscious of the motives which had been deposited by years of experience upon him, he wrote pages upon pages about the glories of Judaism, and the superiority of the Semites over all other races.

That he bolstered up his theories of race with a false ethnology and a still falser anthropology, and that he misquoted the facts of history to prove his somewhat bizarre contentions — bizarre they are when we realize that they came out of the otherwise intelligent mid-nineteenth century (a time bound up so thoroughly with scientific research, science which he lampooned so generously in so many of his works and in his addresses) is simply testimony to the fact that when he touched these particular associations in memory and experience, he threw caution to the winds, and wrote only as a man in whom a reconversion of a profound spiritual sort had taken place. I cannot otherwise account for so large a treatment in his trilogy of a religion and a race to which he had less reason to tie himself in his full manhood than did his father, Isaac D'Israeli, who apparently had no intercourse whatever with Jews from the day he had himself stricken from the list of "yehedim" (contributing members of the synagogue) in King's Road, Bedford Row, in 1817, to the year of his death in 1848. And if his father, a literary recluse, found it incumbent — in the face of his cosmopolitan intellectual theories and for the advantage of his social and mental well-being — to detach himself forever from his race and his religion, how much more reason must that son have had to do so who grasped at every kind of political and social influence and beat down every wave of difficulty, the son who aspired to become the Parliamentary leader of the proudest and the most exclusive aristocracy of Europe?

CHAPTER V

THE PRIME MINISTER'S CONTRIBUTION

SECTION A — LOTHAIR

THE span of years which bridges the period from the publication of the trilogy to the appearance of *Lothair* in 1870 is replete with extraordinary interest in the career of Disraeli, the parliamentarian. It marks, at the start, the protracted duel between him and Sir Robert Peel; the latter — hitherto the ostensible head of the Conservative party — ultimately finding himself unable to withstand the terrific punishment which Disraeli dealt him and surveying around him a party which was repudiating his leadership and falling in pieces, closed his career forever as an English Minister. From then on, Disraeli, not through wealth or noble blood or a great alliance, but because his superior mental quality made him stand head and shoulders above his contemporaries of the Conservative association, began the realization of his ambitions. Upon him was placed the onerous duty of the leadership of the Conservatives, and the task of rehabilitating that shattered party. From the time of this crisis in his affairs there begins a constructive career which was to encompass almost thirty-five years of Conservative power held in his hands; it was to see him a Chancellor of the Exchequer three different times under Lord Derby — in 1852, in 1858-9, and in 1867; he was to be twice Prime Minister of England.

In 1868 Disraeli was forced to resign from his first incumbency of the Premiership, which he held for so brief a period after the passing of the Reform Bill of 1867 and the retirement of Derby. He beheld, in the coming of Gladstone and the

Liberals into power, an apparently impregnable majority standing behind his great political antagonist. Disraeli accepted his fate with his accustomed grace as a good loser, and used the presumable leisure which he, as leader of the Opposition, was now to have for some time, to turn his mind once more into literary channels. The man who was to become the author of *Lothair* was now in his sixty-sixth year. He was at a stage in his career where he needed none of the aid which might be gathered from propaganda clothed in the tissues of romance; he was a statesman of settled convictions who could no longer afford to dream of 'Young England' vagaries; he could afford, in the course of time that was now to be his, to survey with some detachment and poise a world upon which he had already exerted the hand of a master, and to satirize it, to lampoon it, and to glorify it without fear of punishment or without asking for reward. *Lothair* is therefore important to us, aside from its value intrinsically as a political novel, for two reasons: it exhibits the author's literary powers broadened and steadily deepened as he himself had grown older; it is not a novel with any expressed or premeditated purpose, but it is rather the comment of a statesman, a Chancellor of the Exchequer withal who could write the most glowing kind of romance, upon historical and political events which had fallen within the decade that was just closing. And being a novelist and not a biographer or an historian, Disraeli chose only to reflect out of the critical years in European history upon which this novel is based, those historical and political phenomena which interested him as a novelist — though they may not have been, from the viewpoint of the professional student of affairs, the most important phenomena in history-making, or at least, not all of them the most important.

Let us glance at a few of the events and note some of the influences which were powerful in their operation in making the society of England, and the nationalities of Europe, under-

go certain extraordinary changes in the years from 1860 to
1870, and more particularly from 1866 to the end of 1868 —
which are the years reflected in the novel. We shall then
better understand what Disraeli does with them.

Historians tell us that this decade was the turning point in
the history of modern Europe. During this period of storm
and stress in international affairs, the power of Prussia was
exerted against Austria so as to turn the centre of interest
of central Europe from Vienna to Berlin. The beginning of
the decade marks the emergence of the state of Piedmont in
Italy, exhibits the diplomacy of Cavour in full blossom, sounds
the presence of the forces of Napoleon III of France to aid
Piedmont against Austria, and marks the final beginnings of
the great unification of Italian States under the leadership of
the model Piedmont. Garibaldi and his 'Red Shirts' appear
upon the scene. Sicily is taken and then the kingdom of
Naples. Garibaldi's first contemplated attack upon Rome is
frustrated by Cavour who fears to alienate Napoleon III by
the action, but is followed by the successful attack of Victor
Emmanuel against the papal states, excepting their capital,
Rome. By the year 1866 the unification of Italy was practically completed. To Venetia, to the kingdom of Sardinia,
and to Tuscany, Modena, Parma, the kingdom of the Sicilies,
the Marches and Naples — all of them now under the banner
of the king, Victor Emmanuel II — there yet remained this
holy city of Rome and its surrounding territory to be gathered,
in order to consummate that United Italy which had been the
dream of Mazzini, and of the Carbonari who had cried for
constitutional freedom and for freedom from the foreigner,
Austria. Throughout the year 1867 Garibaldi is once more in
arms against the Roman territories, but in spite of all the
changes of fortune which followed his forces throughout that
year he is at length defeated in November at Mentana, by the
combined French and Papal armies. An Italian army was not

to triumph over Rome until 1870 when Napoleon, struggling in the Franco-Prussian war, withdrew his French garrison from the papal seat and gave the Italian king a chance to enter it in triumph. Then, by a plebiscite, the Romans overwhelmingly declared in favor of annexation to Italy. And thus the temporal power of the Pope, which had held sway for over a thousand years, came to an end.

In England during this period, aside from the great political revolution which ushered in the Reform Bill of 1867, two marked facts lying under all other political phenomena need to be noted. First there was the patent struggle between the new forces of science and evolutionary thought and the old forces of devout religious faith. By the side of one of these stood the papal power, with its English Cardinals who, in their desire to pluck every brand from the burning, were not squeamish in the subtle and adroit methods they employed to further their ends. Next was to be noted the state of Ireland, and in particular, immediately following the close of the American Civil War, the beginning of the activities of the Fenian Societies against English rule in Ireland by their use of Irish soldiers, who had borne arms in the war in America, to pillage and murder English officials in Ireland, and to start general uprisings there. From 1866 to the close of 1867 and even to 1870, when Michael Davitt, who afterwards aided Parnell in the Land League, was given fifteen years' penal servitude for participation in the Fenian conspiracy, the story of this 'secret society' is one of murder, burnings, and then of retaliation and of punishment by the English authorities.

That Disraeli chose to reflect these political and historical influences and episodes without making any mention, in the novel, of the acts of his own ministry or of the acts of his predecessor and friend, Derby, and that he kept strictly away from actual doings in Westminster Palace, and as far as possible from discussing the acts of the Political Opposition who were

then in power, is, first, proof of his good taste — particularly
so of one who had looked into the Holy of Holies in the parliamentary life of Downing Street, and of one who had stood on
almost intimate terms with the Queen. Secondly, it is the
best proof that we are dealing here with a work in which the
author is impelled to write not because he has some secret to
give away, or some ideal to impose, but rather because it was
a pleasure for him to talk of things that his fancy liked to play
about, to reflect a patrician society with a freedom and a
buoyancy which only a mystical and a romantic nature could
afford to allow itself. It is because of this fact that we find
here the style of Disraeli characterized by an ease and a natural-
ness that are absent from all his earlier works in like degree.
In this novel, as Mr. Gosse admirably says, Disraeli "is like
an inspired and enfranchised boy set free from the trammels
of reality, and yet bringing to the service of his theme the results of an extraordinary inherited experience. If the picture
is not reality we may take courage to say that it is far better
than reality — more rich, entertaining, intoxicating." [1] Both
Mr. Gosse and Anthony Froude believe *Lothair* to be the most
remarkable of all of Disraeli's novels. Certainly, to judge
from the extraordinarily wide reading public to which it
appealed, it was one of the most popular — if not the most
popular — of all his novels. [2]

The plot may be here worth recalling, and because so com-
pactly presented by Mr. Buckle, and so nicely drawn together
by him, will be told in his words. "The Hero, one of those
fortunate beings whom Disraeli loved to paint, an orphan
peer — apparently a marquis — of fabulous wealth, brought
up and educated quietly in Presbyterian fashion in Scotland,
is thrown, as he reaches adolescence, fresh upon the world,
first of Oxford, and then of London and the great country
houses. The priggishness born of his early education leads
him at the outset to say, 'My opinions are already formed on

every subject; that is to say, every subject of importance; and, what is more, they will never change.' But he is in reality very impressionable, and anxious to discover, like Tancred, what he ought to do and what he ought to believe. All the influences and all the teachers of the day are naturally concentrated upon one whose adhesion might be expected so materially to benefit any cause which he espoused. The main struggle is between three forces, represented by three women, with all of whom Lothair falls successively in love. These forces are, first, the Church of Rome; secondly, the international revolution and what might be called free religion; and thirdly, the Church of England and the round of duties and occupations natural to Lothair's birth and station. Clare Arundel, the representative of the first force, is an attractive and ardent saint; Theodora Campian, the representative of the second force, has great personal charm, lofty character, and high purpose. But Theodora dies and Clare Arundel enters a convent; and the victory is won in the end by the Lady Corisande, the representative of the third force." It might be well to add to Mr. Buckle's summary that the main part of the action occurs in London, and for the rest is divided between Italy and the environs of Rome, where the hero — through the inspiration of Theodora — fights under the banner of Garibaldi against the papal forces, and then on the Mediterranean and in the Holy Land where Lothair, like Tancred before him, is made subject to the purifying influences of the fount of Christianity. Here Lothair meets a 'mysterious stranger,' a forceful personality named 'Paraclete, the wise Syrian-Christian who gives final force and definition to the conservative spiritual perceptions already at work in the soul of the young nobleman, so that he emerges thereafter a man of settled and of firm convictions.

Lothair is a political novel but without a political purpose such as we found in the trilogy. It deals with the currents of thought that flowed through the great ruling classes of the English period of the 60's; a patrician class at the very height of their magnificence which the industrial stimulus of the age had augmented; a class which, for want in part of the simple homely virtues, were drifting everywhere aimlessly, and in increasing instances were falling to 'the seductions of the Roman harlot.' Around these are heard the echoes of a great European revolution — particularly as it was typified in the varied efforts and in the personalities presented in the growing unification of Italy. And within the very gates of the English ruling classes there sounded the notes of their own impending dangers — the Fenian societies, the wily and brilliant maneuverings of the great Catholic Church, the ingenious and dangerous shakings of Conservative faith by such a Pantheistic worship as was represented in the intellectually distorted mind of the artist, Mr. Phoebus.

The outstanding character of the novel next to the hero, Lothair, is Theodora. As drawn by Disraeli she is no ordinary woman. She is, as Froude has happily observed, the incarnation of the Genius of the European Revolution. Her cosmopolitan character, the sort of response which she calls out in Lothair — always a spiritual and never a physical thing, her extraordinary influence among the leaders of the Garibaldian camp (including its General), her mysterious place in English society where she remains only for a comparatively short time, her courage and hardihood which is more than masculine even in actual battle, the manner of her death, and finally the sudden and unexpected appearance of her Presence to Lothair after her death, when he needs, in the greatest spiritual crisis of his life, a guiding hand: all these make of her personality a sort of allegory, an allegory spun like a thread of gold through the book, and not an elaborately conceived flesh-and-blood heroine. She is, after all, a Spirit — as Disraeli almost unconsciously calls her when he tells us that as a girl of seventeen she had sat for the head of 'La République Francaise.' She is a spirit embodied for us here in a matron of almost classical beauty who, Italian by birth, French from inspiration, American in marriage, a keen and generous sympathizer with all movements for freedom everywhere in the world, proves to have in this novel the power and the devotion and the high purpose of a veritable Jeanne d'Arc, as she organizes, as she fights, as she lays down her own life for her own land in the high cause of Liberty.

If Theodora is a sort of Margaret Fuller in intellectual accomplishments, and a Jeanne d'Arc in action, other characters in the book appear to take on a symbolism as well, though perhaps not so obviously intended as hers. There is Cardinal Grandison, whose imperturbable dignity and gravity, and whose masterly handling of an intelligent but an impressionable youth, by exerting the superb and audacious powers of his intellect upon him through treacherous and evasive diplomacy, remind one of the Church of Rome in its full panoply and grandeur, and also in the profound subtlety of its intrigues. If Cardinal Grandison stands for the greater panoply, Monsignor Catesby, whose name is patently chosen by his creator for the part he plays in the novel, represents the petty tricks and the usual artifices of the same significant religious force working upon English life. For the England of the 60's, when men of this sort — cardinals, monsignori, and others — were gaining a dangerous hold among the intellectual classes, and too many members of the nobility, men as well as women, turned to Rome as a natural reaction from the infusion of scientific doubt in religious faith, Disraeli was drawing attention to a great and growing political evil in public life.

More conscious, too, than were most writers of his time, was Disraeli of the great political significance of 'secret societies': the Mary Anne associations of France, the Fenians come out of America to work in Ireland and England, the

Madre Natura in Italy. Of their vast historical importance for good and evil, history has since proved that his emphasis of them in a novel, romantic and chimerical as it must have appeared to his own time, was wisely made with regard to two countries at least — Italy and Ireland. Not that he sketches the intricate maneuverings of these organizations with too firm a hand, in this novel. Lothair's single but exciting contact with the Fenians at Hoxton, the French Ambassador's affirmation that the Mary Anne societies are vigorously at work in his land, seem almost to dispose of two of the secret forces. Only the Madre Natura is drawn firmly, and Captain Bruges is a practical embodiment of their power in action, as Theodora is of their spiritual vigor.

Because the novel had no specific political purpose to impede the natural flow of plot and of characterization, and because here, and for the first time, Disraeli could sit back and survey with particular detachment the society of which he was now a guiding hand and a leader, he talked about it with a freedom and an intimacy and with a lack of restraint that is unknown in his earlier works. The dazzling pageantry which forms around the lives and the homes of the English ruling classes as here painted is unsurpassed elsewhere in Disraeli's novels, — in its elevated tone, its oriental magnificence, the beauty, benignity, and *ennui* of its noble ladies, and the superb wealth and the boundless power of its men. This novel is literally an Arabian Nights' entertainment transplanted into the city houses of London's noble families, and into their country-seats as well. It is a book, as Edward FitzGerald called it, "like a pleasant Magic Lantern." Its hero is as rich as Aladdin when he left his cave: he plans to build a cathedral, and he actually finances a revolution with less personal interest than when he purchases 'ropes of pearls' for Theodora, and a crucifix of gold and emeralds with its earth from the Holy places covered 'with slit diamonds' for Miss Arundel. The extraordinary brilliant, dramatic, and costly scene of the coming-of-age ceremonies at Muriel Towers is only fitting and proper in a work that abounds with marquis, merchant prince, dukes and their daughters, Phoebus, an artist of colossal wealth who has a steam yacht named Pan and an island in the Aegean sea, and the Lord St. Aldegonde — he of many humours — whose wife Albertha's sole and engrossing anxiety is to save her master "from being bored."

The style of the work is in keeping with the people who inhabit it. Radiance of rhetoric, vivacity and cheerfulness of temper, the glow of romantic description appear in page after page. The intention of the author to breathe into his chapters the very atmosphere of the elegant patrician life which he knew so well, allowed him a freedom of expression that makes his language always highly pictorial, and which often reaches stages of floridity and exaggeration. There is the description of Muriel Towers, the Tournament of Doves at the Putney Villa, — typical of some settings in England. There is the gorgeous outline of the ride through the Apennines, the view of the Campagna, the vision of Rome in twilight, and the pageantry of rites and ceremonials in the holy seat of the Catholics. Here is a description of a rich evening sky: "the clouds of the summer evening were glowing in the creative and flickering haze of the vanished sun, that had passed like a monarch from the admiring sight, yet left the pomp behind." Here are the Christian names of his ladies, whom Disraeli's rhetoric does not spare: *Theodora, Euphrosyne, Albertha, Corisande, Apollonia, Claire.* Nor has Disraeli's old epigrammatic quality of expression, and the richness of his humor, decreased in those years when he poured over Exchequer accounts, and stood Leader of the Opposition. On the contrary, they appear to have ripened like good wine since the days of the 40's and the composition of the trilogy. Phoebus declares that he will not undertake an important mission to

Egypt — and then he recalls the fact that no one has yet painted a camel, and if he went a camel would be painted. There are the social aspirations of Mrs. Putney and of Mr. Pinto; the Cardinal's analysis of what is a perplexed Church; the definition of 'a ladies' council'; Apollonia's version of the effect of climate upon religion; the picture of St. James Square; "Pantheism is atheism in domino"; the hansom cab — "'tis the gondola of London"; the small round breakfast tables at Brentham suggest the early Republics. After the Garibaldian defeat at Mentana, and the subsequent illness of Lothair, there is a scene in Rome between Cardinal Grandison and the convalescent youth in which the former, with a superb and almost classic audacity, attempts to convince the Garibaldian hero that he had actually fought, and had fallen fighting, on the side of *the papal forces*. For the vision of the Virgin which was supposed to have come to him, for his great political service, the Cardinal promises the young and now perfectly astonished revolutionary hero, that he is to become another St. Thomas to Christendom! That the Holy Father would himself receive him into the Church! All this is said by Grandison in the face of the most vigorous denials by the astonished youth; and said with an imperturbable countenance, and in the manner of one who is talking to a spoiled child. This particular scene would be a masterly example of high comedy in the book if it were not intended by Disraeli more obviously for keen satire.

Because of the very gorgeousness of the imagery and the splendor of the rhetoric, Disraeli's satire — for a grand satire of the ruling nobility this book is, if ever there was one — becomes all the broader and therefore the more effective in the presentation. Froude hits the nail squarely on the head when he says that in painting these patrician families like flowers in a hot-house, artificially forced to splendor, Disraeli shows how far they have been paralyzed by the enchantment which condemns them to uselessness. Under the surface of this vast patrician life there sounds, throughout the book, the stir and action of political revolutionary forces and the menace of a great political-religious organization — both in and out of England — which would threaten to engulf the whole of English noble life, but which these men and women, heedless of the dangers, pay no attention to, and yet which must eventually mark the destruction of their great power. The author places his contrasts without comment; he does it even while poking fun at his own "Semitic hallucinations" (by which, says Phoebus — speaking for the author — there has come a disturbance of Aryan society and of Aryan manners, and therefore all the evils of modern life); but the serious reader, who can see below the surface of his sardonic countenance and read the mask of this 66-year old statesman who appears to be writing a fantasy, learns his serious intentions!

And so, in spite of all the occasional tawdry rhetoric, and of a world seen through a looking-glass of magic, the ingenuous Lothair — weak as he sometimes appears to an unsympathetic reader, is yet a youth with a heart touched with beauty. He is a pilgrim wandering in a perplexed world and seriously seeking light. If he finds, in the end, that he cannot reconcile the various churches, that he is unable to make his financing of a Garibaldian venture against the papal forces a success and so a stroke for Liberty, that he cannot remove the poverty from the great world around him — if he learns, with something of despair, that the world (like his own Club, which had been unaware of his absence, and cared nothing for his great experiences since he had last left London), that the world has no special interest in the ardent devotion of young idealists for Great Causes, he knows that his failure, at least, has come only after he had attempted to do Great Things. He was considered one of that race which Phoebus had compared to the ancient Hellenes; in three respects they were like the

Hellenes: "they excel in athletic exercise, speak no language but their own, and never read." But he was in reality not like one of them. He had proved himself a manly individual, quick to perceive the great political and social issues marking a changing world, and ready to hurl himself into the midst of them, for better or for worse. He, the wealthiest of them all, with estates so many that he had no permanent home, with a title so noble that his creator does not even mention it, a youth, an orphan, is thrown like a frail bark into a great eddy of conflicting forces. Yet he battles his own way out. For Lothair, at the close of the volume, is a man of settled political and religious convictions, and the woman he marries — Corisande — is of a sweet and reasonable nature, with sound and honest English sense. Here was a fitting mate for one who had battled for the right, who had learnt what is public duty, who had an innate love of humanity, who was struggling to undo great wrongs, and in whose own soul there breathed the perfume of a flower that told of a love for things that are true and of good report — a flower to match the one that Corisande gave him in the garden.

"And they returned almost in silence. . .

'What has become of you, my good people?' said her Grace; 'bells have been ringing for you in every direction. Where can you have been?'

'I have been in Corisande's garden,' said Lothair, 'and she has given me a rose.'"

And with these words the book ends. Two sincere and honest natures had plighted their troth.

SECTION B — ENDYMION AND THE UNFINISHED NOVEL

ENDYMION, the last novel written by Benjamin Disraeli, now the Earl of Beaconsfield, was published in 1880. He was then seventy-six years of age, and approaching very close to the final curtain which, within one year, was to be rung down upon his own extraordinary life. Appearing precisely a decade after *Lothair*, this final work came at the end of the most dramatic single period of his public career — of ten years filled with great triumphs, great accomplishments, the receipt of the highest national honors, and of general admiration and esteem. Yet in this, the final complete product of his imagination, the author was pleased to make no reference either to his own part or to that which his contemporaries played in this great decade of his life, any more than he was intent to leave at the close of his long parliamentary career (what many fastidious moralists find fault with him for not leaving)[3] some instructive lessons and some noble reflections garnered from his own public experiences. That he chose, at the end, to clothe none of his characters in grave attire, emitting profound moral platitudes, — that his political hero succeeds in life without positing lessons of ethical significance, and inspires no reader with solemn conclusions, was after all Disraeli's own affair. No novelist should be criticized if he prefers to act, to the very end, the artist rather than the political philosopher or the political moralist; if he depicts political life as he finds it rather than as others think he ought to have found it.

That Disraeli chose in *Endymion* to ignore the strenuous period that fell between the 70's and the 80's for his material of contemporary politics, and that he reverted to the days of his early manhood, is, however, a cause for regret. For if ever the story of a man and of an historical period of thirteen years, offered likely grist for a novelist's or a dramatist's mill, it was that of Disraeli arrived at the culmination of his political ambitions in the years from 1868, when he first reached "the top of the greasy pole" (as he himself once described his first Prime Ministership), to 1881, after the cause of Imperialism had been definitely planted in the life of Great Britain, and the author of the cause was himself about to be called back to his fathers.[4] The casual reader of history will recall some of the outstanding facts of the time.[5] Disraeli's first Administration lasted but nine months of the year 1868, and was a hectic period for him, who tried, after accomplishing one of the most striking acts of his career — the introduction and the passage of the Reform Bill which had been more democratic and sweeping than any that the Liberals had hoped and prayed for ("the leap in the dark" which had "dished the Whigs," they called it) — to carry on a government without a majority in the House of Commons. Upon his resignation, the peerage which had been offered him for his services to the Crown, he had asked Queen Victoria to bestow upon his wife, — a dramatic request which the Queen graciously complied with. Lord Derby died in 1869. Disraeli passed now from being the nominal head of his party to its real and acknowledged leadership, a power which he held uncontested until the day of his death. Aiding in the full reorganization of the Conservatives in 1872, it was a proud boast indeed which he made on the following year when, in his address at the University of Glasgow where he had been re-elected Rector, he declared that he had led his party in the Commons for an unbroken period of twenty-five years, "the longest period of leadership on record." [6] In 1870 it was Disraeli who, during the Franco-Prussian War, urged the armed neutrality of Great Britain; and it was he who saw thereafter the importance of insisting upon securing the independence of Belgium. Declining the Prime Ministry in 1873, when the Queen offered it to him upon the resignation of Gladstone, he assumed it again, however, the following year and held in his hands thereafter the fate of his country until the year preceding his death.

Two great programs carried on to fruition marked the period of his final Ministry: first, the passage of a series of important social and educational reforms which in some respects revolutionized the internal life of England; second, the establishment of that Imperial Foreign Policy with which his name was ever thereafter associated in the history of nineteenth century Britain. The details of the first of these programs have been presented already in this study. The second is remembered generally by most persons for a number of outstanding events. There was the purchase of the Suez Canal shares from a bankrupt Khedive, in which Disraeli outwitted France, and the money for which he obtained secretly (the 'archconspirators' being the Queen, the Cabinet, Rothschilds, and Montagu Cory, Disraeli's devoted secretary). Calling together Parliament for the purpose "would have blown everything to the skies, or to Hades," he said in a letter to Lady Bradford later.[7] There was the assertion of British interests in Turkey and in Egypt, thus committing the country to an aggressive policy in the Near East. Nearer home the Prime Minister argued that "Bismarck was really another old Bonaparte" and so, when in 1875 Germany again threatened France, Disraeli successfully "bridled" him, and thus assured the integrity of France. The formulation of Disraeli's Far Eastern Policy, the presentation to the Queen of the title of "Empress of India," and the annexation of the Transvaal, in 1877, are all matters well recalled to-day. What Disraeli did in the following year, at the Berlin Conference — the influence he had upon the provisions of the Treaty of Berlin, and the effects of his influence upon the subsequent history of Russia, the Balkans, Greece, and upon the Far East, as well as upon Germany and France, spells the most important and far-reaching international work of his entire career. By that, as Mr. Buckle well observes, his reputation as a European statesman will always stand or fall. His return to England from Berlin at the close of the Conference was then, at least, marked by no doubts or questionings by the masses of the people. He had brought back "Peace with Honour," and the enthusiastic reception which greeted him in London, the congratulations which poured in upon him, the reception by the Queen and the warm indorsement by Parliament of the treaty — all these, added to the opinions held of him by foreign potentates and not the least by Bismarck, marks Disraeli at the zenith of his long public career. When, two years later, the Liberals under Gladstone succeeded in returning to power because of a period of commercial depression which Disraeli's Government could have done nothing to prevent, and which the Opposition used as their opportunity for condemning that Government as they likewise used the unfortunate wars which had broken out in Afghanistan and Zululand, Disraeli's real work had of itself reached a natural climax so that he was ready to bid his final farewell. All these facts Disraeli preferred to leave to the historian, perhaps to the dramatist who chooses to exploit modern English history for the material of his pageants. [8]

With the discovery, among Disraeli's papers, of an unfinished novel, which was first published in 1905 by *The London Times*, it is now clear that one great contemporary, at least, Disraeli had planned to draw in a novel which he had begun writing after he had retired from the Prime Ministry in 1880. That contemporary was his greatest rival in Parliament during the maturer years of his activity, and one who, during the years of Disraeli's Ministry, was his severest critic: William Ewart Gladstone. The fragment which has come down has but nine thinly sketched chapters, but bears genuine evidence of the hand which had composed *Coningsby* and *Lothair:* it contains all the old touches of irony, of familiar satire and of humor, and there is even the suggestion in it of the creation of another man of mystery who might have become another Sidonia. As one now re-reads snatches of characteristic description and notes the portrait-analysis in it one is eager, indeed, to know how far Disraeli might have gone with his arch opponent, whom he calls, in this unfinished novel, Joseph Toplady Fal-

conet. What kind of satire, what scenes of religiosity and of
moral melancholy, might he not have incorporated into the
drawing of this man who, during the last years of his political
life, followed his administration of the Government with
personal animus.

"Joseph Toplady Falconet had been a child of singular
precocity. His power of acquisition was remarkable, and, as
he advanced in youth, his talents were not merely those which
ripen before their time. He was a grave boy, and scarcely
ever known to smile; and this not so much from a want of
sympathy for those among whom he was born and bred, for
he seemed far from being incapable of domestic affection, but
rather from a complete deficiency in the sense of humor, of
which he seemed quite debarred. His memory was vigorous,
ready, and retentive; but his chief peculiarity was his disputatious temper, and the flow of language which, even as a
child, was ever at command to express his arguments. In
person, with a commanding brow, his countenance was an
exaggeration of that of his father; austere even to harshness,
and grave even to melancholy." Falconet senior, Disraeli goes
on to tell us, had political ambitions for his gifted son, and
the first step toward their realization came when a Minister
of State, upon whose West Indian property, as it happened,
the house of Falconet held a mortgage (a considerable embarrassment for the noble lord), was made aware that if the son
Joseph could be allowed to succeed to the representation of a
borough over which the nobleman had control, the gratitude
of the house of Falconet toward him would remain no shadowy
thing thereafter. "And so it came about that Mr. Falconet
and his son were invited to spend the Whitsun week at the
great house, and a public meeting in the borough, *on the revival
of the slave trade in the Red Sea*, having been arranged, Mr.
Joseph Toplady Falconet had the opportunity of making a
speech, which literally electrified the audience. The speech,

indeed, became not only famous in the place where it was delivered, but it was reported in the London papers, and leading articles were written, attesting its commanding eloquence, and announcing the advent of a new and powerful candidate for the honours of public life. True it was that it subsequently appeared that there had been no revival of the slave trade in the Red Sea, but that the misapprehension had occurred from a mistake in the telegraph, manipulated by a functionary suffering from a *coup de soleil* or *delirium tremens.* But this did not signify and made no difference whatever in the eloquence of Mr. Joseph Toplady Falconet, or the result which that eloquence was to accomplish."

Joseph is successfully returned from the borough and takes his place for the first time in the House of Commons. The Falconets give a dinner in their home to celebrate the victory. The noble lord was glad to appear at the dinner, and to grace the occasion with his presence. Dinner over, the young ladies of the party, sweet voices and skilful musicians, sing some psalms, but his lordship, the personification of tact and of polished sympathy, "did not find it out. He sat on a sofa . . . between Mr. and Mrs. Falconet. Joseph Toplady sat on a chair opposite to them, looking earnest and rather grim. They discussed his new life in the House of Commons, and Joseph took the opportunity of remarking that he had received new information respecting the slave trade in the Red Sea and thought of bringing the matter forward. 'I think I would leave the Red Sea alone,' said the Earl. 'It was a miracle that saved us from being drowned in it before.'" That Disraeli's skill in phrase-making which he had exhibited in all of the political novels had not deserted him in this last work must be clear enough already. It is more confidently affirmed when we note such further observations as the fact that there is a free masonry among prigs, and that all prigs spoke of Falconet as the coming man; that 'Lady Bertram was a perfect parent — in theory: she wished her daughter to have every advantage and enjoy every delight that was alike proper and practicable, only she was too much interested about herself to be able to spare any time to carry her theories into practice'; a Buddhist missionary is to be given a congregation among the Chinese about the Port of London, by his lady neophytes: there must be made the elements of a congregation; 'the English like a congregation. The moment there is a congregation they think the affair is practical!'

The fragment of the novel left us — a work in which Gladstone was to have been, possibly, the principal character — cannot help calling to mind some thoughts about the relationship of these two unusual men. The purpose of this study of a literary *genre* can hardly permit our entering the field of political history, much less of discussing the relative merits of the two Victorian figures in statesmanship. And yet, because the great leader of the Liberals played so important a part in the parliamentary life of Disraeli that he could not resist the temptation of wishing to present Gladstone in his romances, it seems almost essential to hazard some opinion at least why Disraeli and Gladstone, men of the world that they were, failed to appreciate one another at their full value; and why Disraeli, even in the fragment of less than a dozen chapters that he left of his unfinished novel, appears to be so completely unfair to the moral greatness of his rival. Certainly, in the latter years of his life, Disraeli failed conspicuously in realizing the great qualities of Gladstone. What was the reason?

In the first place, it must be remembered that Gladstone was a man distinguished for a sort of 'apostolic fervor,' for a parochial righteousness of conduct, that showed itself from his earliest youth when he himself preferred to take holy orders rather than to enter public life, and the Parliament to which his father steered him. He too, like Disraeli, had intellectual sincerity, but it was a sincerity which showed itself in a moral earnestness in the conventional sense: I say this to contrast it with Mr. Monypenny's analysis [9] of Disraeli in this respect. "Though Disraeli knew and practiced intellectual sincerity, he permitted his mind to play too freely and sincerely over everything that came before it to convince many outsiders that he possessed moral earnestness in the conventional sense." Disraeli had humor, wit, and was a master of satire; Gladstone was a man too conscious of the mission of high statesmanship, too much filled with grave principles of conduct, too earnest — with an earnestness unrelieved by any sense of humor, or of gayety of spirit, to see any virtue in his rival's *flippancies*. To his rival, on the other hand, some of the best writings of Gladstone were always *prosaic*. "It was," says Mr. Buckle,[10] speaking of Gladstone's attacks upon Disraeli's Indian and Eastern Policy, "it was perhaps the most conspicuous instance of Gladstone's tendency in the latter half of his life, to believe and to preach that all the most important political questions involve moral issues." And then, comparing Disraeli's attitude in this regard he goes on to say: "As a matter of fact, and as Disraeli saw, political questions seldom present clear-cut moral issues, so that you can definitely say that one course is morally right, the other morally wrong. But the politician who, like Gladstone . . . can persuade a serious and religious people like the English, and still more the Scotch, that such an issue is involved, has a tremendous electoral and Parliamentary advantage. This method of conducting political controversy was repugnant to Disraeli, who despised it as savouring of cant; hence, no doubt, came much of the suspicion and misconstruction which he (Disraeli) was never able to dispel. He took the commonsense view that in politics it is generally a question merely of the more expedient course; and that the prime duty of a British statesman is to regard British honour and promote British welfare." Here, it seems to me, is the more obvious reason, the one which must occur to the average mind, why the men could never truly understand one another. And in these facts, as we see them now, lies the explanation to my mind for Carlyle's bitter comment upon them both, Gladstone and Disraeli. To his rough sincerity of conscience, which hated above all things to see a politician have recourse to supernatural inspiration for every argument which had to be used to support the merest dictates of Parliamentary tactics, it appeared that Disraeli, though a clever, conscious juggler, was outmatched by his rival, Gladstone, who was the greater rascal because he was *unconscious* of his juggling.[11] But there was another reason for the misunderstanding between them which, in their later years, took on upon Gladstone's side, in 1878, a bitterness of personal attack unmeasured in its violence and akin to personal animus,[12] and upon Disraeli's a belief that Gladstone had gone "mad": "What restlessness! what vanity! . . . Easy to say he is mad. It looks like it. My theory about him is unchanged: a ceaseless Tartuffe from the beginning. . . ."[13] That reason is that Disraeli, actor in politics, fervid and intense and romantic in emotion, was after all a solitary figure in the nation that he loved, solitary by his race which he always championed, and detached from those whom he governed. He was primarily a man of ideas, rather than of emotions. Gladstone was the very opposite in every respect. The man whom Disraeli charged with being "carried away by the exuberance of his own verbosity" was a high-minded, honorable English gentleman, fired by emotions that were intelligible to the average Englishman, with nothing in him of the artist, the romantic poet, the Orientalist. He had something of the narrowness of the Victorian, something of the Philistinism of the practical-minded Briton, but he was too much the moral idealist to reckon with temperament, and too conscious of the call of Duty within the borders of England to appreciate the imagination of a political rival whose "wings" spread out to encompass an imperial Great Britain, a country which might take for its standard the Roman motto: *Imperium et Libertas*.

Gladstone's mind was like the clear shaft of sunlight which played against his rival's, with its resplendent colors of the rainbow. In these congenital differences lay the cause for the misunderstandings between them. And being congenital differences it is easy now to understand why, as they each neared the fulfillment of their respective missions — Disraeli with the development of his far-flung Imperialistic programs, and Gladstone with his genius for finance and his interest in things at home, which finally flowered into his Home Rule bills for Ireland — the breach between them widened so far that it became not merely a parliamentary breach but a personal one. The portrait of Gladstone which Disraeli began to draw in the nine chapters of a novel which was to be another addition to his political novels, has enough in it to show off the greatest weaknesses of Gladstone, but, at the same time, it exhibits the prejudices of the artist.

If the Unfinished Novel appears to have, for its *motif*, in part at least, the levelling of Disraeli's great rival, and would seem to promise 'a man's book' in which men, indeed, play the most significant part, *Endymion* is a novel altogether constructive in intention, purporting to show the influence which women have upon political character. The writing of this novel had been begun shortly after the publication of *Lothair* but it was completed only after Disraeli had retired from the premiership in 1880, when the leisure he now had, as Leader of the Opposition in the House of Lords, gave him the necessary few months with which to finish his work. And though this novel avoids making any comment upon the acts and the personalities which figured during his own great administration from 1874 to 1880, in one respect, and that an autobiographical one, it reveals a series of influences which reached their culmination upon him in the very years whose

politics he leaves untouched. I refer to the feminine influences
upon Disraeli's own political life, and the complete power of
which is only now revealed, and for the first time, with the
publication of the last two volumes of Mr. Buckle's biography,
wherein we study the extraordinary series of letters which
passed, almost daily, between him and Queen Victoria,[14] as
well as the letters which passed, after the death of Disraeli's
wife, between Disraeli and Lady Chesterfield (some 500 of
which have been preserved), and Lady Bradford (of which
some 1100 are in existence). To Lady Bradford, as Mr.
Buckle shows, he sometimes wrote two and three times a
day, carrying on a "lovers' comedy . . . during the 1874
Administration."

A "septuagenarian who had the governance of the Empire
and the conduct of the Commons on his shoulders, and who
necessarily was leading a public life of incessant and laborious
occupation, nevertheless traversed in his private life the whole
gamut of half-requited love — passionate devotion, rebuff,
despair, resignation, renewed hope, reconciliation, ecstasy;
and then traversed it *da capo*." [15] The perfect courtier he
always was to the Queen, a courtier tactful, witty, flattering,
respectful, sagacious. Shall we recall the gorgeous verbiage
with which he sometimes adorned his epistles to her, a Queen
to whom he sometimes referred as 'The Faery'? The spring
flowers with which that Queen filled his sick-room during his
last illness, and the several letters couched in terms of the
warmest affection and solicitude which this sober old lady
sent him upon that occasion? The romantic journey she took,
alone, to his grave four days after his interment, walking upon
the very path across which his body had been borne to its last
resting place, and on the reopened vault of which she laid
in silent majesty a personal wreath to her beloved Minister's
memory? All these are evidences of a strange loyalty and an
exquisite affection rare in the annals of English public life

between a Minister of State and a woman Sovereign. To the account of these one must add both the record of his marriage, and the unusual female influences upon his earlier life, in order to see the continuity of inspiration unbroken, and to see it in its completeness. That was a passionate devotion which Disraeli showed for his beloved 'Mary Anne,' who was twelve years older than he, and who, at her death was eighty when he was sixty-eight. It marked a period of thirty-three years of extraordinary affection which, because of the perpetual romance in it, is rare in modern days. To her, for whom *Sybil* was dedicated in an exquisite tribute,[16] he turned during this extraordinarily happy marriage as a young poet might turn to a Muse from whom he receives constant inspiration. Next to his wife, during twelve years of that marriage, and with the exception of one other, his sister Sarah, there existed a romantic intimacy between him and the strange Mrs. Brydges Willyams, which in influence, at least, was next only to that of these other two; it was an intimacy which Froude calls "a curious and delicate idyll"[17] and it fed Disraeli not alone with perpetual sympathy and devotion, but with material gifts as well. Mr. Buckle devotes an entire chapter to this episode in Disraeli's public life, and notes the dramatic fact that Mrs. Willyams' last request, to lie buried beside her idol and his beloved wife, was honored by them. "All three, benefactress and beneficiaries, now lie together just outside the east end of the church (at Hughenden), and one monument, on the outer wall of the De Montfort Chapel, records the names and legends of them all."[18] I have already mentioned Disraeli's sister. Between him and her there existed, to the day of her death in 1859, a "mystical affection" that rejoiced in his triumphs, persistently encouraged and fortified him in his defeats, trusted always in his coming greatness, and supplied him always with a confidante upon whom he poured innumerable letters[19] which breathe the devotion he had for

her "angelic spirit," as Lady Beaconsfield called it, and which
spell the intelligent sympathy with which she fed his mind and
his soul. Next to these one may not close this record without
mentioning Mrs. Austen [20] whose encouragement and criticism
brought *Vivian Grey* to be published by Colburn in 1826, and
whom Mr. Monypenny calls Disraeli's "literary Egeria" in
these early years; and Lady Blessington whose London home,
in the thirties, became the rendezvous of the dandies, and by
whose interest in him he was first introduced into great society.
His devoted sister, his affectionate wife, a grateful Queen, the
benefactress Mrs. Willyams, Mrs. Austen, Lady Blessington,
Lady Bradford to whom he paid an extraordinary courtship
in his late years, her sister, Lady Chesterfield, to whom he
proposed marriage when both he and she were septuagenarians:
here is a record of feminine influence which seldom falls to
most men in active life, and least of all to a busy public character in the great days of a profoundly important historical
epoch.   By the kind of sympathy and affection which he
craved from all these ladies, and by the bountiful measure of
it which they gave to him because they saw always that their
gift was but the return to a man who was devoted to an Ideal,
one may properly say that for him, at least, there was truth
in the lines of Faust's mystical Chorus:

> " Das Ewig-Weibliche
>   Zieht uns hinan."

But to return to our novel. The plot of *Endymion* is woven
around the England of Disraeli's own youth and his early
manhood. It opens with the death of Canning, in 1827, and
sweeps across thirty years of political life — to the first Ministry of Lord Derby in 1852 when Disraeli received his first
Cabinet position as Chancellor of the Exchequer, then to the
Crimean War and finally the defeat of the Coalition Government in 1855.   In the life of Disraeli, the politician, it is a

period marked by the following events: His own apprenticeship in politics, the time when he became the leader of the Young England group and when he wrote the three novels which embodied his ideas upon the origins, the historical positions, and the duties of the great political parties of England. It was during this period that he assumed the leadership of the Conservative Party in the Commons. It was after 1846, and following the so-called Corn Law debates, that he had succeeded in driving Peel out of political life. From the leader of the Opposition, to Peel's place as leader in the House of Commons, he became Chancellor of the Exchequer in the Derby Ministry. Disraeli, as the Liberal historian Herbert Paul says of him, had at last *got a status*. It was now to be discovered whether "the best Leader of the Opposition that the House of Commons has ever known" [21] could prove himself a statesman as he had already proved himself a great Parliamentarian. It is to my mind a tribute to Disraeli's discretion as well as to his prudence that he stopped his last novel with the very moment when he himself began to play a most important rôle in English public life.

The story of *Endymion* may be briefly told. The opening of the book introduces us to the London mansion of William Ferrars, a distinguished statesman wielding great power in the Duke of Wellington's Government, to his proud wife, and to his two children, Endymion and his sister Myra, the proudest ornaments brought out by their mother-Cornelia, — the jewels which are always admired by her aristocratic and distinguished guests. Upon the magnificence and the pageantry which fills that family mansion there suddenly comes, like a bolt of lightning, the crash of the Wellington Ministry in 1830, and on top of that the entrance of the Grey Ministry which, after the passage of the Great Reform Bill, 1832, "promised now to stay on indefinitely." To Ferrars that political catastrophe, which turned England from a strong Tory régime to a

Democracy, spelt immediate and utter ruin. He retires to his country home. There he realizes, for the first time, that his lavish London living and his riots of entertainments, always encouraged by a mad belief that his party would hold its place in public life indefinitely, have brought him to the verge of bankruptcy. He tries to support his family by writing for a Tory paper but fails. He goes to London, in his extremity, to find some position which he may hold with dignity, but he is ignored and humiliated, and learns that younger men are now in power and that with the great change in the political arena he has been made useless and is now deliberately forgotten. On top of all the rest of misfortune comes the death of his unhappy and broken-hearted wife. Completely prostrated by this final blow, Ferrars takes what appears to him the logical step out of the situation: he commits suicide. Endymion Ferrars, and his sister Myra, find themselves orphans in their early youth, and penniless. It suddenly, therefore, becomes the task of these two unhappy children, alone, lacking the power which existing family connections might have given them but which they do not own, without any ties to a London aristocracy which had now completely forgotten them during the number of years in which their unhappy father had retired to his country home — it becomes their common task to revive the prestige of their family name, to replenish with abundance the empty family coffers, and to resume their rightful places among the socially great and the politically all-powerful. All this they succeed in doing in the course of the story.

Endymion accepts an inconsequential Somerset House clerkship at the age of sixteen, without finishing his formal education. Myra replies to an advertisement in *The Times*, and becomes by that the companion to young Adriana Neuchatel, the only daughter of one of the greatest bankers of England, a power in the State no less than upon the Exchange. How

the genius and the masculine purpose of Myra mould her own
fortune so that she may the better mould her brother's; how
this somewhat commonplace and soft-mannered youth first,
through the irresistible power of his Divinity Myra, and then
through the influence of a number of other great women (each of
them leaders in the political drawing-rooms of England) feed
the flame which his sister had kindled in him, and finally help
him to attain the highest political place which England has to
offer — these things make up the central scheme in *Endymion*.

It will be seen, from the start, that in this political novel
Disraeli has plotted well, and is dealing with political circumstances which might be used with admirable effect in a work
of this *genre*. It is a story told in two generations: the older
generation is seen at the zenith of its power; then comes the
great 'political accident' of 1832 and with a sudden climax
the older generation is swept off the boards, politically which
means also economically; and out from under the shadow of
this older office-holding generation arises the younger, which
is portrayed against a background of the most vital public
issues that entered with the stirring age of the thirties. From
this younger generation the product of a combination of two
wills forms the main thread of the novel — one, the plastic
masculine, which is subjected to an energizing, constructively
moulding and inspiring feminine will; the masculine made
purposely subordinate to the other in order to show how,
when great women of intuitive force rally around it, and
inspire it, the man is uplifted, and himself presses forward to
place and to power. On this score, then, the novel is one of
'causes' rather than of 'effects.' It would emphasize the
importance of the drawing-room in the making of a political
character, of the manoeuvrings of brilliant women placed in
strategic positions, and of the power of their penetration and
their sympathy upon the sterner virtues which are needed to
control a nation.

This objective of the novel — the part women play in moulding masculine character, particularly political character — is
the one generally recognized by critics of *Endymion*. To
Mr. Buckle, for example, it is "the main argument," "the
dominant idea." [22] But there is, to my mind, another equally
important purpose pervading this political novel, one which
has escaped all of Disraeli's critics, including even this admirable biographer. The existence of this other purpose accounts
perhaps for the failure of the work in certain other well-recog-
nized respects: the lack of inventiveness, for instance, in it;
the fact that Myra, the leading character next to her brother,
is altogether unconvincing because she has no other individuality given to her than a determination to have her brother
'get on in the world.' "My life," she says to a suitor whom
she rejects at the age of seventeen, "my life is devoted to
Endymion. There is a mystic bond between us, originating,
perhaps, in the circumstances of our birth: for we are twins.
I never mean to embarrass him with a sister's love, and may
perhaps hereafter see less of him than I see now; but I shall
be in the world, whatever be my lot, high or low, — the active,
stirring world — working for him, thinking of him alone.
Yes; molding events and circumstances in his favour." And
she spoke with fiery animation. Now in spite of this determination we find her acts, from her youth to her maturity
when she is finally made a Queen of France, lacking in real
cohesion and consistency, so that some of the exhibitions of
her character seem accidental and even meaningless. This
lack of consistency in the leading woman character, as we
survey all of her acts, makes her appear somewhat extraordinary beside the other, better drawn though less important
women. It is the existence of this other controlling purpose
which has made a critic like Schérer find fault with the work
because "Lord Beaconsfield has velleities of creation rather
than the faculty of it." *Endymion* appears to him a pageant,

a drawing-room performance, a play for which we make up the audience.[23]

"Quidquid agunt homines" is what Disraeli has placed at the opening of his novel, and by that he has given us the keynote to a purpose of his novel which we must discover for ourselves. The historical period set forth here was one of the most dramatic in the political life of the English nation: we are to watch the breakdown of the old despotism, to hear sound the knell of the full power of the hereditary aristocracy of the Georges, and to see the new propelling political forces come into their own. What kind of transformations were to take place, as a result, in that Old Régime, what new forces were to be born and to develop in the heart of parliamentary England, how great careers were to cross with those just beginning, and private intrigue was to attempt to hold public favor, what diversity of passions and of motives came in during that period when England was changed from an hereditary monarchy to a democratic parliamentary government: these are what Disraeli proposes to set before us. Whether Disraeli actually succeeds in making vivid and real the many forces which played upon that period is to be questioned; certain it is that *there* lies an important purpose of his work. There can be no question, however, that he succeeds in presenting graphically and convincingly enough the tenacity, the determination, the spirit of continuity, of the aristocratic classes still to govern the State, to remain the conquerors, in spite of the new-born forces which attempted to revolutionize England. So side by side with a man like Lord Montfort, "the only living Englishman who gave one an idea of the nobleman of the eighteenth century . . . totally devoid of a sense of responsibility," and in a book which describes the aristocracy and the nabobs of the twenties in the reign of George IV, you sweep to the rise of the manufacturers, Lancashire and the Corn Law Leaguers, the philosophy of Free Trade, the principle of Co-

operation, the Bedchamber Plot, Secret Societies, the potato
famine, and the rise of Napoleon III, the appearance of the
railroad magnates and of Mr. Vigo in Parliament, the coming
in and the going out of Ministries for thirty years with a theory for each Ministry, and a summary for each result. "The
French Revolution had introduced the cosmopolitan principle
into human affairs instead of the national," [24] says Disraeli,
and it is something of the transition from the one to the other
in England from the twenties to the fifties that he desires to
exhibit in this novel.

Before passing on to an examination of the political material of a more general nature it may be well to dispose completely of certain outstanding figures. First there are the
Women who are all-significant. In Myra you see exhibited
one who deliberately sets out to accomplish a great purpose
and who *calculates* every step and every consequence in order
to fashion her acts to serve a pre-determined end from which
she never deviates. Once established in the home of a great
English banker she gains the adoration of her ward almost
immediately for one quality, by the kindly and retiring banker's
wife she is loved for another, while her common sense and her
clear intelligence gain the respect of the great Neuchatel
himself. Made a full member of their Hainault home, she
takes, honorably indeed but no less swiftly, full advantage of
her great opportunities. She lives now in a world that is
energetic, restless, and various, through which streams regularly men of commerce, diplomats, great men in public office,
artists, and even a pretender to a foreign throne who, now
living incognito, eventually becomes a distinguished foreign
monarch. Here she meets an elderly statesman, Lord Roehampton, a man of extraordinary wealth and, at the time,
Foreign Secretary in the Cabinet. She wins his devotion and
marries him. The significance of all this she communicates to
Endymion on the day following the betrothal. "Now you know

all, dear darling; it is so sudden, and so strange, that you must be almost as much astounded as gratified. What I have sighed for, and prayed for — what, in moments of inspiration I have sometimes foreseen — has happened. Our degradation is over." She sees now, she says, a career and a great one open to him, and she sees wonderful things for herself. "We have now got a lever to move the world!" she shrewdly closes, and the brother accepts with her their common fate and the possibilities of the future as if they were gifts out of the laps of the Gods.

Endymion I do not find to be the "colorless and insipid" character which Mr. Buckle paints him.[25] He is not, it is true as Mr. Buckle points out, akin to "the brilliant and adventurous heroes of Disraeli's earlier novels," yet he has gifts that are peculiarly his own. When we recall the politically adventurous spirit and the abandon of Vivian, or the dreamy, aspiring mysticism of Tancred, the brilliance and the moral courage to fight for new political ideals such as characterized Coningsby, and the social sympathies and the luxurious enthusiasms of Lothair, this hero of Disraeli's last novel appears somewhat tame. Still, like all of them, he has the charm of youth, he is handsome, he has ambition, pride of class, and energy. He can be, when necessary, quite as vivacious as they and as clever. Lacking their exuberance, he is, after all, the creation of Disraeli's imagination in the days of its seasoning and its quietness, when the author had no further desire to surround his characters with the atmosphere of the Ishmaelite, whose young right hands were against every man because they expected every man's hands to be against theirs. Endymion is therefore of a rather more earnest, possibly more plodding nature, sedate, sober, and somewhat prudential of morals, willing to learn from every experience, and grateful for every step upward. He gains much from his plodding fellow clerks in knowledge of miscellaneous life such as a man

of public affairs must have, he reflects always upon the political
conversations which he has had with Baron Sergius, Prince
Florestan, the Count of Ferrol — all of them distinguished
statesmen, as is afterwards shown. He attends the meetings
of a debating society where future members of the Commons
are in the making, and he listens and himself takes part; he
visits the galleries of the House of Commons and compares
one debater with another to his own advantage; after his
sister's entrance into the Neuchatel Mansion he has opportunity to cross opinions with distinguished parliamentarians,
great wits, and important diplomats. All this may seem slim
preparation for the rapid and extraordinary political good fortune which marks his rise, step by step, in public life after his
sister Myra has become the wife of a Cabinet Minister. This
would be slim indeed if Disraeli were not desirous here to subordinate his hero, to make him plastic, responsive, in order to
permit the greater forces of the novel to work upon him.
That is why Endymion is made of stuff that has not the dynamic vigor, the straight self-reliance, to be found in the
earlier heroes of Disraeli's novels, to whom Mr. Buckle
refers.

Having taken up again the thread of the plot, I may as well
follow the fortunes of the hero to the end. The marriage of
Myra assures her brother entrance into the best political
drawing-rooms, as it gains for him shortly a promotion to a
higher position in the government service, which culminates
at once in an undersecretary's place under Lord Roehampton.
From then on his rise is, it is true, somewhat miraculous. He
is 'taken up' at once by Lady Montfort, Queen of Society
and the Feminine Genius of the political party in power. Her
unflagging interest in his career (which is excelled not even by
Myra), together with Lord Montfort's attachment for him (all
the more remarkable in Lord Montfort, a character representative of the old aristocracy, whose sole function in life appears

to be to fight his ennui, and the depression and the monotony
of the commonplace), is a combination which gains for Endymion a seat in the House of Commons. This, however,
not before another powerful feminine influence, that of Lady
Beaumaris, who is the Feminine Genius of the opposite political party to that in power, gives him negative aid. Lady
Beaumaris had remembered how, in her youth, Endymion's
father had, in his palmy days, done many kindnesses for her
father, and so now, out of consideration to that memory, she
secures from her powerful husband his willingness to give up
all political rights to a borough which had originally been
offered to the young politician by Lord Montfort, but which
Lord Beaumaris could by every legal right contest. With
political opposition staved off, and with an unexpected gift of
some twenty thousand pounds made to him anonymously
(but actually through another feminine source, this time the
wealthy Adriana Neuchatel), there is nothing more left for
this golden youth to do but to take the road that the Gods
had provided him. Houses of the greatest social prestige now
open to him upon every side; his conduct in the House of
Commons, though not marked by any brilliance or power, is
·yet altogether commendable. Thus, when Fortune is smiling
so generously upon him, and he still hesitates to ask Adriana
Neuchatel for her hand because he fears she will think he
wants her only for her wealth, his dearest patron, Lady Montfort loses her husband. The story moves swiftly to its end
thereafter. Lady Montfort offers herself, and all her wealth
to her young protégé, which he accepts in all happiness; Lord
Roehampton, his brother-in-law, then conveniently dies and
leaves Myra free to accept an extraordinary offer in marriage
whereby she becomes the Queen Consort of a French Sovereign;
the Whigs, furthermore, remain in office and so the former
Lady Montfort, now the wife of Endymion, holds intact her
power as "the famous Berengaria, Queen of Society, and the

Genius of Whiggism." The career of the hero now reaches its natural conclusion: from an Undersecretaryship he becomes the Secretary for Foreign Affairs, and from that he finally attains the goal of all political ambition in English public life — the Prime Ministry!

It is to be noted that in depicting powerful women characters Disraeli is not intent upon presenting, necessarily, persons mature in years, but rather those who, possessing all the charm that is feminine, are ripened in experience, seasoned in their contacts with affairs of the world; and whose intuition is a quality so exquisitely fine that, without themselves possessing a formal knowledge of parliamentary procedure (such as might be more common to-day, among public persons represented by Lady Astor, than it was in the mid-nineteenth century), they were yet able to inspire and to energize men of action at great crises in their careers. In Endymion's mother Disraeli painted the helpless early Victorian lady, who broke completely under a crisis because she lacked all intellectual resources; her, therefore, he swept away at the opening of the novel; but his great Tory and Whig ladies, who followed her in the next generation, come closer to our own time. To Lady Montfort, known politically as 'Berengaria,' who is skillfully made into an animated, highly intelligent, altogether brilliant character, the charms of office hold out the main purpose which should motivate a young man's life. "Not go into Parliament!" she cries out once [26] to Endymion, when the latter pleads his youth and inexperience as reasons for not undertaking the career which she is moving various forces to open up to him. "Why, what are men made for except to go into Parliament! . . . It will not cost you a shilling. I and your sister have arranged all that. . . . All you have to do is to write an address and make plenty of speeches, and you are M.P. for life, or as long as you like." To this lady who broods over the "great coup in foreign affairs," who plans out great marriages in

order to keep the right people in power, who was the centre of
the "Bedchamber Plot" since she it was who failed to resign
with her own Government, — to this lady the charms of
political office were as real as they were for one of the active
Secretaries of the Cabinet: ". . . they all arrayed themselves
before him. The social influence, the secret information, the
danger, the dexterity, the ceaseless excitement, the delights of
patronage which everybody affects to disregard, the power of
benefiting others, and often the worthy and the unknown
which is a real joy. . . ." Lady Beaumaris, or Zenobia, the
acknowledged leader of Tory society, is hardly as vivid a
portrayal as her rival. She makes up in her "gentle and
natural manners, blended with a due degree of self-respect,
her charming appearance, her ready but unaffected sympathy
. . . and her greater intellectual range" to that of her sister,
for what she lost in her unwillingness to engage energetically
in political theories and principles when discussion of them
opened. She is the more feminine of the two society leaders,
permitting her own husband, Lord Beaumaris, who was himself actively engaged in the arena of politics, to profit by the
social prestige which her natural qualities of character had
gained for her. To the parties which took place at the home
of Beaumaris, to the power which emanated from Montfort
Castle, one must add the political influence which was represented by Hainault House, the palace of the Neuchatels,
where the only daughter, the wealthiest heiress in England,
was surrounded by wealth "which controlled the destinies of
governments."

"Forty years ago," says Disraeli, "the great financiers had not
that commanding, not to say predominant, position in society
which they possess at present, but the Neuchatels were an exception to this general condition. They were a family which not
only had the art of accumulating wealth, but of expending it with
taste and generosity — an extremely rare combination. Their
great riches, their political influence, their high integrity, and their

social accomplishments combined to render their house not only splendid, but interesting and agreeable, and gave them a great hold upon the world.''

This description, set forth in the early part of the book [27] (portraying as it does, in reality, the English branch of the Rothschild family with which the author was upon intimate terms), helps us to understand, as the story advances, the significance of the great bankers when they furnish aid to the pretender, Prince Florestan, to bring about the revolution which lands him finally upon a throne.[28]

The English historian Trevelyan has somewhere declared that the English aristocracy has always been and still is essentially political in its tastes and its aptitudes. In painting the general background for his last novel, Disraeli, the Prime Minister, makes that fact even clearer than he had in the political novels preceding this. Nor are the types he presents here repetitions of those he had already produced. Lord Pomeroy, for example, is vividly portrayed in a single sentence.

"Lord Pomeroy was . . . the great lord who had returned William Ferrars to Parliament — a little man, quiet, shy, rather insignificant in appearance, but who observed everybody and everything; a conscientious man, who was always doing good, in silence and secrecy; and, denounced as a boroughmonger, had never sold a seat in his life, and was always looking out for able men of character to introduce them to public affairs." [29]

Or take these lines of the Earl of Montfort,[30] a character admirably depicted.

"Under the old parliamentary system he had the greatest number of nomination boroughs possessed by any Whig noble. . . . Although he affected to take little interest in politics, the events of the time forced him to consider them and to act. Lord Grey wanted to carry his Reform Bill, and the sacrifice of Lord Montfort's numerous boroughs was a necessary ingredient in the spell. He was appealed to as the head of one of the greatest Whig houses, and he was offered a dukedom. He relinquished his boroughs without hesitation, but he preferred to remain with one of the oldest earldoms of England for his chief title. All honors, however, clustered about him, though he never sought them, and in the same year he tumbled into the lord-lieutenancy of his county, unexpectedly vacant, and became the youngest knight of the garter. . . . Lord Montfort was the only living Englishman who gave one an idea of the nobleman of the 18th century. He was totally devoid of the sense of responsibility, and he looked what he resembled. . . . With the exception of the memorable year when he sacrificed his nomination boroughs to the cause for which Hampden died on the field and Sidney on the scaffold — that is to say, the Whig government of England — Lord Montfort had been absent from his country for ten years; and one day in his statued garden at the Belvedere, he asked himself what he had gained by it. There was no subject, divine or human, in which he took the slightest interest. . . . No one could say that Lord Montfort was a bad-hearted man, for he had no heart. He was good-natured, provided it brought him no inconvenience; and as for temper, his was never disturbed, but this not from sweetness of disposition, rather from a contemptuous fine taste, which assured him that a gentleman should never be deprived of tranquillity in a world where nothing was of the slightest consequence."

Side by side with this eighteenth century type, living, almost as an anomaly, in the middle nineteenth, you have the newer generation which was soon to make itself a force of profound consequence in public affairs. Mr. Vigo, director of the great railroads just about to interlace the country, master of details in his business, of dynamic energy and enterprise, "in his first session in Parliament had passed quietly and almost unnoticed several bills . . .," and woke up one day to find himself famous. "Suddenly it would seem that the name of Mr. Vigo was in everybody's mouth. There was only one subject which interested the country, and he was recognized as the man who best understood it. He was an oracle, and naturally, soon became an idol." Vigo stands for the railroad mania of the 40's, but his vigorous political personality stands no less for the manufacturing interests in Parliament than did Mr. Millbank in *Coningsby*. Are the agricultural interests of any less consequence in political life? Endymion, just returned from a visit to the manufacturing districts of northern England, where he had gone to get first-hand information about the Corn-Law League, does not find it so.

"In the midst of all this physical prosperity, one fine day in August, Parliament having just been prorogued, an unknown dealer in potatoes wrote to the secretary of state, and informed him that he had reason to think that a murrain had fallen over the potato crops of England, and that, if it extended to Ireland, the most serious consequences must ensue.

"This mysterious but universal sickness of a single root changed the history of the world.

"'There is no gambling like politics,' said Lord Roehampton, as he glanced at the *Times* at Princedown. 'Four Cabinets in one week! The Government must be more sick than the potatoes!'"

Among the figures of a new world which appeared in the forties in England none is sketched by Disraeli with more animation than that of Job Thornberry, a man who, as Mr. Buckle says, shows "touches both of Cobden and of Bright." Exponent of the economics of Free Trade, Thornberry teaches Endymion not alone the extent of the energy, the inventiveness, and the great skill which lay in the textile works of Manchester, and what political effect their development of the nation's resources were bound to have upon other nations, but also the animus which lay in his heart (it is that of a great manufacturer) against what seemed to him the false science of Exchange that prevailed in the minds at Downing Street.

"If there were free exchange," Thornberry tells Endymion, "we should find employment and compensation in other countries. . . . No, my dear Mr. Ferrars; the question is a very simple one, and we may talk forever and we shall never alter it. The laws of this country are made by the proprietors of land, and they make them for their own benefit. A man with a large estate is said to have a great stake in the country because some hundreds of people or so are more or less dependent on him. How has he a greater interest in the country than a manufacturer who has sunk £100,000 in machinery, and has a thousand people, as I had, receiving from him weekly wages? No home market, indeed! Pah, it is an affair of rent, and nothing more nor less. And England is to be ruined to keep up rents! . . . Say what they like in the House of Commons and the vile London press, the thing is stirring!"

Passing from home to foreign matters, we find Disraeli introducing into this political novel at least three distinguished European figures in disguise, with all of whom he was destined to become well acquainted in his own life, and one of whom gives him, in *Endymion*, an opportunity for tracing the career of a great 'political adventurer' (if Napoleon III may be so called), and for commenting upon foreign diplomacy. Describing the political status of England of the period of 1842, Disraeli makes Lady Montfort say to Endymion one day: "This is a political economy Parliament, both sides alike thinking of the price of corn and all that. Finance and Commerce are everybody's subjects, and are most convenient to make speeches about for men who cannot speak French and who have had no education. Real politics are the possession and the distribution of power. I want to see you give your mind to foreign affairs. . . . But foreign affairs are not to be mastered by mere reading. Bookworms do not make Chancellors of State. You must become acquainted with the great actors in the great scene. There is nothing like personal knowledge of the individuals who control the high affairs. . . . What I think you ought to do is to take advantage of this interval before the meeting of Parliament, and go to Paris. Paris is now the capital of diplomacy." [31] One of the greatest of these actors Disraeli portrays in *Endymion* as Count Albert, the man who later became Napoleon III. Mr. Buckle succinctly presents [32] the character as Disraeli portrays him in these

pages. "The plots and vicissitudes which diversified Louis
Napoleon's exile are reproduced in the career of the pretender,
Prince Florestan, who first appears in London society as
Count Albert . . . a mysterious, silent, and solitary figure.
An inveterate and shifty conspirator from his boyhood, he
excuses the breach of his solemn parole by the plea that he is
'the child of destiny,' that his action was 'the natural development of the irresistible principle of historical necessity'; but
he is a romantic personality who interests women, being gifted
with tender and gentle manners, and ready with unobtrusive
sympathy, save when lost in profound abstraction. . . . 'The
Tories did not love revolutionary dynasties, and the Whigs
being in office could not sanction a pretender, and one who,
they significantly intimated with a charitable shrug of the
shoulders, was not a very scrupulous one.'"   In this novel
Disraeli shows him off moving from banker to foreign secretary, from drawing-room to tournament, promoting his cause
through political dinners and good-fellowship.[33]   By the side
of Prince Florestan we have the Count of Ferrol, a portrait of
Bismarck in the days when he was at the London Legation.
To no person in the novel does Disraeli make him so significant
as to Prince Florestan, evidently to suggest how these two
men were later to contend for great stakes.   Endymion, from
the start, had taken a violent dislike to him and frankly says
so to Florestan, with whom he has become a great favorite.
Florestan tries to make our hero appreciate what greatness
there lies in the man.

"The Count of Ferrol is the man of the future. . . . It is an
advantage, a great advantage, for me to observe the Count of
Ferrol in this intimate society," said the Prince speaking slowly,
"perhaps even to fathom him.   But I am not come to that yet.
He is a man neither to love nor to detest.   He has himself an
intelligence superior to all passion, I might say all feeling; and if,
in dealing with such a being, we ourselves have either, we give
him an advantage." [34]

The Count of Ferrol made himself a great favorite in English society, but his greatest favorite was Lady Montfort. "He told her everything, and consulted her on everything; and though he rarely praised anybody, it had reached her ears that the Count of Ferrol had said more than once that she was a greater woman than Louise of Savoy or the Duchess de Longueville." Many conversations between these two keen-witted persons are given in the novel, in each instance self-revelations of both the man and the woman. In the Count of Ferrol none is more significant than the following:

"'You may have troubles here,' he said to Lady Montfort, 'but they will pass; you will have mealy potatoes again and plenty of banknotes, but we shall not get off so cheaply. Everything is quite rotten throughout the Continent. This year is tranquillity to what the next will be. There is not a throne in Europe worth a year's purchase. My worthy master wants me to return home and be a minister: I am to fashion for him a new constitution. I will never have anything to do with new constitutions; their inventors are always the first victims. Instead of making a constitution he should make a country, and convert his heterogeneous domains in a patriotic dominion.'
'But how is that to be done?'
'There is only one way; by blood and iron!'
'My dear Count, you shock me!'
'I shall have to shock you a good deal more before the inevitable is brought about.'" [35]

Disraeli's love for putting things sententiously was never better illustrated in his political novels than in this one, and, as has already been shown, most effectively, through the mouths of continental public men residing temporarily in England. A character not so well conceived as Prince Florestan but yet as real as the Count of Ferrol, is Baron Sergius, a figure based upon Baron Brunnow who in 1840 represented Russia in the London Legation and who was mainly responsible for the Quadruple Alliance of 1840. It is Disraeli, the mocker,

who speaks through this figure now and then, — and also the
Disraeli who seeks for startling effects. Here is one example.

"'I should like to be a public man,' said Endymion. 'Why?'
asked the Baron. 'Well, I should like to have power,' said Endymion, blushing. 'The most powerful men are not public men,'
said the baron. 'A public man is responsible, and a responsible
man is a slave. It is private life that governs the world. You
will find this out some day. The world talks much of powerful
sovereigns and great ministers; and if being talked about made
one powerful, they would be irresistible. But the fact is, the
more you are talked about the less powerful you are!'"

Endymion then suggests the names of a monarch, of an em-
peror, and of a prince, — all of whom are universally believed
to be all powerful. The baron replies that the monarch, at
the moment, happens to be governed by his doctor; the em-
peror is directed by his mistress; and the prince is being
inspired by an altogether obscure individual who "may be,
at this moment, like ourselves, drinking a cup of coffee in a
hired lodging."

"'What you say about public men amazes me,' said Endymion,
musingly.
'Think over it,' said the baron. 'As an Englishman, you will
have difficulty in avoiding public life. But at any rate do not
at present be discontented that you are unknown. It is the first
condition of real power. When you have succeeded in life according to your views . . . you will, some day, sigh for real power,
and denounce the time when you became a public man and belonged to any one but yourself.'" [36]

Upon the young Endymion this baron had a powerful influence
for he had much to do with his 'political education.' He poured
forth to him, apparently without reserve, all his vast experience
of men and things. He initiated him in the cardinal principles
of the policies of different nations; he revealed to him the character of the chief actors in the scene. "The real requisite,"
Baron Sergius would say, "in the successful conduct of public

affairs, is a personal acquaintance with the statesmen engaged. It is possible that events may not depend now, so much as they did a century ago, on individual feeling, but, even if prompted by general principles, their application and management are always colored by the idiosyncrasy of the chief actors." [37] In such sentences as these, scattered generously throughout the novel, Disraeli shows the cumulative experience of a great statesman who had taken his part in the moulding of public affairs, and who now, in a romance, gives something of it, in the form of reflection upon events, back to his readers.

It is impossible to escape the conclusion, as one reviews the place of *Endymion* in nineteenth century English literature, that Disraeli has really left us pages of English history fashioned into fiction and framed on all sides with biographical material. Peel, Palmerston (known in the novel as Lord Roehampton), Sidney Herbert — the statesman in Peel's administration (in the novel as Sidney Wilton, Endymion's political chief), the Earl of Derby, Disraeli's political master (Earl of Beaumaris in the novel); George Smythe of the Young England group (Waldershare), Lady Jersey and Lady Holland (who together formed Disraeli's portrait of Zenobia, feminine genius of the Tory party in the 40's), the Honorable Mrs. Norton (the Berengaria-Lady Montfort of the book), Cobden and Bright in 'Job Thornberry'; Cardinal Manning in the character of 'Nigel Penruddock, the Anglican clergyman who becomes a Cardinal'; and finally Napoleon III and Bismarck and Brunnow [38] — these are some but not all of the many figures, contemporaries of Disraeli in the period which lies within *Endymion*, employed to weave a critical period of English history into the form of a romance. Disraeli has personified the last period of a parliamentary régime when the houses of government in England were still the propelling forces in shaping action and in moulding opinion upon public matters; it was the last period when a directing class, an heredity nobility, *gave* the impulse to all action in public affairs, rather than received the impulses from without. If, therefore, the book has an 'excess of grandeur,' it is because the circles of people with which Disraeli here deals are 'enchanted circles,' and the rhetoric with which he describes them must be, like the dishes that served up Adriana Neuchatel's dinners, not dinner-dishes but 'covers' for banquets. Disraeli was painting the lives of the English aristocracy in the days when these reflected into English political life all the glow and the color of a society whose daily actions were like the variegated pictures of a magic lantern; the light through which he reflected the pictures is made the more resplendent because the shadows thrown upon those pictures, now from this side and now from that — new and serious influences creeping in out of Industrial centres, Agricultural interests, Anti-Corn Law Leaguers — can then be seen with their full import. The tableau of the politically noble and the extraordinarily wealthy suffering a sudden revolution of fortune due to a great political constitutional change is set forth only once; but it is set forth in the most dramatic chapters of the novel, and at its very beginning. And so it hangs, in memory, upon the reader's mind like the ghost of something inexorable which must some day take toll from all the pageantry that is thereafter placed before it. In some of us, altogether out of sympathy with the society which Lord Montfort represents, there is yet enough charity left to appreciate the humor of making *him* say, as Disraeli does, "I cannot stand those ortolans stuffed with truffles and those truffles stuffed with ortolans." If we will appreciate that humor, there is a reward left for us in this political work. I mean there remain those solid passages, which intersperse the romance, wherein Disraeli sums up the political history of thirty years of parliamentary changes. These, though they impede the progress of the plot, add weight and value to the pictures.

CHAPTER VI

THE LITERARY SIGNIFICANCE OF BENJAMIN DISRAELI

SECTION A — WITH THE CURRENT OF SIGNIFICANT MEN AND MOVEMENTS

THE author of the novels which began with *Vivian Grey* and ended with *Endymion* had one of the diversified minds of his century. He remains, indeed, one of the most interesting personalities in all English history. Disraeli unconsciously reflected the legal and speculative tendencies of his race. He inherited their strong sense for practicalities and for finance: his first venture as an author was at twenty-one, when he published two pamphlets arguing against the passing of restrictive legislation toward English mining companies formed to exploit Spanish-America; his record as Chancellor of the Exchequer in Derby's administration is creditable; his *coup* in outwitting France by getting possession of the Suez Canal shares, and the bargain he made with the Khedive of Egypt for them, will always remain one of the dramatic episodes of his time. At thirty he wrote his *Revolutionary Epick*, a long poem intended to be a fourth to the *Iliad*, the *Aeneid*, and the *Divina Commedia*, which his biographer Kebbel calls "a modern Dunciad." In the next three years appeared *Henrietta Temple*, a pure love-story, and *Venetia*, a novel in which the lives of Byron and Shelley are portrayed. Fraser's Magazine for 1833 greeted *The Wondrous Tale of Alroy* which had just been published, with a page of criticism beginning as follows:

"O Reader dear! do pray look here, and you will spy the curly hair and forehead fair, and nose so high and gleaming eye, of

Benjamin D'Is-ra-el-i, the wondrous boy who wrote Alroy, in rhyme and prose, only to show, how long ago, victorious Judah's lion banner rose . . ."

Amusing as this attempt of Disraeli to portray a twelfth century Judas Maccabaeus now seems, and far-fetched and histrionic as his *Revolutionary Epick* is, they have value, nevertheless, in exhibiting still another side of the man's genius. He was something of a poet, a mystic, a sentimentalist. Disraeli, in short, was remarkable in that he was intensely sensitive enough to absorb whatever complex and brilliant influences lay around him — in an age of diverse thought, and yet astonishingly practical enough to combine whatever of them he could to serve best his own ambitious ends.

The romances of Benjamin Disraeli which we have now examined, and which constitute an unsurpassed account of the English political life of his time, contributed a new *genre* to the history of English letters. These political novels, as Disraeli wrote them, assimilated many of the literary influences and forces that composed the rich, many-sided, and strenuous thinking of the earlier and the middle nineteenth century. They formed a fresh outlet which came pouring from the main body of ideas that made nineteenth century England memorable in the history of civilization. The peculiar course of that stream was defined and fixed by one who, among his contemporaries, is an outstanding figure for a career unusual, strange to men of his time, and remarkable to us. It remains now to trace the stream back to its source. We must link Disraeli to his literary age. Let us see how the novels reflect the great diversity and complexity of thought of the nineteenth century as these were presented to their author.

First, in order of time as well as importance, we see in Disraeli the force of the ROMANTIC MOVEMENT. Indeed, it was the romantic in him that gave him his significance as a statesman in the nineteenth century.   Two examples, each significant, will prove the statement.   First, there was the impassioned emotion and the intuitive in him which led him to attempt to create a so-called Young England Party, as if he were dreaming the dreams of Mazzini who, for an altogether different reason, had founded the Young Italy Movement.   These were the very qualities which, when rationalized later, Disraeli employed to build up, for the old Tory Aristocracy of the Georges which was losing its grip upon England after the first Reform Bill, a new platform of political principles, and therefore a renaissance of power.   The Conservative Party as conceived by Disraeli was one which, building altogether upon the reanimated traditions of the English landed proprietors, became sensitive to the needs of a new age of Individualism and of grave social issues.   This rejuvenation of an old party by the infusion of new blood was Disraeli's contribution to history.   This political party, though threatened from within by disruption among its members and from without by the successive shocks of Reform Bills, survived to form the basis of the Primrose League in perpetuation of Disraeli's memory.   It was the mystical in Disraeli, the passionate intensity of his thought, the unbounded egotism of a fascinating personality which could withstand furious attacks upon his policies, together with the use he made of his peculiar imagination, which help to explain his historical function.   The second example of Romanticism is akin to the first.   The man who had succeeded in pouring the new wine of Democracy into the old bottles of Toryism was, while Prime Minister, less interested in devoting himself to the domestic needs of England than he was to developing a grandiose foreign policy for Great Britain.   The Imperialism in English politics of the nineteenth century with which his name is mainly credited in every school-boy's history-text to-day was a policy built upon the picturesque, the esoteric, the Oriental. Disraeli's persistent interest in the Eastern Question while Gladstone's interest, for example, was forever centred at home and upon Ireland; his determination, for better or for worse (as subsequent history of the year 1914 showed) to preserve in 1876 'the territorial integrity of the Turk,' as well as his life-long affection for and idealization of the Holy Land; the dramatic manner in which he stole a march upon France in his purchase, in 1875, of 177,000 shares of the Suez Canal from the Khedive of Egypt, and the still more dramatic manner in which he announced the completion of the secret business to Queen Victoria;[1] the almost boyish delight he took in bringing about a posture of affairs whereby he was able to see his Queen crowned the Empress of India, and the pomp and ceremony which occurred in both England and India upon that occasion; — all these are typical of the political imagination which wrote a whole romance upon the Holy Land, and which as late as 1870 sends his hero Lothair, at the climax of his wanderings, to Galilee, and to the inspiration of a mystical figure named Paraclete.

In the novels of his young manhood, particularly, Disraeli showed himself almost an embodiment of the Romantic Movement — as that was represented by Lord Byron and then by the series of historical romances of Walter Scott. In these early years of the century, wonder and mystery vibrated in the English air; the effects of the French Revolution and the influence of Rousseau, together with the writings of Chateaubriand, had brought a revolt against material conditions, against established state-institutions; nature had been set up against convention, human rights had been declared greater than the rights of all authority; men still strove for a lost youth and believed that they could find truth and beauty only when they fell back upon their own instincts. It was an age of 'impassioned recollection,' of the deification of the imagination, of the power of the lone individual, of the potency of ideas. *Don Juan* and *Childe Harold* filled the air with a magic which permitted men still to tolerate *The Castle of Otranto*.

The underlying idea of *all* Disraeli's political novels is the power of the Imagination to do the greatest practical things. Vivian Grey might be called a Don Juan in Politics, who rises and then sinks in his career of riotous ambition by the aid of that faculty alone. "I think," says the hero of the next novel, *Contarini Fleming*, "that ere long science will become again imaginative and that as we become more profound we may also become more credulous.[2]   The speaker's whole life, as he recounts the details of it in this novel which is told in the first person, remains for the reader either a tragedy or a farce (it depends upon the mood of the reader) altogether because that life has been guided by the imaginative faculty. "Man is only truly great," says Sidonia, the mightiest character in *Coningsby*, in a sentence which he recalls over and over again in slightly other forms, "when he acts from the passions; never irresistible but when he appeals to the Imagination."[3]   The hero in *Tancred* revolts against the hum-drum quality of English public life, and goes to the Orient to seek out 'the great Asian Mystery' (in a pilgrimage which encompasses the larger part of the novel) because of the transcendent quality of his imagination.   Indeed, so strong a motivating force was the imagination upon almost all of the novels of Disraeli that without it for a key we should be unable to understand the meaning of them, and never be able to solve the riddle of a fascinating personality.   Every careful biographer of Disraeli's political life dwells upon this faculty in him. Brandes declares that we should not understand anything of the character of the man if we overlooked the fact that over all his theories and fantasies there is the impress of the great romantic reaction of the nineteenth century.[4]   Lord Bryce dwells upon the 'passion,' the 'intensity,' the 'process of intuition or divination' which characterized his speeches and writings.[5]   Professor Butler, in his study of the Tory tradition in English statesmanship, says:[6]   "In imagination Disraeli excelled. He recognized the powerful agent that lay at hand in the forces which created the Romantic Movement."

Look more closely at some of the romantic materials in his novels. If *Vivian Grey* is the Don Juan of Politics, episode, background, and idea paint the comparison. The book is full of Byronic dash and glamor. There are hectic descriptions of many scenes upon the continent, strange adventures which follow Vivian when he is forced to take up his travels. One needs but to recall the supreme individualism and egotism of the hero, his cynicism, his false and exaggerated rhetoric, his brilliance, his fearlessness, his utterly unscrupulous character, his calculating selfishness, and the total disregard in him for all social morality and his defiance of all established conventions in ethics and in society. All these are presented in a pyrotechnic display of rhetoric, by a writer whose mind has been energized by the intensities of his racial heritage. Let us again recall the melodramatic quality of Mrs. Lorraine, the strange moonlight scenes in which she plays a part, the queer mountebank Essper George, the mysterious woman who would poison Vivian and upon whom he wreaks an awful vengeance. There is the extraordinary character of the Duke of Johannis-berger and his equally extraordinary companions, the experiences with the supernatural which Vivian encounters during his travels at the small German courts, the robbers on the wayside, and the languishing heroine, Violet Fane, who serves by contrast to set off the blackness in the soul of the adventuress who appeared earlier in the story. If all these are even more extravagant than the Byronic school would have painted them, they are not too extravagant for the lingering memories of the Gothic school of literature which Disraeli revives in this novel. And so he brings his tale to a wild and melodramatic end, with a storm, a flood, a landslide, and the death of every living creature except his hero Vivian, who seems to be spared only for enduring increased misery.[7]

LITERARY SIGNIFICANCE OF DISRAELI 149

"Modern English letters," says Heine[8] of *Contarini Fleming*, the second novel which bears so markedly the Romantic impress, "has given us no offspring equal to *Contarini*. Cast in our Teutonic mould, it is nevertheless one of the most original works written: profound, poignant, pathetic; its subject, most interesting, if not the noblest imaginable — the development of a poet; truly psychological; passion and mockery; Gothic richness, the fantasy of the Saracens, and yet over all a classic, even a deathlike repose." Heine's praise is altogether extravagant, and can be accounted for only by the fact that the novel, to a Teutonic mind like his, appeared to be an English edition of *Wilhelm Meister* with which it has much resemblance, and that Heine without doubt displayed a strong racial sympathy for Disraeli. The hero is a character imbued with vagaries of poetic sentiment and of theatrical isolation; he can shout, shriek, swoon, and roll upon the ground with the same recklessness with which he suddenly becomes a man of politics and begins to cut a presumably brilliant figure totally out of proportion to the merits which the author gives him, and of which we never see any proof in action. Contarini's leadership of a rebellious clique at the University, his expulsion because of his revolutionary principles of conduct, and then his subsequent adventures as the head of a group of young 'highwaymen' who live in the woods in an old deserted ruin; his persistent love affairs with women, married and unmarried; the continued mysticism and passion of his nature; his introspection and his melancholy, and the inspired and exalted feeling with which he glows on his travels through the Orient, Jerusalem, Cyprus, Damascus, Albania, and Italy — these remind one of the travels and character of *Childe Harold*. This is a Vivian Grey in a new attitude, and to him has been added an exotic mysticism, overpowering personal emotion, a strong thread of Orientalism, and finally suicide. "Milman who reviewed the novel said it was in no way inferior to

Childe Harold," says Froude in his *Biography of Lord Beacons-field.*[9]

Mysticism and a love for the exotic and the Oriental turn altogether into religion in *Tancred,* a novel which is Disraeli's spiritual autobiography. Here is another Contarini upon a pilgrimage to the Holy Land to unravel 'the great Asian Mystery,' a 'mystery' which the author never defines. The adventures of this youth during his travels in Syria are but the adventures of a Vivian Grey — Contarini transported from the German castles and principalities to the fastnesses of the Holy Land. His capture by Arabs on a lonely desert, the stronghold of Scheriff Effendi where Tancred is held for ransom, the visit to the mysterious Queen of the Ansarey and what the hero sees there of the Queen and her 'mysteries'; the idealized portrait of the 'Rose of Sharon' who is Eva, Lady of Bethany, the wild dreams of gaining an empire which develop in the subtle mind of Fakredeen Sheaab and which almost enlist the energies and the means of the young and impressionable Englishman — all these are reminiscent of the machinery, better ordered perhaps here but no less significant, of the earlier novels. It must be clear enough to the reader that the close of that novel does not reveal what 'the great Asian Mystery' is, or whether the hero ever unravels that mystery, any more than the opening of the book did. It may well be that the unfathomable quality of the religious motive of the novel is itself part of the author's purpose in writing it. And even in the novel *Sybil,* primarily sociological as that work purports to be and dealing as it does with the conditions of the working classes in England, the author cannot deny himself at least one melodramatic and startling scene. At the close of the book, when a violent mob is attacking Mowbray Castle (the stronghold of 'the other half of Society'), Morley, heretofore an intelligent leader of the working classes, whom Disraeli had painted in his various attitudes with much sympathy, is suddenly transformed into a melodramatic villain and has to be shot as he escapes from the castle tower; Sybil, sweet and convent-bred eighteenth century heroine, saves all the ladies of the castle by discovering a subterranean passage heretofore unknown to the owners of the castle themselves; Egremont, the hero of the story, arrives at the precise dramatic moment and rescues her!

William E. Henley, in one of the most sympathetic reviews of Disraeli which has ever been written by a man of letters, says of the extravagance of the novelist's imagination in painting his backgrounds: "If they (the novels) fail as stories they are unexceptional as canvasses. Our author unrolls them with a superb audacity, and rapidly and vigorously fills them in with places and with people. . . . Nothing is too lofty or too low for him. . . . It is but a step from the wilds of Lancashire to the Arabian desert. . . . You suspect the presence of the born mocker but you remember that one of his most obvious idiosyncrasies is an inordinate love of all that is sumptuous, glittering, radiant, magnificent; you incline to suspect that he keeps his sneering for the world of men, and admires his scenes and his decorations too cordially to visit them with anything so merciless." [10]

I have attempted to show wherein Disraeli reflected the Romantic Movement. But I must not be misunderstood. Disraeli, the political novelist who made a *genre* of the form, Disraeli, the statesman who became the leader of the conservative landed aristocracy of England, was never in sympathy with nor an exponent of any part of that extraordinary claptrap which is sometimes attached, in our text-books, to definitions of the Romantic Movement. Disraeli never desired "moral solitude," and was never "conscious of the trammels of an ordered, conventional life." The 'romantic wonder' of Wordsworth, and the 'romantic strangeness' of Coleridge were not in him. The feeling for 'religious voluptuousness' the 'sense of longing and of melancholy' were not his. You cannot conceive Disraeli borrowing some of the 'exoticism' from Chateaubriand, and accepting from the latter the 'sentimental primitivism' with which he endowed Indian savages of America. There is no record that, once having passed the exciting days of his youth, he ever suffered from nostalgia or shut himself up in 'an ivory tower' to escape 'le mal du siècle.' And — to complete the unhappy list — there is never any evidence in Disraeli's active life that he ever sympathized with Revolution, or that he ever contemplated suicide. If any part of these things, or their offshoots, crept into his early books, the novels of his youth, they were due only to the first flush of interest which the fashion of the time, still reflecting the influence of Byron and of the eighteenth century, called out. When he steered out into mid-stream, and his own influence became potent, they dropped out of his imaginative writing. In his great parliamentary debates, treatises, and argumentative writings they cast not even a shadow. In short, when Disraeli came into his full maturity, both as statesman and novelist, the Romantic elements which remained in him were such as might have been found, for example, in the novels of Walter Scott written so many years earlier than his: I mean, only the simple, the permanent, the masculine aspects of the movement remained.

Chief among these in Disraeli, as in the historical romances of WALTER SCOTT, was a belief in the continuity of history. In Scott this amounted almost to an impassioned idealization of the great Past in England and Scotland; with Disraeli (particularly in *Coningsby* where he preaches for the benefit of 'Young England') impassioned idealization characterizes all that the hero Coningsby reflects upon. With Scott, too, Disraeli shared in idealizing the old English hierarchy: that feudal state of society where there was a simple social order, where the protector knew his duty to his subjects, the vassal knew his place, and where both together, closely united and economically related, made an admirable union which worked for the common weal, and protected the whole from the alien and the stranger.   Professor Beers, in his excellent work upon *English Romanticism in the Nineteenth Century*, points out that one of the significant contributions which Scott made to the English novel was 'the crowd,' 'the mass of humanity' — an element unknown in the novel before Scott's day.   In *Sybil* we find that Disraeli, too, reflects this mass-element, but, though this is done through vigorous and graphic pictures, Disraeli does not employ them for the purpose of pageantry with which Scott is mainly interested.   He uses them rather for emotional or sociological effects, not after the manner of Scott.   Here he is more akin to Carlyle.   The relation between Carlyle and Disraeli was, in many respects, a far closer one than that between him and Scott.   But of this later.   One can hardly recall more diverse types of men than these three: Scott, Carlyle, and Disraeli.   Yet they meet on common ground in their passionate love of country, and their common belief in a well-ordered patriarchal society such as Carlyle, too, pictured — after borrowing inspiration from Scott — in his *Past and Present*.   "Gurth," says Carlyle in chapter III of that work, "a mere swineherd, born thrall of Cedric the Saxon, tended pigs in the wood and did get some parings of the pork."   It is this character of Gurth, chosen for illustration by Carlyle from the first chapter of *Ivanhoe*, and used by him in his "Manchester Insurrection" to show its significance, that is multiplied in Disraeli's imagination, and made into a number of figures in his social novel, *Sybil, or the Two Nations*.

"Sir Walter Scott," Professor Irving Babbitt once said to the writer, "was too fine an English gentleman to 'get himself messed up' with the French Revolution.   He ignored altogether the gap which that event had made between the Past and the Present, and wrote as if the cataclysm had never occurred!"

Disraeli appears to have ignored that event in *his* writings no less than Scott did. And though one may not accuse Disraeli, any more than one may Scott, of seeking De Vigny's "stoic silence" or indulging in his moods of 'solitude,' still Disraeli and Scott, in spite of their apparently complete "ignorance" of the event of the French Revolution, shared something with a thorough Romantic like Chateaubriand: they both possessed what Professor Babbitt defined as "his sense of relativity, his outlook upon life as an endless flux that was filled with infinite, picturesque, and dramatic phenomena"; and they both knew — and I quote Professor ·Babbitt again upon Chateaubriand — "his art of travelling in time and space, and with variety and change of scene which satisfies great emotional and intellectual curiosity." These things they shared in because both Scott and Disraeli were, first and always, 'men among men.' They lived with a keen relish of all the senses, and they saw in the social and the political world which surrounded them men and forces which they energized: the one did so in imagination, and thus covered great canvasses with an 'impassioned past'; the other did so in reality, and became the leader of a great political party.

That Disraeli shared in common with Scott his impassioned view of English history, but that, most of all, he carried over Scott's presentation of the beauties and charm of an English patriarchate (which developed in Scott into an idealization of the old Feudal régime) into part of his political philosophy, is not surprising. By nature Disraeli was a Conservative. His inheritance would have tended to put him out of sympathy with any force that was violently revolutionary. Though it is quite true that Jews played a great part in the formulation of 19th century Socialism, the fact remains that the great rank and file of them are altogether peace-loving, and are among the last in the world to believe in the creative force of Anarchy. It is therefore quite probable that in 'ignoring' the violent

events which had closed one century and opened another, he
was unconsciously reflecting an inheritance from his own people.
So it is not at all surprising that we find him, as late as 1870
(which was after the passing of the second Reform Bill in
Britain), saying in the General Preface to his collected novels:
"The Feudal System may have worn out, but its main principle
— that the tenure of property should be the fulfillment of
duty — is the essence of good government." The ingrained
sympathy with the Past which Disraeli here shows, that ideal
which looked upon the great landowner as a father who ought
to exhibit generous solicitude and beneficence for his tenantry,
and which considered the Crown a suzerain that had feudal
responsibilities and that demanded from Aristocracy and
Proletariat alike the services due it, are fundamentals in
Disraeli's serious life. They are sentiments uttered again and
again in the novels of his maturity, and they serve to form
the very foundation upon which he builds his political-
philosophical reflections in his treatises.

This psychological fact may help to explain why Disraeli,
as the acknowledged leader and the very soul of the YOUNG
ENGLAND MOVEMENT of the forties, presses so constantly upon
the stop which issues paeans of glory about his own people
when, in writing the trilogy of novels, he presents the sym-
phony of ideas which comprised the Young England philosophy. That movement, be it remembered, was, strangely
enough, inspired by the contemporaneous rise of reactionary
liberal movements upon the continent, and most notably the
rise of 'Young Italy' and 'Young Germany.' There they reflected concentrated reaction against the results of the Congress
of Vienna, and against the subsequent absolutism which had
been inaugurated by Metternich. 'Young Italy' and 'Young
Germany' represented the very epitome of Liberalism. In
England, however, the movement was inaugurated as the very
antithesis of Liberalism. It showed itself distinctly opposed to

the growth of Liberalism in England, particularly as that took
form in a growing materialism, and in industrial changes that
destroyed the essential unity of the nation. Young England
pleaded for a return to the old Feudal ideal of Society which it
wished to see socialized; it pleaded for a renaissance of art, for
a deepening of spiritual feeling, and an awakening of the Church
to its grave duties; it cried out for a return to the old English
customs and ceremonies which it believed were being forgotten
in the face of a growing Liberalism that seemed Anarchy.
The extreme expression of its views is to be seen in the poems
printed by one of the most ardent of its disciples, Lord John
Manners, some of whose lines I quote. The first selection [11] is
typical of a lyrical enthusiasm for 'the good old times' when
all the virtues of Royalty and of the Church flourished.

> "Each knew his place, king, peasant, peer, or priest;
> The greatest owned connexion with the least;
> From rank to rank the generous feeling ran,
> And linked society as man to man."

The second [12] sings the need of the revival of the good old customs, when lord mixed with vassal, and thus retained his
respected, personal authority.

> "Oh! But it was a goodly sight
> The rough-built halls to see
> Glancing with high-born dames and men,
> And hinds of low degree.
> To holy Church's dearest sons,
> The humble and the poor,
> To all who came the seneschal
> Threw open wide the door. . . .
>
> And now, of all our customs rare,
> And good old English ways,
> This one, of keeping Christmas-time,
> Alone has reached our days. . . ."

The Young England Group consisted essentially of high-born youths, Cambridge University graduates, who rallied around Disraeli (who was neither aristocrat nor university-bred) because he could best express their noble ideals. Lord George Manners, the second son of the Duke of Rutland, Disraeli afterwards converted into Lord Henry Sydney of *Coningsby* and of *Tancred;* George Smythe, the 7th Lord Strangford, and most brilliant of those who made Disraeli their leader, became the hero in *Coningsby*, and was not forgotten in Disraeli's last years, when in 1880 he published *Endymion* and recalled him again as the character Waldershare; there was Alexander Bailie Cochrane, a young Scotch laird, who became Buckhurst in *Coningsby;* Ambrose Lisle Phillips, the Eustace Lyle of *Coningsby;* and young Henry Hope of Depdeen, at whose estate Disraeli wrote part of his *Coningsby*. As the movement began slightly to penetrate into the House of Commons, in the late forties, several of the more brilliant of the younger men joined it — "Stafford O'Brien, a master of epigram, who was popular on both sides of the House; and William Busfield Ferrand, a Yorkshire squire with a Dantonesque appearance . . . who denounced the crimes of the manufacturers and the woes of their employees. Monckton Milnes fluttered uneasily around the group, hesitating to commit himself." [13]   The young Alfred Tennyson ought to be added to the group as one who joined it outside. The movement never actually succeeded, of course, in developing any political force upon English public life. It is significant, however, for two reasons: first, because it inspired Disraeli to write his political novels of the forties which glowed with the idealization of youth, with the promise which resided in the younger nobility, and which helped to fuse, in the author's imagination, a concrete programme of political principles wherewith he might set out upon the leadership of the Conservative Party and hasten the downfall of Peel.[14]   Its second significance lay in the fact that the same class of sentiments which inspired, through Young England and Disraeli's trilogy of novels, a new life in the politics of the old Tory Party, had been the cause, at about the same time, of the great Anglican Revival which had gained power through the vigorous mind of Cardinal Newman. Eventually this was remembered as THE OXFORD MOVEMENT.

The literature concerning this great event in the English Church is enormous. For our purpose here it will be unnecessary to do more than sum up, in a few sentences from the pen of a brilliant French critic,[15] just what it represented in English life. While reading these let us recall what has already been said about the philosophy of the trilogy, and in particular Disraeli's sentiments upon the English Church, and we shall see how closely his thought lies to the thoughts under the Oxford Revival.

"The Oxford Movement is the expression of the mystical and the sentimental needs of the human soul. Its activity in all places is inspired by the same profound exaltation. It is a psychological shock to awaken certain dormant tendencies. The religious life, up to that time prosaic and cold, is warmed and inspired; it overflows in a lyrical joy in the poetry of Keble, in moving adoration in the sermons of Pusey and Ward, in impassioned argument in the polemical tracts of Newman. The aesthetic splendor of worship, the great dignity of the ecclesiastical body, the power of the Church, all of the grandeurs and the sensible beauties are invoked by the intensity of the inner feeling. Religion becomes beautiful, poetic, enriched, like the soul of the believer."

There are several remarkable resemblances between Benjamin Disraeli and the great leader of the Oxford Revival. Both were descendants of Jews: Cardinal Newman came from a family of Dutch Hebrews, the Newmanns. Each was a leader of a party, the one in the State, the other in the Church. Each was resented in his respective camp by members of his own party. The one wrote an *Apologia pro Vita Sua*, the other set forth his ideals in *Coningsby*. Each went East for inspiration.

Both had a common love for great ceremonial. Each had a great influence upon his time. The one rejuvenated the old English Church, the other reanimated the old Tory Party.

By choosing these type examples of 19th century thought in England, and noting the relation of Disraeli to them, we are tracing a stream back to its source, and gathering a knowledge of relationships which helps us better to understand his own mind, and the material with which he formed his political novels. It is inevitable that we turn now to the HUMANITARIANISM which was so characteristic of the middle of the century. And, in literature, to say a word or two about Charles Dickens, and to mention as well Kingsley and Mrs. Gaskell. At first thought it appears a far cry from Dickens to Disraeli. He "kept out of Parliament which he thought the dreariest place in the world"; [16] he was essentially a realist lashing contemporary vices — as he believed, with not the slightest interest in the pageantry of English history and English society such as Scott presented, and which Disraeli, in part, inherited, for Disraeli's political novels of the forties were in a sense an off-shoot of the historical romances of Scott. Dickens sought only to discover the imperfections in the body politic, and once having discovered an injustice, "it became for him the germ of a structure as delightfully fantastic as a tale from the 'Arabian Nights.'" Here was a writer primarily of "the literature of feeling," filled with the pathos of dying little children, and the horrors of "workhouses, debtors' prisons, pawnbrokers' shops, hovels of the poor, law offices, dark streets and dark alleys, all the London haunts and lurking-places of vice, crime, and pain." A writer whose "theme was always the downtrodden and the oppressed. He was their advocate; for them each of his novels after *Pickwick* is a lawyer's brief. He did not believe it possible for the lower and criminal classes to raise themselves by the elective franchise to a higher moral and intellectual plane." Between such a writer, crying out to "the heart and the conscience of Britain," and Disraeli, the author of the *Vindication of the English Constitution* who was intellectualizing the conservative property owners, and firing the younger nobility, in his political novels, to their great 'feudal' responsibilities, it seems a far cry indeed. Nor does there seem to be much alliance between him and Kingsley, the author of *Yeast* and of *Alton Locke*, "two red-hot ingots hissing with passion and with indignation . . . these social sermons," who preached a Christian Socialism, hated the Oxford Movement, and hated no less the Young England Party.

With Charles Dickens Disraeli held several things in common. The Disraeli of *Sybil, or the Two Nations* was as truly a popularizer of the Chartist ideas and showed, for an intellectualized character like him, as much sympathy for the poor and the unfortunate as did Dickens. Only it should properly be said, he was less interested in the souls of the poor than he was in their practical needs. This interest is an outstanding one of his in *Sybil*. He believed in the efficacy of Parliament to right their wrongs, but he thought that Parliament needed to be educated, and that the education had to come from those who were born with responsibilities for the land, and who had to feel it first. Disraeli's interest in 'the other half' is less psychological and sentimental than Dickens'; he finds the remedy for the wrongs in a more enlightened intelligence rather than in warmer hearts. Perhaps here, too, we see a characteristic inheritance showing itself. Yet with Dickens, and with Kingsley, Disraeli, too, was opposed to the Utilitarians; he saw no sense in the science of Political Economy (which, we recall, he actually satirized in several of his sketches); he never appeared to be impressed with the theory of Evolution any more than did Dickens or Kingsley. Once or twice, in his novels, he deliberately goes out of his way to make fun of it.

Disraeli, like Dickens, was a master of satire, but where the latter's shafts are Anglo-Saxon, so to speak, Disraeli's satire is actually Hebraic. It lashes the vices of the aristocracy with something of the fervor and mentality which was exhibited by the Old Testament prophets when they tried to reawaken their people to the duties of their own heritage. We may designate that form of satire as corrective rather than derisive; we find that it concerns itself, furthermore, with society at large rather than with actual individuals, and that in that society the satirist has a sort of cosmic interest. The Hebraic satire has for its end, unconsciously, national destiny or national doom. It is a satire which never laughs. "Les peuples semitiques manquent presque complètement de curiosité et de la faculté de rire," says Renan [17] — a sentence which comes aptly to mind to illustrate my thesis about the Hebraic quality. Now, by comparison, Dickens' satire is the satire of exaggeration, of burlesque, and of invective. It has a range, a gamut, which runs from the lightness of the *Pickwick Papers* to the intensity found in *Oliver Twist*. And, conversely, Dickens, with his impassioned observations and his sensitive heart, was unable to think of the wrongs and the sufferings of the poor without 'seeing red' when he thought of the rich. Disraeli, more objective where sentiment is concerned, and somewhat stunted to a feeling of the pathetic in life, and somewhat too cerebrative to sense all the grace that lay in the virtue of Christian charity, was able to look upon the aristocracy with more indulgence than Dickens, and could see greater possibilities of their reformation. That reformation would take place if only the nobility fashioned their ideals into actions that might meet the demands of a new age. Dickens had the love of his public; the author of *Sybil* never did. And that was not because Disraeli fails to show an understanding of the sufferings of the poor. Neither was it because he fails to present sincere sympathy with the demands of the Chartists. But Disraeli is too often merely the painter looking for picturesque effects, rather than the humanitarian concerned primarily with portraying the tremors of the heart. For him 'the two nations,' i.e. the rich and the poor, are separated not by a sort of sensibility (as they are in Dickens), but by an unfortunate economic geography. He sees on the one side a refusal to recognize the virtues of an Aristocracy which had made England great; on the other a stupid unwillingness to mark the appearance of new industrial forces, with a consequent challenge upon them to face new responsibilities and to awaken to grave duties.

SECTION B — DISRAELI AND THOMAS CARLYLE — AN EXCEPTIONAL RELATIONSHIP

"A SUPERLATIVE Hebrew conjurer spell-binding all the great lords, great parties, great interests of England to his hand in this manner, and leading them by the nose like helpless mesmerized somnambulist cattle to such issue! Did the world ever see a *flebile ludibrium* of such magnitude before? Lath-sword and scissors of Destiny, Pickle-herring and the three Parcae alike busy in it. This, too, I suppose we had deserved; the end of our poor old England (such an England as we had at last made of it) to be not fearful tragedy, but an ignominious farce as well!" [18]

With these words Thomas Carlyle greeted Disraeli and the part he played in the passage of the Reform Bill of 1867. Some six years after this was written Disraeli, as Prime Minister of England, offered to Carlyle, in the Queen's name, the Grand Cross of the Bath (a distinction never before conferred upon any English author) with a life income corresponding to the rank. The act was one of the first of the new administration and was a tribute, from Disraeli, to one of the greatest influences upon his life. When one recalls all that Carlyle had said and done against "the superlative Hebrew conjurer" during his lifetime, and then measures the full importance of the Prime Minister's act, there is revealed a picturesque and dramatic episode unique in the history of the nineteenth century. A study of the relationship which existed between Carlyle, the greatest moral force of the century, and Disraeli, the Tory politician and 'Jingoist' of his enemies, adds an extraordinary chapter to the narrative of English literature of all time. James Anthony Froude,[19] admirable biographer alike of both Disraeli and Carlyle, points out that for half a century before a Prime Minister of England chose to recognize his merit, Carlyle had worked his way in disregarded poverty. "The wise throughout Europe had long acknowledged in him one of the most remarkable writers of the age." The German Empire, admiring him for his genius and reverencing his stern integrity, had bestowed upon him its most distinguished decoration. "In England Carlyle had been left severely alone in his modest home at Chelsea under all the changes of Administration, while peerages and titles were scattered among the brewers and the City millionaires." It remained for Disraeli, adds Froude, about whom Carlyle had never spoken except with contempt, to perceive the disgrace which would attach to England if such a man were allowed to pass away as one of the common herd. In one of the most dignified and touching letters that must, I truly believe, ever have been written by an English statesman to a man of letters, the Prime Minister implied that he did not offer him a peerage, because an hereditary honour would be a mockery to a childless old man, but he pressed him to accept the other, and more useful distinction.[20] Carlyle, sensible of the compliment that had been paid him, and touched by the source from which it came, nevertheless declined the honor on the plea of old age.[21]

The episode has considerable significance for us at this point. In spite of the strangely differing personalities which the sturdy Scotch moralist and the brilliantly ingenious politician present at first thought, and much as the first would have denied that he had anything whatever in common with the political and social programs of the other, there is, in truth, an astonishing resemblance between them. It would, of course, be nonsense to declare that a large part of the body of thought expressed in the works of Carlyle during his life was transmuted in the sensitive mind of Disraeli, and then converted into the trilogy of his novels. No such close and immediate influence, of Carlyle upon Disraeli, could be proved. Disraeli was, however, a man of intellect, with a character sturdily independent and vigorous, and of a curiously religious nature. By inheritance, by his traditional apperceptions, and by the positive good that was in him, and by what he desired and accomplished for his contemporaries, he proved himself a sort of Hebrew seer converted — or, corrupted, if one pleases — into a Victorian statesman. The nobler side of Disraeli linked itself to Carlyle, the Carlyle of "sledge-hammer moral abstractions," of an intensely religious nature, contemptuous of mediocrity but with generous sympathies for the sufferings of the working classes and the peasantry, who hated Democracy, Utilitarian philosophies, and the contemporary doctrines of political economy. It linked itself to the author of *Chartism* and *Past and Present* where politics is shown to be "the principal agent in making history"; to Carlyle who believed in the powers and the leadership of an intelligent aristocracy, and who, in "the fiery glow of enthusiasm or indignation" could wield "the very sword of Goliath" over all England.[22] The better side — the philosophic side — of Disraeli was attracted to the strength of Carlyle, and responded to his influence.

Carlyle's social, political, and ethical views had found expression long before Disraeli published his trilogy. There were all the Edinburgh Review articles of 1829, 1831, and 1832, including respectively, *Signs of the Times, Characteristics,* and *Corn-Law Rhymes*.   *Chartism* appeared in 1839, *Heroes and Hero-Worship* in 1841, and *Past and Present* in 1843.   The first of Disraeli's trilogy did not appear until 1844, while *Sybil* and *Tancred* followed in the next three years.   Disraeli's *Vindication of the English Constitution*, which presents his first compact, careful outline of a new program for a Tory Party did not appear until 1835, — at least six years after Carlyle had begun to write for the Edinburgh Review.   If we recall an analysis of this important treatise which was made earlier in this study when we discussed the principles underlying the philosophy of Tory Democracy, and then compare it with the content of Carlyle's Edinburgh articles, it will be clear enough that Disraeli's conceptions of the place of the populace, the power of the Crown, and the great destiny of the English nation had been considerably influenced by these early writings of the moralist.   Our purpose in this book being interpretation rather than dissection let us lay aside the probe and pick up the looking-glass.   What we shall find there reflected from the works of both men will give us an account interesting enough of 'relationships.'

First in interest is a series of ten articles, written by Disraeli for the "London Times" in 1838, and deliberately mirroring the style and phraseology of Carlyle to disguise the sentiments of their author.   Writing under the pseudonym of *Cœur-de-Lion*, Disraeli, who was about to enter Parliament as 'member of the Opposition,' desires to show that a real crisis has been reached in England due to the deadlock in the working of the Government, and that only by a moral regeneration in public life would the Government be able once more to function.

I quote from three that are typical.

"Note ever, John, the difference between a true Nation-cry and a sham Nation-cry.   Reform House of Commons, wise or unwise, true nation-cry; Reform House of Lords, sham nation-cry.   Respecting the voice of the nation there can be no mistake;

it sounds everywhere, in town and in country, streets and fields,
lordly mansion, ten-pound tenement, unglazed hovel.   Great
chorus wherein all join, prince and peasant, farmer and factor,
literate and illiterate, merchant and artisan, mariner and land-
lubber.   The same thought stamped on the brain of everyone,
from him who wears a coronet to him who drives a coster-monger's
cart; same thought on the brain, same word on the tongue."

From the article entitled: *Nation-Cries.*

"'How is the Queen's Empire to be maintained?'   What if
this question be only thine in another guise?   But nation will be
answered; nation is omnipotent; will be omniscient; will go to
everyone; will clutch them in the street, in House of Lords,
House of Commons, Quarter-sessions, town-councils, mechanics'
institutes, will come, among others, to thee, to wait for response
beneath the far-spreading branches, old oak of the forest!   Nation
will go to Brocket, to Woburn, to Drayton, to Knowsley, ay!
even to Lambeth and Finsbury, but answer it will have.   If not
from the palace, from the cellar; if not from the common man,
from man inspired, from prophet; if no prophet, will make one,
will believe in one.

"This is Tekel-Upharsin work; gold chains and fine linen, and
robes of purple, honour for whomsoever will expound, but answer
there must be.   Notable the difference between moral and material
questions: King's Government, a spiritual essence;   Queen's
Government, form substantial;   one asked by a far-seeing statesman, no reply;   the other asked by a whole nation, by all, even
by the mob, and must be answered."

From the article entitled: *The Duke's Question.*

"Remember what the great Prussian said, old iron-hearted
Frederick, when affairs were very desperate, though his salvation
was nearer at hand than he deemed it: 'After seven years of
struggle, all parties began to know their own position.'   You,
too, have had your seven years' war, John.   Let us see whether
all parties in your case do not begin to know their position also.
And, for the first, what may be yours?   'Tis seven years and more
since Old William the Fourth, who also had a lion heart in his
way, did *not* dine in the city; and the great question has not yet
been answered, 'How is the King's Government to be carried on?'

Great question of a great man! True hero-question, prescient, far-seeing, not easily answered by common men."

From the article entitled: *Asleep.*

Within six years after the writing of these articles [23] appeared the first of the trilogy, *Coningsby*, followed by the others a few years later, wherein Disraeli developed his completed philosophy of Tory Democracy and showed how close was his thought with Carlyle's. There is, in these, first and obviously, the belief in the Great Man and the Hero in whose influence alone lies the hope of civilization. Only through Hero-worship can reform be brought about. "Man" says Sidonia to Coningsby, "is made to adore and to obey; but if you will not command him, if you give him nothing to worship, he will fashion his own divinities, and find a chieftain in his own passions." [24] The speaker, whom Monypenny calls the principal character in the novel as embodying Disraeli's own personality, and whom Disraeli consciously fashions into the very epitome of a Great Man and Hero — his is the very soul of influence upon Coningsby's complete life thereafter — is the literary embodiment and expression of his Hero philosophy.

"'I perceive,' said Coningsby,[25] pursuing a strain of thought which the other had indicated, 'that you have great confidence in the influence of individual character. I also have some confused persuasions of the kind. But it is not the Spirit of the Age.'

'The age does not believe in great men, because it does not possess any,' replied the stranger. 'The Spirit of the Age is the very thing that a Great Man changes.'

'But does he not rather avail himself of it?' inquired Coningsby.

'Parvenus do,' rejoined his companion, 'but not prophets, great legislators, great conquerors. They destroy and they create.'

'But are these times for great legislators and great conquerors?' urged Coningsby.

'When were they wanted more?' asked the stranger. 'From the throne and the hovel, all call for a guide. You give monarchs constitutions to teach them sovereignty, and nations Sunday schools to inspire them with faith.'

'But what is an individual,' exclaimed Coningsby, 'against a vast public opinion?'

'Divine!' said the stranger. 'God made man in His own image; but the Public is made by newspapers, Members of Parliament, Excise Officers, Poor Law Guardians. Would Philip have succeeded if Epaminondas had not been slain? And if Philip had not succeeded? Would Prussia have existed had Frederick not been born? And if Frederick had not been born? What would have been the fate of the Stuarts if Prince Henry had not died, and Charles I., as was intended, had been Archbishop of Canterbury?'"

The selection is from the opening of the third book of the novel, and recounts the first meeting of the two men — soon to prove master and disciple — in the forest inn where both had taken refuge from the storm. Sidonia appears again in *Tancred* and though he has no such dominating position in the moulding of a young man's character and thought as he does in *Coningsby*, he is yet the only person among Tancred's family and friends who is in full sympathy with his religious perceptions, and is, in a practical way, the key which opens the doors of the Holy Land to him.[26] And, again, in a strategic chapter in *Sybil*[27] wherein Egremont (a character showing the Carlyle influence) discusses with the radical leaders, Morley and Gerard, what hope there lies in a social revolution that may be brought on through the philanthropy of such generous patrons as Mr. Trafford, we are given to understand that such generosity hinders rather than aids the solution of the great social question, since it limits the powers of the great individuals, the great 'heroes' in whom the hope of the century must necessarily lie.

Sidonia's teachings are vitally significant in the trilogy. Toward the close of *Lothair*, which Disraeli published in 1870, appears the character of Paraclete who, though borrowed bodily from *Pilgrim's Progress* (where, it will be recalled, he is the Interpreter), shows here much of the religious feeling which

makes the great Sidonia so peculiar. He is, in truth, a transformed Sidonia. Like Sidonia he first appears as a 'mysterious
stranger'; like Sidonia he is drawn not so much for his personality as for the symbol of an ideal; and again like him he
cuts the Gordian knot of a young hero's perplexities. To
Lothair, whose mind and heart had been perplexed and
troubled by intense experiences (recounted in the preceding
parts of the volume) he comes as a spiritual guide and comforter. In a picturesque setting upon the Mount of Olives,[28]
which reminds one of the vision which taught Tancred on
Sinai, this great Interpreter, a Syrian-Christian, proves his
church to be more ancient than that of the East or the West;
he disposes for Lothair of the nature-worship theories of the
artist, Mr. Phoebus, and gives Pantheism its true definition to
the young and distracted nobleman; he sweeps away "in five
pages of conversation" all the minute points of learning and
controversial criticism about Church Councils, Creeds, and
Successions; he instructs the young man that there is a higher
unity and a more ancient one than that of mere Catholicism,
whether it be Roman or Anglican. As the result of the teachings, and the influence of the character of this seer, peace
comes to his mind and heart. Lothair finds happiness and
satisfaction in a broad Christian belief. He returns almost
immediately thereafter to England. Upon his arrival there we
find that he proves his strength: for Miss Arundel despairs
now of making a Catholic convert of him and so is forced 'to
take the veil.' Lothair has become a man of firm character
and of fixed convictions.

That Disraeli was well prepared to become disciple to this
Hero-philosophy may be seen in a natural tendency which he
first showed in his earlier novels. In *Contarini Fleming* there
is the artist Peter Winter, a 'stranger' who meets Contarini
while he is on a lonely and solitary walk, and whose subsequent
influence upon the hero [29] is strangely reminiscent of the meet-

ing of Sidonia with Coningsby, and of his profound influence upon Coningsby's character thereafter. And in *Vivian Grey* there appeared, for the first time in the novels, the personality of a really strong man, a unique individual who is not controlled by circumstances but who controls both his environment and destiny itself. This is Mr. Beckendorf, the somewhat mysterious and brilliant personality whose speeches have, supposedly, a considerable effect upon Vivian.[30]

Throughout Disraeli's novels there is the ingrained belief that the natural leaders of the people are to be found in the aristocracy — a rejuvenated aristocracy, indeed, established by their youth, and one fully conscious of their national duties to the common people, and of their responsibilities to the Throne. This is an integral part of his Tory philosophy, the cumulative message of his political novels. In his portrayal of the large and showy aspects of the English nobility, their hunts, their great country estates and their city entertainments, the processions of their women, their retainers, and such noise and bustle as they show in action (withal political action or social action) he links himself, in a stroke, with the historical novels of Sir Walter Scott. His, however, are no mediaeval portraits; and the leaders in his 'tourneys' and 'battles' having passed from the Middle Ages to the parliamentary lists of the nineteenth century, show the metamorphosis everywhere. Living in the nineteenth century Carlyle is therefore closer to him than is the author of the *Waverley Novels*. He did not, any more than did Carlyle in *Past and Present*, preach an actual return to the Feudal system. But, like Carlyle, he considered the aristocracy as "the least corrupted part of the community"; that they, "in alliance with the people, . . . could return the English nation to the lines of true progress."[31] Stripped of their idleness and their self-indulgences, they would still show "the characteristics of a high-born race" that was once England's, and they alone could bring the necessary authority with which to deal with the Radicals and the problems of an industrial revolution. He, too, like Carlyle,[32] castigated the Nobility for their weaknesses, their dilettantism, their grotesque and time-consuming habits, the effeminacies of their 'dandies,' and the hollow and superficial knowledge of their great landowners and their women-folk about public affairs, and the phantom and mockery of their sense of responsibility to the body politic. He went farther even than Carlyle in satirizing these foibles.[33] With Carlyle, whose *Chartism* shows a direct influence upon *Sybil*, he saw the danger in the rise of the Chartists, and preached with him the doctrine that to the landed proprietors of his day there must return that grave sense of paternal duty, that profound authority based upon personal excellence, that willingness to undertake the leadership in the solution of grave public problems, which characterized the chiefs of the great estates, and the abbots over their country-sides in the days of the Past, when men lived under a purely paternal government.[34]

For somewhat different reasons both Carlyle and Disraeli opposed the Utilitarian philosophy and the political economists of their time. Sidonia teaches Coningsby that though the principle of Utility has been powerfully developed in England, and though serious attempts have been made to reconstruct English society on a basis of material motives and calculations, it has failed because it is a principle founded on Reason; but the great achievements of mankind have been due not to Reason but to the Imagination. Just as Imagination once subdued the state, only the Imagination can now save it.[35] The disciple shows the influence of the master toward the close of the book when, in conversation with Millbank, representative of the great industrial power, he says: "The Utilitarian system is dead. It has passed through the heaven of philosophy like a hailstorm, cold, noisy, sharp, and peppering, and it has melted away. And yet can we wonder that it found some success, when we consider the political ignorance and the social torpor which it assailed?" Several years before, in his political satire, *Popanilla*, Disraeli had castigated without mercy the whole "greatest good for the greatest number" school, and his "Mr. Flummery Flum" had already passed down into literature as *the* joke upon the professional political economist. His hatred of the movement appears frequently in his writings.[36] To Disraeli the movement was based upon false principles of social psychology, and therefore produced a totally false political philosophy for a result. To Carlyle the "Professors of the Dismal Science," as he named the professional political economists, sinned against both God and human nature. "That brutish god-forgetting Profit-and-Loss philosophy and life-theory, which we hear jangled on all hands of us in senate-houses, spouting-clubs . . . everywhere as the ultimate Gospel and candid plain-English of man's life," he calls it in *Past and Present*. "Respectable Professors of the Dismal Science, " he greets them again. "I perceive that the length of your tether is now pretty well run, and that I must request you to talk a little lower in the future. . . . I perceive it is not now the Gigantic Hucksters, but it is the Immortal Gods, yes, they, in their terror and their beauty, in their wrath and their beneficence, that are coming into play in the affairs of this world!"[37]

Both men, then, castigated the science of political economy, for the same reason that both opposed the Free Trade doctrines, and any others that proved ultimately to be based on motives of personal interest. Prosperity, they believed, would come not by cheapness of markets, formed out of an ignorant profit-and-loss arithmetic built into a science, but by excellent workmanship of the artisans, by the superior character of the English people, and by the willingness of all classes in England to work harmoniously together. Hence both recognized the tremendous power that lay in the new industrial class of England, and the need of coping with it if England was to realize a great future, a future not to be swamped by what Carlyle called Mammonism. "The Age of Ruins is past," says Sidonia. "Have you seen Manchester?" [38] And with the entrance of Coningsby into Manchester, and the meeting with Millbank, the full power of the young nobleman's education reaches its zenith. And Carlyle, in *Chartism*,[39] "Manchester, with its cotton-fuzz, its smoke and dust, its tumult and contentious squalor, is hideous to thee? Think not so: a precious substance, beautiful as magic dreams, and yet no dream but a reality, lies hidden in that noisome wrappage. . . . Hast thou heard, with sound ears, the awakening of a Manchester, on Monday morning, at half-past five by the clock; thousand times ten thousand spools and spindles all set humming there, — it is perhaps, if thou knew it well, sublime as an Niagara, or more so." To Carlyle this was the symbol of his doctrines of Work, of Productivity, which he preached in *Past and Present*, become action. To him Manchester was a comment upon the wastefulness and the lethargy of the noble classes, — it was a call of Power, Energy, which England had to heed if she would not face a 'Dilettantism' swallowed by 'Mammonism.' To Disraeli all that Manchester represented — its vast energy and daring and its inventiveness, the pristine qualities of character in men like Millbank and Trafford — became the lesson for the moral regeneration of the English aristocracy through its younger sons. If the authority of the nobles would but combine intelligently with the energies of the former, and if both then worked for a common weal — over a contented peasantry and ruled by a Crown respected by all — there would never again arise a Condition-of-England question, and the greatness of the Empire would be thereafter assured.

I have attempted to show within what compass Disraeli held common thought with Carlyle, and have suggested how, in some regards, he was directly influenced by him. There are other links between them. For different reasons they were both, for example, infected with enthusiasm for the general reform movement instituted in 1832 which gave power to the middle classes. Both regretted the loss to the English church of influence among the people. Carlyle bewailed it,[40] Disraeli satirized its unimaginative leadership.[41] In Carlyle's writings one discovers a persistent faith in the energy of the English race, and a mystical confidence that with the coming of their moral regeneration they must lead the world to better things.[42] In Disraeli the same belief gained for him a devotion from Queen Victoria such as Gladstone, his great political rival, never had; as a statesman once in power, it formed the very basis of his Imperialistic ideas. But there were of course violent differences between Carlyle and Disraeli as well, and even on parliamentary issues. Not the least of these — to choose but one example — was the Reform Act of 1867, the bill which gave the franchise to every householder in the kingdom, and for whose passage Disraeli was primarily responsible. To Carlyle it appeared to mark the beginning of the end for all England! "The shooting Niagara" he called it, and its author "a superlative Hebrew conjurer." "How long," he cried out in his wrath, "will John Bull permit this absurd monkey to dance upon his stomach?"

However, much as Carlyle differed with Disraeli on the relative value of even this measure of parliamentary reform — and differences with parliamentary acts were after all congenital in Carlyle — history has since shown that the great measure of reform in 1867 which gave the artisans throughout England the power of the ballot, was but part of that mass of humanitarian and social amelioration for which Victorian England has gone down blessed by other generations. To that program of social reform the days of Disraeli's leadership contributed no small share. To the Act of 1867 Disraeli, when he became Prime Minister in 1874, tied a comprehensive series of measures for which history only now has seen fit to give him and his government a just meed of praise. Mr. Buckle points out in one of the final volumes of the Disraeli biography what the full nature of those measures were. Applying the act which furthered public education among the masses, the Artisans' Dwelling Bill which assured better housing conditions for the English poor, sound measures instituted for the protection of the peoples' savings, and two important laws which assured greater protection of the workingmen in court cases against their employers, and which secured for their unions greater freedom of action (measures which, says Mr. Buckle, drew from a Trade Union Manual of Labor Laws of the day the remark that "these were the charter of the social and industrial freedom of the working classes") were conspicuous humanitarian contributions of Disraeli's Ministry. The hours of factory labor for women and children, the policies for giving enjoyment to the masses of parks, commons, and playgrounds in congested quarters of the city, the whole intricate series of factory laws as they affected the working classes, the English sanitary code, measures affecting Irish education, laws governing the extended usefulness of the Church of England, the protection from the dangers of unseaworthy vessels of the English merchant seamen, — all these were carefully examined and in every case conspicuously, in some cases very notably, bettered. This, says Mr. Buckle, was 'Tory Democracy' in action; it won, he adds, from Alexander Macdonald, an important Labor Member of the House of Commons, his warm thanks to the Government, and in 1879, the remark to his constituents: "The Conservative Party have done more for the working classes in five years than the Liberals have done in fifty.[43] What, in a word, do these ameliorative acts of the Prime Minister Disraeli signify to the reader of his novels? They prove that with their author once in, power, the aspirations of *Sybil* and of *Coningsby* had been converted into legislation. The key to the acts of the Ministry from the years 1874 to 1880, not alone of social and economic welfare but also as they concern foreign policy and English Imperialism, must be sought in the years 1844, 1845, and 1847 — in *Coningsby*, *Sybil*, and *Tancred*.

Even before many of the acts here outlined had been given direction by the Prime Minister of England, Disraeli, the man, paid his tribute to the great moralist Carlyle. It was, as we know, one of the first desires which Disraeli wished to. gratify when once in office, and though Carlyle would not accept the Order of the Bath, he could not help showing how touched he had been by the offer from *that* source. "The letter of Disraeli," he said to his friend Sir William Fraser, "was flattering, generous, and magnanimous; his overlooking all that I have said and done against him was great!" In the light of our review of the relationship between these men as seen through their writings, does not this act of Disraeli take on significant meaning? To me, it was the graceful recognition from a genius of a master.

Section C — A Valuation of Disraeli in English Literature

The "Primrose Sphinx" of English politics has left something of his mystery to the history of English letters. Himself a fascinating figure in his time, product of a peculiar race who combined in a curious manner the stirring influences of his own age, Disraeli perfected a new form and launched it upon the literary world. The Political Novel, as Disraeli conceived it, is as fascinating and various a production, when measured by the side of the novel-forms of the time, as its author was unique among Victorian statesmen.

It is especially true of Disraeli that *le style est l'homme même*. All his characteristic intensity flames in his written word; all his great strength struggles for utterance. The novel-forms of his day were incapable of embracing the stretch of his ideas, of enduring the speculative intrepidity of his mind. They offered no vehicle for the development of 'programs,' for launching manifestoes, for the destruction of adversaries, for exposing plans that would rejuvenate England. He chose to present a form of his own. The path out of the main highway upon which he, more than any other, trod, has since his day been widened, paved, and used by many travellers. The course of time has made the journey a familiar one. The life of politics, particularly to people like our own — active participants in a thoroughly popular government — is now a well-known story. But to the masses of people, in the days of Disraeli's novels, when England was passing from behind the shadows of rule by close corporation to the dawn of a new day of democracy, the inner life of politics was not familiar. Even less so was it to Americans: by that fact they showed the greater curiosity. The spectacle of a Prime Minister presumably revealing, in the form of romance, what 'made the wheels go around' in the English government, encouraged many to buy his novels — at one time at the rate of 1000 copies a day, 80,000 in a few months. Disraeli, however, far from desiring to make any such revelation, whether as minister or member of the Commons, perceived only a world of men, women, and customs which had never before been adequately portrayed in the novel. More intimately familiar with that world than any other writer of his time, he resolved therefore to present it. He was not disturbed by fixed artistic principles which govern every form of creative work. He was probably not conscious of their existence. He simply accepted certain facts: that the novel is capable of holding and shaping real experience of any kind, as it affects the lives of men and women; that it is, in literature, the most adaptable of forms; and that no man has a right to set limits to its range. So he rode audaciously across the impediments which the very nature of his material would have made into stumbling-blocks for a more conscious artist, a better educated writer than he, and his very audacity landed him safe on the other side. For not only in England, but in America and upon the continent Disraeli has had a great reading public.

Disraeli was a pioneer in English letters. The definitive biography of him which has been completed, and which reveals now and for the first time that this highly imaginative and romantic character had, from early manhood, laid out a course from which he never deviated, that he possessed the qualities which went to form a great statesman, obliges us also to give more importance than we have given heretofore to his place in our literature. In his own time friendly contemporaries who had perceived the difficulties he encountered gave voice to an appreciation of his accomplishment. He had taken — so they declared — the barren field of politics and had founded upon it a new school of novel writing. He had breathed a soul into dead bones, genius into facts, power into mechanics! Here, they said, is a man who by means of the novel has established what are the principles of power; by what method the English people may sustain their realm; by what social and political measures the nation may assure future happiness; how the individual, by a visit to the founts of Christianity, may, in an age of doubt and perplexity, come back to a broader and nobler faith. Some of his admirers, particularly those of the Young England group, believed that for what he did for his party, Disraeli was as truly an elemental force in English politics as Lord Byron had been in English poetry. Upon the very classes whom he had chosen to lead he poured satire, lampoon, and ridicule; he showed off their self-contentment, their superciliousness and frivolity, their self-indulgence, their aversion to originality and genius, their disinclination to self-sacrifice; he did all this until he aroused them out of their languors and stung them into action. Though he succeeded only at first in earning their hostility, he eventually educated these proud men up to his own level, and forced them to accept him as their leader! The man who could transpose the first three letters of his own name, and use them to begin that of an intellectual Messiah leading Coningsby to a Promised land, himself became a sort of 'Sidonia' to the English nobility. Of all men of his time Disraeli was least under the sway of current influences, though he shows that he was familiar enough with them. Less than most of his contemporaries was Disraeli enslaved by the authority of accepted opinion. He dared to be eccentric, individual, audacious.

Something of the same spirit is what he brought into literature. Here, too, he was self-reliant, surprising, unconventional. Less than others did he depend upon the forms of the past; less than others did he follow the established methods of his contemporaries. His descriptions of certain types of national character have not been equalled by any other English writer. He was the first to give us the satire of politics in a novel. His pictures of social and political England undergoing democratic transformation must remain a permanent and moving record of historical phenomena. Much of what he gave us is unique in Victorian literature, because there was none other, at the same time a novelist, who was so conversant with the machinery of public affairs. The same hand that signed Exchequer accounts and executive orders of the First Minister in Downing Street, busied itself at Hughenden Manor with the most glowing kind of political romance. In that political romance Disraeli was one of the first of the nineteenth century to defend the right of women to rank as intellectual beings. He was one of the first to appraise the rôle they may play, through their charm and their sympathy, in the lives of great men — particularly men of public affairs. There are few writers who have had as great an affection for youth as he, and who show that the world is for the young. To him "youth were the trustees of posterity." His heroes are almost always young men of power, filled with energy, resolution, adventure, and high idealism. With the single exception of Endymion, they are youth trying to emancipate themselves from the tyranny of custom, from the conventional, from the accepted, and they are usually either permanently or temporarily conquerors in their struggles. His young women are always charming, sweet, and gracious, and though in his portrayal of them he seems to follow the 18th century conventions, still they are never the colorless, flabby persons one associates with that period of 'heroines,' but are always creatures of ardent affection, lively imagination, and independent spirit. Toward them the author is supremely courteous, — gallant, almost, to the point of adoration.

These are a few of many things upon which one likes to pause and comment as one recalls what it is that Disraeli has incorporated into his novels. The whole, however, is greater than its parts. In their own day these materials out of which Disraeli compounded his political novels, achieved a remarkable result. By the side of *Don Quixote*, which is said to have annihilated Chivalry, and *Tartuffe*, which dealt a powerful blow to the Church; *Vanity Fair*, which relieved us of much snobbery, and *Bleak House*, which gave an impulse to law reform; beside works like these Frederic Harrison would place *Coningsby* and *Sybil*. These created a 'new political party' and thus directly achieved an effect upon English history.

His style is a reflection of his fascinating personality. It is invariably lively, ardent, colorful. Usually it is a pageantry of rhetoric, a verbal orchestration of thought. Much has already been said of Disraeli's riotous imagination, of his oriental tastes; how he surrounds his schemes of power and sets off his vistas of genius with fabulous wealth, elegant patrician life, Babylonian terrace and ideal cathedrals, alabaster tombs and ropes of pearls. The society to which he sometimes introduces us appears to have stepped out of an Aladdin's cave, laden with the spoils of centuries. The worst of these descriptions are so extravagant as to be altogether unreal. Some of the best of them — such as the famous passage recounting the accession of Queen Victoria, the description of Jerusalem, the mountain scene during Tancred's prayer — have become part of every biography written of Disraeli. Not so well known are passages in his novels which, for swiftness of narration, rival the work of Sterne. Still more surprising in Disraeli, and unfortunately never quoted, are descriptions in every one of his novels that are filled with the beauty of nature and characterized by the highest simplicity of art. Where, for example, can one find in the range of nineteenth century English literature a more natural, a more simple pastoral picture than this, in which Disraeli is presenting the effect of a summer shower?

"The oppressive atmosphere had evaporated; the grey, sullen tint had disappeared; a soft breeze came dancing up the stream; a glowing light fell upon the woods and waters; the perfume of trees and flowers and herbs floated around. There was a carolling of birds; a hum of happy insects in the air; freshness and stir, and a sense of joyous life, pervaded all things; it seemed that the heart of all creation opened." [44]

The man's airiness of invention, his shimmer of wit, the hundred and one resources of his fresh and frolicsome genius, never show themselves to better advantage than in the short, epigrammatic descriptions of persons and scenes with which his novels abound, the sparkling, vivacious dialogue of his clubs, lobbies, and drawing-rooms, and his phrase-making. There are none in the comedies of Congreve and Sheridan better than Taper and Tadpole, the young and romantic Lady Bertie and Belair, Count Mirabel, Mrs. Guy Flouncey, Leander the French chef, Lady Firebrace, Lord St. Aldegonde. "Nature had intended Lucian Gay for a scholar and a wit: necessity had made him a scribbler and a buffoon." From the same novel, *Coningsby*, we choose a description of a noblewoman. Lady Gaverstock's "mother having been divorced, she ever fancied she was paying a kind of homage to her parent, by visiting those who might some day be in the same predicament." Here is one of a nobleman from *Lothair*. "Every day when he looked in a glass, and gave the last touch to his consummate toilet, he offered his grateful thanks to Providence that his family was not unworthy of him." Of a lesser character in Parliament: "Bertie Tremaine was one of those who always walked home with the member who had made the speech of the evening," and welcomed at his table "every one except absolute assassins." Of the Utilitarians: "Their dogma is — rules are general, feelings are general, therefore property should be general." Of his political enemy, Peel: "Peel caught the Whigs bathing and walked off with their clothes." "Peel's precedents are tea-kettle precedents: he traces the steam-engine always back to the tea-kettle." There were politicians who were "Forcible feebles," "Tory men and Whig measures," "Patricians in a panic." He once defined the Austrians as "the Chinese of Europe," and diplomatists as "the Hebrews of Politics."

These imaginative works of a peculiarly subtle character, whom a contemporary once described as able to "maintain the mingled gravity of Oedipus with the *insouciance* and *diablerie* of Robert Macaire," show unfortunately much unevenness of writing, and certain organic defects. They should, perhaps, be explained as due to a novelist whose active life was devoted primarily to the lists of party strife, and to the busy affairs of state; only occasionally could he find that repose, that retirement, which could sustain even short periods of contemplation so necessary for an artist. Disraeli too often irritates the reader by his complete detachment from the class of society of which, in active life, he desired and did become both philosopher and leader. He lampoons out of all reason the stock whose children he idealizes, making a separation in his novels between the older nobility and the younger generation that violates every natural and historical law. How can one believe, in novel after novel, that the same atmosphere of England, the same sun, produces such dissimilar fruits? What means can perform such a miracle in a single generation? Take another example. There is not, in all of Disraeli's political novels, a single portrait of a statesman, or of a minor public character, in whom love of country and desire to give service to the state is the sole and moving passion. Disraeli was too much the cynic in his worst moments, and too much the actor at his best, to be able to speak feelingly of the statesman of great integrity, or to analyze ambition which thinks only of serving the nation. Surely, in Victorian England, there must have been such men in active public life! When we turn to examine closely his occasional defects in English composition we must believe that many a sentence was placed upon a page "as hot and as hurried as ever was penned." Again and again he fails to command the English idiom, and sometimes he employs constructions that are so bad that his statements are quite ridiculous. Of some of these, the less said the better.

Historically, the place of Disraeli in English literature is assured. Time alone will fix his permanence and convince men of his importance. He smashed through the traditions of English literary forms, broadly interpreted laws or altogether ignored them, and established a *genre* in modern literature. He did so by widening the technique of the novels already in existence, and by employing it to absorb a new kind of material. Preceding him there is but one exception: the novel *De Vere* by Robert Plumer Ward. Strictly speaking, however, Plumer Ward is only a forerunner of the master: *De Vere* was but a link between *the novel with a purpose* of the 18th century and the political novel as Disraeli firmly established it in *Coningsby* and *Sybil*.   Disraeli, therefore, poured new wine into old bottles. He did that for the novel which Ibsen, in more recent days and in another fashion, has done for the drama: for Ibsen broke through the technique of the so-called "well-made play" and thus enlarged the scope of the drama for all future playwrights. The publication of *Coningsby* was an event of no less importance to the history of the novel than the appearance of *The Doll's House* was to modern dramatic literature. Disraeli has not, like Ibsen, founded a school. Still, the writers in both England and America who have used the *genre* that he established have been persons of prominence and great influence. Taken all together they make a very respectable showing. What each of them has done in that *genre* is to be analyzed in the course of this book. When that analysis has been made it will be found that the great political novel has yet to be written. So has the great problem play. Neither fact, however, can lessen the historical significance which both Disraeli and Ibsen hold in their respective fields of literature, nor can it undervalue the contribution which their establishment of special forms has made for the creative artist of to-morrow.

Chapter VII

ANTHONY TROLLOPE: THE VICTORIAN REALIST
IN THE POLITICAL NOVEL

THE knowledge which Anthony Trollope shows of the English ruling classes and of the great and small parliamentary leaders in his series of political novels which began with *Phineas Finn* and ended with *The Duke's Children* is certainly not accounted for by any great parliamentary experiences of his own. Here is a prolific English writer who, possessed of little formal education and in a life busied with commonplace official duties, made a distinct place for himself in English letters. He left more than the ordinary novelist ever hopes to leave behind him. In the very large number of his works he contributed a series of *Parliamentary Novels* which show a kind of insight into public characters and political habit that, coming from him, is somewhat surprising. It is surprising because there is little or nothing in Trollope's life to account for his interest in political matters. Only once did he run for parliamentary office and he was not successful. The experience of it he describes half humorously in his Autobiography. It was in 1868. He had made a contribution to the election funds of the Liberal party, and, as custom then permitted in England, that party in gratitude gave him the opportunity of offering himself as a Liberal candidate for the district of Beverley, in Yorkshire. In canvassing for himself in this district, and on the Gladstonian side, there is no evidence whatever that he took the great political issues of the day (it was the time immediately after the second Reform Bill) with any great seriousness, that he was known or backed by any of the great

political clubs, or that his desire to enter Parliament was for
any reason greater than might be that of any other gentleman
who wished to be made a member of "a great gentlemen's
club." Trollope went at his electioneering duties seriously for
a while, then he began soon to feel the drudgery of them, and,
in spite of many effective speeches made and of voters gained,
he dropped matters almost abruptly and allowed the Liberal
organization of the district to finish up the work. The result
is best told in Trollope's own words: "I did not get in, yet
was in at the death, for the effort of my defeat involved Beverley's own parliamentary demise. . . ." Defeated by the unscrupulous bribery which was used by the winning candidates,
he later had the satisfaction of seeing the borough disfranchised
in consequence. Trollope never took this defeat seriously, and
never again in the course of his life even hinted at a desire to
try for parliamentary office. His knowledge of the temper of
political life and of the issues and the personages which formed
the political kaleidoscope at the passing of the Reform Bill
appears to have been at no time greater than that which might
have been in the possession of any other well-informed but
ordinary English citizen. How little of intimate knowledge
Trollope had of parliamentary life, and how little this rough-
hewn, homespun, self-taught Englishman had of contact with
the great political clubs or with primary or secondary political
leaders, are shown by two facts: first, that when in 1882 he
published his *Life of Lord Palmerston* he tells us that he had
undergone a period of sustained reading and study of political
matters during the preceding ten years [1] (yet the larger number
of his political novels were published before 1872, and the
others within a few years thereafter); secondly, there is his
own statement that for his first and perhaps ablest political
novel, *Phineas Finn*, which was written a year before he had
gone through his one personal experience in borough campaigning at Beverley, he had attended the galleries of the

House of Commons for "a couple of months" in order that he might correctly describe the life of a member of that body.[2]

Of some sixty novels written by Anthony Trollope there were but half a dozen included in the so-called Parliamentary series, and these alone have a place in our study. *Phineas Finn, the Irish Member* was written in 1867 [3] and was followed in 1874 by *Phineas Redux*, a novel in which the political adventures of Phineas are broadened, deepened, and where much of the political paraphernalia of the first novel is made more significant. The two works may be very properly considered together, — the second work being read as a sequel to the first. One of the great politicians of the second work, introduced as a Chancellor of the Exchequer who has inherited a ducal tital and has become the Duke of Omnium, had previously appeared in *Can You Forgive Her?*, published in 1864, as Planty Pal. This same well-developed political type who, upon his uncle's death in *Phineas Redux*, is sent to the Upper House and while there becomes "the oracle, the good genius and presiding potentate of his party," is carried on to still another political novel, *The Prime Minister*, published in 1876, where we find him the First Lord of the Treasury and head of the Government. The last-named novel does not yet exhaust all that Trollope has to say about this political favorite of his. In 1880 there appeared *The Duke's Children* wherein the widowed Duke of Omnium is obliged to see his own children breaking away from all the fine aristocratic traditons of which, in politics and in old English society, he had been an ornament. A character who appears in both *The Prime Minister* and *Phineas Redux* was one who had been carried over from an earlier novel of 1873 where, as Lady Eustace, she had given her name to *The Eustace Diamonds*. These six novels constitute the Parliamentary series. They are, as must already have been made clear, held together by a peculiar family relationship — at least, each contains one or many figures that have been brought over from another novel in the series. To this series stands "a biographical prelude," as Mr. Escott, Trollope's biographer, has called it,[4] in *Ralph the Heir* of 1871, wherein Trollope's own adventures in the Beverley campaign are graphically reflected. These seven works, then, constitute the full vein of his 'political diggings,' but in actual pages they represent five thousand four hundred and twenty-six as originally published, small octavo, divided among sixteen volumes!

Because these novels were published so close together, revealed the author's desire to portray in varying degrees parliamentary methods, political issues and customs, and the characters of the ruling classes, and because there is, after all, little variation in the author's merits and defects as political novelist from one book to the other, we shall consider them as a whole rather than individually.

As evidence of the particular emphasis which Trollope (in comparison with Disraeli, for example) gave to his political novels, and as showing some aspects of the human canvas — so rich and various in his day — in which he expressed no literary interest, one fact stands out at the start as preëminent as we survey the backgrounds of these seven works. Written, all of them, at a time when the verve and passion of extended suffrage and economic reform filled the air, when England was being transformed from an agricultural community to an industrial democracy, from a land of parochial interests to one of imperial dominion, and when the great struggle between Gladstone and Disraeli defined so sharply and dramatically party issues, these realistic novels, photographing the outward aspects of the daily life, and making a pageant of lords and ladies, dukes, country gentlemen and ambitious Commoners, portray few, if any, of the most significant public issues of the time. There is much talk of Phineas's strong political convictions, and of his political fidelity to the standard of Mr.

Monk, who Escott believes is evolved entirely from the creator's inner consciousness, but who, to my mind, has some of the traits of the Liberal Gladstone. There is the very virile and universally-admired Gresham, the great Liberal leader, who once offers Phineas a place in his Cabinet as an Undersecretary. There are many speeches of ranting radicals and pussyfoot Liberals in *Ralph the Heir*. When in *Phineas Redux* the hero is brought out of his retirement from Ireland (his home to which he had to return, in the earlier novel, because of his attitude on an Irish question), and is again seated in Parliament, we watch his chequered career through three volumes, during the space of which there are a multitude of speeches on 'purity of politics,' on 'church disestablishment,' on the ideals of the 'Tory aristocracy,' on borough disfranchisement. We see the 'conjurer Daubeny' — Trollope's portrait of Disraeli — matching his wit and brains against the 'masterly Gresham' (who is closer to his original Gladstone than Trollope's biographer believes). We are present at the labors of bringing a new Cabinet to birth. We are made intimately acquainted with the private and the public life of a leader of a Coalition Cabinet and listen to the many various difficulties which beset him in *The Prime Minister*. Yet no part of this elaborate web of political life spun for us through so many episodes ever reveals the few very necessary supporting strands: a consistent and logically-developed set of political principles which bear the name of a program of political philosophy.

The only situation which Trollope deliberately creates (deliberate because the episode has no other purpose in the novel in which it is found) in order to present the reader with a carefully thought-out political creed such as he might employ wherewith to interpret the actions of men and the meaning of measures, is in *The Prime Minister*. Here the Duke of Omnium, leader of the Cabinet and a strong Liberal by political conviction, on a ramble through his country estate with his promising young disciple Phineas, whom he is tutoring in party philosophy, has the following to offer in illustration of the integral differences between the Conservative platform and the Liberal ideas of the sixties. For a man of his importance they appear entirely superficial observations.[5]

"I began life with the misfortune of a ready-made political creed. . . . It was a tradition in the family and was as inseparable from it as any of the titles which (I) had inherited. . . . Since then I have satisfied myself that chance put me into the right course. . . . When a man has to be on the alert to keep Ireland quiet, or to prevent peculation in the dockyards, or to raise the revenue while he lowers the taxes, he feels himself to be saved from the necessity of investigating principles. . . . I have made (since) no grand political invention, but I think that I have at least labelled my own thoughts. I suppose what we all desire is to improve the condition of the people by whom we are employed, and to advance our country, or at any rate to save it from retrogression. . . . I give credit to my opponents in Parliament for that desire as readily as I do to my colleagues or to myself. . . . But . . . the Conservative who has had any idea of the meaning of the name which he carries, wishes, I suppose, to maintain the differences and the distances which separate the highly placed from their lower brethren. He thinks that God has divided the world as he finds it divided, and that he may best do his duty by making the inferior man happy and contented in his position, teaching him that the place which he holds is his by God's ordinance. . . .

"That is the great Conservative lesson. . . . The doctrine of Liberalism is of course the reverse. The Liberal, if he have any fixed idea at all, must I think, have conceived the idea of lessening distances, — of bringing the coachman and the duke nearer together, — nearer and nearer, till the millenium shall be reached by —.

"'By equality?' asked Phineas, eagerly interrupting the Prime Minister, and showing his dissent by the tone of his voice.

"I did not use the word, which is open to many objections. In the first place the millenium, which I have perhaps rashly named, is so distant that we need not even think of it as possible. Men's intellects are at present so various that we cannot even realize the

idea of equality, and here in England we have been taught to hate
the word by the evil effects of those absurd attempts which have
been made elsewhere to proclaim it as a fact accomplished by the
scratch of a pen or by a chisel on a stone. We have been injured
in that, because a good word signifying a grand idea has been
driven out of the vocabulary of good men. Equality would be a
heaven if we could attain it. How can we to whom so much has
been given dare to think otherwise? How can you look at the
bowed back and the bent legs and abject face of that poor ploughman, who winter and summer has to drag his rheumatic limbs to
his work, while you go a-hunting or sit in pride of place among the
foremost few of your country, and say that it is all as it should be?
You are a Liberal because you know that it is not all as it ought
to be, and because you would still march on to some nearer
approach to equality; though the thing itself is so great, so glorious, so god-like, — nay, so absolutely divine, — that you have
been disgusted by the very promise of it, because its perfection is
unattainable. Men have asserted a mock equality till the very
idea of equality stinks in men's noses."

Throughout the full career of the speaker, from our first acquaintance with him as Plantagenet Palliser in *Can You Forgive
Her?*, through the *Phineas Finn* and the *Phineas Redux* novels
where he comes into his own by the attainment of a great
landed inheritance and a ducal title and is soon looked upon
as the prophet of his party, until, in *The Prime Minister* he is
rewarded for his profundity of statesmanship with the highest
office in the public power, we presumably follow the fortunes
of Trollope's beau ideal of a Liberal statesman. The declaration of political principles which I have quoted above represents, in the sum total of the four novels mentioned, the highest exhibition of his political sagacity. That Trollope fails to
give us, of a character whose thread of parliamentary existence
we follow through a dozen separate books, anything more
satisfactory for an interpretation of the great Liberal convictions of his day, is *prima facie* evidence that his interest lay
in directions other than the delineation of great parliamentary

ideals, or of the impelling forces which explain the actions of even first-rate statesmen.

In point of fact, when one surveys all that is to be found in Trollope's political novels, and seeks, so to speak, the common denominator of them, one is forced to the conclusion that Trollope's main interest, first and last, is to tell 'a rattling good story.' It was to weave a plot that would hold the reader's interest from first page to last, to infuse, wherever possible, a strong 'heart interest,' and to make all other things subordinate to that primary end. Long before he came to write his political novels Trollope had found his *métier* (which was to tell a straightforward English tale as Thackeray had told it [6]), and he had found his audience, which was the world of average, normal human beings, less interested in psychological discernments and in the tracing of cause and effect than in the chronicles which dealt with broad surface values in human character and the portrayal of every-day domestic affections. Having therefore gained his reading public — a public which had learned to look for these definite things in him — Trollope, upon approaching the political *genre* of the novel, came to it with certain limitations already imposed upon him. The audience which had grown used to his 'style' necessarily sought only for those things which had interested them in his earlier novels and which they expected to find in these of the political *genre* as well. Had they missed here what they had learned to love in his other works (he had written some twenty novels before the publication of *Phineas Finn*, among which were included his popular Barsetshire series), that reading public, always fickle, might easily have deserted him. Trollope, therefore, took no chances, but reproduced in this *genre* part of the world and much of the method which he had made popular in his earlier works. So, in these seven political novels we have again mainly the narrative writer, the clever draftsman filling his canvasses with English squires, country gentlemen, lords of the chase and the hunt, grand ladies of the drawing-rooms, fine gentlemen of the clubs. In all of these the social emotions are more significant than the play of intellectual wit and fancy, and in depicting the social emotions Trollope was a master. In the political *milieu* Trollope found another, a new, background as a source for story-telling, and he took seven distinct novels in which to exhaust the material of it. Upon characters which he knew well, and had drawn elsewhere with great success, he imposed a political emphasis, without forgetting to deal here, too, with the domestic and social emotions, and the 'heart interest' which had earned him in his own day a very wide reading public. That he was successful, in spite of the limitations under which he worked here, in making some definite contributions to the *genre* of the political novel — as we shall soon see — is evidence of his great resourcefulness as a writer, and of his fertility as a story-teller, as well as of his acquaintance with widely-varying types of human beings.

Since the method of one is the method of all, let us take for our fuller analysis the two *Phineas* novels, and here discover in what consisted Trollope's art as a political novelist. Phineas Finn is the son of an Irish physician, of Killaloe in county Claire, a man well-thought of but with only limited finances, against whose conservative traditions Phineas so far revolts as to determine to enter public life (even though a youth without a great family name and poor) by going to London as a member of the House of Commons. The father's good name and local influence, together with pressure made upon an already lean purse, as well as a contribution from the Reform Club in London among whose members Phineas, already in London studying law, had made himself well-liked, wins a constituency for him, and Phineas finds himself, in spite of the advice of the conservative Mr. Low in whose chambers in London Phineas was studying law, graciously blessed with a seat easily gained in the House of Commons. To a decidedly minor degree, but there nevertheless, we have at the very start of these novels the sound of the revolt of the younger against the older, the more steady-going and conservative, generation [7] which was so vigorously portrayed in Disraeli's *Coningsby;* with Disraeli it was, however, a revolt against worn-out political ideals and by that a reflection on the history of the times, whereas in Trollope the differences grow out of matters of expediency. Phineas's father cannot understand how a poor country-doctor's son, born in Ireland, can dare to fly in the very face of honored political traditions of England so far as to hope to mingle as an equal with the younger nobility in the Commons. Mr. Low is well on in middle life; he looks forward to the attainment of a seat in Parliament as the fruit of a life-time of hard labor. To him it is nothing less than madness for the young and untrained Phineas to expect to succeed in Parliament without having either means of his own, a distinguished name earned by a life-devotion to a profession, or that intellectual training which might assure a man some independence of action when he attains a seat in the great assembly. The traits of courage and audacity are unfamiliar to him. In Disraeli's young political heroes they comprise, however, the first essentials of character, and the parliamentary life of Phineas Finn is no less an illustration of their significance.

Now, as a matter of fact, Phineas wins a kind of public success, but when all is said it is a success greater in its promise than in its performance. At the close of the novel in which he first appears, after attaining (and certainly for no great qualities of his which the reader can see) an Undersecretaryship in the Government, his loyalty to a great parliamentary leader of high ideals named Monk causes him to break with his party on an Irish question, by which he loses not only his Ministerial office but his seat in the Commons as well. He returns therefore to his home in county Clare, marries his first sweetheart,

Mary Flood Jones (after having had three different love affairs
in London), and settles down in Dublin as an Irish poor law
inspector. All this has happened during but a single session of
Parliament. Reviewing the nature of the success that Phineas
had attained at the close of the first novel which bears his
name, the reader is almost inclined to sympathize with Mr.
Low's opinion that Phineas might have done better to have
followed the hard mistress of the law rather than the will-o'-
the-wisp of politics. How far does he go in *Phineas Redux?*
Certainly, measured in terms of political 'adventure' his life
in the second novel does not suffer from lack of variety. He
has exciting adventures upon 'the hustings' before he is again
returned to Parliament. The scope of his insight into the
kinds of men who make up the political world is enormously
widened. He listens to endless debates between great parliamentary leaders, he attends drawing-room political conclaves,
he gains our sympathy for his patient and trying efforts to
make his first successful speech in the House of Commons.
He learns the power of 'the Third Estate,' or the Press, in
public life and its ability to make and to destroy public reputation. He crosses opinions with unscrupulous office-holders and
learns the might of political venom; he sees the forces of
Labor pitted against restrictive legislation imposed by an unintelligent but powerful aristocracy; and, most of all, he feels
the tremendous force which women may exert in the making
and the breaking of public careers. All this, including a tremendously exciting court trial for murder of a dull but a very
useful politician, with whose death Phineas is charged but of
which he is eventually cleared by the aid of a resourceful and
a devoted woman, Madame Goesler, is what Phineas goes
through before we close the last pages of the second novel.
At the very end we find him married to Madame Goesler (his
sweet little Irish bride had died in the first chapter of *Redux*
conveniently enough to send him hurrying back to London

and the political harness), and in command of that lady's great wealth. He is now "a prosperous middle-aged M. P.," who prefers the domestic tranquility which goes with that anonymity to a place in the Cabinet which is offered to him finally, but which he does not now care to accept because it comes to him too late.

As a study of the character of a rising young politician battling his way to high office and to power Phineas is of course a complete failure. But then Trollope was not interested in delineating ambition in public office. If Phineas lacks any of that wit, culture, refinement, all those graces and the supreme idealism and the poetic quality which characterizes Disraeli's youth, and by force of which they often attain high place enough 'to move the world,' we must remember that Trollope's imagination is not Disraeli's. That this prosaic, homespun, altogether worldly youth finally succeeds in making Commoners sit in wrapt attention while he rises to make his commonplace remarks, that lords of the Treasury confide their political philosophies to him, and a titled lady of a great family (having made an unfortunate marriage) acquires the bad habit of throwing her arms around his neck and burying her face upon his bosom for sympathy, are significant evidence that Trollope was less interested in drawing the character of a zealot touched by a great public cause, or a highly trained and highly spirited youth hungering to right great social or political injustices, than he was in setting forth a man made of common clay who was to be a focal point for as much as possible of domestic tragedy and romance, and one who would furnish 'copy' out of his political adventures for an absorbing tale. When it comes to penetrating the soul of statesmen, and the idealism which may inspire a noble youth to go forth and fight a battle for the common weal, we can say of Trollope on this score all that need be said of him, when we mention Nathaniel Hawthorne's criticism of his works in general: "solid, substantial, written on the strength of beef and through the inspiration of ale, and just as real as if some giant had hewn a great lump out of the earth and put it under a glass case, with all its inhabitants going about their daily business, and not suspecting that they were being made a show of." [8]

If Trollope's knowledge of the intricacies of the political game is so imaginary, and his attachment to political convictions is so slight, as to make his primary political heroes altogether unconvincing (by which facts he stands at the very antipodes from Disraeli), we must, in his political novels, move away from the centre and seek for his contributions to the political *genre* in their 'outskirts' so to speak, upon the rim of the wheel which keeps the hub of it in motion. First in importance in the *Phineas* novels are the WOMEN. Lady Laura Standish, daughter of the Earl of Brentford, cousin to Barrington Erle who is secretary to Prime Minister Mildmay at the opening of the story, and who is mistress of her father's home, is the feminine political genius of his great drawing-room until her subsequent marriage to Mr. Kennedy, a powerful M. P. She loved so much to meddle "with high politics, to discuss reform bills, to assist in putting up Mr. This and in putting down Mr. That," that she is not only the cause of making her father accept the Privy Seal and of taking active part in the House of Lords debates but of inspiring Phineas with a great desire for parliamentary life. To him this woman of active mind, to whom "the cause of Women's Rights was generally odious" but who delighted in the thought that "she might be useful by being brought as near as possible to political action," becomes a political guide, philosopher, and friend. In her drawing-room, at the gatherings of Liberal political notabilities, he is made to meet the right persons; from her keen mind which had grown up in the atmosphere of public duty he receives the right interpretation of men and of measures; and from her warm sympathies he obtains again and again

courage and comfort in the face of apparent failures endured
when he was trying to find himself, in his early days in Parliament. She was the Mentor to his Telemachus. Unfortunately,
however, this was a female Mentor, whereby follows the inevitable consequence that the Telemachus whose interests she
has been so intent in advancing falls heels over head in love
with her. But Lady Laura, as we are clearly enough made to
see from the start, is guided by her mind principally; impelled
therefore by prudence, she beats down a growing affection
which she has herself begun to entertain for Phineas, and
thus marries Mr. Kennedy, because his wealth, she argues, will
give her that great power which her father's growing poverty
could never give. In the end she pays for her calculating
prudence. Her married life becomes the story of another
Dorothea Brooke with another Mr. Casaubon. While she is
thinking great thoughts about public duty and public service,
and is planning to make her new home the greatest gathering
place for distinguished men in parliamentary life, he sets her
down to learn lessons upon how to keep accounts of their private expenditures, to read endless letters to him from 'guagers
and landing-waiters' asking for jobs; he becomes so severe in
his ordering of her daily life, her church-going, her reading,
and even her human contacts, that life with him soon passes
from wearisomeness, to virtual imprisonment, and then to
sheer tyranny. The man whom she had married that her
mind and heart might realize their full development becomes
a log of wood to block the very entrances and exits of her
daily existence. Her spirit broken, she finally abandons her
husband. Her life thus sacrificed by her too prudential philosophy, she eventually causes the death of her husband (Kennedy
dies of the mortification which comes upon him as a result of
his wife's abandonment). She breaks the pride of the noble
earl, her father, and she almost brings ruin upon the public
life of her protégé Phineas. He, remaining faithfully devoted

to her almost to the very end, had previously drawn the hatred of Kennedy (because the latter charges him with having been the cause of their separation, a charge altogether untrue), who, after an unsuccessful attempt to kill him, dies himself. The whole story of the entanglement finds its way into the hands of an unscrupulous editor who uses it to blackmail the rising young member of Parliament. Lady Laura reaps the fruits of her initial mistake — she goes completely to pieces, loses both her head as well as her heart, finds that Phineas has promised himself to another, and that her mere friendship, in a time of crisis for him, has become a serious embarrassment to his political future. Phineas remains true to his friendship for her to the very end. She, however, is left by the author a pitifully broken wreck of her former high-minded self, without children or husband, a victim of her own ambition, suspicious, envious of others' good fortune, — a picture all the more pitiful to the reader who recalls her as the most high-minded, intelligent, perhaps the noblest woman character in all the political novels of Trollope, now completely fallen from her high estate. All this because she wished, in her own way, to be "politically powerful" [9] and believed, after her father's straightened circumstances, that she could best remain so through a marriage.

A political *grande dame* of a totally different temper is Lady Glencora Palliser who, in *Phineas Redux*, serves to protect and to advance that young parliamentarian's interests with weapons which are mainly used in a skirmish in that work when we see with what prevailing and consummate power she employs them in *The Prime Minister*, where the advancement of her own husband's great political position is concerned. In the first work, having taken a great fancy to the young Irish politician, and conscious herself of her social power as the wife of the distinguished statesman, the young Duke of Omnium (the Plantaganet Palliser of *Phineas Finn*), she becomes the centre of a women's conspiracy to force upon a new Premier

the necessity of taking Finn into his government. How she
invites the Duke and Duchess of St. Bungay to her home for
the Easter recess in order to enlist their help in her enterprise
but fails, how she flatters her husband and chastises Barrington
Erle in behalf of her favorite, how she leads with much skill
a Mr. Bonteen, who is the greatest difficulty in the way of
Finn's advancement, to offend the personal reticence and the
official discretion of the Duke in her own home so as "to prove
himself an ass," how the Duke thereupon losing faith in Bonteen prevails upon the coming Prime Minister, Mr. Gresham,
to give him no place in his Cabinet — through which Lady
Glencora wins her battle by her shrewdness and strategy, and
gains more power, as she believes, for her Phineas — all this
is earnest of the greater skill she employs as the wife of a
Prime Minister, in the later novel.

It has been pointed out that in drawing rising statesmen
Trollope is altogether unsuccessful. This is shown clearly
enough in the portrait of Phineas, who, when all is said and
done, appears to be a young politician running amuck in public
affairs, and leaves the reader with the final impression that he
was a better model for a Lothario than he was for a promising
politician with the ambitions of a Younger Pitt. Certainly,
it would be a sad day for England if men of his weak moral
fibre and mental flabbiness became samples of 'an ambitious
younger generation' struggling with public affairs. Trollope's
portrait of Lady Glencora's husband who gives his name to
The Prime Minister is not more successful. A slow, plodding,
unimaginative and therefore peculiarly conscientious aristocrat, who was never as happy as when in *Phineas Redux* he
spent his days and nights, while Chancellor of the Exchequer,
in studying decimal coinage, shy, fretful, a man of stiff reserve
so that he was too cold for friendship, uncommunicative,
sensitive to the point of morbidity at the attack of a single
public organ upon the acts of his Ministry, we can never

understand how such a fearful specimen of a statesman could ever have been made the Head of a Coalition Ministry. Yet this he is for the space of three volumes, and three years: years in which his time appears to be divided among differences with his wife (who seems by far the more masculine character of the two), differences with his colleagues which arise as he makes more and more enemies through his unfortunate personality, fears that he is not doing his duty, terrors at the attack made by a 'yellow journal' whose editor is running rampant, hopelessness at the nightmare thought that he never had a gift for governing men, and finally coddling by the Duke of St. Bungay (the Warwick who had made him) and by his wife (the power behind him fighting with every weapon at her command to make him popular). All of Trollope's principal politicians have this same unconvincingness and unreality. Let us name Gresham, Daubeny (who is called England's "political Cagliostro," a picture of Disraeli as bitter as it is unintelligent), Bonteen the politician who is useful, dull, unscrupulous, well-acquainted with all the back-doors and by-paths of official life and therefore 'invaluable' to his party. There is the poor, blundering Lord Fawn who represents the lay-figure in English public life; Sir Orlando Drought, type of sublime mediocrity of talent and energy who never went astray on the Treasury Bench "because he always obeyed the clerks and followed precedents." Mr. Monk is here — prosperous tradesman who prospers in politics because he is the most advanced of Liberals, the beau ideal to Phineas of what a statesman should be when he becomes a member of the Cabinet, and who expresses his consequent loss of independence to Phineas in the following characteristic words:

"Give me the full swing of the benches below the gangway, where I needed to care for no one, and could always enjoy myself on my legs as long as I felt that I was true to those who sent me there! That is all over now. They have got me in the harness, and my shoulders are sore. The oats, however, are of the best, and the hay is unexceptionable." [10]

Measure all these various types by those created by Disraeli and you see the *pastiche* in them, the counterfeits of their make-up, and with what little insight into political psychology their author was endowed when he created them or imitated them from some living characters about whom he read in his contemporary press or whom he knew.

With his women Trollope stands on firmer ground: here he deals not with silhouettes and shadows but with the substance. The Duchess of Omnium acting the proud wife of a Prime Minister, stirred into great political ambitions of her own, a wealthy woman whose feelings and convictions only help to keep her straight rather than her scruples, is blazing her way in the London social season in order to advance her husband's greatness and popularity. She flatters people she dislikes in order to hold them, as she believes, in service to her husband, and spends and squanders a fortune at the ancestral Castle Gatherum to entertain the great world as she supposes she is in duty bound to do it, indeed. She reminds the reader, for two volumes at least, by her lavish hospitality, of another lady who came down the river Cydnus on a barge whose poop was "beaten gold, purple the sails," and by her ambition for her husband and herself, of Lady Macbeth.

"I was made to marry," she says to her confidant Mrs. Finn, "before I was old enough to assert myself. . . . He's Prime Minister, which is a great thing, and I begin to find myself filled to the full with political ambition. I feel myself to be a Lady Macbeth, prepared for the murder of any Duncan or any Daubeny who may stand in my Lord's way." [11]

"A man of his rank," she once said to herself, shortly after his appointment, "to be a minister should be a great minister — at any rate as great as circumstances will make him. A

man can never save his country by degrading himself." Finding
therefore, at the very start, that she may not have the position
as Mistress of the Robes given to her, she becomes determined
that he, at least, should not be degraded by any failure of hers
to show him off as "the leading man in the greatest kingdom
in the world." She knew him to be full of scruples, "unable
to bend when aught was to be got by bending, unwilling to
domineer when men might be brought to subjection only by
domination. . . . To win support by smiles when his heart
was bitter within him would never be within the power of her
husband. He could never be brought to buy an enemy by
political gifts." She works, therefore, to do those things for
his magnified political position which he would not do for
himself. In London, she promises herself, there will not be
a member of Parliament whom she would not herself know
and influence by her flattery and grace — or if there were
men whom she could not influence they should live as men
tabooed and doomed. Money was to matter nothing in carrying out these objects. We watch this lady playing her grand
game first in the London political drawing-rooms; we are
then transported to the great Castle of Gatherum where the
magnificence of her display and the comprehensiveness of her
hospitality toward every possible person who may be of some
or of no use to her husband's political position, suggests, when
we see it all, an Arabian Nights' Entertainment transported
to a Victorian English country castle. Here, however, the
lady overreaches herself. She does this, first, by interesting
herself in the political aspirations of Lopez, a young adventurer
and — as he turns out later — a miscreant, whom she urges
to stand for the borough of Silverbridge, a seat once in the
possession of her husband. But this (as she learns later when
she is severely taken to task by the Prime Minister for having
'got him into it'), under the new election laws, it would have
been a legal offence for the Prime Minister to offer to give

away to any man. In the end Lopez loses the election (failing
the support of the Duke) and uses the incident both to blackmail the Prime Minister into giving him money to keep silence
about his wife's meddling, and then to reveal it to the editor
of an opposing newspaper who makes bitter capital of it in his
attacks upon the Leader of the Coalition Cabinet. She makes
her other most serious mistake when she fails to send an invitation to Sir Orlando Drought for one of her great 'affairs' at
Gatherum because he had shown some slight difference of
opinion with her husband's political ideas; by which fact she
makes an enemy of Orlando for her husband. Orlando, now
leader of the House of Commons, and influential member of
the Coalition, resigns from the Cabinet after the breach between him and his chief had widened, and in resigning throws
the first bombshell into the official family so that trouble for
the Prime Minister thereafter becomes more and more serious.
In the end the quickly-born ambitions of Orlando serve as the
entering wedge for what eventually marks the overthrow of
the Omnium government. These two grave errors, but only
two among many committed while 'meddling' in her husband's
affairs, lead him to philosophize over her 'wickedness.'

"If it were to go on he must throw up everything. Ruat caelum,
fiat — proper subordination from his wife in regard to public
matters! No wife had a fuller allowance of privilege, or more
complete power in her hands, as to things fit for women's management. But it was intolerable to him that she should seek to interfere with him in matters of a public nature! And she was constantly doing it. She had always this or that aspirant for office
on hand; — this or that job to be carried, though the jobs were
not perhaps much in themselves; — this or that affair to be managed by her own political allies, such as Barrington Erle and Phineas
Finn. And in his heart he suspected her of a design of managing
the Government in her own way, with her own particular friend,
Mrs. Finn, for her Prime Minister. If he could in no other way
put an end to such evils as these, he must put an end to his own
political life. Ruat caelum, fiat justitia. 'Justitia' to him was

not compatible with feminine interference in his own special work." [12]

Trouble at home is only symptomatic of the troubles in the Government. The gathering of the clouds when the budget of Monk, of the Exchequer, had failed to relieve the taxes in the licences of certain 'interests' (brewers' interests, they were, and the "deputations which they sent to Downing Street had been most respectful and respectable . . . it was quite usual for a deputation to have four or five county members among its body, all brewers; and the average wealth of a deputation of brewers could buy up half of London"), — the gathering of the clouds presaged by these deputations the coming of the storm. In the end, after three years of unhappy administration as the Leader of the Coalition Cabinet, unhappy to himself though useful enough to the country, he resigns and retires, much to his gratification, out of the public limelight, but to the chagrin of his ambitious wife, who could not so easily give up her 'Cabinet.'

It is easy enough to see that Trollope, who knew more about the domestic life of the English aristocracy than he did about the ways and means of the ruling classes at Downing Street and in the political clubs and committee rooms, had some definite convictions about the place of women in English public life. This he shows by both affirmative and negative methods. He shows it affirmatively in the fact that his two greatest 'political ladies,' Lady Laura and the Duchess of Omnium, when they once over-reach that natural measure of influence which the laws of Victorian propriety permitted them, become not helpers but meddlers, and their meddling is fraught with danger and even ruin for him whom they would aid. Negatively he proves that he had definite convictions by the fact that Madame Goesler, who afterwards becomes the wife of Phineas Finn (a rising young statesman in the last novel in which he appears before us in the Parliamentary

Series) seems to be his picture of a model wife for a politician.
As Escott puts it in describing her, she "knows exactly when
to help her husband by appearing in the foreground, and how
to advance his interests by *unadvertised activity* behind the
scenes." We see little of her maneuvering above board to
give her husband place, but we remember, from her ingrained
common sense and her practical measures taken in the *Phineas
Redux* novel to save both the name and the life of her hero, as
well as from the fact that she turns down a coronet when
offered her by an idle duke and then becomes the bosom-friend
of his nearest female relative who is afterwards the Prime
Minister's wife, that in *her* Trollope paints the active woman
with whom he had the greater sympathy. One of the most
charming among the many women characters which Trollope
knew so well how to draw, and which fill these novels, is Violet
Effingham. Vivacious, high-minded, spirited, but absolutely
independent in her judgment of men and of character, she is
laid siege to, for month upon month, by Lord Chiltern, brother
of Lady Laura. She continues to refuse to marry him because
she sees in him a wealthy nobleman, aimless, restless, undisciplined, without an object in his life to turn his mind to
usefulness, or his heart to loyalty. When she finally capitulates
to him and he wins her it is only because she is convinced that
he may yet make something of himself, and if it is not to be
in the service of his country (she was quite eager that he
should enter the Commons) it may be in some other useful
activity. She finds after marriage that her hopes are not to
be disappointed.

It appears to me that as one looks later into the thoroughly
happy home of this charming, keen-minded, altogether energetic matron, one finds in her the spokesman of Trollope's
views upon woman's place in England. "I do not," she says
in one place, "I do not think I shall marry Oswald. I shall
knock under to Mr. Mill and go in for woman's rights, and look

forward to stand for some female borough." But as a fact
Mill's liberal views about Women's Rights was the very last
thing that Violet ever thought of accepting. She wished
rather to live a fuller life, a completer life, under the sure
guidance of one whom she could trust, and whom therefore
she could in turn help with her quick sympathies. When Lord
Chiltern, as afterwards happens, turns out to be the man she
hopes he might become, she appears to have found her complete happiness and the fulfillment of her desires. In the days
of these novels, when Mill's theories of Feminism were beginning to startle some women, Trollope showed in these persons,
for example, that a woman might live a broad and a full life
under her husband's care, and so live it as to help him sanely
and well. But her Liberty was to be guided according to him,
we may be safe in saying, by an old-fashioned Puritan Principle: it was Liberty under the Law. If Trollope had some
guiding conviction underlying his delineation of women who
touched public life it seems to me that the conviction was
embodied in some such Puritan ideal. To him Woman could
be the greatest power in the affairs of England when she served
a purpose, first, for which the Creator apparently chose her:
to preside over the hearth and the home, and to make them
the source of all that was true and of good report. There she
could mother England's future law-givers. Then, by intelligent contacts with a world without that was active and not
too likely to interfere with the home, she could gain that
broadening of vision which might make her an intelligent
help-mate to her husband whose right and duty it was alone
to serve in the lists. As soon as the woman began to have
great public ambitions of her own, however, and began to
over-reach herself by interfering with those things the intricacies of which she knew little or nothing, she became not
a constructive force but a destructive influence. We shall see
later, when we discuss Mrs. Humphry Ward's contribution to

the political novel, as we have already seen in Disraeli's
Theodora of *Lothair* and in the women of *Endymion*, that
doctors sometimes disagree.

A contribution to the political novel of the nineteenth century peculiarly his own is Trollope's recognition of the 'Third
Estate' in Politics, or the tremendous POWER OF THE PRESS
to make and to destroy public reputation. In the figure of
Quintus Slide, editor of "The People's Banner," whose fortunes
we follow both in the *Phineas* novels and *The Prime Minister*, Trollope produced one of his most convincing characters. Unscrupulous, vulgar, but haunted by an unquenchable
ambition to make himself, through his sensational newspaper
organ, a great political force, Quintus Slide is set forth in all
of his black-mailing proclivities, his pandering to an uncritical
audience who perceived that in him there stood the champion
of "the existing rights of the people" and "the new rights for
the people," and in his political inconsistencies. To such as
he the world was divided into two parts: those who supported
him, and those who not being with him were therefore against
him. And not to be with Quintus Slide meant to be filled "with
iniquities from a sink of abomination," to have meanness of
temper, 'duplicity' and 'immorality' of character, a false wife,
an erring husband, or any other or all of the sins expressly
forbidden in the Decalogue. "We go in for morals and purity
of life, and we mean to do our duty by the public without fear
or favour" he once tells Phineas,[13] and finding upon that
occasion, as he had found upon an earlier, and was to find
upon later occasions with the Prime Minister, that the public
person with whom he has to deal has too high a sense of honor
and propriety to want to 'trade' with a man of his type,
he leaves the interview determined to destroy his 'opponent'
by using every vicious means that his poisoned pen is capable
of fashioning. We therefore watch the fearful attack upon the
personal character and the political record of "Purity of

Morals, Finn" (as he names him afterwards in the 'Banner')
and its consequences upon that young man's peace of mind
and upon Lady Laura and her aged father, the earl. We see
the terrible payment which the Duke of Omnium, Leader of
the Coalition Cabinet, must make because he had failed to
yield to that unscrupulous editor's request to be permitted to
enter his home at the Castle of Gatherum to meet the great
men congregated there. For this and other reasons he attacked
the duke. Suppose he was sued by the Prime Minister for
libel, — particularly for libelling his wife who was called the
cause of the self-destruction of the adventurer Lopez? Mr.
Quintus Slide thus thinks of the matter:

"Such an action, even if successful, may bring with it to the
man punished more of good than of evil. Any pecuniary penalty
might be more than recouped by the largeness of the advertisement which such an action could produce. . . . He would carry
with him a great body of public feeling by the mere fact that he
had attacked a Prime Minister and a Duke. If he could only
get all the publicans in London to take his paper because of his
bold and patriotic conduct, the fortune of the paper would be
made. There is no better trade than that of martyrdom, if the
would-be martyr knows how far he may judiciously go, and in
what direction." 14

Thus the unscrupulous editor joins forces with the Opposition
to the Duke's control of the Cabinet, in the person of Sir
Orlando Drought. *His* interests he thereafter furthers, it is
his flag that he thereafter waves in order to confound the other
remaining members of the Cabinet after Orlando's resignation
from it. An opposing journal immediately thereupon begins
to show his inconsistencies. By launching, in return, in the
Banner, an attack upon the opposing organ's "grammar,
paper, and type," by attacking the morality of the wife of
the paper's editor, by revealing what he declares is that
editor's unvarying duplicity, he creates such a storm of wind

between him and his brother craftsman that in the end he succeeds in sailing safely into a fair harbor. "The readers of the *People's Banner* all thought that their editor had beaten his adversary out of the field."

Thus is Slide painted by Trollope, an admirable realistic politician-journalist, moving from sensation to sensation, consciously and unconsciously trading on the ignorance of the great middle classes, ministering to their vulgarities, inflaming the lowest and the most corrupting of their passions. As Trollope paints him there is nothing that shows a saving grace in this man of power in public life — nothing that is magnanimous, beautiful, or clean. It is a portrait of a political power painted in one color — a dirty gray. Had Trollope been as imbued with a serious purpose in dealing with politics as Disraeli had been, he would have made, of this peculiar contribution of his, a more intellectualized character than he does: I mean, he would here, too, have moved from the domestic side of politics to the more comprehensive side, which would have shown the influence that such a man, exercising day after day an enormous power, can have upon the very thought of a great part of the English middle classes — upon their ideas and principles of conduct. He might have shown, for example, what we see in the editors of our yellow press to-day, that though they succeed in stinging the English lion into irritation, they do not always succeed in driving him in the direction they desire. Then he would have had to deal with political issues, with great public problems, rather than with domestic tragedies and personal misfortunes arising out of the boudoir and the drawing-room. But Trollope, as has already been pointed out, is mainly occupied in the social side of politics, with a love interest first, and with great political ambition motivating a story not at all.

And yet in spite of the superficiality of his interest in the real political *milieu*, Trollope made still further contributions to the *genre*. We have mentioned his political grande dame; we have mentioned the press. We must not forget that it is with a degree of almost supreme literary excellence that he spins the home-spun web of BOROUGH-POLITICS in every novel in which he deals with it; for with this he is personally familiar through his own experience in running from Beverley. The small peanut-politics played between the Conservatives and the Liberals at Percycross, the drawings of pompous old Pile 'the father of the borough,' minister Pabsby who shows himself determined to make the most of his short-lived importance when a great man comes to ask him for his vote and his influence; how men were bribed by Browborough and the subsequent trial for the disfranchisement of Tankerville; the story of the candidates at Silverbridge and the subsequent election which has such extraordinary consequences upon Lopez, deepest of villians, and Fletcher, the pink of heroes — these threads, woven in *Ralph the Heir* and in *The Prime Minister*, — woven into novels of emotional intrigue and of social convulsions in high places, are painted with the colors of blunt, roaring, and honest comedy. Sometimes, in these Hogarthian characters, there are to be found touches even of high comedy such as might have pleased the nice taste of Meredith, an artist of supreme excellence when compared with Trollope.

With how much more of interest and sincerity Trollope painted the 'man of the people' in politics, the idealized radical, or the idealized industrial figure fired by political ambitions, than he did the young aristocrat who came to Parliament as a matter of tradition, is to be seen by the colorlessness of Lord Silverbridge — member of the House of Commons in *The Duke's Children* — when compared with such POLITICIANS OF THE PEOPLE as Ontario Moggs, in *Ralph the Heir*, and Mr. Bunce, in *Phineas Redux*. Young Silverbridge, eldest son of the Duke of Omnium — the one-time Prime Minister — looks upon his parliamentary adventures in the House as a social

diversion, to be endured because his father wishes him to hold
the seat in the great Assembly. In a novel in which he and his
sister are the leading characters, we find the political interest
to be no more than a scratch upon the surface of a romance
— a romance which deals largely with his gambling habits,
his horse racing, and his 'amours.' He is in love first with a
fine English girl, Lady Mabel Grex, and then with a charming
American heiress, Isabel Boncassen, consent for the marriage
with whom he does not receive from the great duke until the
last chapters of the third volume of the novel. Ontario Moggs
is only a passing figure in a novel given over to a romantic
hero, Ralph, afterwards the heir to the great country estates
of Old Squire Newton, a rich country gentleman, whose illegitimate son he is. Yet as a passing figure he is ably drawn.
One cannot find anything better in *Pickwick*, where Dickens
tries to show something of the sort, nor even in George Eliot's
Felix Holt, than this portrait of radical candidate Moggs,
noble, demagogic, illiterate Moggs, who walks the streets for a
whole night after making his great speech upon "Purity in
Politics and the Rights of Labor" and dreams vast dreams of
what he, an erstwhile boot-maker brought to power by the
Cheshire Cheese Club, would do for the greatness of England
hereafter, to find on the morrow, after the heated borough
campaign is over, that the polls show him the last man on the
list! [15]

There is the admirable, flesh-and-blood figure of Mr. Bunce,
in *Phineas Redux*. This is the type being introduced into
English politics by the newly-come-to-power Labor interest.

"Mr. Bunce," says his creator, "was an outspoken, eager, and
honest politician, — with very little accurate knowledge of the
political conditions by which he was surrounded, but with a
strong belief in the merits of his own class. He was a sober,
hard-working man and he hated all men who were not sober and
hard-working. He was quite clear in his mind that all nobility

should be put down, and that all property in land should be taken away from men who were enabled by such means to live in idleness. What should be done with the land when so taken away was a question which he had not yet learnt to answer." [16]

Bunce represents all the energy of that growing but untutored mass of the British public which shows an innate spirit of opposition to the exercise of all restrictive power — an energy newly born with the entrance of the great industrial classes into the political arena of the sixties — energy which as often effected the passage of ameliorative legislation for itself through its representatives in the Commons as it got itself into trouble with constituted Authority because of its self-assurance and independence of action. Poor Bunce knew the cost of that when, championing the cause of his great Labor hero Turnbull, member of the House of Commons, in manner too vociferous and in language too loud for the public peace, he is arrested by a London policeman and has to have the help of his friend Phineas to bail him out and then to have his case quashed by the presiding magistrate. Bunce is ignorant, and has his prejudices, but he knows clearly enough what he wants.

"'Wouldn't you have the Government carried on?' Phineas asks him at one point. 'Government! Well, I suppose there must be a Government. But the less of it the better. I'm not against government; nor yet against laws, Mr. Finn, though the less of them, too, the better. But what does these lords do in the Government? Lords indeed! I'll tell you what they do, Mr. Finn. They wotes; that's what they do! They wotes hard; black or white, white or black. Ain't that true? When you're a lord, will you be able to wote against Mr. Mildmay to save your very soul?'

"'If it comes to be a question of soul-saving, Mr. Bunce, I shan't save my place at the expense of my conscience.'

"'Not if you knows it, you mean. But the worst of it is that a man gets so thick into the mud that he don't know whether he's dirty or clean. You'll have to wote as you're told, and of course

you'll think it is right enough. Ain't you been among Parliament
gents long enough to know that that's the way it goes?'

"'You think no honest man can be a member of the Government?'

"'I don't say that, but I think honesty's a deal easier away
from 'em. The fact is, Mr. Finn, it's all wrong with us yet, and
will be till we get nigher to the great American model.'" [17]

Mr. Turnbull, evidence in the House of Commons of the
growing power of the Labor 'interests,' and the great hero of
Bunce, is another convincing reality of Trollope's. This is the
absolutely-upright, vigorous-minded middle class M. P., one
of the most popular politicians of the country, if not the most
popular. "Poor men believed in him, thinking that he was
their most honest public friend; and men who were not poor
believed in his power, thinking that his counsels must surely
prevail. . . . He was certainly a great radical, and as such
enjoyed a great reputation." He used to declare that under
no possible circumstances would he accept office from the
Crown. "I serve the people and much as I respect the servants
of the Crown, I think that my own office is the higher" he was
wont to say, especially to his audiences in Manchester where
he was always received with acclamation.

"Progressive reform in the franchise, of which manhood suffrage should be the acknowledged and not far-distant end, equal
electoral districts, ballot, tenant right for England, as well as for
Ireland, reduction of the standing army till there should be no
standing army to reduce, utter disregard of all political movements in Europe, and almost idolatrous admiration for all political movements in America, free trade in everything except malt,
and an absolute extinction of a State Church — these were among
the principal articles in Mr. Turnbull's political catalogue." [18]

In this man who has an enthusiasm for righteousness, who
shows himself in the struggle he wages for his 'people' so
much finer than some of his colleagues that he is above their

hatred and contempt, Trollope paints the weaknesses as well. Being free from responsibility, his author tells us, he was not called upon either to study details or to master even great facts. It was his business to inveigh against existing evils. It was his work to cut down forest-trees, and he had nothing to do with the subsequent cultivation of the land. Mr. Monk, the great Liberal leader, once told Phineas how great were the charms of that inaccuracy which was permitted to the Opposition. Mr. Turnbull no doubt enjoyed these charms to the full, but, Trollope declares, he would sooner have put a padlock on his mouth for a month than have owned as much.

A character already mentioned in this analysis of Trollope's Commoners is the lawyer, Mr. Low, in whose chambers Phineas Finn first comes up from Ireland to London to read law. Mr. Low plays no great part in the *Phineas* novels except that, in time of crisis for Phineas during his great court trial, it is he whose sympathy and skill the women count upon to direct their efforts that they may tell for Phineas's greatest advantage, and they do not count upon him in vain. Yet, though only a passing figure in the novels he is real enough for the purpose for which Trollope introduces him. A man of great energy, of unquestioned integrity in his profession, conscientious and hard-working, he, too, has dreams about entering the Commons — so he tells Phineas. "But if I ever sit on a Treasury Bench I shall sit there by special invitation," he informs Phineas, "having been summoned to take a high place because of my professional success." Under those circumstances, having succeeded first in his law work so that he could be independent in his acts and judgements while in the House, he felt assured that he then would really be the colleague of a Minister and not his creature; he could then always vote as his conscience dictated and not to please Lord This or Lord That. To his way of thinking, therefore, the entrance into Parliament of a poor man like Phineas, who expected to live upon the money he received from the state for his parliamentary position, was a temptation from the Devil to sell his soul for the sake of place and of power. To this middle-aged successful barrister, for whom a seat in the Assembly with an opportunity to serve his country there to the best of his ability was yet a dream, the entrance to it of an unknown youth like Phineas was madness. What a wealth of wisdom lay in Mr. Low's words, and how well Phineas's subsequent experiences prove their wisdom, is to be seen in part of a conversation which we quote here out of the last chapters of the *Phineas Redux* novel wherein our political hero gives some of his own conclusions to his wife, conclusions based upon the experiences which had served material for six volumes preceding. "Do you think that public life then is altogether a mistake, Mr. Finn?" asks Madame Goesler, the lady whom he marries in the last and final chapter of the novel. And this is his reply:

"For a poor man I think that it is in this country. A man of fortune may be independent; and because he has the power of independence those who are higher than he will not expect him to be subservient. A man who takes to parliamentary office for a living may live by it, but he will have but a dog's life of it." [19]

As one surveys all that Trollope has contributed through the political novel one is forced to the conclusion that if Trollope held a brief for anything in the political world it was his faith in the COMMONER as a coming benign influence in English public affairs. This we see as well in the class from which his principal political hero Phineas comes, and the Liberal tendencies toward which his mind drifts, as we see it in the last political novel (if it may be called that, so slight is the political material in it), *The Duke's Children*, where the youth of the people, Frank Tregear, finally succeeds in breaking some of the opposition to himself for the hand of Lady Mary, daughter to the Duke of Omnium and sister to Lord Silverbridge, only after he becomes a member of Parliament by his own wit and energy.

Trollope being no platform-preacher in the novel, holding no thesis which he wishes to set forth convincingly to the reader, having once shown the dawning influence of the Commoner in English public life, lets it go at that. In every case the youth he has placed before us as a possible parliamentary constructive force, is retired, and then made at once into a hero of romance. That is why, in presenting his political figures one and all, Trollope never shows, in the political world at least, the inter-action of character upon character; what help or injury there comes from one person upon another is always in material things. It is a misfortune that Trollope did not penetrate deep enough to paint these dramatic contrasts. It is a misfortune because Trollope's field was his own, — it was not Disraeli's, nor Meredith's, nor even George Eliot's, though the last-named writer comes closest of all to him. Trollope's political heroes are unconvincing *as* political characters: his prime minister, his Cabinet members, are men whose minds he shrewdly infers from their manners, and not because he knew them intimately; the slight reality they have for us is due to the fact that Trollope refrains from bringing them too close to the reader. Yet despite the fact that his political characters are unconvincing, there are still, in these novels, glimpses of profound knowledge of the parliamentary system of England. There is no sounder passage in all of Disraeli's novels than this which comes from *Phineas Redux*. It would be hard to find one with more insight.

"A man destined to sit conspicuously on our Treasury Bench, or on the seat opposite to it, should ask the gods for a thick skin as a first gift. The need of this in our national assembly is greater than elsewhere, because the differences between the men opposed to each other are smaller. When two foes meet together in the same chamber, one of whom advocates the personal government of an individual ruler, and the other that form of State which has come to be called a red republic, they deal no doubt weighty blows of oratory to each other, but blows which never hurt at the moment. They may cut each other's throats if they can find an opportunity; but they do not bite each other like dogs over a bone. But when opponents are almost in accord, as is always the case with our parliamentary gladiators, they are ever striving to give maddening little wounds through the joints of the harness. What is there with us to create the divergence necessary for debate but the pride of personal skill in the encounter? Who desires among us to put down the Queen, or to repudiate the national debt, or to destroy religious worship, or even to disturb the ranks of society? When some small measure of reform has thoroughly commended itself to the country — so thoroughly that all men know that the country will have it — then the question arises whether its details shall be arranged by the political party which calls itself liberal, — or by that which is termed conservative. The men are so near to each other in all their convictions and theories of life that nothing is left to them but personal competition for the doing of the thing that is to be done. It is the same in religion. The apostle of Christianity and the infidel can meet without the chance of a quarrel; but it is never safe to bring together two men who differ about a saint or a surplice." [20]

In conclusion, then, one must mainly emphasize what has already been said of Trollope, as political novelist, in other words. Desirous first and always of picturing human nature as it shows itself in every-day, domestic surroundings, wishing to tell a good love-story in an easy, good-natured manner, he approaches his best characters (which are always the middle-class characters) with an observant, tolerant, and somewhat humorous outlook. Never offensive in his portraiture, with a comfortable interest in England and her sacred institutions, and the men who go up to make her laws in Parliament, he has no philosophy about public life, no ideas about what changes historical necessities call for, only opinions. They are opinions of his own gained by hearing, as might a gallery-auditor hear, the clash and the noise of political differences exhibited in a great law-making Assembly. To such a person comes only the reverberation of an internal tumult within.

If he had glimpses of a political *Weltanschauung* which might have served to help penetrate below the surface of his political characters, if he ever felt the power of Disraeli, for example, to *create* political character and situation, to intellectualize the elements of his political *milieu*, Trollope was content not to exercise that power, but rather to *depict* his characters and his situations, to gratify his world of readers with the easily jogging narrative of sentiment to which they had already become accustomed in his earlier works. Dead earnestness and daring dreams of power in the mind of an aristocrat Trollope preferred to paint, or could paint merely, as the somewhat domestic and social manoeuvrings of the pale shades of the upper classes. The political life of England was never the integral part of Trollope's literary personality that it was of Disraeli's, to say the least. His political cabinets feed therefore always upon small talk and small ideas. His principal actors are somewhat mechanically-minded public leaders, when it is of them that he treats. Only when he steps down among the people that he knew most intimately, and whose daily fortunes, in their middle-class environment, he could easily follow, does he give us convincing situations and real flesh and blood. With the exception of the great ladies (whom he paints admirably, because he assumes them to be middle-class persons 'risen' to the level of 'high society,' but still with middle-class habits) his flesh-and-blood people are not the leaders in the fight, only the secondary characters. Trollope never took his politics more seriously than as a means of creating another background for the portrayal of human beings, for the telling of a good story, for the chance of reflecting more 'heart interest.' As a result he never created a big figure or evolved a great ambition. The reader therefore never gains the intellectual stimulus which a novel with a political thesis is likely to give because he never is interested in novelizing a 'point of view,' a platform, a philosophy of conduct. What the reader does gain from these works is the sense of an "aggressive cordiality" in the story-teller, of a warm-hearted personality "perplexed by no ethical or philosophical media," who is chronicling some part of the English world of men and women just as they lived before his eyes as he watched them in his travels as Post Office Inspector up and down the breadth of the kingdom.

Chapter VIII

GEORGE ELIOT AND RADICALISM

"NATURAL talk, like ploughing, should turn up a large surface of life, rather than dig mines into geological strata," says Robert Louis Stevenson. To the lively but not too critical reader that sentence sums up the passing distinction between Trollope's political novels and George Eliot's *Felix Holt, the Radical*. Trollope's parliamentary series of novels keeps close along the lines of an every-day humanity, near the bosoms and businesses of public men and ambitious women, and at a level where the history of Cabinet ministers and general politicians, the intrigues and scandals revealed in ladies' drawing-rooms, and the experience of rising and hopeful Commoners intersect and illuminate each other. George Eliot digs into spiritual strata: her political philosophy is the reflection of a single noble and earnest soul, her public stage is a pin-point of a pocket borough upon the vast map of England, her prominent actors are a wealthy young country gentleman with political conceits and the son of a weaver, himself a poor working man, struggling one against the other for the confidence and approbation of a handful of uneducated miners, ill-educated tenants possessing votes, and a rough lump of penurious humanity which represents Public Opinion. Upon these she asks you to level the large end of your telescope, and, having thus brought them in magnified form close to you, to discover the pathos, the blindness and the injustice of conduct, and even the heroism which were among the effects of the passage of the 1832 Reform Bill as revealed not alone in Treby and Sproxton but among the wage-earning classes over the length and breadth

of England. Anthony Trollope's political paraphernalia came
sweeping out of a Victorian chronicler's mind that was troubled
by no psychological or ethical dicta; George Eliot's political
ideas were the product of her spiritual moods.

Measured in terms of the political *genre*, *Felix Holt, the Radical* is, in spite of its name, a political novel without a political
hero. I mean by that, there is no leading figure in the work
with a soul aflame to enter Parliament to right the wrongs of
a down-trodden class, or to awaken in another class a consciousness of their national duties. Of such characteristic stuff were
Disraeli's heroes made. Harold Transome has the same selfish
love of ease, the same want of principle, and also the same
sense of honor and tradition that usually were attributed to
the Tory families of which he was a typical offshoot — landed
country gentlemen who if they did not preach the beauties of
a Feudal society yet did what they could to put it into practice,
and believed the passing of the Reform Act a national catastrophe. That he decides, upon his return from Smyrna to his
maternal home at Treby Magna, to run for Parliament as a
Radical is due to no sympathy for the under-dog, or the down-
trodden, but because, being a younger son who had carved out
his own fortunes as a merchant in the Orient, he returns to
England out of patience with his own hereditary caste, and
anxious to show that he is tied to no class conservatisms. "He
was addicted at once to rebellion and to conformity, and only
an intimate personal knowledge could enable any one to
predict where his conformity would begin," so his creator tells
us. The profundity of his political convictions are easiest
measured by the brittleness of his first disciple — his uncle,
Mr. Lingon, the Tory parson of the parish. At the end of the
second bottle of port, upon the night of Harold Transome's
return, it requires little effort to convince him that Toryism
is a dead institution and that Whiggery is a monstrosity. On
the next morning, however, the Vicar's mind being somewhat

clearer, he becomes aware that he may have let himself in for more than he had bargained in promising his support to a Radical in that Tory stronghold. But the nephew easily dissipates his doubts by declaring to him that he is a Radical only in desiring "to root out abuses."

"'That's the word I wanted, my lad,' said the Vicar, slapping Harold's knee. 'That's a spool to wind a speech on. Abuses is the very word, and if anybody shows himself offended, he'll put the cap on for himself.'"

When Felix Holt returns from Glasgow, where working as a watchmaker he had received his education, to his native town, he comes imbued with a determination to advance the spirit of reform, and to make more cohesive the cause of the laboring-man.

"I'm a radical myself, and mean to work all my life against privilege, monopoly, and oppression. . . . I shall go away as soon as I can to some large town, some ugly, wicked, miserable place. I want to be a demagogue of a new sort; an honest one, if possible, who will tell the people they are blind and foolish, and neither flatter them nor fatten on them."

Political progress to him must go hand in hand with intellectual breadth and moral elevation; and because it is the interest of his own class that he has deeply at heart, he makes himself one of the "Sugar Loaf" and lays plans to preach weekly to the illiterate miners about their duties to themselves and their children; he scorns a 'white-collar job' in exchange for his humble watch-making duties because he wants to labor among the working men as one of themselves and not as one raised above them; and he never entertains for an instant the thought of personal ambition wherein either his eloquence, his learning, or his profound purpose may make him a leader of his class, and thus advance its own peculiar ends. He sounds the Carlyle doctrine of the holiness of labor, he shows a sans-culottian fierceness for gentility and sentiment, he has the asceticism and the practical wisdom of the Puritan as Macaulay painted him in his essay on *Milton*, and the disdain for the aristocrat that the early Christian martyr had for his sensual tormentor. He is not a Chartist — and that in the days when the Chartist movement was gaining momentum. When a radical demagogue fighting for favor in behalf of Harold Transome makes his loud-mouthed promises to his audience not alone of universal suffrage but of the other points of the Charter, too, Felix Holt later hurls the words 'back into the speaker's mouth.[1]

"All the schemes about voting, and districts, and annual Parliaments, and the rest, are engines, and the water or steam — the force that is to work them — must come out of human nature — out of men's passions and feelings and desires. Whether the engines will do good work or bad depends on these feelings; and if we have false expectations about men's characters, we are very much like the idiot who thinks he'll carry milk in a can without a bottom. . . ."

He is not a popular leader, nor does he show any ambition to become one. There is in him something of the high purpose and the self-effacement of the early Christian, combined with the political vision and the moral fervor of a great patriot.

If the sketch I have drawn of Felix Holt leaves him a hazy figure in the reader's mind it is because George Eliot has given us, in this man, an idealized character, a creature of the understanding rather than one of romance or of the passions. In 1866, England was in the midst of a great political agitation concerning the issue as to the best method of extending the franchise among the working-classes as well as the householders — an issue in which Disraeli and Gladstone were upon opposite sides. That agitation was the climax of a fight first made by the Radical, Joseph Hume, and carried on by John Bright later.[2] In this year George Eliot thinks back thirty years, to the passing of the first Reform Act; she tells us that she studied the *Times* of those years [3] in order to make herself more familiar with episodes which had occurred in her childhood, and within her own memory. She becomes convinced that nothing very good has come out of violent reforms — at least, nothing of import has resulted for the working classes. Amid all this great talk about further extension of the ballot privilege through a more comprehensive Reform Act, she feels it incumbent upon herself to show that though she is a true Liberal so far as party alliance is concerned, she looks upon the ballot as merely a clumsy mechanical means of gaining that morality in political life which ought to be — by every law of human nature — a spontaneous growth, a natural and not a forced development. She becomes convinced that no political reforms without can amount to much if they are not first the effects of a moral reform within. Possessed of this thesis she is not willing, however, in spite of the intensity with which it held her, to enter into the arena of political partisanship and controversy. Expression, nevertheless, she had to give it: and expression had to come for two reasons. First, there was the sheer human one — the good of those classes whose interests lay close to her heart was at stake; second, there was the purely artistic and moral impulse — to show that in political life no less than in social life those who sow the wind must reap the whirlwind. Her duty, as a writer, was therefore twofold: to record, at the start, clearly and convincingly, that a mechanical parliamentary reform, originally intended to better the status of one class of society, had failed to do so for certain obvious reasons; to appeal, finally, in a direct and impassioned address, to those working classes whose interests were hers, pointing out to them what folly would be theirs if they permitted mere political gestures to be taken for a national panacea while the body for which the medicine was intended was totally unprepared to digest it. It may well be doubted whether George Eliot began her writing of *Felix Holt*,

Radical, with a program in her mind as articulate as I have suggested. I am certain, however, that long before she had completed the writing of that novel the full plan was there. Hardly had she laid down her pen upon the completion of its last pages, when she took it up again to write her *Address to the Working Classes by Felix Holt.* It was an address published in the very first days of the year 1868,[4] and was written immediately upon the passing of the Reform Bill of 1867 — an act of democratization which almost doubled the voting power of the masses as compared to the Reform Act of 1832 by adding, to the already enfranchised middle classes, the vote of the householders in all boroughs, and the votes of all the better-class laborers. Since this address is in only a more contracted and precise form a summary of the principles of political conduct which are set forth in the novel, and furnishes furthermore a key for the understanding of the author's own program of political philosophy, it may be well to pause, for a space here and set forth with some fullness the substance of that paper.

George Eliot begins by pointing out the need of realization, by the working classes to whom she addresses herself, of the heavy responsibility which has come to them with the new franchise. It is a responsibility which involves terrible risks — the risk of "electing platform swaggerers, who bring us nothing but the ocean to make our broth with," the risk of working for "class interests" rather than for "class duties" and the common weal, the risk of losing one's force in a passion of indignation against the evils of others instead of looking first into one's own heart and there gathering strength. Gathering strength means the cultivation of knowledge, sobriety, the exercise of patience with those endowed classes who hold the precious inheritances of the Past in their hands — even if these classes sometimes stumble; it means cultivating energy and industry to further the common weal of England, and gaining that discernment which is quick to see wickedness in low places no less than in high; it means watching for that wisdom which knows that in co-operation with all classes, and that in the proper submission to the great laws of inheritance which have garnered the precious thought of the ages, can one hope to mould a future England closer to the heart's desire.

"Whether our political power will be any good to us now we have got it, must depend entirely on the means and materials — the knowledge, ability, and honesty we have at command. These three things are the only conditions on which we can get any lasting benefit, as every clever workman among us knows."

We may feel bitterly enough that the evils under which the country now suffers are the consequences of the folly, ignorance, and self-seeking of those who wielded all of the power in the past, but we must for that very reason refuse to clamor for measures of half-relief hastily passed, even if these may promise an immediate good, in order that we may not ourselves fall into these very sins and so leave a vicious inheritance for our children. Human lives are linked together. A society, a nation, is held together by the dependence of men, one upon another, and their common interest in preventing injury. No class of society is so much in danger of forgetting this truth as Workingmen. When these talk of their 'interests,' as if they were altogether apart from a common body of interests, as if they believe that a nation can exist without being composed of different classes each performing its peculiar function, they are but sowing injuries and resistances which will leave everything worse and not better for the voting power that has come to them. "The only safe way by which society can be steadily improved and our worst evils reduced, is not by any attempt to do away directly with the actually existing class distinctions and advantages (as if everybody could have the same sort of work, or lead the same sort of life) . . . but by the turning of Class interests into Class Duties or Functions. What I mean is that each class should be urged by the surrounding conditions to perform its particular work under the strong pressure of responsibility of the nation at large." The franchise exercised by the working-classes will bring them good only in proportion as they use it with judgement, conscience, and knowledge.

Right knowledge, she loftily conceives to mean, a sympathy with and an understanding of that wealth of science, poetry, refinement of thought and feeling, of manners, great memories and the interpretation of great records, which is passed down from the minds of one generation to that of the other. As things now stand she warns the workingmen to remember that this precious heritage of knowledge and refinement, resident for the most part in those who must always have a necessary leisure and ease wherewith to cultivate and to magnify it, will be broken into a thousand pieces if jealousy and wrath and the brutal passions so sway their judgement that they become revolutionaries, iconoclasts, possessed by the sole desire to make absolutely predominant "a class whose wants have been of a common sort." For the sake of having all things more fairly shared the members of that class desire to bring about the passage of hasty measures of relief which would, in the end, debase the very life of the nation. They must, therefore, exercise much patience with the institutions of wealth and with the methods still obtaining by which it is accumulated: for though there are many evils still part and parcel of these methods, it is yet true that "this treasure of knowledge, which consists in the fine activity, the exalted vision of many minds" is bound up at present with these institutions. Since the blessings of knowledge are ready for all, — the moment persons show evidence that they are prepared to receive them, — it behooves all men therefore to strive, first and foremost, to break the yoke of ignorance that surrounds them. "If we demand more leisure, more ease in our lives, let us show that we don't deserve the reproach of wanting to shirk that industry which, in some form or other, every man, whether rich or poor, should feel himself as bound to as he is bound to decency. Let us show that we want to have some time and strength left to us that we may use it, not for brutal indulgence, but for the rational exercise of the faculties which make us men. Without this no political measures can benefit us."

Right knowledge, Felix Holt argues, will best show itself among the workingmen when they begin to recognize their duties to their country; which means when they begin cultivating in themselves the essentials of great character. Good character in them will shame members of the higher classes to feel their own duties. What is the evidence of right character among the working classes? It is their possession of the responsibilities of parenthood, and their determination to give their children all the schooling that is possible. Let the Labor Unions preach this duty to their members. Let the working classes remember, furthermore, that wickedness among them no less than among the more wealthy will leave disease for their children, and will breed pauperism and brutality enough to debase not merely their offspring but the race. If the working classes will only cultivate right knowledge, a kind of truth which walks hand in hand with right character, they will gain wisdom. This enlightenment will reveal to them who are the wise and the intelligent to whom they may confide their newly gained political power. They will then know whom to trust in government assemblies, and what measures those are that can develop the best in all citizens and the greatest good in the whole nation.

Such is the summary of George Eliot's address to the working men of England. It is the very thesis of her political novel. We may now return to that work, better able to interpret it.

In spite of the name which George Eliot gives that novel, the chief actor in it is not any single individual. It is, in point of fact, rather a certain class in the body politic — the working people, in short, shown in their slow awakening to a consciousness of their impending importance in the English political fabric. During this gradual discernment in the masses of their possible powers and their opportunities, in a nation undergoing a transformation, we see revealed the wicked men and pernicious evils that came with that reconstructing age, in the rural districts of the country. There was the typically selfish aristocrat and Tory in Sir Maximus:

"whom every one called a gentleman of the right sort, who condescended to no mean inquiries, greeted his head servants with a 'Good evening, gentlemen' when he met them in the Park, . . . willing to endure some personal inconvenience in order to keep up the institutions of the country, to maintain his hereditary establishment, and do his duty in that station of life — the station of the long-tailed saurian — to which it had pleased Providence to call him"; [5] —

a landed proprietor who made the most of the natural veneration of the lower for the higher classes of society; who looked upon the entrance of radicalism into politics as if it had been a pestilence come upon the populations of England; and who, during election, snapped the whip of his influence over the heads of his recently enfranchised tenants to vote 'the right way' with as much force as the shepherd could over his bleating sheep. There were shown the crafty and unscrupulous methods of canvassing employed in behalf of a wealthy candidate by his political agents — by lawyer Jermyn, a type of middle-class pushing gentility, whose calculating logic occasionally garnished with Latin phraseology, answers away, to his own mind at least, every dictate of honor and decency when the business of getting votes for his principal is concerned. Jermyn's theories are put to practice for us [6] by his field agent

Johnson, a glib, sycophantic, noisy, and dishonest wretch, whose fine phrases, and generous 'treating' and bribing among the colliers and navvies of Sproxton delude and demoralize those workingmen, and transform them, eventually, into a mischievous and ignorant rabble. Having sown the wind these two political agents eventually reap the whirlwind.

George Eliot paints a dramatic picture of the subsequent election day at North Loamshire, where all of the preceding Sunday drinkings among the miners, all of the electioneering slanders spread by the political agents, together with the unscrupulous play upon the prejudices of the mob by self-seeking political candidates, have their effect: the great Treby riot occurs on the day of the election, and ends in an orgy of untold brutality visited upon the innocent, with a great conflagration and even a murder to boot.[7] To this tragic side of the immediate effects of the Reform Bill upon the poor and the illiterate, George Eliot adds the humorous as well.[8] Mr. Pink, the saddler, who professed a deep-dyed Toryism for business reasons, appears at the polls upon election day and is there so hectored by the mob that, upon being stopped on the way, declares that he is to vote for Debarry, the other candidate.

He "got himself well chalked up as to his coat, and pushed up an entry, where he remained the prisoner of terror combined with the want of any back outlet, and so never gave his vote that day."

Goffe, a Transome tenant, trailing along at the end of the line of the Transome tenants who were being led in a body by the bailiff to cast their votes for their Radical landlord, is cut off from his companions, hemmed in;

"asked, by voices with hot breath close to his ear, how many horses he had, how many cows, how many fat pigs; then jostled from one to another, who made trumpets with their hands, and deafened him to vote for Debarry. In this way the melancholy Goffe was hustled on till he was at the polling booth, — filled

with confused alarms, the immediate alarm being that of having
to go back in still worse fashion than he had come. Arriving in
this way after the other tenants had left, he astonished all hearers
who knew him for a tenant of the Transomes by saying 'Debarry!'
and was jostled back trembling, amid shouts of laughter."

Chubb, the publican, had just got his vote as a householder
because he was landlord of the "Sugar Loaf," and he was
determined — conscious as he was of his importance as voter
— so to dispose of it as would most profit him. In the page
and a half which sketch his 'political machinations' his creator
draws an unforgettable figure.

"He called himself a straightforward man, and at suitable
moments expressed his views freely: in fact, he was known to
have one fundamental division for all opinion — 'my idee,' and
'humbug.' . . . The coming election was a great opportunity for
applying his political 'idee,' which was that society existed for
the sake of the individual, and that the name of that individual
was Chubb."

To these figures one should add others — particularly of those
men who actively engaged in arousing the public interest in
the political issues, and in the candidates who were to come
up at the hustings. One can never forget the impression of
moral greatness which Felix Holt's public reply makes, when
Holt discloses to his audience the cant and the hyperbole in
the words of the professional politicians. George Eliot draws
that saintly Christian character, the Reverend Rufus Lyon,
with so much sympathy and affection, and portrays him — his
apostolic zeal, his great humility, and his courage and kindness
— in so many pleasing and inspiring situations, that he seems
for a time to dominate the stage, and to be the controlling
interest in the story. To the Reverend Mr. Lingon, rector of
the English privileged classes, whose campaign speech to the
Tory farmers is only a chance to give an appealing, tempera-
mental viewpoint of their favorite "Parson Jack," or "Cock-

fighting Jack," the dissenting little minister was a thorn in the flesh. What particular political function he served, what power his independence of thought had upon the opinions of 'the masses,' is best revealed through the words of his bitterest critic — the Tory clergyman who was seeking 'a spool to wind a speech on' for a Radical nephew.

"Let me tell you, Phil, he's a crazy little firefly, that does a great deal of harm in my parish. He inflames the Dissenters' minds on politics. There's no end to the mischief done by these prating men. They make the ignorant multitude the judges of the largest questions, both political and religious, till we shall soon have no institution left that is not on a level with the comprehension of a huckster or a drayman. There can be nothing more retrograde — losing all the results of civilization, all the lessons of Providence — letting the windlass run down after men had been turning at it painfully for generations. . . ."

When we study these characteristic incidents and observations, most of them serious, some of them fantastic and humorous, all of the events so dramatically colored, we see, in the totality of the effect which the full book produces, George Eliot's consummate skill in penetrating to the very core of a crucial period in English history, and in drawing therefrom a serious lesson. That lesson raised the question whether those who had received the right of the ballot were fit to exercise political power: whether, in short, something else were not necessary before any good might be expected from that parliamentary reform. It raised the question as to the effect which certain political ideas might have upon one class of society should that class fail to receive guidance from above — from those whose responsibility it was to know that the new conditions might produce evils hardly less pernicious under the régime of popular power than they had been in the days of pure aristocratic supremacy.

George Eliot's heart lies with the rights and the safeguards of the working people. Her hand is busied in revealing their pitiful ignorance and their consequent inability to take advantage of the new power given them, power which is being used by the agents of Darkness against them because they are themselves unprepared to use it. That men should tug and rive for what will benefit them most, — particularly men of the upper classes; that they should do so without caring how that tugging must act upon the fine and widespread network of society in which all classes form a single plan, — that is what makes her heart bitter, and what gives to this novel a sense of seriousness and gloom that is foreign to any of her other books. There is no warm sunlight in this novel, not even in the love scenes between Felix Holt and the charming young Esther. Between these two the relations are so serious and elevated in purpose, so entangled in the business of mental development on the one side to meet the moral greatness upon the other, that it robs the single day upon which they walk out together of all its sunshine and summer, and it makes of their companionship something that is the natural resultant of the old clergyman's ecclesiastical library (a room, by the way, in which they carried on much of their courtship), and of the gloom of the walls of a jail into which Esther enters to see her lover.

If Felix Holt is not — as I have already pointed out — the dominant actor of the novel, what then is his place in it? To the wage-earners of Treby Magna and Sproxton, of whom he is one by birth, and to whom he deliberately returns after his education in Glasgow in order to sink his individuality among them, he is what the spire struck by morning sunlight is to the country chapel of which it is a part, standing in the valley below. He had caught the first rays of the dawning light while the others beneath him were still groping in total darkness or in the shadows. His missionary zeal led him to forget and to ignore all thought of self in the firm determination to spread among those others who were of his flesh and blood something of that intelligence which had penetrated into the windows of his soul, and without which, as he knew, there could be no future growth for them. Because of this inborn nobility, because of his great moral integrity, because of his almost Carlylean fierceness to right wrongs, he becomes for the reader not a typical every-day Radical out of the period about which George Eliot was writing, but rather an idealized figure, a perfect Radical of the Future in England's great parliamentary transformations. Like all great reformers he is made, by his creator, to pay a great price — the price of misunderstanding, of anger, of final persecution — in part at the hands of those very persons among whom he had conse-crated himself to spread a light which had already fallen upon him. I can see no better method of showing George Eliot's ultimate purpose in this novel than by repeating Felix Holt's lines in his great speech to the colliers, just before the North Loamshire election, and suggesting by those opening lines the sweep of thought that encompasses the novel.

". . . While public opinion is what it is — while men have no better beliefs about public duty — while corruption is not felt to be a public disgrace — while men are not ashamed in Parliament and out of it to make public questions which concern the welfare of millions a mere screen for their own petty, private ends — I say, no fresh scheme of voting will much mend our condition. For, take us working men of all sorts. Suppose out of every hundred who had a vote there were thirty who had some soberness, some sense to choose with, some good feeling to make them wish the right thing for all. And suppose there were seventy out of the hundred who were, half of them, not sober, who had no sense to choose one thing in politics more than another, and who had so little good feeling in them that they wasted on their own drinking the money that should have helped to feed and clothe their wives and children; and another half of them who, if they didn't drink, were too ignorant or mean or stupid to see any good for them-selves better than pocketing a five-shilling piece when it was

offered them. Where would be the political power of the thirty
sober men? The power would lie with the seventy drunken and
stupid votes; and I'll tell you what sort of men would get the
power — what sort of men would end by returning whom they
pleased to Parliament. . . ."

He does tell them, indeed. And as the collected hearers
begin to feel something of the force behind his words, as they
grasp the sanity and the seriousness with which those words
are freighted, and as there comes now from one and then from
another of the listeners some evidence that the shafts have
struck home once for all, we see before us the growing articula-
tion of that group-consciousness with which George Eliot is
absorbed from the first page to the last of her story. We
seize the promise of a Future when the light caught first on
the steeple will have passed not merely upon the full structure
below, but will have flooded the entire valley in the surrounding
country.

CHAPTER IX

GEORGE MEREDITH — "BEAUCHAMPISM," THE IDEALIST IN POLITICS

MEASURED by the intense seriousness, the propagandist spirit which is the urge back of George Eliot's political novel, the work of George Meredith's political hero, is, so far as results are concerned, writ in water. Radicalism in politics — here the support of a chivalric, intense, and fiery English youth whose absorbing interest in national affairs forms the pin-point upon which gyrates a body of conflicting characters and ideals — is the defining *motif* of the only political novel written by George Meredith, namely, *Beauchamp's Career*.[1] After that fact — the common political ground of both books — the comparison ends. *Beauchamp's Career*, published a decade after *Felix Holt, Radical*, is miles apart from the other in artistic purpose. The Radical here dominates every thought and incident in the story; his association with politics is only his greatest expression of an absorbing determination to work and to fight for something greater than self, and to exhibit a chivalric love of country. So far as 'results' or 'effects' from that life are concerned, the span of it proved to be but the journey of a flaming meteor — there was some pyrotechnic display but the end was oblivion. Compared with George Eliot, Meredith's purpose was never to propound a lesson out of a man's career or to preach Liberalism or to cry a warning. True it is that Meredith, like George Eliot, was a Liberal by party, that he shows elsewhere a strong faith in democracy,[2] that he has an easy sneer for the vestiges of the mediaeval aristocracy which still existed in his England, and a high respect for the mercantile classes who were hitting with sledge-hammer strength the venerable body of English Conservatism, but it was not to air these things that the novel was written. Still, some of these are in the novel, and more besides — flashes of political sympathies, half-lights of satire upon the remnants of English Feudalism, skirmishes with political formulae, paradoxes, and with high idealism in public service.

Let Meredith make his own apology for this and explain his own purpose.

"It is artless art and monstrous innovation to present so wilful a figure, but were I to create a striking fable for him, and set him off with scenic effects and contrasts, it would be only a momentary tonic to you, to him instant death. He could not live in such an atmosphere. The simple truth has to be told: how he loved his country, and for another and a broader love, growing out of his first passion, fought it; and being small by comparison, and finding no giant of the Philistines disposed to receive a stone in his fore-skull, pummelled the obmutescent mass, to the confusion of a conceivable epic. His indifferent England refused it to him. That is all I can say. . . . Blame the victrix if you think he should have been livelier." [3]

Style is so conscious a force in the structure of this novel, and so singular is the strategy the author employs in depicting both his political hero and the politics (singular by comparison with all the other novels of the political *genre* studied here), that no possible square and plumb-line can be used to guide our estimate of the work, or to control our judgement of it. By the side of the others this is, somehow, *sui generis*. By which it must not be inferred that there is anything capricious about its texture. There would be nothing capricious in a political novel written by Thomas Carlyle or by Robert Browning. The comparison between what they might have done and what Meredith did do is, in any discussion of *Beauchamp's Career*, an apt one to make. That fact the reader will quickly see for himself. Nevil Beauchamp is like the diver with whom

Browning's Paracelsus compares himself· he knows himself to
be a beggar while preparing for the plunge; he thinks himself
a prince if he can but arise with the pearl. Why, unlike Paracelsus, he fails to attain the object for which he made the
plunge we shall discuss later. For Nevil Beauchamp, too, his
"political mentor and the mouthpiece of his ideals" throughout
the novel is a Dr. Shrapnel, who has a soul as violent, as enthusiastic, as savage, and as void of measure, taste, and order
as Carlyle's; who suggests something of the colossal range of
Carlyle's opinions; who certainly talks in none other than in
Carlyle's semi-chaotic language. "His favourite author," says
Meredith — attempting early in the novel to fasten a beam
of Carlylean radiance upon his young hero —

"was one writing on Heroes, in (so she esteemed it) a style re-
sembling either early architecture or utter dilapidation, so loose
and rough it seemed; a wind-in-the-orchard style, that tumbled
down here and there an appreciable fruit with uncouth bluster;
sentences without commencements running to abrupt endings and
smoke, like waves against a sea-wall; learned dictionary words
giving a hand to street-slang, and accents falling on them hap-
hazard, like slant rays from driving clouds; all the pages in a
breeze, the whole book producing a kind of electrical agitation in
the mind and joints." [4]

If, with all this in mind, the reader is left with some confusion
of ideas after a first reading of this political novel, it will not
help him to fall back upon any four-square set of 'first principles' wherewith to measure and then to interpret Meredith's
pages. A second reading and then a third will prove that
the initial confusion is the result of no obscurities in the
novel but rather the result of the intensity of the author's
vision. Close study will bring out, as does the warmth of a
steady fire upon sensitized ink of parchments we read about,
one after another of familiar images.

In an investigation of this kind whichever of these images

belong appropriately to the political *genre* of the novel need proper attention. Let us examine them, as they appear, one by one.

In the first place there is the motivating political philosophy of the main character — which is of the school of Cobden and Bright. That Meredith sets forth the principles of any political platform at all is because Beauchamp is a man to whom "political activity must be the summit, or almost the summit, of human endeavour," and because this Englishman, "passionately moved by abstractions" (which are focussed in a love of country), subordinates one after another of his private relations for a sheer political objective. Here is the reason for including this novel of Meredith's in our study of the political *genre*, as it is also the fact which distinguishes this work of his from all his other novels. That he sets Nevil Beauchamp out to fight upon the steed of Radicalism in politics is, as has already been pointed out, not for any ulterior reason of the author's (as was profoundly the case in Disraeli's heroes when they fought for a democratized Toryism), but because Radicalism of the 1870's was the farthest possible thing away from the mediaeval Conservative politics of Nevil's own social set and of his own family traditions as most sharply presented by his uncle, the Honorable Everard Romfrey, eventually the Earl of Romfrey. The result therefore was that Nevil had the longest possible journey to make, and, being what he was by heritage, by taste, and by natural inclination, he had the most difficult possible fortress to besiege. "All of which," we can imagine the author saying of him, "was as it should have been." So much to show why Radicalism rather than some other political philosophy lies back of the hero's actions. And it is clear that Meredith, by virtue of the futility which comes of his protagonists' efforts to spread their creed, has himself no brief to offer here. The very opposite was the case with George Eliot.

Indeed, *Beauchamp's Career* is rather a satire upon English political Conservatism than it is an encomium upon the political thought of Bright and Cobden. On the one side there is Dr. Shrapnel. He is described as "the dreaded doctor" by Nevil's friends and relatives. A man of sixty-eight, immoderately tall, immoderately lean, carelessly clad in a long coat of no color, loose trousers, and huge shoes each of which top off "a league of a leg" as they appear to one of his guests, he writes thirty-two page epistles to his political disciple, the revolutionary and inflammatory contents of one of which (as it appears to Colonel Halkett, father of Cecilia Halkett who is in love with Nevil, to Lord Palmet, Captain Baskelett, and others of the camp of the landed aristocracy) draw upon his head, from the disgusted and amazed listeners, such epithets as "the flaccid frog!", "mad, mad as a dog!", and finally "the man deserves hanging!". Upon their own beloved Nevil it appears to them that this presumably insane Radical philosopher exerts the influence of another Svengali. Because of his influence Nevil Beauchamp, man full grown and Commander in Her Majesty's Royal Navy to say nothing of being nephew to the great Earl, punishes his devoted friend — that high-bred English gentlewoman, Rosamund Culling. He quarrels with his uncle Romfrey and almost breaks the heart of this man who so deeply loved him. He raises an almost impenetrable barrier between himself and the family of the noble Cecilia Halkett — that magnificently independent and beautiful creature to whom every law, human and divine, appears to point that he should have married. He rides out like another Don Quixote to tilt with political windmills as exponent of the great Doctor's ideas about 'the rights of the workingmen' and 'the power of the people,' and thus draws upon himself, for his acts, the laughter of his friends, the satire of his enemies, and 'the pitch and tar' of his political opponents. So much for Dr. Shrapnel, Radical prophet and philosopher. Does Meredith have a profound partiality for him? For the answer read what Seymour Austin, the thoroughly sane person of the novel, says of him in summary.

"Dr. Shrapnel is the earnest man, and flies at politics as uneasy young brains fly to literature, fancying they can write because they can write with a pen. He perceives a bad adjustment of things; which is correct. He is honest, and takes his honesty for a virtue: and that entitles him to believe in himself: and that belief causes him to see in all opposition to him the wrong he has perceived in existing circumstances: and so in a dream of power he invokes the people: and as they do not stir, he takes to prophecy. This is the round of the politics of impatience. The study of politics should be guided by some light of statesmanship, otherwise it comes to this wild preaching. These men are theory-tailors, not politicians." [5]

On the other side, and as the implacable opponent of this Radical philosopher, you have Stephen Denely Craven Romfrey (the Honorable Everard, afterwards the Earl of Romfrey) whose magnificent personality stands beside the tatterdemalion monstrosity of the other (I speak of the first impression that Dr. Shrapnel made upon Rosamund Culling, afterwards the Earl's wife) as might, in the mind's eye, the spectacle of an ancient baronial castle in an English country-side flanked by noble friends and guarded by old retainers, standing beside a present-day Workingmen's Union building, tolerated upon the off-street of a strenuous modern metropolis, and inhabited nightly by intellectually hungering toilers, dumb idealists, a few fanatics, — all of them dreaming of some future Millenium. The Honorable Everard Romfrey, in appearance a magnificent gentleman, "in mind a mediaeval baron" of the twelfth century, had been at one time "a hot Parliamentarian, calling himself a Whig, called by the Whigs a Radical, called by the Radicals a Tory, and very happy in fighting them all around." In spite of the fact that a Liberal had deprived him of a seat he had held in the Commons for fifteen years, he yet "stood for King, Lords, and Commons. . . . Commons he added out of courtesy." He came of a long race of fighting earls with "a savour of North Sea foam and ballad pirates" hanging about the early family chronicles. Inheriting his family passion for land, the Honorable Everard, at the beginning of the story, had some hopes of eventually possessing with the family title all of that property which the Earls of Romfrey of old saw "from their topmost towers . . . spied few spots in the wide circle of the heavens" that were not their own. In the course of the narrative he assumed, himself, the responsibilities of the "good landlords, good masters, blithely followed to the wars. Sing an old battle of Normandy, Picardy, Gascony," and you sang of the celebrated deeds of his family. Between the traditions of such a man and the political ideas of an extraordinary Dr. Shrapnel what could there possibly be in common? All through the novel the struggle between the two forces represented by these men continues — on the one side it is a conscious and bitter fight, on the other side the Radical doctor is utterly unaware of what 'havoc' he has been the cause. Only when the Earl, finally unable to contain himself any longer, makes an imagined discourtesy, which Rosamund Culling hints that she may have suffered from the extraordinary language of the Doctor, the inciting impulse for summary action, he swoops down upon him, as might an eagle upon a chattering crow, and punishes the old man 'within an inch of his life.' Then, indeed, does Dr. Shrapnel realize what it costs to be a prophet in his own country.

And here is the satire on Toryism and the grin of the Comic Spirit: that "a mediaeval gentleman with the docile notions of the twelfth century, complacently driving them to grass and wattling them in the nineteenth," having flogged a Radical doctor without doing him first even the courtesy of discussing with him the nature of his guilt, eventually goes back of his own accord to him, and abjectly apologizes for having made a 'mistake'; afterwards laughs "in his dumb way" when he learns that Nevil is to marry Jenny Denham (niece of Dr. Shrapnel) in whom he had already discovered a natural distinction that not even Cecilia Halkett possessed; and in the end, to cap the climax, takes Jenny and her son, the son of Nevil Beauchamp, to his home at Mount Laurels, and with them her uncle, Dr. Shrapnel! Let us take a page out of the closing chapters for quotation here.

"'I cannot endure the thought of his marrying a girl who is not in love with him . . . of whose birth and blood we know nothing.' (This from Rosamund, now the Earl's wife, to her husband).

'Just as you like, my dear.'

'Oh, what an end to so brilliant a beginning!'

'It strikes me, my dear,' said the Earl, 'it's the common sense beginning that may have a fairish end.'

'No, but what I feel is that he — our Nevil — has accomplished hardly anything, if anything.'

'He hasn't marched on London with a couple of hundred thousand men: no, he hasn't done that,' said the Earl, glancing back in mind through Beauchamp's career. 'And he escaped what Stukely calls the nation's scourge, in the shape of a statue turned out by an English chisel. No: we haven't had much public excitement out of him. But one thing he did do: *he got me down on my knees!*' Lord Romfrey pronounced these words with a sober emphasis that struck the humour of it sharply in Rosamund's heart, through some contrast it presented between Nevil's aim at the world and hit of a man: the immense deal thought of it by the Earl, and the very little that Nevil would think of it — the great domestic achievement to be boasted of by an enthusiastic devotee of politics! She embraced her husband with peals of loving laughter. . . ." [6]

Let us look more closely at the object of this discussion and at a few of the places in the novel which the radiance of his image reveals. Nevil Beauchamp is a romantic figure who is not a romantic hero. His author prepares us to accept him as such with a warning early in the story: "Beauchampism, as one confronting him calls it, may be said to stand for nearly everything which is the obverse of Byronism. . . . His faith is in working and fighting." At the age of fourteen he is already a hero worshipper, "possessed by a reverence for men of deeds," when he is sent away by his uncle, whose ward he has become, as Midshipman in the Navy. The fire of Chivalry is already burning within him, the passionate love of his England is already rooted in his boyish heart, and the first evidence of it is seen in the challenge by means of a letter which he addresses to the Colonel of the First Regiment of the Imperial Guard at Paris — a letter issued in his name and addressed to the whole French Guard — to meet him in combat because the Press of France had sneered at the English Navy and at the English Government! With the help of his Rosamund Culling, housekeeper to his uncle after her heroic husband had died in the service of his country, and now the one who pours out the love of a mother and a sister upon this fiery youth, — with the help of Rosamund, who humors the boy because she cannot dissuade him from sending the letter, the challenge is written in correct French and mailed. Nevil does not believe in dueling — so he informs Mrs. Culling when she gravely tells the artless youth whom she dotes upon that she "hoped bloodshed would be avoided." "A man," adds Nevil in explanation of his act, "may do for his country what he wouldn't do for himself." Of course the very foolish letter never receives a reply. Nevil thereupon proposes an expedition to France, but being ordered to join his ship, he must forego that venture, all the while suffering from a slight "which now affected him personally" since he felt that it was "the country that suffered, not he at all." However, he is finally convinced "that the letter had served its object: ever since the transmission of it the menaces and insults had ceased. But they might be renewed and he desired to stop them altogether. His last feeling was one of genuine regret that Frenchmen should have behaved unworthily of the high estimation he held them in. With which he dismissed the affair."

It is this heroic, handsome, passionate youth, in whose fiery countenance his uncle Everard "traced him back by cousinships to the great Earl Beauchamp of Froissart," that could never be spoiled because he would never think of himself. "How could he think of himself, who had done nothing, accomplished nothing, so long as he brooded on the images of signal Englishmen whose names were historic for daring, and the strong arm, and artfulness, all given to the service of the country?" This fiery youth it is that sets out upon his romantic journey — unconsciously does so — to make himself worthy of his English heritage, and to gain self-respect. Issuing a challenge to the entire French Imperial Guard to save the honor of his beloved England when he was but a Midshipman, was but a characteristic gesture in a life shot through with chivalric and ennobled service meant always for his country or for the good of others. This was the earliest and one of the most dramatic of episodes. At home he fights another youth for what he thinks is a fancied slight upon his beloved Rosamund's name; a year or two later, during the Crimean War, his uncle Everard hears reports that Nevil is doing more than his duty and must write him: "Braggadocioing indeed is only next bad to mouthing it. Remember that we want *soldiers* and *sailors*, not *suicides*." He is wounded, receives military glory for unusual bravery, goes to Italy to recuperate, meets the sister — Renée was her name — of the young Count Roland, a French youth whose life he had saved, and falls madly in love with her. He decides to save her from marriage with the Marquis de Rouaillout to whom she is virtually betrothed. She, with the help of her brother, manages to break away "from this hurricane of a youth" who had swept her off her feet and was determined to decide her destiny; and, not caring to be saved, in the end marries the Marquis even though he may have been close to forty-nine when she was but a charming young girl.

Now all these things are but forays, skirmishings, in preparation for the great thing to come. The war being over, "the first to come home received the cream of the praises." In England they are waiting for him to give him his due. But the youth does not return. Instead, while the French affair is presumably waiting to be settled, Uncle Romfrey, Cecil Baskelett, Rosamund Culling, Cecilia Halkett and her father, and a world of friends, awake one fine day to learn that the electors of Bevisham, an English borough, are "summoned, like a town at the sword's point, to yield him their votes" (so began the letter from Cecil to Mr. Romfrey). With it came a copy of Nevil's proclamation to the electors of the borough — "an address, moreover ultra-radical . . . an amazing address . . . museums to be opened on Sundays; ominous references to the Land Question, etc.; no smooth passing mention of Reform, such as the Liberal, become stately, adopts in speaking of that property of his, but swinging blows on the heads of many a denounced iniquity!" And thus Rome is set on fire for the eminent Mr. Romfrey and for all the others. Of course the source of it all is traced at once to the infamous Dr. Shrapnel. So off goes Rosamund to the 'scoundrel of a Doctor' to pluck her beloved brand from the burning. As well might she hope to catch an eagle lodged upon a mountain fastness by crooning to it from below. The deed was done and "Commander Beauchamp R.N. . . . the illustrious Commander Beauchamp, of our matchless navy, who proved on every field of the last glorious war of this country that the traditional valour of the noble and indomitable blood transmitted in his veins had lost none of its edge and weight since the battle-axes of the Lords de Romfrey, ever to the fore, clove the skulls of our national enemy on the wide and fertile champaigns of

France" (so read the leading article of the *Bevisham Gazette* about their illustrious Radical candidate), — Nevil Beauchamp was off again, and this time with a vengeance. How did Mr. Romfrey take it? It was the act of a donkey, a monstrous joke, the source for volleys of laughter about him and his rascal Doctor to whom he had now tied himself — this youth whom he pitied only because "as a practical man his objection lay against the poor fool's choice of the peccant borough of Bevisham." Still, thought Romfrey, it will serve its purpose: he will need money, he had none of his own, and the immediately compelling need of disbursing a lot of it among the Bevisham electors will "be the surest method for quickening his wits. Thus would he be acting as his own chirurgeon, gaily practicing phlebotomy on his person to cure him of his fever."

The particular 'fever' in this instance was, however, a more raging one than the Honorable Everard Romfrey, or any of his aristocratic friends, gave it credit for ever being when it first showed itself. What occurs in the course of it requires four-fifths of the book to tell. There is Beauchamp portrayed in his political colors attempting to convert his own people; there are acts of canvassing to recount, and the little effect, or rather the humorous effect, which the view of them had upon Lord Palmet. There are side-looks at the election, and at the editor Turbot with his ideas about the proper kind of political publicity. There are the long epistles of Dr. Shrapnel and the baiting of him by Cecil Baskelett and Lord Palmet. All these things, as well as the exquisite love story of Cecilia, the reappearance of Renée, and the introduction of the figure of Jenny, have to occur before the fever has spent itself and a cure has been found for it. And, after all, was it a cure? That question only the reader may answer when he learns that the poor youth, in whose soul and body a flame had spent itself, was finally taken from the world at the moment when everything promised well for him and his; and that all that was left to us of him was "the flat result of an optically discernable influence of our hero's character in the domestic circle; perhaps a faintly-outlined circle or two beyond it." "But," so the author generously concludes the paragraph from which I am quoting, "but this does not forbid him to be ranked as one of the most distinguishing of her children of the day he lived in." He is speaking of those among England's children who have fought and died for her — for her honor, her government, her venerable traditions.

His failure to win a seat in the House of Commons from the Bevisham electors, the fact that his project to found a Radical-politics newspaper entitled *The Dawn* ended aimlessly like the final splutter of a spent pin-wheel, that he, with all the ideals and aspirations which possessed him, seemed hardly to have made a dent upon his own class who stood for lingering feudal traditions — all these do not make him the less one of "the distinguished children." Neither does the final episode in the career of this chivalric youth detract from his distinction. It was the episode which closed with the loss of his life, and deserves recounting. They were sailing home from Italy where he had gone to recuperate from his terrible illness — he, Jenny his wife, a son just born, and Dr. Shrapnel. A little older, made more sober by his defeats and therefore the more tenacious of his beliefs, he reaches the shores of his beloved England again, determined now to make his early rebuffs but stepping-stones to greater usefulness, not alone for his own country but for all of the humanity within it. The family had landed at Bevisham, but Nevil was determined to deliver his vessel at the very moorings in Otley from whence he had taken her. (The vessel was Cecilia Halkett's yacht). Some poor fisherman's boys, larking upon their father's boat, on that December night in sight of the twinkling lights of English shores, fell overboard just as Nevil was rowing by. He jumped up and dived in after them. He got one of the boys immedi-

ately, swam to the vessel with him where he remained safe, and
then dived again for the other boy. He was down a long time.
Finally he appeared with the second boy, but either because
of a sudden cramp or because of the bursting of a blood-vessel
— for he had been rowing hard and long and must have been
hot when he plunged in to save the boys — he went down
again. They dragged for hours but they never found his body.
Two men stood upon the bank that day, one of them directing
the dragging "since five in the evening, and will till he drops
or drowns, or up comes the body." That was the great Lord
Romfrey. The other beside him was Dr. Shrapnel, whom he
had "once flung to the ground" but whom he was now supporting from falling by his arm linked in the arm of the other's.
The Earl had ordered Jenny and her baby to go to his home,
soon to be accompanied by her uncle Dr. Shrapnel, whom the
Earl was himself to bring there later. The book closes with a
picture of the two men standing together upon the bank —
these two who had loved Nevil Beauchamp with a great love
— looking down upon a little urchin whose face was being
wiped by a crying but grateful mother, — "an insignificant bit
of mudbank life" for which Nevil had given his own. "This
is what we have in exchange for Beauchamp."

Does the struggle between the younger and the older generations as found in *Beauchamp's Career* furnish us with illustration
of Meredith's Comic Spirit, as Professor Joseph Warren Beach
would have us believe? [7] It appears to me to be anything but
that. Is the story a tragedy, as Arthur Symons suggests? [8]
This critic has gone too far in the other direction. Of such a
youth as Nevil, whom Robert Louis Stevenson might have
taken for his inspiration of a "happy-starred, full-blooded
spirit" who shot "into the spiritual land," in his essay *Aes
Triplex*, it might be said that at whatever age death overtook
him he would have died young. Next comes the distinguished
Mr. Brownell with his proof, presumably, that Meredith always

keeps his "personages in arbitrary control," which he illustrates from the life of Beauchamp. I quote Brownell.

"You never warm to his personages. You are not allowed to. He banters you out of it generally; even when such favorites of his own as Nevil Beauchamp are concerned, he is almost nervously timorous lest your tenderness should be unintelligent. This is carried so far that one rarely cares much what becomes of these personages. You know in advance that they will never be the sport of any spontaneity. Their fate is sealed. They are the slaves of their creator's will, counters in his game. And this is why, in playing it, though he constantly challenges our admiration, he does not hold our interest. The air of free agency that he throws around them does not deceive us. We don't at all know what is to befall them, how they are going to act, but we have an ever-present sense that he does, and this sense is only sharpened by the knowledge, born of experience in reading his books, that he is going to make them surprise us. The induction he would have us make is, no doubt, that they are unaccountable, like human nature itself; but the one we make is that it is he who is unaccountable." [9]

Finally comes Mr. Hammerton who, having quoted this passage from Mr. Brownell in his own book, does so to show that he thoroughly agrees with him that "in the death of that true hero (i.e. Beauchamp) the novelist is 'unaccountable'," adding — and thus making confusion more confounding — his own interpretation of the reason for Nevil Beauchamp's death. "It is," says Mr. Hammerton, "obviously meant to illustrate the slaps in the face which Fate loves to deal out to idealists, and it could be supported with any amount of evidence from real life." [10] At this last sally, for its naiveté at least, the Comic Spirit of George Meredith, if only we could evoke it, would have uttered its heartiest laughter! No, there is nothing very comic in the life of Nevil Beauchamp as expressed in the struggle with his uncle; nor is his death the inevitably tragic thing that another implies: if there is any 'tragedy' in it the great loss is England's. Least of all can we believe anything 'unaccountable' or even arbitrary about that death, and to say that the loss of him was intended by Meredith to show "the slaps in the face which Fate loves to deal out to idealists" is to utter an absurdity.

When so many critics appear, at the same time, to look through their glasses darkly, and when each has not even the same maladjustment of glass as the other, as shown by the report of what each of them finds, we had better return to our original manuscript and ignore the glasses altogether. There, fanned with the flame of our warm affections for the main character, and prepared quickly to translate one image after another as they appear because our study of the *genre* of the political novel has endowed us with a key to the symbols, the author's purpose becomes quickly intelligible and there is consequently little room left for conflicting interpretations.

The career of Nevil Beauchamp is a parable, and the loss of him and what happens to that which he leaves behind are parts of an allegory. In the England of the mid-nineteenth century, the buoyant youth, the youth sensitive to the great changes, political and industrial, going on around them, were caught between two extremes. On the one side were the traditions of the old Conservatives, which were represented in their complete form in Nevil's uncle and in his family friends; on the other were the smashing forces of men like Cobden and Bright. In their generation the reconciliation *had* to be made between these two naturally antagonistic parts of the body politic. Loving his country more than himself, Nevil Beauchamp gives up his heritage, sacrifices the love of Cecilia — representative of his own class — for the greater patriotic purpose, ignores the satire of his family and friends just as he brushes aside the devoted personal ties which would bind him to Old England. He does all this and gives himself, mind and soul, in discipleship to a philosopher of the New Democracy, and in marriage to his niece, Jenny. In Jenny's veins flowed the blood of the working classes; her mind was consonant with the new influences beginning to be felt in English public life; her soul reflected a natural nobility of character which not even Cecilia possessed. That fact the Earl finally discovered for himself When the great crisis came, when Nevil battled for his life in the course of a serious illness contracted while serving one of the common people, it was the Earl again who discovered that in Jenny there was a quality of fineness, and a deep sense of appreciation of the value which Nevil Beauchamp's life and his great heritage meant for the glory of future England, that Cecilia could never have realized. And this in spite of the fact that Cecilia, symbolizing in her own sex the youth of the mid-nineteenth century of her social class, begins to grasp, toward the latter part of the story, fully, the great significance of Dr. Shrapnel's teachings. Cecilia's appreciation of Nevil was primarily emotional; Jenny seized the precious value of the man through her understanding. Jenny Denham may have been less beautiful than Cecilia; she certainly was but a beggar girl in comparison with the other when it came to material wealth. But Jenny might have posed for the statue of a Modern, a democratized England. Cecilia Halkett was still part of the Feudal life of an old England.

In the union by marriage of the niece of a Radical philosopher with the nephew of a twelfth century baron you have the consummation which must bring forth the newer generation demanded by a Parliamentary Democracy. Jenny Denham cradled the son of herself and of Nevil Beauchamp. But that issue could not be born without a great sacrifice: the gods did not decree that the transition from the Old Conservatism to the New Democracy was to be made without a great price. The price had to be paid in that period when the dawning just rose upon England: upon that generation of youth who first caught the light and who were ready as missionaries to give their very lives to spread it. Nevil Beauchamp — symbol of his own, the younger generation — was wasted. He was wasted by the grinding battle and the prejudices of mediaeval England, the old aristocracy, when these pitted themselves against what was almost the fanaticism of political revolutionaries, of Radicals. Yet above this wasted generation there gleamed a hope, there was born a vision, of a new, of a democratized England that came in the heat of the conflict. In that new England there was the merging of the two opposing ideals, the happy blending of two kinds of blood, — enriching and humanizing forces were both at work. Less picturesque than the mediaeval aristocracy, more sane than revolutionary England, this newer nation had come out of pain and travail; it came only after the older had made 'a pilgrimage' to the other, had shown itself ready to learn from it, and had served a penance. Thus was the new life born, and the house which it thereupon built stood as a temple, a memorial marking a debt to the idealism of a wasted generation.

These things are parables. Our diver was a beautiful and entrancing figure as he prepared to make his plunge. The passage of him across our field of vision is the story of the political transformation of the English nation.

Like Paracelsus speaking to Festus, in the closing verses of Browning's poem, we may say of our hero:

> "Yes, it was in me; I was born for it —
> .   .   .   .
> . . . a searching and impetuous soul
> Might learn from its own motions that some task
> Like this awaited it about the world . . ."

Chapter X

MRS. HUMPHRY WARD AND FEMINISM

As we have examined one after another of the writers of the nineteenth century who have contributed to the *genre* of the political novel, it has become clear that each of them gave some particular emphasis to, or made some individual interpretation of, the history of their own period or of a period that had just passed. From this they build their political pageants. In order of time there is nothing singular in the type of persons, or in the kind of ideas, which defines the contribution made at the close of the century by Mrs. Humphry Ward. On the contrary, and provided the comparison is not drawn too literally, it may be said that *Sir George Tressady*, which appeared two years after Mrs. Ward's *Marcella*, and which is really a sequel to that novel, exhibits quite unconsciously, but as if it were a natural step in the evolution of a *genre*, the refurbishing of earlier threads of nineteenth century thought. These threads, caught in the mesh with later products, produced the new pattern: this new pattern sums up Mrs. Ward's full contribution to the *genre*. Something of the lofty purpose and the high idealism which we found in many of Disraeli's younger men, which appears in Plumer Ward's *De Vere*, and which shows itself in America in Henry Adams's novel, is reflected by Mrs. Humphry Ward in her principal male characters. We see it in that fine old Tory gentleman Lord Maxwell, in Aldous Raeburn with his sensitive conscience trained in university circles, in his noble old friend Hallin, lecturer, economist, social reformer, whose 'legacy of feelings and ideas' passed on, at his death in the closing pages of *Marcella*, to Aldous, takes shape later, in the political novel, in a parliamentary bill upon the passage of which the crux of *Sir George Tressady* rests. The spirit of political reform which energizes the aristocratic youth in Disraeli's trilogy of novels, and in particular the impelling need of social amelioration set forth in impassioned language in Disraeli's *Sybil, or the Two Nations,* find a clear reflection in Mrs. Ward's novel written almost half a century after Disraeli's. H. D. Traill says very properly here:

"There is hardly a moan of suffering from the victims of our industrial system, hardly a sigh of sympathy with the sufferers, hardly a cry of passionate indignation against the iron law whereby they suffer, which is not equally audible in the utterances of these two writers divided from each other by an interval of more than fifty years. Nor, to all appearances, is the earlier writer less profoundly convinced than the later that English society is treading the edge of a volcano. To him, as to her, it seems as if the State must solve the problem of poverty, must compose the everlasting quarrel between the Haves and the Have-nots finally and forthwith, or perish." [1]

This profound interest in the fortune of the working classes, and her sincere desire to spread light among them, Mrs. Ward proves convincingly in her own *A Writer's Recollections,*[2] wherein she gives page upon page to William Forster's Education Act, and even describes her interest in it as a girl of eighteen, and then her own social experiments of the nineties through such foundations as Toynbee Hall, in East London, and the Passmore Edwards Settlement which, Mrs. Ward says, "has played a large part in my life . . . during twenty years." It is this same interest which links her work with that of the author of *Felix Holt, Radical.* Only the sweep of time has made some change in the names of the philosophies: George Eliot presents in 1866 what she calls Radicalism; thirty years later, after Karl Marx's influence had spread well beyond the boundaries of Germany, Mrs. Humphry Ward portrays, in

her Marcella and in her friends the 'Venturists,' reflections
of Marxian Socialism. Between Anthony Trollope and his
commonplace middle-class political characters and his complete emotional detachment and Mrs. Humphry Ward's ardent
propagandist spirit and her deadly earnestness in the portrayal
of ministers of the Cabinet, great Parliamentary speeches for
or against a Measure, men and women agitators among the
working classes, there would seem to be little in common. Yet,
all unconsciously, Mrs. Humphry Ward has taken one figure
from Trollope's political canvas. It is a person against whom
he presumably held a strong Victorian belief that once out of
'her natural sphere' she became a negative, indeed, even a
destructive influence when she entered public life. Mrs. Ward
has given that figure a modern interpretation. I refer to the
place of the Woman in public life.

Marcella Boyce, who might well, as Lady Maxwell, have
appeared beside Sir George Tressady in the title of the political
novel of that name, is a portrait of the Awakened Woman of
the close of the century, and is a complete foreshadowing of the
thoroughly emancipated political woman of the century thereafter. Marcella Boyce is a vibrant and sensitive and thoroughly
independent creature, who feels called upon to make herself
familiar with the terrible injustice and poverty visited upon the
people around her by an industrial age, and which is made no
less so owing to the strong caste feeling of a landed aristocracy.
Having become familiar with the problems, she makes herself
responsible, in the arc of her own little world at least, for
finding a solution for them. Led astray by her own impassioned nature, by a heart undisciplined because of an unfortunate bringing-up and an imperfect education, she mistakes
high integrity of character and disciplined emotions in two fine
aristocrats (in Aldous Raeburn, to whom she becomes betrothed,
and in his splendid old grandfather, Lord Maxwell) for a lack
of humanitarian feeling and for a lack of kindly sympathy for

the poor. Only after she has herself gone out into the East End of London to serve as a nurse in the homes of the poor and the unfortunate, and has thus given herself the discipline which subordination in a great social organization is apt to give to a thoroughly over-wrought emotional nature; after she discovers that in a time of crisis the great Labor spokesman in Parliament named Wharton proves to be only a political chameleon, having neither sincerity of purpose, nor depth of principle — and remembers that she had once declared that upon him her 'awakening' had depended; after all this has happened is she able to distinguish the true from the false, and to weigh at full value the richness of the character of him whom she had thrown away. And precisely as she learns, after the world's bitter schooling, that great character, refinement of soul, can be obtained only by self-surrender, and that self-surrender comes of love rather than of knowledge, so Aldous Raeburn learns, in the many months of estrangement from her, and because of the whips and buffets of an outrageous fortune upon himself, things similar. He learns, furthermore, that even if he "had no comforting faith in what seemed to him the rule of the multitudinous ignorance," still, the world had "taken the road of democracy; and the key to the future, for good or ill, lay not in the revolts and speculations of the cultivated few (as he had learnt in his university days, and as had been instilled in him through his love for his friend Hallin), but in the men and movements that can seize the many." Each of the two, therefore, had, in the course of a long estrangement which meant for them both discipline and education in their own respective ways, come unconsciously closer one to another. Marcella learned to look up; Raeburn looked more closely when he looked down upon the people for whom Marcella wished to consecrate her life. What wonder, therefore, that at the close of *Marcella* the woman realizes that in this age her greatest service can come politically and socially only by being a helpmate to a strong man, and not by stumbling on alone; the man finds in her that intelligent sympathy, that perfect understanding with his own ideals, without which his life was like a ship without a rudder, his aspirations for his fellow-men like sails without a driving breeze. For two such as these, children beloved by the gods, Mrs. Ward's solution is marriage. And that is the conclusion of this earlier novel.

In *Sir George Tressady*, Marcella, now called Lady Maxwell (since her husband Aldous had, upon the death of his grandfather, inherited the family title and estates), is portrayed as a feminine force altogether invigorating and thoroughly constructive in her influence upon English public life. In a story which is primarily political, because the House of Commons is the main stage upon which the entire drama unfolds itself, she stands throughout graphic and dominating, an intelligent and profoundly energizing force, tremendous in her influence with those who fall under the spell of her feminine charm and her gracious character, active in a world of labor unions, settlement houses, and drawing-room political discussions, cooperating with the forces making for righteousness, and giving life and new energy to a husband whose position in the Cabinet was 'the keystone of its arch,' as his great Factory Bill marked, in its fortunes, the final fortunes of an entire Ministry. In this novel we watch a brilliant woman become a vital part of the political world, because through her vision, her aspiration for common humanity, and her peculiar spiritual and mental endowments, she labors with her husband to find a solution for some of the perplexing economic problems of her day. We watch her drafting acts of Parliament — resultant, with her husband's proposal, of a common desire to make their beloved Hallin's 'feelings and ideas' exert their influence upon the land he loved so well; "feelings and ideas all largely concerned with this contrast between the huge and growing tyranny of the working class and the individual helplessness or bareness of the working man." In support of this great measure, entitled in Parliament the Maxwell Factory Act, we hear her speaking upon public platforms, conscious that she is as capable of reasoning with her critics as she is of persuading those in whose interests the Act is drawn, that the passage of the Act is essential to the good of the individual laborer and to the ultimate good of England. We see her, again and again, haunting the gallery of the House of Commons, the lobbies, and the terrace of that chamber, listening anxiously, watching eagerly and patiently the rise and fall in the fortunes of a Measure which had taken two years of their common labor, two years which, in her husband, "had aged and marked the labourer."

In these facts, therefore, Lady Maxwell as a political influence is a very modern figure indeed. She is a step in the evolution of the Woman in public affairs well beyond anything conceived even by Disraeli. Instead of exerting merely an indirect influence upon an eminent statesman of her own household, or her own affections, either through her social position or her natural talents or her material wealth, Mrs. Ward's creation has a heart and a mind of her own. The Maxwell Bill fell into three parts; two of those three parts were remedial clauses by which it became a penal offence to practice certain trades (tailoring, boot-finishing, and shirtmaking, for example) in the home which a worker used for eating and sleeping; and it forbade an employer engaging either a man or a woman for a longer period than ten and one half hours a day (with a few exceptions concerning some necessary over-time). These remedial clauses had been the contribution of Lady Maxwell herself to her husband's bill; they had been founded upon her own experience amongst the wage-earners of every sort and kind, amid whom, in the earlier novel *Marcella*, we had watched her spend many exciting and

enlightening months of her life. In fighting for the Maxwell
Bill both upon East End platforms of London, and in the
drawing-rooms of the West End, she was fighting for a measure
drawn co-operatively with her husband, and fighting in the
name of those countless workers who sought a voice in the
halls of legislation. The whole story of *Sir William Tressady*
hangs upon the outcome of this bill. Its vicissitudes and fortunes in the House of Commons mark the political novel with
which we are here dealing into sections far more natural than
do the chapters of the romance recounting the marital experiences of Sir William and his insignificant little wife. This second *motif* of the novel — the married life of Sir William —
appears, indeed, to be altogether dependent upon the first: if
there had been no Maxwell Bill in Parliament there would have
arisen no vital interest initially in Lady Maxwell for Sir George
Tressady; lacking that initial interest there might never have
been stimulated in Sir George an "attention which became concentrated on the convictions, the temperament, and the beauty"
of this remarkable feminine personality; without that influence
upon Sir George Tressady's life (and later upon his wife's), the
plot of the novel would not have been worth drawing to a
climax.

After we recall the excitement aroused in us who see the
ebb and flow of parliamentary strife in the novel, and after we
watch, entranced, how a highly intelligent modern woman
develops in her own husband, who is a product of a great
Tory heritage, a strong sense of his social responsibilities —
strong enough to make him sponsor a parliamentary measure
of economic amelioration, and upon which there hangs in the
balance an entire political career,—after we recall these things,
the tale then of the domestic bickerings between Sir George
Tressady and his worldly and vulgar wife Letty appears to be of
little moment indeed. In the political novel that episode (an
almost sordid account of the extremes which a shallow nature

feeding upon aimless social rivalries and ambitions may go)
serves mainly to propel the noble husband. He becomes aware
that he has been "dazzled by a brightness and fascination"
— the gay plumage of a parasitic bird, and is now in the radius
of influence of a lofty, zealous, and intensely serious nature
which is fighting for the realization of a noble social ideal.
Small wonder, then, that the effect of the contrast, added to the
instantaneous sympathy which Lady Maxwell shows for his sin-
cerities, his enthusiasms, and even his prejudices — a sympathy
and an understanding which he had not found in any other
person before, least of all in his mother who had shown herself a
vain, jealous, and pleasure-hunting creature — win him to her
cause, finally, mind and soul. Upon the critical night when the
final division for or against the Maxwell Bill was to take place
— that night which meant the fruition or the destruction of
months, years of thought and labor on the part of Lord and
Lady Maxwell — we come to the crisis of the novel: Sir
George Tressady, the most important figure in that small
group of Commoners who, under the leadership of Lord Fontenoy, held the balance of power between the two great parties
in the Chamber, and whose action in the political crisis raised
by the Maxwell Bill was expected to be decisive in defeating
that measure, rises in his place, makes a profoundly telling
speech in favor of its clauses (and this in the face of his own
party chief), and succeeds on that night, by his powerful
personal influence, in swinging enough favorable votes with
him to pass the Bill!

The situation is the most dramatic in this political novel,
and bears quoting.

"Before the speech was over many of those present had already
recognized in it a political event of the first order. The speaker
had traced with great frankness his own relation to the Bill — from
an opinion which was but a prejudice, to a submission which was
still half repugnance. He drew attention to the remarkable and

growing movement in support of the Maxwell policy which was now spreading throughout the country, after a period of coolness and suspended judgement; he pointed to the probable ease with which, as it was now seen, the 'harassed trades' would adapt themselves to the new law; he showed that the House, in at least three critical divisions, and under circumstances of enormous difficulty, had still affirmed the Bill; that the country, during the progress of the measure, had rallied unmistakably to the Government, and that all that remained was a question of machinery. That being so, he — and, he believed, some others, — had reconsidered their positions. Their electoral pledges, in their opinion, no longer held, though they would be ready at any moment to submit themselves to consequences, if consequences there were to be.

"Then, taking up the special subject-matter of the clause, he threw himself upon his leader's speech with a nervous energy, an information, and a resource which held the House amazed. He tore to pieces Fontenoy's elaborate attack, showed what practical men thought of the clause, and with what careful reliance upon their opinion and their experience it had been framed, and, finally — with reference not lacking in a veiled passion that told upon the House, to those 'dim, toiling thousands' whose lot, 'as it comes to work upon the mind, is daily perplexing if not transforming the thoughts and ideals of such men as I' — he, in the plainest terms, announced his intention of voting with the Government, and sat down, amid the 'usual mingled storm, in a shouting and excited House.

"The next hour passed in a tumult. One speaker after another got up from the Liberal benches — burly manufacturers and men of business, who had so far held a strong post in the army of resistance — to tender their submission, to admit that the fight had gone far enough, that the country was against them, and that the Bill must be borne. . . . But they made their purpose plain, and the Government Whip, standing near the door, gleefully struck off name after name from the Opposition list."

In real life such a defection of a noble lord from his party chief in time of great parliamentary crisis, and for the reason which Sir George Tressady himself gives for his action, seems incredible. "I should never have taken the part I did but that I had come to have a strong wish to give Lady Maxwell her heart's desire. She has been my friend. I repaid her what I could." These are his words of explanation for his astonishing action, as he gave them soon to his wife. How astonishing the action was, Mrs. Ward herself notes later. In her *Writer's Recollections* of several years ago, she said, apropos of this novel and of her friend Gladstone's criticism of it: "When *Sir George Tressady* appeared he sent me a message through Mrs. Drew that he feared George Tressady's Parliamentary conduct 'was inconceivable in a man of honour'; and I was only comforted by the emphatic and laughing dissent of Lord Peel, to whom I repeated the verdict. 'Nothing of the kind! But of course he was thinking of *us* — the Liberal Unionists.'"[3] Now whether Gladstone or Peel won the argument, the most significant comment for us is Mrs. Ward's apparent valuation of the whole volume. In her own account of her work at the close of her life it is interesting to note that whereas she gives a full chapter to the discussion of her *Marcella*, and another full chapter to the novel which immediately followed *Sir George Tressady*), namely, *Helbeck of Bannisdale*, she seems so little interested in her hero Tressady, upon whom she spent two years of thought, that she passes the story of him with scarcely more than the sentence I have already quoted. It is obvious enough that the earlier novel *Marcella* has received the warmer meed of praise, and that Mrs. Ward was very naturally aware, in recounting the days of her writing, on which of her novels the attention of her past readers had been centered. Certain artistic defects are obvious enough as we read the work to-day.

For one fact, there is the kind of influence which Marcella, or Lady Maxwell, really exerts upon Tressady. She is really made to exert an emotional rather than an intellectual force upon him: it is never clear that his natural political beliefs had ever been changed by argument of hers. All of which makes unintelligible his sudden and extraordinary defection

MRS. HUMPHRY WARD AND FEMINISM   265

from his party and his leader Fontenoy, upon an occasion when the place of a ministry was at stake. One must agree with Gladstone that in a man of honor, of whatever party, such a conversion is inadequately presented. Lady Maxwell, herself, is portrayed here as a presumably normal woman, wife, and mother. She is a late nineteenth century Englishwoman discontented with remaining in the decorative Victorian frame in which her sisters of an earlier generation sat calmly, in shadowy leisure. She steps out, and falls willingly into the procession of those who represent a new age, new and revolutionizing forces which call for independence of action. She focuses all her rational powers, her intuitions, her idealism, and fights one great fight upon her own account for God and for Country.

In such as she is, just made aware of her powers, Mrs. Ward draws a character with almost too firm a hand. The zeal with which Marcella plies her cause in season and out, in drawing-room no less than among invited guests in other people's country houses; the straight course she runs in behalf of her working classes, the wives and children of the poor; the high aim of her purpose which leads her to attempt to persuade members of the working classes against their own convictions to fight for a measure which was to have the *immediate* effect — whatever the final effect might be — of taking the bread temporarily from their mouths: all these take the reader's breath away. All these send us soaring with her into regions so high, so detached from the common work-a-day world of mixed motives and ideals where much which we gain comes only by compromise and bargaining, that we sometimes cry for a little foolish sentiment from her, a grain of hearty humor, a little lightening of the strings that stand always so taut and sensitive. We have to believe that even Lord Maxwell, as one critic of the novel puts it, "must sometimes have sighed for repose."

Next to the introduction of the enlightened woman who has

chosen to take a vital interest in public affairs, Mrs. Ward has given us in her political novel, for the first time among the writers whom we have recounted here, the elements of organized labor, trade-unionism, the voices of working men and women, making themselves felt as a profound force on the floor of the House of Commons in the actual moulding of legislation. In *Felix Holt, Radical* the forces of reaction, the cry of the toilers, were just about to be revealed: as yet, however, they had gained no momentum. They were but voices pleading their cause half-dumbly, and upon a day just a-dawning. In Mrs. Humphry Ward's two novels we are transported to a cosmopolitan London, with the forces of conservatism and of progress fighting out their battles in the glaring light of midday, and nothing loathe to rend the whole country asunder with a discussion of the merits of their respective sides. When Sir George Tressady entered Parliament, in the novel that bears his name, we begin to see what point and consequence comes of the forces of reaction — there the teachings of Socialism — which play around the character of Marcella in the earlier book. "A Liberal government, embarrassed by large schemes it had not force enough to carry through, was sinking towards inevitable collapse. When the crash came, a weak Conservative government, in which Aldous Maxwell occupied a prominent post, accepted office for a time without a dissolution. They came in on the cry of 'industrial reform,' and, by way of testing their own party and the country, adopted the Factory Bill for East London." The Bill split the party but the ministers appealed to the country to support them, and in their programme the Maxwell Bill held the leading place. The law they desired to pass was actually intended to be of an experimental nature: it was first to be put into effect in East London, and if it was found to work there the operation of it was to be extended through the rest of the country. The appeal to the country was not made in vain. Organized labor everywhere rallied to the support of the measure. "Every trades union, every working-man's club throughout the United Kingdom, was ringing with this project." In the end a Cabinet in which Lord Maxwell, sponsor of the measure, was made President of the Council, was backed by the people with a sufficiently large majority. They took the reins of government at once into their own hands. With the situation here presented taking up some quarter of the novel, the other three-quarters of it trace the conduct of that Bill, its fortunes and set-backs, through the Commons. Then comes the fatal night when Sir George Tressady swings his own influence strongly for the measure; it passes into a law, and by that we see the full fruition of Lady Maxwell's socializing influence not alone upon her own aristocratic husband but also upon other members of her Conservative class.

Thus does Mrs. Humphry Ward introduce upon the floor of the House of Commons the gigantic force of the working classes, thoroughly martialed and organized; and she shows how, by means of that new force, a breach is made in the traditional ranks of the old parties — a breach large enough to admit those revolutionizing political influences which in our own day have transformed the United Kingdom.

Chapter XI

MR. H. G. WELLS AND THE CULT OF
INDIVIDUALISM

HISTORICALLY speaking, Mr. H. G. Wells takes up the
political novel where Mrs. Humphry Ward lays it down. In
Sir George Tressady one still feels firmly beneath one the
granite structure built by the members of a traditional aristocracy. Aldous Raeburn, and his noble grandfather before
him who appeared in the earlier novel, sensitive to the great
Past which their forbears had left to England, are desirous in
their own time of serving their country as their sense of honor
and their interpretation of their national duties dictate. Raeburn, the younger man, living as he does in Marcella's changing
world and not in Victorian England, proves that he is nevertheless too patient with tradition, too much in mental bondage
to 'initial circumstances,' and to the documented, well-worn,
respected things; he must suffer himself therefore to be broken,
and he is forced to compromise with things, before he may
win his heart's desire. In him, as in Sir George Tressady, you
see the drift toward the new age of liberalizing thought. That
new age unfolds, however, toward the close of the second novel,
when the Maxwell Bill is passed, and not at the opening of
either story. In both books, for the most part, party lines
still hold firmly together and they do so along conventional
ways; when there *is* a defection in the ranks (as in Tressady's
action) you are at once faced with a parliamentary crisis, so
unique is the occurrence. Gladstone's own comment upon that
fact in Mrs. Ward's novel was the finger of scorn pointing out
a great political immorality in his time. In *The New Machia-*

268

velli [1] the world of English politics has taken a leap ahead. Party ties have no longer the force which they held throughout the century of Disraeli and of Gladstone. The ruling forces show themselves altogether impatient with political bondage of the past, or with old traditions. The force of education has been to universalize and to liberalize the mind, so to speak; men seem to be sorting themselves more and more by their intellectual temperaments and less and less by their accidental associations. Says Mr. Wells, speaking through his main character, Remington: "Men are becoming increasingly constructive and selective. . . . The past will rule them less, the future more. It is not simply party but school and college and county and country that lose their glamour. One does not hear nearly as much as our forefathers did of the 'Old Harrovian,' 'Old Arvonian,' 'Old Etonian' claim to this or that unfair advantage or unearned sympathy. Even the Scotch and the Devonians weaken a little in their clannishness. A widening sense of fair play destroys such things."

The breach made in the traditional ranks of the old parties by the forces of a new time, forces which had but only begun to work in Mrs. Ward's second novel, shows itself so vast and so complete in Mr. H. G. Wells' work that the reader is left, at first shot in that novel, with a conception that in political life nothing permanent exists, that all is either flux or chaos. The old Conservatism appears undermined because it ties altogether to old Westminster traditions, and seems not at all alive "to the greatness of the Present and to the vaster Future." The Liberals showed "tremendously clear what they were against. The trouble was to find out what on earth they were for!" The third imposing party, the Socialists' Party, had become a "sort of big intellectual No-Man's-Land"; it appeared to be made up of a great many different kinds and sects, each of which "had pegged out claims upon that No-Man's-Land," all of them beset by a sort of "quarrelsome uneasiness," with a total want of a common intimacy in its leaders, and with no, or at least, few, unanimities common to them all. One of the most outstanding of agreements was

"that every one should be a little odd in appearance, funny about the hair, or the tie, or the shoes or more generally, and that bursts of violent aggression should alternate with an attitude entirely defensive."

Then there was the Labour Party, with leaders constructive-minded indeed, but with the mass of the members of it suspicious of education and of all discipline, hostile to higher education, and — except for an obvious antagonism to employers and property owners — almost destitute of ideas. With the two main parties "more or less heterogeneous in composition," with "the rider groups" not in themselves carefully rationalized but seeking only to gain an end here and there "in the event of a small Government majority," the time of *The New Machiavelli* is one of innovation, sudden change and experiment, of insecurity in political leadership, and of political opportunism. The years of which these things are painted are those of the first decade of the new century. The turning point at which the leading character, Remington, finds a means in politics of "organizing, and disciplining, of building up a constructive and controlling State" out of the public confusion around him, is the actual year 1909, when the famous Budget of that year, denounced everywhere by the landed and aristocratic interests as destructive of their traditional rights, actually led in England to the passage of the Parliamentary Bill, the effect of which was to sweep, once for all, enough power and prestige from the House of Lords to transform English public life.

Not alone in the portrayal of the evolution of the status of political parties does Mr. Wells pick up the thread of the political narrative where Mrs. Ward had left it. There is the new status of Woman, as well, ushered in with the new century, that is to be reported. In *The New Machiavelli* it is not merely that women, having dropped from their shoulders the Victorian draperies of timidity, false modesty and propriety, and having rolled up their sleeves themselves to battle for industrial and economic amelioration in legislative hall and by means of influencing law-makers (profoundly the case with Marcella), now do these things on a still vaster scale than ever was dreamt of by Mrs. Ward's heroine, but that in this political novel Woman as Woman becomes one of the most serious subjects determining legislation. Here is Altiora Bailey giving point, intellectual direction, and initiative to a husband whom she married in order to advance both herself and him; giving fire and energy to the leaders of a party of reform who come to her for direction and knowledge as they might come to a political chief; and whose dinners and gatherings bring together all sorts of interesting people in or about the public service. From this "self-constituted guardian of reform's Thermopylaean Pass" we turn to the whole Suffrage agitation ushered in with the new century, and to a description of its campaigns, its "absurdities and follies, its courage and devotion." Says Remington, describing his first parliamentary experiences at Westminster at which the besetting of Woman as a political and national problem was destined to have so strong an influence upon his later public life:

"There were aspects of that unquenchable agitation that were absolutely heroic and aspects that were absolutely pitiful. It was unreasonable and unwise, and, except for its one central insistence, astonishingly incoherent. It was amazingly effective. The very incoherence of the demand witnessed, I think, to the forces that lay behind it. It wasn't simply an argument based upon a simple assumption; it was the first crude expression among modern educated women that the conditions of their relations with men were oppressive, ugly, dishonouring, and had to be altered. They had not merely adopted the Vote as a symbol of equality; it was fairly manifest to me that, given it, they meant to use it, and to use it perhaps even vindictively and blindly, as a weapon against many things they had every reason to hate."

Finally we see Remington making his group out of the Pentagram Circle the nucleus for a rejuvenated Tory party, a nucleus which begins to develop force and followers in Parliament only after he had himself become a Feminist, and his measure, the State Endowment of Motherhood as a practical form of Eugenics, had got into public life. It is the problem of Woman, the "besetting of sex" as Mr. Wells calls it, which, having made him a man of promise in English public life because of the ameliorating forces which he had set in action, finally unmakes him as well. It is when he has begun to feel himself a real force in English politics, when he appears to be leading toward the apogee of his career, that all the false education (or lack of education) in such matters during his youth, which "had put the kink into him," now plays the deuce with him: he abandons his wife Margaret, he runs away with his mistress Isabel (who is in the story a type of the emancipated woman), he throws over all those devoted political friends who had begun to look up to him as their leader, and thus ends his promising public career by making a wreck of all his great political theories, his national ambitions, and by permanently warping the lives of three human beings. Marcella and Aldous Raeburn permitted themselves to be chastened and educated by suffering the whips and scorns and bitterness of common human experiences; they become in the end, therefore, two persons fit to mate one with another. In the second novel Mrs. Ward shows them helping each other to bring their lives to a glorious fruition. Mr. Wells' man and woman are too strongly individualistic, too thoroughly independent, too little given to a respect for the Past, and too much children of an emancipated present age, to permit any sorrows of the daily life to get so close to them that they can show the evidences of being chastened emotionally. Product of a false upbringing in a time of superficial educational theorizings and vaporings, these two are set before us by Mr. Wells, who is himself a scientist and almost a fatalist when it comes to dealing with the human passions. We watch the man growing out of the "chaotic indiscipline, ill-adjusted effort, spasmodic aims" of his home life, taming successfully, apparently, an education of disorderliness and of confusions, and set upon the road of public service and patriotic endeavour which seems to be leading to a noble end; we see the woman, university graduate and with splendid mental equipment, suddenly carried away with a passion that is "formless, inconsiderate, and overwhelming." So these two mentally independent and peculiarly vigorous people, being the products, however, of shabby subserviences, "mean discretions, and unreasonable prohibitions" where matters of sex were concerned, are obliged to pay for the hypocrisy of their parents, their schools, and the nation which fostered these stupidities, by falling without reason, at a critical time in their lives, upon their primary sexual desires, and thus destroying their promising careers in the full light of mid-day. "That is what you get," so Mr. Wells would say to us, "for the evasions and the suppressions and the false delicacies with which you bring up your children to-day!"

If what has already been said of this political novel suggests that it stands for Mr. Wells as propaganda to spread his well-known sociological criticisms of our modern world, and in particular of the English nation of his own time, that impression gathers force as one penetrates more deeply into the novel, and compares the deductions of its main character with the general teachings of Mr. Wells, the reformer. For, in truth, to understand the *modus operandi* which Mr. Wells the political novelist employs, one should recall the sociological essays which appeared some years before this political novel was published: namely, *Anticipations, Mankind in the Making,* and *A Modern Utopia.* To the novel of 1910 these philosophic-sociological reflections have the equivalent relationship which Disraeli's *A Vindication of the English Constitution* had to his political novels of the forties. Mr. Wells' political novel may be said to be, generally speaking, a powerful picture of the social and the moral discontent of his time; of a society, restless, experimental, given to innumerable programs, muddling on in its education as in its politics, trying to heal the moral crack in a universe which, to the utopian Mr. Wells, appears to be a wretched mending of what ought to be completely remade. The economic and social disorder, the incoherence and plan-lessness, the unequal struggle of reason with the natural ener-gies and instincts of human life — unequal because of the physical disorder in which the battle is taking place, — all of which paint the picture of our present-day political and eco-nomic world in *A Modern Utopia,* and against which "the Owner of the Voice" argues and argues for the better world, are all focused in and around the life of the young English statesman who dissects his soul for you in the autobiography which is entitled *A New Machiavelli.* In this novel a man of great imagination, of high and sincere aspirations, indeed, of powerful initiative, and possessing the gift of leadership, seeing the waste and the ill-adjusted effort and the confusion around him, finally hits upon what appears to him and to his followers to be a way out of the muddle — a program, in short, of amelioration if not of a practical renascence. In this program you see, again, Mr. Wells, the sociologist, directing, guiding, and planning a world that may come closer to one's ideal. But his hero, Remington, is not strong enough to carry the work through to completion. *His* political progress moved faster with him, so to speak, than his education had prepared him for. The edifice of constructive statesmanship became too heavy for the frail foundation which his country had given him of character, of spiritual integrity, of sheer physiological awareness about himself and about the passions of the opposite sex as well. The result is that the whole edifice topples over just when it is expected to bring its full reward to the one who had so patiently raised it. The man outstrips the statesman.

The significance of this work for us, as a contribution to the political *genre*, lies mainly in the diagnosis which Mr. Wells makes of the political ills of his time, and in the autobiography he sets forth of a rising young gentleman whose political development is as clearly revealed as was "the portrait of a brainy gentleman, sliced in half and displaying an interior of intricate detail and much vigour of coloring" which hung over the mantle of his father's home in that statesman's very early youth. To this portrait the author refers several times, as if to suggest by it what it was he was himself doing. Let us dwell, therefore, on the main significance of the work and less upon the particular 'accident' which occurred; the pebble, so to speak, which, once loosened, started an avalanche and toppled the entire structure. For the first of these things lies within the scope of this investigation; it is among those thoughts and part of those forces which have concerned the other political novelists. It must contribute something, therefore, to the story of the evolution of a literary *genre*. The other is but a singular incident, even though it unexpectedly destroys a great scheme of constructive statesmanship built up after years of thought and effort. We must deal here with the facts of a political evolution rather than with a particular 'accident.'

Richard Remington's story of his life is that of a contemporary man discovering himself. It is an attempt at a survey of "the relation of the great constructive spirit in politics to individual character and weaknesses" of the present day, much as Niccolo Machiavelli's *The Prince* was to the sixteenth century. Remington, type product of "the splendid disorder

of forces" (so Mr. Wells calls it) which marks his own age,
begins his political thinking in terms of a "vast, vague humanitarianism." That came during his 'school-days' when he
began to feel

"the massive effect of that multitudinous majority of people who
toil continually, who are forever anxious about ways and means,
who are restricted, ill clothed, ill fed and ill housed, who have
limited outlooks and continually suffer misadventures, hardships
and distresses through the want of money."

It was in this period of adolescence while he is still at Cambridge University that he hears Chris Robinson, the great
Labor leader; that he has great debates with his fellows on
Socialism; and that he passes through, with his undergraduate
friends, that Young Imperialistic stage which made Kipling
so prevailing a force in those early days. His first holiday
upon the Continent with his philosophical friend, Willersley,
throws him into contact with "that great multitude of function-
less property owners which encumbers modern civilization";
that gives him much food for thought later, and incidentally
offers him a splendid chance to discuss vast plans for the socializing of England. It is upon this trip that young Remington
shows off a moral weakness, in the very midst of his plans
for doing political service for his nation, which is to prove
afterwards the deep rut in the road that is to wreck him. He
comes home to analyze his uncle, a type of prosperous business
man and industrial owner, of a tough-minded attitude toward
all higher education, with a curb-stone intellect toward all the
things of the spirit, who hated everything and everybody that he
could not understand; a man who was "about as much civilized,
about as much tamed to the ideas of collective action and mutual
consideration as a Central African negro." Between this man
and his workers there always existed a state of war, and toward
them he never concealed his feeling of "mingled contempt and

animosity." It was the study of this uncle, who became for
Remington but a symbol of the vast hordes of industrial owners
who were to be found all over the kingdom; — it was the
thought of his two cousins, Sybil and Gertrude, who showed
themselves such brainless creatures and such wasters of what
men and women were producing by the sweat of the brow, —
that forced Remington finally into the ranks of Liberalism,
and, in particular, under the banner of Socialism.

Passing from the narrow industrialism of his uncle's world
at Staffordshire, he enters London. Here begin five years of
"definition" for him. He publishes two books, he writes
several articles which bring him friends of his own thinking,
he establishes his relations with reviews and Liberal clubs and
dinner parties — all of which appear to push him forward
toward the goal of his ambitions: to enter politics and to make
himself a great force in the public life of England. "My
political conceptions," he says, summing up the significance of
this period in his life,

"were perfectly plain and honest. I meant to leave England and
the empire better ordered than I had found it, to organize and
discipline, to build up a constructive and controlling State out
of my world's confusions. We had, I saw, to suffuse education
with public intention, to develop a new better-living generation
with a collectivist habit of thought, to link now chaotic activities
in every human affair, and particularly to catch that escaped,
world-making, world-ruining, dangerous thing,.industrial and financial enterprise, and bring it back to the service of the general good."

Intent upon that mission he is successful, through the help
of his Socialist friends, the Baileys and their set, the aid which
his wife Margaret brings him (as much by her small fortune
as by the "radiant reconciliation" she meant for him in the
"darkling disorders of lust and impulse"), and the publicity
given to him by his own writings, in having himself returned
to Parliament as a Liberal from the Kinghamstead Division.

Once in the halls of the House of Commons, this "primary, intuitive, illogical" person (as we might define him in William James's terms), filled with vast ideals and grandiose conceptions of what needs to be done for the Empire by the reactionary forces of which he appears to himself to be a natural leader, is suddenly obliged to square with realities of procedure and definite methods and personalities which existed before the appearance of his impatient and impetuous spirit in the halls of legislation. He begins to feel — when he finds himself being sworn in with the scores and batches of other new members of the Commons — that he is like one of a lot of sheep being branded. There comes suddenly upon him the thought of how infinitely small a chip was his personality which had come "swirling in like a flood" in that tide of Liberalism; and how natural it would be that he, with all of his 'fine thinking,' should be overwhelmed. All about him — at the National Liberal Club, in the lounging rooms of the Commons, among small groups — after that general election of 1906, there was fuddled talk about "doing things," and questionings concerning "just what we shall do"; in Parliament, however, in the three years that followed, he saw his own party "enormously taken up with moribund issues and old quarrels," with never a great leader standing at the rudder, and with the chaos and the planlessness of the outside world merely transferred to the halls at Westminster. On the night of his first visit to Parliament, when he walked away alone to the pillars of the Lambeth Bridge and in sight of the two Houses, he already sensed what was to come. And so he prayed to his Maker, in the sound of the rushing waters of the Thames.

"I prayed that night that life might not be in vain, that in particular I might not live in vain. I prayed for strength and faith, that the monstrous blundering forces might not overwhelm me, might not beat me back to futility and a meaningless acquiescence in existent things." . . . "'Break me, O God,' I prayed at last, 'disgrace me, torment me, destroy me as you will, but save me from self-complacency and little interests and little successes and the life that passes like the shadow of a dream.'"

God heard Richard Remington's prayer. But before He destroyed him, and in order to save him from 'the little interests' and 'the little successes' of the normal politician's career, He sends him through an evolution of political thinking so complex, woven in a web so multifarious, that Remington himself, reporting this most important part of his life in that large part of the novel entitled "The Heart of Politics," is able to indicate only the main strands, only the details most graphically colored of the interior of "that brainy gentleman sliced in half," to whose portrait reference was made earlier in this chapter.

First, in the course of his parliamentary career, comes the realization upon him of the utter futility of holding to any strong party ties. Then, as he matures in thought and penetrates more closely into the very core of party philosophy, he begins to see something of the bleakness, the hypocrisy, and the unimportance of his Young Liberal group, and the want of any constructive political philosophy in the older Liberals. The National Liberal Club eventually takes on for him a sort of landscape view of the entire party: clumps of men, writers, journalists, Jews, Irish politicians, a few East Indians, anglicised Germans, some eminent Rationalists, self-indulgent and pompous Aldermen, respectable and make-believe young Fabians, Altiora Bailey with a 'bony soul' and her dynamic little husband who took himself with such profound seriousness as the great political publicist. Where, he asks himself, can you find in this variegated mass of human beings anything but their special and narrow concerns, a 'universal littleness of imagination,' little pools and eddies of selfish purposes stretching out and out into infinity? Where in this reservoir was to be found any creative imagination? 'Any giantry, or immense valiant synthesis?' "What but a common antagonism would ever keep these multitudes together? . . . antagonism against the Lords — against plutocrats — against Cossington's papers — against the brewers. . . ."

So he breaks with the Liberals and turns for a time to the Socialists. Here, it at first appeared to him, there might be something real beneath the air that surrounded them "of coherent intentions." But the disillusioning comes only too soon. He finds these as dissociated, one from another, as their individual temperaments will permit. Once, at an assembly which he and his wife Margaret gave, in 1907, he tried to bring together "a representative collection of the parliamentary leaders of Socialism, the various exponents of Socialist thought and a number of the young Liberal thinkers into one room." They were all there, from Chris Robinson up or down. The evening was a total failure. "I could not have imagined," says Remington, drawing a conclusion to his experiment as a Comforter among Radicals,

"I could not have imagined it was possible for half so many people to turn their backs on everybody else in such small rooms as ours. But the unsaid things those backs expressed broke out, I remarked, with refreshed virulence in the various organs of the various sections of the party next week."

He turns to the Labor Party, and finally concludes that these stand primarily only for "the expropriated multitude, whose whole situation and difficulty arise from its individual lack of initiative and organizing power." They favor all sorts of reforms without the least conception of the great difficulties involved in carrying out these reforms; their logical absurdities he finds typified in the single example of their demand for the complete nationalization of land and capital, while they remain bitterly opposed to "the equally reasonable socialization of individuals which is implied by military service."

As a result of all this thinking he finally concludes, both of

himself and of his associates of the several parties that have
been mentioned, that they

"were oddly narrow, priggish, unreal, that the Socialists with whom
we were attempting co-operation were preposterously irrelevant to
their own theories, that my political life didn't in some way comprehend more than itself, that rather perplexingly I was missing
the thing that I was seeking."

What was the way out? It lay, evidently, in getting away
from the personal, from immediacy, from the attempt to
scheme out a plan as a whole which should be the panacea for
all the ills, political, industrial, and educational, and in turning
to the business of laying altogether new foundations: in devoting one's forces "to the development of that needed intellectual life without which all (one's) shallow attempts at fixing
up are futile." It lay, in short, in providing first for "the
mental hinterland in the individual and for the collective mind
of the race."

And thus Remington comes to his great phrase: love and
fine thinking. This is when he arrives at the climactic period
of his political progress: when he definitely allies himself with
the Aristocracy of the understanding and of purpose, with
those 'hinterlanders,' in short, who were the big people, the
wealthy people, the influential people, among whom it was
worth while starting an intellectual renascence. Or, quoting
him in his own words, "my general conception in politics (now
became) the conception of the Constructive Imagination working upon the vast complex of powerful people, clever people,
enterprising people, influential people, amidst whom power is
diffused to-day, to produce that self-conscious, highly selective,
open-minded, devoted aristocratic culture, which seems to me
to be the necessary next phase in the development of human
affairs." It behooved him now to seek associates among these,
the fittest of the nation's children, and to co-ordinate them, to
energize them, to unite them all into 'one great constructive

effort for the betterment of the whole human race.' In his own so-called Pentagram Circle he finds the handful of followers who set out to realize this political reformer's dream. The phrases of his disciples show how earnestly they have caught the spirit of their master. Says Gane, one of them, "we're working altogether too much at the social basement in education and training. Remington is right about our neglect of the higher level." Says Crupp, another: "We've got to pick up the tradition of aristocracy, reorganize it, and make it work." And Britten, who becomes, later, Remington's right hand man, agrees with him at this early meeting of organization when he rebukes Thorns for the scepticism he shows toward launching any revival of Toryism. "Revivals and revisions of Toryism have been tried so often," said Thorns, "from the Young England Movement onward."

"Not one but has produced its enduring effects. It's the peculiarity of English conservatism that it's persistently progressive and rejuvenescent." Remington is talking. "One thing emerges. Whatever accidents happen, our civilization needs, and almost consciously needs, a culture of fine creative minds, and all the necessary tolerances, opennesses, considerations, that march with that. For my part I think that is the Most Vital Thing. Build your ship of state as you will; get your men as you will; I concentrate on what is clearly the affair of my sort of man, — I want to ensure the quality of the quarter deck!"

Having gathered his young group around him, having founded an organ to spread his political philosophy, he seeks now for the first tool which he, as a practical-minded man of political affairs, must have in order to put into effect the teachings of his party. He finds this in a measure intended for the "Endowment of Motherhood — which involves the independence of woman, the control of all great educational forces in the common interest, and the breeding of fit children for the

future State." His *Blue Weekly* ably edited, his group of followers ardent, the high dignity with which he planned his lines
of attack upon plutocratic selfishness, and the appeal he made
to age-old duties and responsibilities of the ruling classes — all
of these began to show their effects. There came then that
fight over the 1909 Budget wherein the House of Lords placed
their veto upon a measure which they declared was a piece of
infamous class legislation, — deliberately intended against the
rich, and destructive of all property rights. How the general
election in England supported the Commons, how the Lords
were forced into accepting the Budget in the end, and how, on
the following year 1911, the famous Parliamentary Bill defined
once for all the relations of the Deliberative Assembly over the
Hereditary Body, are all now matters of history.[2] For Remington in 1910 the crisis that had suddenly risen in which the
whole future power of the Lords was concerned, seemed a
heaven-sent opportunity to launch once for all under the best
possible auspices the program of constructive politics of which
he was now the champion. For, in the period of reconstruction
which he was certain would follow after this crucial parliamentary event, what better time was there for an intellectual
renascence of Conservatism?

And then comes the 'accident.' The disturbed 'pebble' dis-
places a volume of effort painfully expended by this political
champion, and the avalanche which follows buries him and his
hopes and ideals forever. We suddenly discover that in the
man himself progress has run ahead faster than civilization;
that the intellectual powers of him have been intently at work
erecting a structure upon a frail spiritual foundation.

However efficient as a political leader Remington has proved
himself, and however superior is his imagination in matters of
constructive statesmanship, the great moral truth is suddenly
revealed that in matters involving the passions he is a man
thoroughly lacking in discipline, and that the totally false edu-

cation of his youth in matters of sex which had permitted him
his indulgences when he became a man full grown, cause now
the catastrophe of the statesman. For in this, too, Remington
is revealed as but the product of his time. That at the very
height of his promise Remington should abandon his wife
Margaret, she whom he later thought back upon as an exquisite
woman of 'silvery splendour' of 'triumphant kindliness' and
of 'enormous generosity,' and that he should run off with
Isabel, a person like himself experimenting with life, egotistic,
energetic, fired by intense impulses and unstable emotions,
was the great tragedy. The evolution of this man's political
thinking led him to believe that he had outgrown the first
woman, and had to cling to this other, a type of the twentieth century emancipated creature of vigorous cerebration, who
was irritated with all convention, and who loved only independence of action. That Remington, of all men, should have
made this choice was but a proof that even in his age one cannot
get away from trivial human limitations. The pride of the
statesman outweighed the conscience in the man. The sense
of efficiency in the first had been fed so intemperately in a
world of material things that it drowned out the voice of
conscience and numbed the spiritual feelings. In his fall
Remington, the man, wishes to show that he was the victim
of a normal instinct, a natural passion by which the race is
continued, but which in him had been distracted through the
hypocrisies and the suppressions of his time. His defence of
himself for bringing on the domestic scandal which destroyed
his political future, and which suddenly sent his great plans of
constructive statesmanship flying into the air, begins early in
his autobiography when he describes his youth.

"That age which bore me," he explains, "was indeed a world
full of restricted and undisciplined people, overtaken by power,
by possessions and great new freedoms, and unable to make any
civilized use of them whatever; stricken now by this idea and

now by that, tempted first by one possession and then another to ill-considered attempts. . . ."

And then, in the very last pages of the story, speaking with hot indignation to his friend Britten of the justification of the action to which both he and his mistress had been led:

"What in God's name was to be expected of us but what has happened? I went through my life bit by bit last night, I recalled all I have had to do with virtue and women, and all I was told and how I was prepared. I was born into cowardice and debasement. We all are. Our generation's grimy with hypocrisy. I came to the most beautiful things in life — like peeping Tom of Coventry. I was never given a light, never given a touch of natural manhood by all this dingy, furtive, canting, humbugging English world. Thank God! I'll soon be out of it! The shame of it! The very savages in Australia initiate their children better than the English do to-day. Neither of us was ever given a view of what they call morality that didn't make it show as shabby subservience, as the meanest discretion, an abject submission to unreasonable prohibitions! meek surrender of mind and body to the dictation of pedants and old women and fools. We weren't taught — we were mumbled at! And when we found that the thing they called unclean, unclean, was Pagan beauty — God! it was glory to sin, Britten, it was a pride and splendour like bathing in the sunlight after dust and grime!"

It is when we come to the close of the book and to passages like these that the full force of Mrs. Humphry Ward's criticism of it occurs to mind: the work itself she found lacking altogether in charm, and of Mr. Wells she says that she was always impressed with his "grossness of mind," with his being "earthy." As for Remington's action, his friend Britten's criticism of him and of his defence, is the more searching comment. "You're throwing yourself away," he says in reply to the man's speech I have just quoted, "and accusing your country of rejecting you!" And we are inclined to agree with Britten. Wells' passion for dissection was transferred to his political hero. And he, caught in a tortuous, giddy, chaotic world

which he has determined to set straight so far as he can, is led
unfortunately to probe the domestic scheme that enfolded
him, the soul of his Victorian wife, her loyalties, triumphs,
expectations, forgetting the fact that analysis here, though it
may reveal the structure of the flower, wipes away the blush of
it and kills its perfume. And the whole virtue of marriage
and of domestic companionship lies in these intangible things,
and not in the physical facts and the gross material laws which
tell us just why and how things are as they are. Margaret was
always prepared to meet him, step by step, as he moved forward
and away from *her* initial Victorian impulses. That fact is
revealed clearly enough to him as soon as he runs away with
his mistress, and it is driven bitterly home to him — it strikes
into his very soul — when he reads the extraordinary letter
which Margaret sends him after he had run away with the
other woman. It was a letter of renunciation, one showing
the most searching insight, and full of almost divine forgiveness for the two of them. Margaret's letter is the best possible
antidote to Mrs. Ward's criticism of Mr. Wells. "You are,"
Margaret says in part to her husband,

"you are always talking of order and system, and the splendid
dream of the order that might replace the muddled system you
hate, but by a sort of instinct you seem to want to break the law.
I've watched you so closely. Now I want to obey the laws, to
make sacrifices, to follow rules. I don't want to make, but I
want to keep. You are at once makers and rebels, you and Isabel,
too. You're bad people, — criminal people, I feel, and yet full of
something the world must have. You're so much better than me,
and so much viler. . . . My beauty is still beauty, and yours, is
excitement. I know nothing of the fascination of the fire, or why
one should go deliberately out of all the decent fine things of life
to run dangers and be singed and tormented and destroyed. I
don't understand . . ."

In that failure to understand, both Margaret and Mrs. Ward
at least agree.

Chapter XII

THE PIONEER AMERICAN POLITICAL NOVEL
OF HENRY ADAMS

To read the shy, over-sensitive, and questioning account of that "eighteenth century Bostonian" in the now famous book, *The Education of Henry Adams,* and then to recall the dashing, adventuresome, and calculated life of Benjamin Disraeli, in another recent biography, is to marvel at the strange tricks Mother Nature loves to play upon her children. That two such extreme types of men — alien by temperament, antipodal by inheritance and education, completely dissimilar in political ambition — should stand shoulder to shoulder as pioneers in the same field, and that field literature as exemplified in the political novel, is to upset almost all conservative judgement, and to spell order, chaos. *Democracy — an American Novel,* by Henry Adams, is the first true political novel written in America. Its theme is "government under a system of universal suffrage" (which we should now call manhood suffrage); its action takes place among leading figures in the United States Capitol. It is the work of one whom his brother very properly placed among the most cultivated and stimulating men of his generation (in his acquaintanceship, "the most cultivated and stimulating"), unloading his heart, and pronouncing bitterly over the greatest disappointment of his hopes and dreams.

Henry Adams was one of the patriots of our time. Great-grandson of John Adams, signer of the Declaration of Independence and our second President, grandson of John Quincy Adams, our sixth President, Henry Adams was by heritage, by knowledge of European conditions gained through periods of residence abroad, by familiarity with England first made while private secretary to his father, Charles Francis Adams, our Ambassador there during the critical years 1861–1868, and by the brilliance of intellect shown in his American writings, fitted to be a distinguished expositor of the country. He tells us in his autobiography that he had known Washington, D. C., for fifty years, and to that number a dozen more of his knowledge of the Capitol needs now to be added following the publication of that work. *Democracy* was published, however, in 1880, at a time when he was actively engaged as political reformer. Papers of his written in recent years and collectively entitled, after his death, *The Degradation of the Democratic Dogma*, convincingly prove that the political philosophy of despair which was given dramatic and narrative form in the novel, was a philosophy held to the end of his life. Pioneer in America, as Disraeli was in England, in expressing his thoughts upon public affairs in the form of the novel, he stood side by side with him because of the motive which actuated publication: the desire for Reform. There the resemblance ceases. Disraeli published the trilogy to "hold the mirror up to Nature"; to show the country the foibles and weaknesses of the ruling classes. So did Adams in America. But Disraeli went farther: he presented in his works a developing political philosophy; he wished to impress his own personality upon his readers; he showed himself ready to offer his services. That was the last thought in Adams's mind. He was mainly "primed to awaken the moral conscience of America," to show whither the "spoils system" was leading, to have the book discussed and not the author of it. The mere assumption that *Democracy* was written to exploit Henry Adams is ridiculous. The anonymity of its publication during all these years — a secret kept after the book had gone through sixteen editions — no less than the character of Henry Adams would put such a thought to shame.

This novel is evidence that a man possessed by a message may find a vehicle for his ideas sufficiently satisfactory and engrossing to his readers, in spite of the want in him of a literary education. The urge of what *must* be said appears to help the author to seize intuitively upon the right things, where the professionally-trained novelist must toil methodically, and in accordance with "the rules of the game." Disraeli was an illustration of this no less than Adams. But the remarkable fact is that Henry Adams succeeded in his single work, where Disraeli failed in some of his: namely, in constructing a narrative with a distinct 'purpose,' one that is a bold, strong argument, and an arraignment of the "spoils system," but which is at the same time an admirable work of art. So deftly is the political propaganda, the reform purpose of the novel, handled, that the practical issues at no time overshadow what is imaginative in it. The American political historian avoids the pitfalls which beset the English parliamentarian: he never delays the narrative in order to insert opinions about American political history (of which he had as many as Disraeli had about England); he never neglects his characters in order to discuss theories; he never pauses to dogmatize and instruct, but moves forward from incident to incident, steadily, easily, skilfully, holding all the while the reader's interest in the actual story until he has brought him to the last page. Disraeli, it should be said in all fairness, employed by comparison a much larger canvas. What he left upon that canvas has since given him an historical importance. Realizing the massiveness of his characters, and the complexity of his object, he thought to bring some relief to the onlooker by setting forth his backgrounds in high color, luxuriant decoration, vivid and sharp contrasts in light and shadow. Henry Adams had a lesser object in view and he achieved it with greater skill. When you have finished reading *Democracy* the effect is precisely the same as when you finish reading any other fascinat-

ing novel. You will have been caught by the story the author
has told, and carried along by the gracefulness of the style,
the lightning flashes of plot and counterplot so carefully pro-
portioned. And when you reflect upon your reading, two impressions equally vivid will remain: first, anger and rage at
the political intrigue in public life and disgust with the commonness of mind and tone and the want of dignity and elevation that mark the conduct of public affairs; secondly, the
glow, the thrill that is the after-effect of the characters. What
a charming young girl — you will say — is Sybil! What
dignity and power in the heroine, Mrs. Lee! Was there ever,
in a novel, a more perfect disinherited knight of romance, one
more meritorious and noble, than that splendid young South-
erner, Carrington! Where find a more plausible villain than
that clumsy, unscrupulous, overbearing product of "Main
Street," named Silas P. Ratcliffe?

And now for the story.

Mrs. Lightfoot Lee, a young and charming widow, has tried
life in New York, in Boston, and upon the continent; she has
read philosophy in original German and Spencer 'in the original
Spencerian'; she has plunged into philanthropy and saturated
herself with statistics of crime until her mind nearly lost sight
of virtue. But nowhere had she been satisfied; nothing could
keep her from being ill at ease; every activity ended in ennui.
She had been unable to discover any real nourishment for the
higher moral and intellectual life. She still waited to find
something that "grew more than six inches high, that grew to
be a tree and cast a shadow." A woman sincerely attached to
her country, "American to her finger-tips," she hits upon the
Capitol, at Washington. She determines "to watch the tremendous forces of government at work."

Here, she hopes, she will be able "to see with her own eyes the
action of the primary forces; to touch with her own hand the massive machinery of society; to measure with her own mind the capac-

ity of the motive power. She was bent upon getting to the heart of the great American mystery of democracy and government."

So, with her young sister Sybil Ross — gay, shallow, straight-forward, warm-hearted, and sternly practical — she pitches her wandering tents in Lafayette Square, converts the 'curious barbarism' of their interior into homelikeness and beauty, and awaits instruction and amusement. While Sybil, devoted to millinery and to Mr. Worth's gowns, practices ritualism on Sundays and flits and flirts on week-days, Madeleine, the elder, religiously attends Senate debates, reads American history, politics, and the Congressional Record, and soon succeeds in making her home the centre "for the brightest and the most distinguished in Washington." This she does with the help of a distant connection, John Carrington, a Virginian aged forty, whose mother and sisters remained on the ruins of the family estate after the Civil War while he struggled man-fully, in the practice of law in Washington, to replenish the family fortunes. Thus does Madeleine's apprenticeship in politics begin.

An analysis of the *dramatis personae* among these "brightest and most distinguished" — both those within and those with-out the intimate circle — will reveal the novelist's choice of such types as may, together, give the reader a fairly comprehensive picture of the political-social life of the Capitol, and which will at the same time advance our knowledge of the plot. First, and most important because the interest of the story centres around him, is Senator Ratcliffe, — the Honorable Silas P., otherwise known as "the Prairie Giant of Paeonia" or the favorite son of Illinois, a distinguished politician and one of 'the ornaments' of Congress, the head of a great party who had once been very near the Presidency and who still aspired to it. Madeleine's interest in government soon takes concrete shape in this man, whose language and imagery of speech remind her of Daniel Webster.

"To her eyes he was the high priest of American politics: he was charged with the meaning of the mysteries, the clue of political hieroglyphics. Through him she hopes to sound the depths of statesmanship, and to bring up from its oozy bed that pearl of which she was in search, — the mysterious gem which must lie hidden somewhere in politics. She wanted to understand this man, — to turn him inside out, — to experiment upon him, and use him as young physiologists use frogs and kittens. If there was good or bad in him, she meant to find its meaning,"

Meeting Silas P. at a dinner-party, Madeleine amused herself by angling for this large and powerful fish, and by spinning before his eyes the glittering lure of female flattery. She lands him. Having done so, she soon finds him "decidedly a man to be reckoned with." The Prairie Giant is clever, and though unused to fair society, soon becomes aware that with Mrs. Lee for his wife he might command social successes beyond the dreams of his old ambitions. Besides, he soon falls very much in love with her.

"What equality was there between these two combatants? What hope for him? What risk for her? And yet Madeleine Lee had fully her match in Mr. Silas P. Ratcliffe."

The position of the angler and "the catch" is in danger of being reversed.

Baron Jacobi, Bulgarian Minister, gay, witty, and cynical, who

"despised and loathed an American Senator as the type which to his bleared European eyes, combined the utmost pragmatical self-assurance and overbearing temper with the narrowest education and the meanest personal experience,"

has a special dislike for Ratcliffe, and never misses a chance to bait him and to show off his ignorance before Madeleine. This is one of the most diverting members of Washington society seen frequently at the home of the two sisters. With him is his friend Popoff, "an intelligent and vivacious Russian."

Mr. French, member of Congress from Connecticut, is a type of educated New Englander who is a reformer in politics, wishing "to purify the public tone," and devoted to the cause of Civil Service Reform. Inasmuch as his measures have not the sympathy of such authoritative persons as Ratcliffe, he has as little chance of converting his bill into law as of making a dent with his fist upon a stone wall. From Massachusetts comes Mr. Nathan Gore, poet, diplomatist, and historian, who had made himself famous by his account of Spain in America, and who hoped that the new administration would return him to his ambassadorship at Madrid, a post he had honored during a preceding administration. He was destined to be disappointed this time. An Indiana friend of the President's, who had wanted the Postmastership at Indianapolis — so Gore eventually tells Madeleine — had to be bought off with the exorbitant price of the Spanish mission because it suited the politicians to give the Indianapolis post office to another. The British minister, Lord Skye, one of the most popular men in Washington," has with him an innocent Irish peer, Lord Dunbeg, who becomes the object of solicitude of a charming young flirt and rattle named Virginia Dare — the lady who furnishes so much humor to the novel while showing the Irishman "the phases of American society," and then marries the peer and his peat-bogs. Another lady, no less entertaining, is Mrs. Baker, an exceedingly clever woman-lobbyist who upon occasion enlightens Madeleine and astonishes her with an account of how certain important measures, in which great 'interests' are concerned, are often made into laws. The Schneidekoupon family stand in a class by themselves. The sister Julia cannot understand what there is so hilariously funny in the manners of Cabinet ministers' wives, when she is out making calls with Sybil. Being a 'native' she cannot appreciate what, to the refined New York woman of fashion, is crudity and rusticity. Her brother is a wealthy amateur politician, of a proud Pennsylvania family, an editor of *The Protective Review*,

"who made periodical visits to Washington, where he closeted himself with committee men and gave expensive dinners to members of Congress."

Around this general group, who play a sort of chorus to the principal characters, there are other senators, Cabinet members, foreign visitors who are members of the nobility or of royalty, and young secretaries of foreign delegations, — all of them designed to complete the picture of political life in action.

One principal personage, too important to confuse among the others, remains to be described. This is the President-elect. Let Adams set forth his incomparable portrait.

"The new President was, almost as much as Abraham Lincoln or Franklin Pierce, an unknown quantity in political mathematics. In the national convention of the party nine months before, after some dozens of fruitless ballots, in which Ratcliffe wanted but three votes of a majority, his opponents had done what he now was doing. They had laid aside their principles, and set up for their candidate a plain Indiana farmer, whose political experience was limited to stump-speaking in his native state, and one term as Governor. They had pitched upon him not because they thought him competent, but because they hoped by doing so to detach Indiana from Ratcliffe's following; and they were so successful that within fifteen minutes Ratcliffe's friends were routed, and the Presidency had fallen upon this new political Buddha.

"He had begun his career as a stone-cutter in a quarry, and was not unreasonably proud of the fact. During the campaign this incident had, of course, filled a large space in the public mind, or more exactly in the public eye. The 'Stone-cutter of the Wabash,' he was sometimes called; at others, the 'Hoosier Quarryman'; but his favorite appellation was 'Old Granite,' although this last enduring name, owing to an unfortunate similarity of sound, was seized upon by his opponents, and distorted into 'Old Granny.' He had been painted on many thousand yards of cotton sheeting, either with a terrific sledge-hammer smashing the skulls (which figured as paving-stones) of his political opponents, or splitting by gigantic blows a huge rock, typical of the opposing party. His opponents in their turn had paraded illuminations representing the quarryman, in the garb of a state-prison convict, breaking the heads of Ratcliffe and other well-known political leaders with a very feeble hammer; or as 'Old Granny,' in pauper's rags, hopelessly repairing, with the same heads, the impossible roads, which typified the ill-conditioned and miry ways of his party. But these violations of decency and good sense were universally reproved by the virtuous; and it was remarked with satisfaction that the purest and most cultivated newspaper editors on his side, without excepting those of Boston itself, agreed with one voice that the Stone-cutter was a noble type of man, — perhaps the very noblest that had appeared to adorn this country since the incomparable Washington. That he was honest, all admitted — that is to say, all who voted for him. This is a general characteristic of all new presidents. He himself took great pride in his home-spun honesty, which is a quality peculiar to Nature's nobleman. . . . His cardinal principle was hostility to Ratcliffe, yet he was not vindictive. He came to Washington determined to be the Father of his country; to gain a proud immortality — and a re-election."

The concern of Madeleine in the struggle between this confused politician and the wily, audacious, and unmoral Ratcliffe, offers a fascinating example of how a writer, coating with romance his thesis on the degradation of office of the Chief Executive when he is manipulating schemes with politicians, can present many pages upon the serious faults of American democracy, and preach "reform," without seeming to do so. With the true instinct of an artist, combined with intimate knowledge of his government, Henry Adams seizes upon the most dramatic and at the same time most strategic moment in American political life — when an old administration is going out and the new is coming in, — and all the intrigues, the secret bargainings, and the dishonest compromises that may then occur behind closed doors, he reveals in a masterly fashion.

Once in Washington, the new President is forced, against
every inclination, to make terms with the powerful head of
the insurgent party, in order that he may have the promise
of some peace during his administration. Ratcliffe thus becomes the centre of a series of skilful intrigues and political
maneuvers whereby he forces the leader to be the one led
and he obtains for himself a strategic position upon the new
Cabinet; thus, master of the situation, he gets everything he
desires, not the least of which are countless favors for his hordes
of place-hunters and dependents.   While this is going on
Madeleine is placed in a dangerous position. Ratcliffe has
now become a professed suitor, is frequently at her home,
looks upon her as an "ideal of purity," and makes it seem
to her that in his conduct as a statesman, and in his contest
with the President, he needs "the help of every pure mind."
He succeeds in making himself appear to her the victim of
certain governmental conditions over which he has no control:
a disinterested statesman striving with might and main to
steer a straight and honorable course. The largeness of outline
which he has now assumed in her eyes is nothing lessened by
his confessions of somewhat minute sins of expediency and
opportunism. These make him appear all the more honest.
So, unconsciously, she becomes 'the victim of a kind of partnership; she assumes the weight of interested responsibility.'
Here, she thinks, is "the victim of a corrupt system, and (she)
is not at all sure that it is not her duty to help him reform it."

Thus blindly does she involve herself in a situation which,
however it terminates, must end unhappily for her. No one
sees this more clearly than Carrington. He, too, is now madly
in love with her, a love made all the more intense by his fear
that she will throw herself away on Ratcliffe. And in Washington no man knew Ratcliffe better than Carrington. Through
information which had been in his possession for some time,
he saw in the Senator a man whose moral senses were literally

atrophied; one in whom every question of principle resolved itself solely into a question of power. Here was one immersed constantly in 'bargain and intrigue'; who, even when he sought Madeleine's opinion, did so only on "points of political casuistry." Every effort of Carrington to make Ratcliffe betray himself to her proved fruitless; the ingenious politician was forearmed by his grasp of the fact that Carrington *knew* him and understood the game he was playing. In desperation Carrington is forced to enlist the help of Sybil — who, by the way, detested the Senator no less than Carrington did, and who is likewise fearful of the consequences of that attachment upon her sister. They plot together to save the woman who has professed that she "has lost the path of duty," and who believes that her course points now to sacrifice herself to the political purity of the country, to become the Iphigenia of Democracy, and offer herself on the altar of Silas P's moral nature.

Ratcliffe, aware now that his greatest obstacle is Carrington, sets his forces at work, and succeeds ultimately in ridding himself — as he believes — of that difficulty. A flattering appointment is made to Carrington to go to Mexico, and this he is obliged to accept as much out of pressing family considerations as from the fear that if he did not he would appear vindictive to Madeleine — especially since he is unable to prove, what he suspects — that the appointment had come through Ratcliffe's influence. His departure, however, does not promise that the great man was to have the free field that he had bargained for: he was ignorant of the fact that the other, before leaving Washington, had entrusted into the hands of Sybil a letter addressed to Madeleine, which the younger sister was to use only if affairs grew so desperate that in no other way could Madeleine be dissuaded from accepting Ratcliffe's offer of marriage.

With Carrington out of the way, Ratcliffe moves swiftly to

his goal. He seizes upon the occasion offered at a ball given by the British ambassador, to make a formal proposal. She is about to accept him when Sybil unexpectedly breaks in upon them. Grasping the situation at a glance, and determined to have Madeleine read the letter in her possession before she takes the irrevocable step, she adopts an heroic measure. She feigns sudden illness. Friends rush to her assistance and Madeleine orders the carriage home. Chagrined and annoyed at the upset of his plan, Ratcliffe is solaced with the thought that he will receive an affirmative answer from Madeleine when he calls upon her the following day. In the meanwhile Sybil has a chance to accomplish her purpose. Madeleine reads the letter she presses upon her. She learns — what is to her an astounding fact — that the man whom she was about to accept, and who she assumed was a man of integrity, had some time before taken a bribe of 100,000 dollars to withdraw, as Chairman of a committee, his opposition in the Senate to a certain steam-boat concession. The money had been paid into his hands by a person well known to Carrington; upon the death of this intermediary Carrington came into possession of all his papers, and there found an account of the whole transaction. The nature of this information, together with the extraordinary manner in which Ratcliffe attempts to defend his act — when she confronts him with the letter on the following day — convinces her that she had been dealing, all along, with "a moral lunatic"; a man who "talked about virtue and vice as one who is color-blind talks about red and green." In that single moment the full meaning of her whole political experience in Washington came upon her in one inspired flash (like a picture-puzzle of a hundred and one varied pieces that suddenly assemble themselves, each in its proper place), and to that design the character of Ratcliffe, as now revealed, was the key. And thus this woman who had come to get at the heart of the great American mystery of government discovers, as if by revelation, that the business of democratic government "was nothing more than government of any other kind." She had lived, so to speak, in a masquerade, and that as for Ratcliffe, "she had been in love with a shadow raised by her own vanity."

The close of the story presents a powerful and dramatic scene. The skilful manner in which Adams draws a cultured woman at bay, attempting to free herself from an intolerable situation; the analysis of Ratcliffe's character in its process of disintegration — first, the self-possessed man defending his act, then the use of effrontery, then the passionate personal appeal which closes with an attempt to make a bargain, and finally the harsh violence of the brute: these have never been excelled in modern fiction. Madeleine's last words to him read like the sentence of the American conscience on the corrupt political world exposed in the novel. When the reader closes the book he feels like saying with Madeleine as she completes her preparation for a flight to the desert of Egypt: "Democracy has shaken my nerves to pieces. Oh, what rest it will be to live in the Great Pyramid and look out forever at the polar star!"

Having completed the story, we may now turn to the author's political philosophy — so to speak — which underlies the work.

Democracy, as Henry Adams presented it, is a panorama of a political "Main Street" at the national capitol. It pictures, as no American novel that has ever been written, the commonness of mind, the deadness of tone, and the total insensibility to the nobler aspects and finer responsibilities of national life which he found so characteristic of the body politic, and which have so often struck intelligent European critics. It shows how much the public business is managed only by average men, who are inspired so little by any sense of the magnitude of the interests entrusted to them. In the closing pages of his autobiography, when Adams looked back in reminiscence upon his

active life at the Capitol, he re-enforces there what he had
exposed earlier in the novel. "Few centres of great energy,"
he reflects, "lived in illusion more complete or archaic than
Washington with its simple-minded standards of field and
farm, its Southern and Western habits of life and manners, and
its assumptions of ethics and history. . . ."

In that panorama, certain types peculiar to Washington,
and certain indigenous conditions are especially emphasized.
What some of these are have already been indicated. There is
no doubt that in the portrayal of a few of them the novelist
exaggerated, and even employed caricature. An outstanding
instance of this is the portrait of the "Hoosier" President,
and of his household. But who shall say that there is not to-
day a compelling amount of truth back even of these descriptions? Take the account of a White House reception.

"One evening Mrs. Lee went to the President's first evening
reception. As Sybil flatly refused to face the crowd, and Carrington mildly said that he feared he was not sufficiently reconstructed
to appear at home in that august presence, Mrs. Lee accepted
Mr. French for an escort, and walked across the Square with him
to join the throng that was pouring into the doors of the White
House. They took their places in the line of citizens and were
at last able to enter the reception room. There Madeleine found
herself before two seemingly mechanical figures, which might be
wood or wax, for any sign of life they showed. These two figures
were the President and his wife; they stood stiff and awkward
by the door, both their faces stripped of every sign of intelligence,
while the right hands of both extended themselves to the column
of visitors with the mechanical action of toy dolls. Mrs. Lee for
a moment began to laugh, but the laugh died on her lips. To the
President and his wife this was clearly no laughing matter. There
they stood, automata, representatives of the society which streamed
past them. Madeleine seized Mr. French by the arm.

"'Take me somewhere at once,' said she, 'where I can look at
it. Here! in the corner!' . . . What a strange and solemn spectacle
it was, and how the deadly fascination of it burned the image in
upon her mind! What a horrid warning to ambition! And in all

that crowd there was no one besides herself who felt the mockery of this exhibition.   To all the others this task was a regular part of the President's duty, and there was nothing ridiculous about it. They thought it a democratic institution, this droll aping of monarchical forms."

With this spectacle Madeleine soon had opportunity to compare another — that of a grand ball, given in honor of a visiting duke and duchess, in the rooms of the British legation. This, though no less happy an occasion for her than the other, was eminently successful for a large number of her fellow-citizens because, as Adams remarks, all republicans who have a large income derived from business feel a great respect for English royalty.

The author's opinion of the personnel of the United States Senate is obviously enough focussed in the character of Ratcliffe.   There is no doubt that Adams has endowed this man with the least admirable traits of some American public personages.   Adams certainly goes too far in making one who has confessed to permitting the stuffing of ballot boxes while he was Governor of his state because he believed it was for the good of his party, and who had been guilty of accepting a bribe as Chairman of a Senate committee, a man who might be a probable candidate for the Presidency.   The fact remains, however, that in certain essentials Ratcliffe is no unique figure.   His Websterian pompousness and dignity, his calm self-assurance, his willingness to substitute for moral principle the principle of expediency and the measure of power, the shrewdness and the commercial vigor of him which take the place of culture and refinement of thought, — these are characteristics unhappily too true to-day of many men in the Senate body. What Adams is trying to say here, of the constituency of the upper House and of the methods of the Federal government, as well as what he had said of the "Hoosier Quarryman" as President, is but a reflection of his thought from his articles on

Civil Service Reform, written when he was an editor of *The North American Review*. He would show that the great men of America do not enter politics as often as they should, because the people of the country do not encourage them to do so. Public Opinion, he then declared, must be stirred up, and educated, if America is to have a government that is not apathetic and clumsy and irresponsible. "If the President is weak it is merely because," he adds, "public opinion is silent and support is not to be found."

One of the ablest political historians corroborated long ago in his *Congressional Government* these general sentiments of Henry Adams. Speaking of the quality of United States senators, Woodrow Wilson, before he became president, said:

> "The Senate is just what the mode of its election and the conditions of public life in this country make it. Its members are chosen from the ranks of active politicians, in accordance with a law of natural selection to which the State legislatures are commonly obedient; and it is probable it contains, consequently, the best men that our system calls into politics. If these best men are not good, it is because our system of government fails to attract better men by its prizes, not because the country affords or could afford no finer material. The Senate is in fact, of course, nothing more than a part, though a considerable part, of the public service; and if the general conditions of that service be such as to starve statesmen and foster demagogues, the Senate will be full of the latter kind, simply because there are no others available."

Since this paragraph was written it may be doubted whether anything which has occurred in America, including the passage of the Seventeenth Amendment which assures the election of senators by the people, has materially altered the force of it, or has changed materially the truth in Henry Adams's attitude toward that body as set forth in the political novel.

Unquestionably, the exquisite part of the book is to be found in the faith which Adams has in the cultivated American woman. He makes her the single idealist in the novel, the coadjutor in the proposed work of political reform, a marvel of cleverness, of wit, and charm, and the outstanding figure of distinction. Madeleine is the most high-minded person in the social and political society of Washington. In so portraying her, Adams was not, of course, proposing to hold a brief for women's rights nor was he intent upon showing the probable place of women in some political society of the future. Rather was he interested in expressing his unqualified admiration for the sex, his tribute to the charm and the beauty of the cultivated feminine mind, his pleasure in her personal freedom. The representation of Madeleine as the symbol of an ideal is but another way of expressing in the novel what Adams said later in his autobiography of the sex in general. "In after life," he there reflects, speaking of himself in the third person, "he made a general law of experience — no woman had ever driven him wrong; no man had ever driven him right." The debt he thus pays to Woman, and his expressed admiration for her good influence, remind one curiously of the same feelings held by another novelist; they offer, indeed, a further comparison between Henry Adams and Benjamin Disraeli. It is interesting to note that of all the political novelists of both England and America, the only two who throughout their lives were active participants in public affairs, were the two also who elevated the feminine ideal to a place almost of sublimity.

Of Madeleine, the woman, and her part in the book, there are two lessons of political significance to be drawn. One is that her conclusions about public life as she has seen it in Washington, which express after all the grievance of a high-minded American, is a general grievance. In the very last sentence of the novel, which is a post-script to a letter written by Sybil recounting to Carrington all that had happened since his departure, Madeleine adds: "The bitterest part of all this horrid story is that nine out of ten of our countrymen would say I had made a mistake!" There, after all, is the heart of the problem — as Adams would suggest to us. It is not the mere personal disappointment of Madeleine that is important: what is important is her general grievance against the whole democratic society, rather than the representative portion of it in Washington. If she failed to find evidences of greatness at the Capitol, if no one of the law-makers she met "grew more than six inches high, grew to be a tree and cast a shadow," it was because there were little or no big-minded statesmen in other parts of the country; it was because there was not sufficient desire, among the American people generally, to have only great men sent to the Capitol. A spring cannot rise higher than its source. Yet Madeleine was made unhappy because she believed that America offered an example unlike that of the older, the European countries; but she learned, after bitter experience, that America had many of the failings of other governments and a sufficient number of its own as well.

The other lesson which Adams indirectly indicates is the unfortunate separation in America of the educated or cultured classes from the business of government. These stand aloof and watch either contemptuously or mournfully persons intellectually incompetent and spiritually dispossessed, floundering about in the management of public office. This state of affairs, the author clearly enough shows, is not due to the fact that the cultivated and fastidious minds are unwilling to engage in their proper share of governing, but rather that 'the masses do not look to them for guidance.' If these more fortunate persons 'wish for office, they must struggle for it, avoiding the least appearance of presuming on their social position,' or what may seem to them nobler powers, but must be willing to go through what is sometimes the mud of a campaign and an election, precisely as the others do. The result

is that in America the people who have had the advantages of
education and training, little encouraged to add the benefits
of their superior wisdom to the conduct of public affairs, withdraw, and permit those who will, struggle for what are, after
all, doubtful honors.   The consequence is that the national
capitol has a tone merely of commonness and of mediocrity.
Washington is just "Main Street" upon a national scale.

Yet in spite of all this, there is no cause for despair.   A person
familiar with the author's high purpose, with the life of this
distinguished citizen which was devoted to 'reform,' must
recognize quickly enough that if the political novelist has
exaggerated some facts, or over-emphasized others, he has done
so in order to make certain that he has driven an essential
truth home.   *Democracy* is, of course, one-sided.   There have
been Presidents who have cast shadows like trees; we have
had, and we have to-day, Senators who fall quite within the
compass of Adams's heritage, both of blood and of culture.
The government is not perfect, we know.   But as idealists we
must, like Adams, see the tares in order that we may save the
wheat.   And like Adams, too, we must have a manly courage
in the face of misfortunes, and an undying belief in the future
of America.   When has there ever been phrased so noble, so
perfect, an 'American Creed' as that spoken by Henry Adams
through a minor character of the novel:

"I believe in Democracy. I accept it. I will faithfully serve
and defend it. I grant it is an experiment, but it is the only
direction society can take that is worth taking; the only conception of its duty large enough to satisfy its instincts; the only
result that is worth an effort or a risk. Let us be true to our
time! If our age is to be beaten, let us die in the ranks. If it is
to be victorious, let us be first to lead the column!"

Chapter XIII

WINSTON CHURCHILL AND THE NOVEL OF POLITICAL REFORM

Of all the writers who have followed Henry Adams none of importance has, by a strange perversity, looked again to the national capitol, which has grown with time so rich and infinitely various of character and situation, for his political material. It seems strange that reflective novelists generally have, thus far, neglected this great 'source.' Instead, the works which have followed have dealt with sectional aspects, factional arguments and theories, restricting themselves as most of American literature does, by its local color, its setting in mountain, plain, plantation, or New England farmhouse, by its theses concerning some social or industrial order, its exploitation of the Four Million or the Four Hundred. Not given a comprehensive view of the complex political landscape, we see instead restricted portions of it, presented now here now there either like premonitions in happy moments, just before the drift of opinion begins to set in and the waves are about to inundate some slime and blackness of the sea-shore; or else we have sketches which show the conditions at flood-tide, commonplace and familiar to the native, but interesting nevertheless because of their dramatic focus and coloring. When senatorial bribery and civil service corruption were about to stir the country, the political novelist appeared, and gave the agitation point and direction. The self-made politician, risen in the West, became a force in legislation: Hamlin Garland recounted his career in *A Spoil of Office*. Was it the political status of the South during the Reconstruction period that stirred thinking men, and had the vote of the freedman raised a grave public issue?

A. W. Tourgée defined them in *Bricks without Straw*, and *A Fool's Errand*. The cry of the old economic order against the increasing demands of labor brought forward John Hay's *The Breadwinners*, while agitation favoring Communism gave us Edward Bellamy's *Looking Backward* and laid down the principles and platform of the Nationalist Party of the eighties. The appearance of the professional reformer in city politics bore fruit in Brand Whitlock's *The 13th Ward*. Even the attempt of the woman of fashion to stir up the waters of legislation were recorded. Brand Whitlock shows a trivial instance of it in *Her Infinite Variety*. Gertrude Atherton makes a more imposing attempt, and promises at the start to present a vast conflict of political forces and issues; but she immediately reduces her political machinery to the lowest possible terms, and makes her work a story of emotion, of the temperament of Betty Madison and its influence upon the career of a married senator and his rivals. This is her *Senator North*. It passed through twenty-two editions in three years, showing how eagerly her public turned to what was a unique society novel.

After Henry Adams, the most important writer is Winston Churchill, and the two stand in relationship almost as master and disciple. Mr. Churchill, like the other novelists, has been obliged to deal with particular problems, to narrow his stage in order that he might give more sharpness of outline and concreteness of design to that in which he was interested. But he is like Henry Adams in his essential Americanism, and he carries on the former's work by pointing to the causes of the conditions of which Adams had shown the national effects. The two political novels of Winston Churchill reflect a distinctly national impulse, a national mood. There is an epic quality in his romanticism, a moral earnestness in him, a kind of imagination which shows "an instinctive feeling for the underlying and definitive forces of the country." Though

both his plots are laid in New England, and deal with New
England characters, the reader is forced to the conviction,
after finishing the stories, that their author had developed
them while envisioning the outline of a continent — its movement and expansion, the robustness and the self-confidence of
the American people, their stirring optimism, a memory of an
heroic Past. The historical imagination with which we deal
here had felt the march of the American mind, and had recorded it admirably for the climactic periods of their history.
Thus came *Richard Carvel* and *The Crisis*. Like these two,
and like some of Mr. Churchill's more recent works, his political novels are definitely American stories.

Coniston and *Mr. Crewe's Career* are, as one critic has said of
them, cabinet studies rather than pictures for the gallery;
they are "local, rather than continental, interpretations of the
American spirit." What Hamilton Wright Mabie says of one
of these applies equally well to both. "By localizing his story
Mr. Churchill has gained in concentration, sharpness of outline, convincing clearness of characterization. Without changing his style he has given it a shorter focus, and by narrowing
the field of vision brought his figures more distinctly before the
eye." The stage here no longer dwarfs the actors, and we get,
as a result, sharper individualization and detailed definition of
personality. And though we watch an analysis of a section of
the country, we perceive that it is done to enforce a national
meaning. In both these works we see Mr. Churchill, like
Henry Adams, "primed to awaken the moral conscience of
America"; like him, too, he calls upon us to return to the
principles and practices of the forefathers; like him he wishes
to make us conscious of a great American heritage so that
Americans may cease drifting away from it.

If, in political philosophy, Churchill allies himself with this
thinker of an earlier generation, his zeal as a reformer, and
his energy and vigor in declaiming against specific evils and

persons, link him with a more strenuous generation, and one more virile — the generation of Theodore Roosevelt. Here he is the practical man crying out against definite abuses, and showing the way to correct them. He is 'the younger generation' calling others of his kind to leadership, — calling to the sons of the old native stock. He moves straight to New England in the stories because there is the very soil of the Pilgrim Fathers; and he holds their descendants to strict accountability for the mess of pottage for which they have exchanged their birthright. The world must see, he seems to say, how the native stock of America, by its apathy, its ignorance, its cowardice, its sterility of conscience, is tearing down the fabric which the forefathers had so painfully woven, and had shed so much blood to preserve. Both novels have this common purpose: to protest in the American democracy against the use of *arbitrary power*. *Coniston* is a searching study of the rise of the Boss-system in American politics. *Mr. Crewe's Career* is an exposition of the power over legislation held by corporation interests. The concrete example chosen for portrayal is the domination of government by 'the railroad interest.'

The Boss in *Coniston* is of Puritan stock, in control of his State, and not like the city boss, of foreign origin and parentage "grown up in an atmosphere of oaths and cocktails, with ideas of honour and purity as strange to him as ideas about the nature of currency and the incidence of taxation." This man does not marshal his forces by using the votes of the foreign-born, by stuffing ballot-boxes, holding his ward or wards in awe of his influence with 'the men higher up,' and surrounding himself with hundreds of trusty henchmen and retainers. Jethro Bass is carved out of the granite of New Hampshire. He is a crudely masterful figure, uneducated but having an abundance of native Yankee shrewdness, and with an uncanny knowledge of men. He is characterized by New England rusticity and simplicity, and by a humor both original and picturesque. This is the native son of New England, "the child of democratic traditions."

"The Era of the first six Presidents," says Churchill at the beginning of his novel, "had closed, and a new Era had begun. I am speaking of political Eras. Certain gentlemen, with a pious belief in democracy, but with a firmer determination to get on top, arose, — and got on top. So many of these gentlemen arose in the different states, and they were so clever, and they found so many chinks in the Constitution to crawl through and steal the people's chestnuts, that the Era may be called the Boss-Era." Jethro Bass is an exponent of Jacksonian politics, of "the might makes right" theory. He is a kind of pioneer in professional politics as his ancestors were pioneers in government and in statesmanship. He, however, debases the ideal. By acquiring mortgages quietly among his neighbors, multiplying these as time and added wealth permitted; by doing favors for some men so that they become his debtors, and by frightening others into submission; by the exercise of an irresistible quality of natural sentiment which makes friends of some of his enemies, — by these methods and others he slowly builds up a body of retainers and lieutenants of the native stock around him, a machine of power and influence which controls important legislation at the state capital, and which is even able to exert an influence with the President in Washington. He holds eventually in submission powerful 'combinations' rising in his own state, which are led by college trained men, and by men of 'aristocratic traditions.' These are obliged to make terms with him before they can have favorable laws passed for themselves, before they can be permitted to exploit their own interests. Jethro is, therefore, all the more a real figure because he is not a plutocrat, a monster, but a man of natural instincts, normal passions, and with a few warm but determined affections. He is not a man who wishes to gratify selfish aims for wealth nor is he a man who desires fame. He wants power, power over persons and things, and in order to gain his end he employs the weapon that he knows how best to use, that of intrigue. He is aware that the time is coming when the 'interests,' the corporations, will try to exterminate him, as they would wish to destroy, in his own time, the rights of the people; he is determined not to permit the first, and to remain the dictator of the other in his own state.

Coniston is the history of a system symbolized in Jethro Bass, — its unscrupulous methods, its insidious power, the character of its retainers, friends, and enemies. It is the best chronicle we have, in American literature, of the old-time state boss, and is full of suggestion of the methods of the newer, the more sophisticated political boss, whose wealth and corporate control dominates government sometimes in our own day. As a contribution to the permanent figures of American literature, its leading character takes his place among the best and the most significant creations of American writers.

Passing from the power of the individual Boss to power in the hands of a group of men, a corporation with zealous and loyal retainers, a complete Feudal system, Mr. Churchill gives us his second novel, *Mr. Crewe's Career*. This very naturally follows the earlier work, and may be called a supplement to it. Here are registered the days of American history when the 'interests,' particularly the railroad interests, acquired immense power in the districts they traversed, and exercised an extraordinary dominance in the halls of legislation. It is a picture of how the great companies secretly held in their hands, not necessarily through mortgages, but by strategy and manipulation, the comfort of individuals and the freedom of communities. Under their able but unscrupulous chiefs they exerted immense influence upon legislation by gifts of free passes to members of the legislature, to young lawyers of the state just rising in power who promised to become defenders of clients against them, and by bestowing favors upon significant individuals, and rebates to favored shippers. It is a picture of how the Railroad captured individual legislators, made the governor, and dictated the personnel of committees before whom bills might appear that were either favorable or unfavorable to the corporation. It represents their power over the Press, and over the men who had ambitions to rise in public life.

It is a book which sounds the coming duel between the 'vested interests' on one side, and the people on the other. It shows the autocratic and irresponsible power exerted by the railroads, and consequently their growing unpopularity. We watch their secret control and manipulation of men, and their private fights and intrigues against one another. With governors to watch their interests and to initiate favorable legislation, with chairmen of committees to clear the paths for them, and trusty bands of adroit lawyers and agents to defend them in the public courts, they had only to control the state nominating conventions in order that "the right men" got in everywhere. Clashes between great corporations and an awakened people, between one railroad and another, were more common in the western states than they were in New England. But Mr. Churchill's panorama of the play of forces in an eastern state presents a typical picture. It is a reflection of general conditions that once existed throughout the country. "After the Boss," — so he concludes his opening paragraph of the earlier novel, — "came along certain Things without souls, but of many minds, and found more chinks in the Constitution: bigger chinks, for the Things were bigger, and they stole more chestnuts."

The book is the work of a reformer who had tested his powers, and it is dedicated to men in every state of the Union who are engaged in the struggle for purer politics. Far more profound than the earlier novel, because Mr. Churchill registers in this the sum total of his own political experiences and his reflections upon them, *Mr. Crewe's Career* presents in striking fashion the completely autocratic power of the monopoly in American life, and to what degree its influences had gone: here it practically disfranchises the voters of a state. This it is that marks an era of fraud, of self-deception, of conditions that violated every sacred principle of free government which the forefathers had shed blood to obtain. Lobbying, graft, and place-hunting; threats, cajoleries, and the crushing out of competition; each takes its toll in this vast dark scheme. Who can forget the exciting battle in the arena of the Republican state convention, with men hatless and coatless among the delegates, with candidates in suspense, torture, and confusion, playing *their* game of political strategy, while on the second floor above them a bourse is being openly conducted to run up the price of votes, and close by, at the Pelican House, a little band of seasoned and brilliant henchmen which include a United States Senator — representatives of The System — manipulate the real forces and determine the final strategy which ends in the greatest victory of all for the Corporation! The Convention had opened with these planks laid down first in the platform: "The Republican Party (chosen children of Israel — adds Churchill) must be kept free from the dominance of corporations. Some better method of choosing delegates which will more truly reflect the will of the people." After the dust had flown, and the tumult and the shouting was over, "offices were secure once more, the Feudal system intact, and the rebels (had been) justly punished."

Let us focus our attention upon a few typical figures in the drama, and weigh their significance. The first is a country member, himself fighting the corporation, and with as little power against it as a gnat might have against a lion. One speech tells his story.

"'Well,' said Mr. Redbrook, 'it just makes me tremble as an American citizen. The railrud sends them slick cusses down here to sit in the front seats who know all this here parliamentary law and the tricks of the trade, and every time any of us gets up to speak our honest minds, they have ruled us out of order or get the thing laid on the table until some Friday morning when there ain't nobody here, and send it along up to the Senate.   They made that fat feller, Doby, Speaker, and he's stuffed all the important committees so that you can't get an honest measure considered.   You can talk to the committees all you've a mind to, and they'll just listen and never do anything.   There's five hundred in the House, and it ain't any more of a Legislature than a camp-meetin' is.   What do you suppose they done last Friday morning, when there wahn't but twenty men at the session?   We had an anti-pass law, and all these fellers were breakin' it.   It forbid anybody riding on a pass except railroad presidents, directors, express messengers, and persons in misfortune, and they stuck in these words, *and others to whom passes have been granted by the proper officers*.   Ain't that a disgrace to the State?   And those twenty senators passed it before we got back on Tuesday.   You can't get a bill through that Legislature unless you go up to the Pelican and get permission of Hilary —'

Here Mr. Redbrook stopped abruptly, and glanced contritely at his companion.

'I didn't mean to get goin' so,' he said, 'but sometimes I wish this American government'd never been started.'"

The twenty Senators are the "Descendants of Horatius": "Twenty picked man, and true they were indeed, but a better name for their body would have been the Life Guard of the Sovereign.   The five hundred far below them might rage and at times revolt, but the twenty in their shining armour stood undaunted above the vulnerable ground and smiled grimly at the mob.   The citadel was safe."

Another figure is the Honorable Hilary Vane, scion of fine old New England stock, product of the best American education, and a brilliant lawyer, but one who has prostituted his brains and broken his health during a lifetime of service devoted to the Corporation.   His history is like stern fibre, binding the texture or darkening the outline, of the entire tapestry, and needs to be traced from one end to the other in order to be properly valued.

There is no doubt that in the manifold adventures which mark the career of that gentleman and amateur in politics, Mr. Humphrey Crewe, we have a vivid account of some of the political experiences of Mr. Winston Churchill himself. A representative in the New Hampshire legislature from Cornish, about the time these two novels were written, he learned at first hand, in his own state, something of the methods of the reigning political machine. It was through his agitation, and by his revelations, that the Lincoln Club was formed in the Republican party of the state — an act which marked the first revolt against the political bosses. Mr. Churchill himself, it will be recalled, appeared upon the stump, and aroused the people by his disclosures. In 1906 he was a candidate for the nomination of governorship in his state, but failed to receive the nomination. However, the work which as reformer he had set out to do, he completely accomplished. Stanley Johnson, in his account of Mr. Churchill's political experiment, which he wrote for *The World's Work* in 1909, concludes with these words: "There can be little doubt that had the choice of the governor been submitted direct to the voters, without the machinery of a nominating convention, whose integrity has been severely criticized, Churchill would have been elected. The old leaders barely saved themselves from disaster, and found themselves thoroughly disorganized and badly out of temper with each other." Mr. Johnson adds that the most striking effect of the novel which embodied Mr. Churchill's experiences, was to make the people of New Hampshire aware of the existence of a statute, passed back in 1889, which had been completely forgotten, but which now forced the Attorney General of the state to proceed against the railroads for violating a statutory obligation for over a score of years.

The conclusion to which one is led who follows the adventures of Humphrey Crewe is, that the gentleman in politics, who takes the attitude of a reformer, and who believes that his wealth, fine breeding, and personal influence can advance him to a position of political independence, power, and control, and that he can thus override or ignore established 'interests,' is sadly mistaken. After spending a fortune, and suffering great personal humiliation and disappointment, he learns that in politics a man cannot play a lone hand and arrive anywhere. This was an axiom before Mr. Crewe appeared upon the scene, and it is no less true of American politics to-day. An idealist, incidentally a millionaire, who uses his money to advance all sorts of reforms which he believes are for the good of the state and the nation, possessed of a certain amount of shrewdness and penetration, he ploughs a way through the crowd of the less ignominious 'five hundred'; but in spite of the most generous use of his means, and the rallying of his friends to his cause, he discovers at the critical moment that he has advanced no farther than most of the insignificant members of the legislature, because word has gone forth from the Interests that "he must not pass!" Outwardly he meets with the most generous and hearty sympathy. The politicians in power listen with patience to his grand speeches, accept his countless bills, compliment him on his unselfish activities, and a few even attend his garden-party. Behind his back they lampoon him, bury his bills in committees, laugh at his seriousness, and block his progress at every step and by every means known to clever men. His mere election to a place among the five hundred in the legislature, came about only after he had joined hands with 'the System': had gone to the town boss, Job Braden, and had 'fixed things' with him. After this humiliating experience the "People's Champion" (so his paid press notices eventually call him), made aware of the status of things, begins to play politics with politics, believing that the end justifies the means. But being an initiate, and having a complete grasp of the intricacies of the game, serve no other purpose for him except to make his defeat all the more intolerable. An intelligent man made a scapegoat by the more adroit, has necessarily a longer fall and receives a harder bump at the end of it than a less sensitive person might receive.

In the son of Hilary Vane we have Mr. Churchill's conception of the kind of Young American needed in political life to-day. Austen Vane comes of the best native stock, — a fact also true of Humphrey Crewe. He has, like the other, great determination and aggressiveness, but he does not have his snobbishness and he refuses to be an amateur. To his mind advance in public life can come by no short cuts, but by a slow and steady growth founded upon a complete knowledge of conditions, a thorough understanding of the people, a willingness to get down to the very roots of the soil and thus win the affection and the confidence of those whom one would serve unselfishly. Through this man Mr. Churchill makes his plea for an awakened electorate, for a more sensitive public conscience, for a realization of the truth in James Russell Lowell's words: "Popular government is not in itself a panacea, is no better than any other form except as the virtue and wisdom of the people make it so." His energy is a comment upon the apathy and the shortsightedness of the upper classes in failing to take the initiative in our public life. By his idealism at the very opposite pole from his father, he proves that the sturdy integrity, the vigorous courage, the unselfish devotion to a great moral principle no matter at what cost, — qualities of the men who signed the Declaration of Independence, and fought for the integrity of the Constitution — are not all dead in our own day, but that they can rise again from the ashes of the older generation and, like the fabled Phoenix, appear the more precious in their newer plumage. Thus Austen Vane is made a Rooseveltian figure, for he has his

energy, and cries out upon his own people with something of
the force of that native reformer. The most dramatic situation in the novel, next to that of the nominating convention,
is the scene of another battle, this time not among a half
thousand delegates buying, selling, and manipulating votes, —
that in which Humphrey Crewe is the central figure; but in a
quiet room, the private study of the President of the Northeastern railroads, when Mr. Flint, head of the monopoly and
the embodiment of all its evils, stands face to face with Austen
Vane, and listens to a courageous indictment of all his rotten
practices. Part of what is said there is worth repeating.

"'It doesn't matter,' said Austen, 'whether the Northeastern
railroads have succeeded this time. . . . The practices by which
you have controlled this state, Mr. Flint, and elected governors
and councillors and state and national senators are doomed.
However necessary these practices may have been from your point
of view, they violated every principle of free government, and
were they to continue the nation to which they belong would
inevitably decay and become the scorn of the world.'"

Flint replies by accusing Austen of being a radical in government, and Austen answers that if the refusal to receive a pass
from a railroad which will bind his liberty of action as an
attorney and a citizen is radicalism, he is a radical. "But
my radicalism goes back behind the establishment of railroads,
back to the foundation of this government, to the idea from
which it sprang."

"Mr. Flint smiled. 'We have changed materially since then,'
he said. 'I am afraid such a utopian state of affairs, beautiful as
it is, will not work in the 20th century. It is a commercial age,
and the interests which are the bulwark of the country's strength
must be protected.'

"'Yes,' said Austen, 'we have changed *materially*. The mistake
you make, and men like you, is the stress you lay on that word
material. Are there no such things as *moral* interests, Mr. Flint?
And are they not quite as important in government, if not more

important, than material interests? Surely, we cannot have commercial and political stability without commercial and political honor! If, as a nation, we lose sight of the ideals which have carried us so far, which have so greatly modified the conditions of other peoples than ourselves, we shall perish as a force in the world. And if this government proves a failure, how long do you think the material interests of which you are so solicitous will endure? Or do you care whether they endure beyond your lifetime? Perhaps not. But it is a matter of importance, not only to the nation, but to the world, whether or not the moral idea of the United States of America is perpetuated, I assure you.'"

Flint counters with the remark that even supposing that the railroads have taken an interest in seeing that 'conservative men' get into the government, they have done so to save themselves from being at the mercy of unscrupulous men and of blackmailers. To this Austen comments that such an excuse is ridiculous; that corporations have deliberately carried on essentially criminal practices solely to avoid making unnecessary improvements for safety and comfort, to keep down their taxes, and to pay as large dividends as possible to their stockholders. What would Austen do in Flint's place? He is asked the question, and this is his full reply — one that sums up completely a reformer's philosophy of conduct touching vested interests in America.

"I believe as firmly as I stand here, that the public opinion which exists to-day would protect your property, and I base that belief on the good sense of the average American voter. The public would protect you not only in its own interests, but from an inherent sense of fair play. On the other hand, if you persist in a course of political manipulation which is not only obsolete but wrong, you will magnify the just charges against you, and the just wrath; you will put ammunition into the hands of the agitators you rightly condemn. The stock-holders of your corporation, perhaps, are bound to suffer some from the fact that you have taken its life-blood to pay dividends, and the public will demand that it be built up into a normal and healthy condition. On the other hand, it could not have gone on as it was.

But the corporation will suffer much more if a delayed justice is turned into vengeance.

"You ask me what I could do. I should recognize, frankly, the new conditions, and declare as frankly what the old ones were, and why such methods of defence as you adopted were necessary and justified. I should announce, openly, that from this day onward Northeastern Railroads depended for fair play on an enlightened public — and I think your trust would be well founded, and your course vindicated. I should declare, from this day onward, that the issue of political passes, newspaper passes, and all other subterfuges would be stopped, and that all political hirelings would be dismissed. I should appeal to the people of this state to raise up political leaders who would say to the corporations, 'We will protect you from injustice if you will come before the elected representatives of the people, openly, and say what you want and why you want it.' By such a course you would have, in a day, the affection of the people instead of their distrust. And, more than that, you would have done a service for American government the value of which cannot well be estimated."

Thus speaks the voice of an Era in American history. He who has given embodiment to this voice in its literature, living in our own day, can expect no full judgement yet of the significance of his literary powers. Of Mr. Winston Churchill, the novelist, criticism has too often taken stock to the disparagement of the critics. There can be nothing surprising, for example, that one of the most recent of these, and one of the best among our professional literary judges, finds a place in his *Contemporary American Novelists* for "a masterpiece" that had been written by a little-known writer just a year before his own history was published, but forgets, in his analysis of the novelist Churchill, that the latter has long ago served his apprenticeship in his historical romances. To the mariner searching American coast lines, Mr. Churchill's works, since *Richard Carvel* and *The Crisis*, have offered neither pleasant fair-weather havens where most readers comfortably bask, nor quiet inlets in which others love to dream, nor yet muddy swamps in which some of our 'naturalists' wallow. His works, rather, have become great light-houses warning against the shoals and reefs, and showing the way to the safer paths beyond. Of Mr. Winston Churchill, the sociologist, there can be no conflict of opinion as to the value of his works to American moral development and its national growth. It would be difficult to find another writer of our time with such balanced emotions, such ingrained common sense, possessing his freshness and eloquence in discussing moral issues, and having the contagion of his patriotism. His political novels are a splendid embodiment of all these qualities, and they shed light and utter a warning as well.

Chapter XIV

PAUL LEICESTER FORD AND THE INDUSTRY OF POLITICS

A NOVEL which had a popularity so striking that it appeared in its fifty-third edition a dozen years after its first publication, and was reprinted again a decade later in 1920, deserves consideration. *The Honorable Peter Stirling* by Paul Leicester Ford was a great popular success. The cause for this certainly lay in no distinguished literary merits such as sometimes mark the unexpected work of a not very well known writer. This novel is, indeed, somewhat heavily put together, and is lacking in warmth and in beauty. It has other grave literary defects. The secret of its success lay altogether in its political import: first, it was reputed to be the biography of Grover Cleveland, recounting the facts of his life up to his attainment of the Presidency, in the form of fiction; secondly, it was the first novel to deal seriously with the professional reformer, and to paint the picture of municipal politics as conducted in America in a city so varied in population and so large as New York. The first fact illustrates excellently how the fiction writer may use the material in the life of a favorite who is a contemporary, and, by disguising certain facts and adding other dramatic episodes, may weave a popular romance out of it while at the same time producing a political novel. The second proves that the political novelist, by taking into account the forces which everyone knows to be at play in a community so swiftly moving and so vital as in a great American metropolis, may, by a proper selection of official facts, convert documents and reports into a work of art, and find a public enthusiastic to receive it.

The Honorable Peter Stirling is an exposition of the forces of public life not in the Capitol, and with national figures primarily; this was Adams's contribution. Nor is it of the grip of monopolies upon the forces of State legislation, such as we found in Mr. Churchill's second political novel. This work deals with the great melting pot. It moves away from the American pioneer stock and the rural boss and state control of Mr. Churchill, and passes to the immigrant stock, the ward boss, the saloon, the torch-light procession, and the political primary of a vast American city. Here we have portrayed the complete industry of politics in action: the furnace is seen melting and moulding alien traditions and ideals, and men of foreign birth are being converted into American citizens. We see that mechanism put together part by part, we watch it grinding out justice and injustice, we sound the influence of its productiveness upon the national political and social life. Whereas in Churchill men constituting the political community are well known one to another, and the Boss who arises gains and holds his power over his neighbors as much from the fact that the leader and the led have grown up together in the same community as for any other reason, in Ford's political novel we deal with the great masses of a city, where the individual voice is lost in the sheer weight and noise of the tens of thousands of others which surround it, and where the political Boss, unknown to the great majority of those who support him, deals through a small army of lesser bosses, lieutenants, and henchmen, and reaches out to the inarticulate worker getting his day's recreation in the corner saloon on the one side, and the justices of the courts and the governor of the state on the other. *Peter Stirling* is nearer the political novels of Mr. Churchill than it is to the work of Henry Adams because it helps to complete the panorama of political life set forth in those two novels. It gives you the other side of the shield, and a completed picture of *the* great American industry.

The Career of Peter Stirling is the history of a 'political boss.' The hero is a native young American, the son of a comparatively poor widow in Massachusetts, born in a mill town, whose only endowment is a Harvard education got under hardships, and whose character reflects a sturdy New England conscience, and a love for humanity. Except that he is native born, and has the same integrity of character as Austen Vane in Mr. Churchill's novel, the positions of these two young idealists are totally unlike. This unlikeness is marked from the very start, for whereas Austen Vane is born to wealth and to a place in cultivated society, Peter Stirling goes unknown, and poor, to a great city and knocks at its gates precisely as the lowliest immigrant does who lands from the steerage of an ocean-liner. And like the alien, a stranger in a metropolis, he endures the loneliness, the hardships, the long periods of patient waiting, and finally the triumphs that come to him who is strong enough and earnest enough to rise by his own efforts to leadership. He proves to be what all Americans like: a self-made man. While waiting patient months for a law practice to develop, he lives, himself, in the very thickness of the atmosphere of the alien and the radical, makes friends with their children, spends his evenings upon their door-steps and in their public squares, visits their saloons, and follows them to their homes in the blackness and the unhealthy surroundings of the tenement districts. In time this man who lives in the 'sixt' ward, who has learned the hopes, the tragedies, and the ideas of those who are his neighbors, begins to be trusted by them; and, as he gradually becomes "their bulwark against the greed of the unscrupulous capitalist, and spokesman before the high courts and in the halls of legislation," they learn to love him. And thus this young American, cut off from his own native stock, who has chosen to understand the people who grow up in 'an atmosphere of oaths' and bad whiskey, becomes the Chairman of their political primaries, a delegate from the ward and the city to their political conventions, and ultimately is their spontaneous choice for the Governorship of the state of New York.

Peter's march upward in politics is not an unmixed joy. Party intrigues, the jealousy of bosses fearful of his growing power, all the bitterness and the denunciation of a partisan press which has no use for 'a reformer,' are ranged against him. This opposition and power of the established 'city machine' he feels in those very early days when, in an attempt to punish a wealthy brewer whose diseased cows and filthy stables had been the cause of poisoned milk that had killed children of his district, he is blocked by the justices of the courts and by the district attorney, and is forced to appeal to the Governor at Albany in order to get action. The accumulation of experiences in public life from that time on is focussed into a short soliloquy, at a later day, when he hears that he has received the nomination for the Governorship.

"I am giving up," he says to himself, "everything that has been my true life till now. My profession, my friends, my chance to help others, my books, my quiet. I shall be misunderstood, reviled, and hated. Everything I do will be distorted for partisan purposes. Friends will misjudge. Enemies will become the more bitter. I give up fifty thousand dollars a year in order to become a slave, with toadies, trappers, lobbyists, and favor-seekers as my daily quota of humanity. I even sacrifice the larger part of my power."

In raising this question Ford notes the price which a man often pays who enters political life in America: the alienation of friends, the loss of income, of peace, and independence, and the only return for all this a mere title. Is it any wonder that our government and office-holding are left to the foreign element, asks the author. Is it any wonder that the native American prefers any other work rather than to run the gauntlet of public opinion and the press, and pay so heavy a price merely that he may hold some difficult office for a brief term?

The specific illustration of the tactics employed by partisan press and politicians in a great city in order to discredit an opposing candidate brings us into the heart of the novel, and touches upon the romance which is woven into this exposition of the industry of politics. It is about the time that Stirling is rising rapidly in political power that he falls in love. The lady is the charming young daughter of a former classmate at Harvard, Watts D'Alloi, who had remained in Europe after his marriage for almost nineteen years, and who, upon his return to New York, is ready to introduce Leonore to American society. Peter Stirling is out riding one day in Central Park when he stops a runaway horse, and the young lady whose life he saves and who literally hurls herself into his arms proves to be the daughter of his classmate, with whom he had not corresponded during all those years since he had served as best man at his wedding. Not that Stirling had not known that Watts D'Alloi was in New York before this runaway accident occurred. Almost as soon as that person arrived he sought out his old room-mate, now a well-known lawyer, and confessed to him that he had become entangled, while in Paris, with a Frenchwoman, that there had been a child, and that this woman was now in New York and threatened to expose him to his wife and daughter (who, by the way, worshipped the husband and father, and had not a breath of suspicion about this affair). During this interview in D'Alloi's home, and while Stirling is attempting to make some arrangement for the future with the Frenchwoman who had, during that very conference, forced her way into the presence of D'Alloi and his friend Stirling, Mrs. D'Alloi comes into the room unexpectedly and overhears part of the conversation. Stirling, in the face of a serious and critical situation for his friend D'Alloi, nobly shoulders the entire responsibility: he makes D'Alloi's wife believe that it is

of his son that they were talking, that the woman had followed
him to D'Alloi's home; he thus sacrifices himself to save his
friend. The Frenchwoman touched by the drama in the
episode, and the heroism of the deed, finally agrees later to the
terms which Stirling makes with her in order that she should
return to Paris, and he agrees to become the guardian of the
son while Watts D'Alloi cheerfully pays the money which the
final arrangement calls for to the mother, and is rejoiced to get
out of a serious situation so easily.

This episode has political consequences later. D'Alloi never
assumes the responsibility of his guilt, and that even when his
wife will not hear of Stirling's suit for the hand of her daughter
because she believes that her husband's friend has led an
immoral life. However, two years later, when the opposition
of the mother has been beaten down, and Leonore has made
Stirling supremely happy by becoming engaged to him, both
his political career and his life's happiness stand in jeopardy,
because the reporters have discovered, as they believe, something in the life of the opposing gubernatorial candidate which
they know can ruin him. Headlines in the newspapers of the
opposing party cry out in wrath: "SPEAK UP, STIRLING! *Who
Is This Boy? Detective Pelter finds a ward unknown to the
Courts, and explanations are in order from 'Purity Stirling'.*"
Stirling is powerless to reply when Leonore implores him to
speak, and since Watts fails to explain, Peter, now frantic and
physically and mentally broken, goes quietly away. The
effect of the shock upon the woman he loves, who believes that
her idol has feet of clay, completely unnerves him. A policeman finds him wandering aimlessly about, and takes possession
of him — believing that he is intoxicated — on the very day
when his political ward was to celebrate with a torchlight
parade his nomination. Being an old friend of Peter's, whom
he finally recognizes, and determined now that 'none of the
byes must ever see him like this,' the officer bundles him into

a cab, takes him to his own study, and there leaves him
safely to himself. "He was fined the next morning for being
off his beat and refusing to answer or give any information
which might justify his absence."

The situation is the most dramatic in the book, and the
novelist makes splendid use of it. Of course, in the end, Watts
D'Alloi confesses, the people who love him fight the harder
fight for him to win his election, and Leonore nurses him back
to health from the nervous shock which the episode, coupled
with a recurrence of a fever due to an old wound, bring on.
While Leonore is in his rooms imploring him to look at her,
while Stirling is raving, and roaming, stumbling, and falling,
and then slowly recovering from the fearful shock, and D'Alloi
is confessing for the first time to his daughter that he is the
miscreant, and not Stirling, the streets outside furnish a highly
dramatic setting to the emotional crisis which is being enacted
within. There are bands of music, a procession of dancing
and flaring torches, singing and bawling crowds, tremendous
cheers, the waving of banners and flags, and then silence for a
moment, followed by the burst of a political song, to the tune
of 'Marching through Georgia,' from the throats of five thousand
men:

> "Rally 'round our party, boys;
> Rally to the blue,
> And battle for our candidate,
> So sterling and so true.
> Fight for honest government, boys,
> And down the vicious crew;
> Voting for freedom and Stirling.
>
> Hurrah, hurrah, for Stirling, brave and strong.
> Hurrah, hurrah, for Stirling, never wrong.
> And roll the voters up in line,
> Two hundred thousand strong;
> Voting for freedom and Stirling."

The essential motive of Ford in portraying the character of Peter Stirling is to show *the practical idealist* in American politics, in contradistinction to the so-called reformer. The first is, according to the author, an extreme type of man far from uncommon in America, yet one who is not as well understood as he ought to be by the foreign population, and seldom understood by native Americans. In a conversation which the hero has with the woman whom he desires to marry, and whom he, by his frequent explanations, presumably educates so that she may grasp the burden of his political philosophy, we have the author's analysis of the professional political reformer. "The reformer," says Peter, "is usually a man who has other occupations, and, if I may say so, has usually met with only partial success in them. By that I mean that the really successful banker, merchant, or professional man, cannot take time to work in politics, and so only the less successful try. Each reformer thinks he is right, and as his bread and butter is not an issue, he quarrels with his associates to his heart's content, so that they rarely unite all their force in his favor. Most of the reform movements have been attempted in a way that is laughable. . . . The average reformer endorses thoroughly — a theory. And he always thinks himself the better man. The people won't stand for that. The 'holier than thou' attitude will always be defeated in this country quicker than will any rascality that may have been done."

"But don't you think the reformer is right in principle?" she asks.

"In nine cases out of ten, yes. . . . But politics does not consist in being right. It is in making other folks think you are. Men don't like to be told they are ignorant and wrong, and this assumption is the basis of nearly all of the reformer's educational campaigns. To give impetus to any movement takes immense shrewdness, tact, and many other qualities.

The people are obstructive, in most cases, and need plenty of time." This fact, Stirling goes on to say, is well known by the popular politician. Hence he gains his political power by recognizing that he can have his own way only by making it suit the voters. 'The Boss who does the most things that the people want can do the most things the people don't want. Everytime I have surrendered my own wishes and done what the people of the ward desired, I have added to my power, and so have been able to do something that the people or politicians do not care about or do not like.' He admits that as a result he has been called all sorts of names. 'The papers call me Boss. If the voters didn't agree with me they would call me a reformer.'

Stirling, — or rather Ford through his hero, — draws the lesson: if the reformer were only to build his program as patiently and as scientifically as the Boss does, he might in the end accomplish all that he desired. For, says Stirling, the Boss is never a sudden, a mushroom growth, as the reformer frequently is. He is a man who comes from the ranks, and who has risen upon the backs of his neighbors. He has been far-sighted enough to keep adding to his circle of friends and acquaintances, and to doing whatever will increase his local popularity; he is a born fighter, and a man who has learned that he must be absolutely truthful. He recognizes that he is a block of material in a great and orderly structure. At the top of that structure, at a place which has grown more and more narrow as it rose from the ground, are those few men who are abler, more intelligent, who possess greater executive and administrative ability, than all of those others below them who furnish them their support, and upon whose shoulders they have risen to their place of eminence. In a time of election, particularly a federal election, or a state election, rival organizations try by every means honorable and often dishonorable to test the strength of the structure that has been so painstakingly reared. Then it is that you see, in the great cities of the country, the industry of politics in action, and that you feel the might of powerful organizations.

Not the least interest of this political novel lies in watching this great mechanism in operation, at the time of an important election. You note all the forces in dramatic action, and you see how each group is dominated by a special kind of boss. No man seems too unimportant to have a place in this unique American institution: for it includes policemen, bartenders, tradesmen, and prize-fighters; laborers, milkmen, and munici-pal justices; merchants, district attorneys, the Governor; reporters, detectives, and editors. The primary of the ward conducted by Irish-Americans whose clinching argument is always the fist in action; the methods of attack always em-ployed by the rival organizations which include blackmail and perjury if no other means can be found to attack an opponent's character after it has been investigated and combed from the day, almost, of birth; the torch-light processions and band-wagons and corner-oratory which keep interest alive in the favorite; all these help to make this a highly entertaining and at the same time instructive picture of a vitally important part of national life. Amid the smoke and the turmoil of these things, Ford argues, a man who is a lover of his kind, who comes with a touch of chivalry in his soul and a determina-tion to bridge the chasm between the highest ranks and the lowest of society, has nothing to fear. His efforts alone can destroy the ignorance of the one and overcome the obstructive selfishness of the other, and thus point the way to the develop-ment of a fairer and a more intelligent national life. The melting pot will work if we can find men courageous enough and un-selfish enough to conduct the melting process. In municipal politics that means men of native stock, charged with great American ideals, who have the power of constructive leadership.

So much for the political significance of this novel, which

marks the cause of its popularity. It has been pointed out
that the work has some grave literary defects. These are
largely in character-building. Ford is arbitrary in the uses he
makes of many of his people. Aside from the hero, who is a
good enough embodiment of a man of flesh and blood, too many
of the others are merely persons with a pigeon-hole characterization; they are taken out whenever needed to 'point up' the
story, to develop some further aspect of the hero's personality,
and then put away again after they have served their purpose.
This is too much like the typical trick found on the American
stage, of having a star figure and then a completely subservient
cast. Can you imagine that a man like Watts D'Alloi, "with
two hundred years of Knickerbocker and Huguenot tradition"
back of him, would be such a cad as to permit the deliberate
self-sacrifice of his best friend upon two different occasions,
and take it in the completely nonchalant manner that he does,
postponing to the last possible moment, and only when his
friend's reason threatens to give way, the assumption of his
own responsibility? Does it seem reasonable to believe that
a sweet and charming young girl of eighteen, who knows little
or nothing of the active world, can be wooed and won by conversations which seem solely arguments and expositions about
American political life, analyses of the Boss and the Reformer,
and the strategy of a great gubernatorial campaign? Leonore
D'Alloi, as we know her, is given, indeed, to whole-hearted
hero-worship: but the loyalty of her nature is an emotional,
not an intellectual force; she sees, perhaps, the heroic propor-
tions of the man, but she does so only by learning of the
dramatic episodes in which he had taken part, and not because
she understands his undoubted moral and intellectual superiorities. The mother of Leonore is a still less satisfactory
figure; a plaster-saint she seems to us, in her married life, but
without the saint's presumable determination never to compromise with what must have appeared to her a carnal sin.

In his handling of the immigrant class Ford is more at ease. The robust figure of Moriarty, the German brewer Bohlmann, Costell, Maguire, and Curlew — all leaders in the political primary or forces in the sixth ward; the parents of the children in the tenement districts, and the children themselves; the humor, the pathos, and the tragedy in the lives of the underdog and the poor: — these Ford can draw with a convincingness of appeal that reminds one of Charles Dickens. He knows how to find the natural warmth in the hearts of the submerged classes; he sees how dumb and helpless they are in the face of a great trial, how hearty is their response and quick their reaction to the helping hand held out to them, and how touch-ing is the evidence of their appreciation. He would show that they are quick to seize upon the evidence of real honesty, and can remain loyal and devoted to him whom they love in spite of every inimical attempt to prove that their idol has blemishes. Like a journalist or newsgatherer, Ford enters the homes of the poor, and wanders through their streets, collecting and reporting the local color, the quaintness, and the out-standing qualities in the figures of familiar districts.

CHAPTER XV

COMPARISONS AND CONCLUSION

A COMPARISON of the American with the English political novelists brings out one striking fact: that whereas in England the writers have often enough been interested in presenting the political panorama for the sake of the panorama, — shall we say, for art's sake? — American political novelists have been mainly concerned with Reform. The artistic impulse such as we found expressed in Mrs. Humphry Ward, Trollope's simple desire to tell a good story, the analytic interest in sheer character development of ˜Mr. Wells, to say nothing of the joy in the scene and its splendor which Disraeli so frequently revels in, are all missing in America. Here the several political romancers have been essentially interested in propaganda, argument, exposition.

From one standpoint this has had a value. The eminent popularity of the several American political novels proves that their reading public accepted them not for mere entertainment: the mere pleasure of reading could have been far more easily satisfied in the works of other writers. They accepted them because, amid all the other works of fiction, these works pointed a moral and adorned a tale. In America, therefore, we may say that the political novel has, in a sense, instructed the voter, and explained to him and to his family something of the inner working of political machinery. It has served to make popular government more popular.

From another standpoint, and by far the more important, this has been a great misfortune. The intensity with which these writers have examined their material, the seriousness of

334

their approach to it, have made them lose the sense of depth and the great beauty of the forest by this close attention to the individual trees. The kaleidoscope of American political life is one infinitely more various than was that of England in the time of Queen Victoria. The immense foreign population and their place in the political scheme of things, municipal melting pots, to say nothing of the many state governments each with its peculiar problems, and the life at the Capitol, offer material for fascinating dramatic treatment. So vast and various is the landscape, that we have already taken for granted the fact that 'the great American novel' will never be written because no such work could ever contain a picture of the energy of New England with the charm of the South, and reflect the buoyancy of California and the intrepidity of the middle West. And yet, in the *genre* of the political novel there seems to be offered the one great vehicle where something of the fusion of north, south, east, and west may take place, and where the writer may produce in fiction what is truly typical of the American people just as Walt Whitman produced it in poetry. Here is a form which offers a great latitude of plot development, permits an untold variety of background, and can present countless numbers of national and local types each novel in situation. And in spite of all this flexibility of content, the political novel must deal with one thing common to all, — the great Experiment of popular democracy in America.

For the first American political novel we had to wait until the eighties of the nineteenth century — until the pioneer work was done, after the Civil War had tested the nation, and the Reconstruction period had fused it. Then did Henry Adams appear with *Democracy*. Much water has flowed under the bridges since his day, and the scene is now more graphic than ever, yet few are the writers who seem to see what is before them. How little they see it is proved by the statement that the American national capitol, irrespective of its political im-

port, but solely for its broad human value, has had little reflection in American fiction. One might count upon the fingers
of one's hands all of the works of any importance of American
novelists which set forth Washington for 'the American scene.'
So far as the political significance of the city is concerned, there
seems, astonishingly enough and in spite of all these years,
but one serious reflection of it. Henry Adams still stands a
lone figure.

Yet at no time has American political life been so much
worth recording as it is to-day. The log-cabin pattern quilt
which symbolized, in homely metaphor, the days of Lincoln,
and which was not very much changed in the days of Henry
Adams, is no more. To-day we have a marvellously woven
tapestry, richly wrought and glittering with the spoils that
have been added to it by intimate contact with continental
life, and European thought. To the one who looks closely at
the pattern, the home-dyed calico and the woollen threads
still form the base upon which all the rest has been imposed.
Where is the writer who can describe this uniquely enriched
design with beauty and with justice?

NOTES

Acknowledgment is made to Dr. George W. Ward for his kindness in reading proof. The courtesy of the Macmillan Company was extended to the author to reprint the portrait of Disraeli.

CHAPTER I
FIRST PRINCIPLES

[1] Henley: *Views and Reviews*, Vol. I. London, David Nutt, 1908. Essay on *Disraeli*, pp. 23 ff.

[2] Gosse: Published in *Transactions of the Royal Society*, Vol. XXXVI. London, Oxford University Press, 1918, pp. 61–90, entitled *The Novels of Benjamin Disraeli*. Address made in 1918 before the Royal Society of Literature in the United Kingdom.

[3] Stephen: *Hours in a Library*, second series. London. Smith, Elder & Co., 1876. Essay on *Disraeli's Novels*, pp. 344–393.

[4] W. F. Monypenny and G. E. Buckle: *The Life of Benjamin Disraeli, Earl of Beaconsfield*. In 6 volumes. Macmillan Co. 1916 to 1920.

[5] *Temple Bar*, London, vol. 83, May–August, 1888. Cf. pp. 422 *et seq.*

[6] Lowell: A review of *Tancred, or The New Crusade, a novel*, in the "North American Review" for July, 1847, volume 65, pp. 201–224. This was later reprinted in "The Round Table" under the title *Disraeli as a Novelist*.

[7] Bryce: *Studies in Contemporary Biography*. Macmillan Co., New York, 1903. Cf. the essay entitled *Benjamin Disraeli, Earl of Beaconsfield*, *pp. 1–68.*

[8] *A Writer's Recollections*, Harper and Bros. London and New York, 1918. In 2 volumes.

[9] Vol. XIII: *The Nineteenth Century*, chapter 11, pp. 340–402, entitled "The Political and Social Novel."

[10] A. Lawrence Lowell: *The Government of England*. The Macmillan Co., 1908. Vol. I, opening pages, 50–51; chapter 3; also pp. 409–413. Volume II, chapters 32, 33, 34, 37.

Walter Bagehot: *The English Constitution*, London, Chapman & Hall, chapter VI, "The House of Commons." Cf. also, pp. 68–9, 126–7, 118–119, 130.

Gilbert Murray: *The Pale Shade*, in *World War Issues and Ideals* by Morris Edmund Speare and Walter Blake Norris. Ginn, N. Y. and London, 1919, p. 191 *et seq.*

John Galsworthy: *Diagnosis of the Englishman*. *Ibid.*, p. 116.

Jan Christian Smuts: *The British Commonwealth of Nations*. *Ibid.*, p. 202 *et seq.*

[11] "The ranks of the peerage are recruited every year by new creations; and, to one who does not expect too much of our frail human nature, especially in a region where it is apt to be seen at its frailest, the new

338 NOTES

creations, though far from ideal, are, on the whole, by no means unrespect-
able. The obviously bad appointments attract lively public interest; the
good ones pass by unnoticed . . . If you make a list of the most recent
peers, you will find among them a very large proportion of men who are
at the head of their respective professions or walks of life, especially of
course if they have been engaged in law or public administration. Turn
up the record of a few debates in the House of Lords and notice the
speakers. You will find first several of those recent peers, whose rank is
not hereditary but has been conferred on them for public services: Lord
Morley, the famous radical philosopher and man of letters, friend of Mr.
Gladstone and John Stuart Mill; Lord Cromer, a very great governor who
reformed the finances of Egypt; Lord Milner, an extreme Imperialist,
who is strongly distrusted in Liberal circles but certainly achieved his
peerage by hard work and personal qualities; Lord Loreburn, a great
lawyer and a former Liberal Lord Chancellor; Lord Courtney, formerly
Chairman of Committees in the House of Commons, a leading radical and
pacifist; Lord Parmoor, a Conservative lawyer; two or three Bishops,
some very conservative, some moderate like the Archbishop of Canterbury,
some Socialist, like the Bishop of Oxford. Then there are many peers
whose title is hereditary, but who would have probably attained eminence
in whatever rank of life they had been: Lord Rosebery, the famous orator;
Lord Crewe, Lord Lansdowne, the very accomplished leaders of the Liberal
and Conservative peers, respectively; Lord Curzon, a great traveller, a
distinguished ex-Viceroy of India, and a man of academic distinction.
These are all men whose opinion is of real importance, and who probably
ought to be members of any second chamber, however democratically
constructed. Then there are a number of successful business men, brewers,
doctors, and men of science." Gilbert Murray: *The Pale Shade* (1919)
Ibid., pp. 188–9.

[12] Edmond Scherer: Etudes sur la Littérature Contemporaine. Vol. VII,
pp. 72–3. Paris, Calmann Levy; Librairie Nouvelle, 1882.

[13] Quoted by Reginald Lucas in the *London Quarterly Review* for July,
1907, page 153. The article is in large part a careful analysis of the novel
Lothair.

[14] "The difficulty of treating contemporary characters and events has
been ever acknowledged: but it may be doubted whether the difficulty is
diminished when we would commemorate the men and things that have
preceded us. The cloud of passion in the first instance, or in the other
the mist of time, may render it equally hard and perplexing to discriminate.
It should not be forgotten that the most authentic and interesting histories
are those which have been composed by actors in the transactions which
they record. The contemporary writer who is personally familiar with his
theme has unquestionably a great advantage; but it is assumed that his
pen can scarcely escape the bias of private friendship or political connection. Yet truth after all is the sovereign passion of mankind; nor is the

writer of these pages prepared to relinquish his conviction, that it is possible to combine the accuracy of the present with the impartiality of the future." *Lord George Bentinck — A Political Biography*, Colburn & Co., London, 1852. Page 3.

[15] *The Nation*, (New York) volume 80, page 310.

[16] Disraeli's biographer Buckle (op. cit.), from whom I quote this letter (vol. V, page 166) goes on to say that on June 9, 1870 (Goldwin Smith's letter appeared in the English press on the preceding May 25th) Longman, the publisher, wrote to Disraeli, "The Oxford Professor's letter is doing its work well. . . . etc."

[17] *The Appreciation of Literature*, page 134.

[18] *De l'Allemagne*, pt. 1, chapter 2.

[19] Cf. the English edition entitled *A Writer's Recollections*, by W. Collins and Co., London, 1919. Page 232.

[20] In *The Round Table*, article entitled "Disraeli as a Novelist."

[21] See a History of the Purpose-novel in Appendix, Part 2, *infra*.

CHAPTER II
DISRAELI'S EXPERIMENTAL STAGE

[1] Published originally in 2 volumes by Colburn, London, in 1826. In the following year part II, entitled *A Sequel to Vivian Grey*, appeared in 3 volumes, also by Colburn.

Vivian Grey was published anonymously, but by the following year, 1827, when the *Sequel* appeared, it was generally known that Benjamin Disraeli was the author.

THE BEST EDITION OF THE WORKS OF BENJAMIN DISRAELI is that published upon the centenary of his birth, in 1904–1905, by M. W. Dunne of London. It was printed only for subscribers, was prefaced with Mr. Edmund Gosse's excellent critical introduction, and contains all of the novels, plays, poems, short stories, political essays and treatises, and the more important political addresses which have been worth preserving. The novels published during Disraeli's lifetime, with their dates of publication, follow: Vivian Grey (1826), The Young Duke (1831), Contarini Fleming (1832), The Wondrous Tale of Alroy (1833), Henrietta Temple (1836), Venetia (1837), Coningsby (1844), Sybil (1845), Tancred (1847), Lothair (1870), Endymion (1880). A number of chapters of an unfinished novel, written in 1881, and which were not published until 1905, should be included.

To these romances we must add a number of satirical *jeux-d'esprit* which comprise *Popanilla* (1827), *Ixion in Heaven* (1833), and *The Infernal Marriage* (1834) all of which are political satires; *The Runnymede Letters* (1836) were a series of 19 philippics, altogether political in nature; *The Revolutionary Epick* (1834), intended by its author to be a fourth to the *Iliad*, the *Aeneid*, and the *Divina Commedia*, was a long poem which Kebbel

340 NOTES

calls "a modern Dunciad"; the great political essay entitled *Vindication of the English Constitution* appeared in 1835; the last named work together with the *Runnymede Letters* and his essay on the *Spirit of Whiggism* have been collected, with some of Disraeli's satires in verse that concern politics, and published under the title of "Whigs and Whiggism — political writings of Benjamin Disraeli" by Macmillan (1914) with an introduction by William Hutcheon. Another political treatise, famous in its day and important now for the understanding of Disraeli's political views in his novels, is *Lord George Bentinck: a Political Biography* (1851). This comprehensive work of 588 pages, as it was published by Colburn of London in 1852 for the fourth edition, has been called by Mr. Gosse (q. v.) "a manual of personal conduct as applied to practical politics."

Among other writings not already mentioned were a tragedy of *Count Alarcos* (1839) which is of interest to us only as showing how the number of horrors piled here one atop of another find its author, as late as 1839, with a heart as quick and with a brain sufficiently tolerant of the fantastic that he can still seriously endure some of the worst of the Gothic School's melodramatics. A number of short stories (12) written by Disraeli, and most of which were inspired by his early travels to the Orient and whose plots are laid in Egypt, Syria, Turkey, and the Bosphorus, are to be found only reprinted in Dunne's edition published in 1905, volume 9. Fragments of songs and poems written by Disraeli are to be found only in a single work, a biography published of him the year following his death, by Cornelius Brown, and entitled *An Appreciative Life of the Earl of Beaconsfield* (London, Harrison & Sons, 1882, 2 volumes). Disraeli also edited the works of his father, Isaac Disraeli, and wrote prefatory introductions for all of his father's works as they were reprinted in various editions extending from 1849 to 1881, the year of Benjamin's death. There were also a number of contributions to the Press by him of political articles of one sort or another, dating from 1833, when he was campaigning for a seat in Parliament and wrote an account of early political ideas in a political-autobiographic article entitled *What is He?*, to various additions made in 1836, 1852, and 1853. In the last named year at his inspiration there was founded a political weekly review entitled *The Press*, which lived until 1866 and was intended to advance his party's interests. To this Disraeli made a number of contributions, but since these, with the rest of his journalistic activities mentioned, are ephemeral material there is no need of making further mention of them.

Three University Addresses made by him upon certain occasions in his political life are worth noting. The first was an address at the Manchester Athenaeum, on October 3, 1844, and is to be found in America in the Barton-Ticknor Collection of the Boston Public Library, in a volume entitled "Addresses made at The Manchester Athenaeum 1835-1885." For the intellectual power it shows, and for the high seriousness and nobility of appeal in it, it is an address worth reading today. And worth contrasting, too, with the flatness and the paucity of thought of an address made by his predecessor at the Athenaeum the year before, who happened to be Charles Dickens! In 1864 Disraeli delivered at Oxford his famous so-called "Ape or Angel Speech" which is interesting for the issue he there took with the Darwinians, and for the objections he raised to the Evolutionary theory in explaining the descent of man. His Inaugural Address delivered in 1873 at the University of Glasgow, made as Rector of the University, was thought good enough to have published by Longmans, Green & Co., in London, at the close of that year. The New York City Library alone has a copy of this in America.

To enforce the notion of the range of writing which Disraeli did — as one must already have judged by this tabulation of his works — it is necessary to add another word: that the first appearance of Disraeli as an author was in 1825, when he was 21 years old, and when Murray of London published his two Mining Pamphlets! The first of these was "An Enquiry into the Plans, Progress, and Policy of the American Mining Companies"; the other "Lawyers and Legislators; or Notes on the American Mining Companies." They have, curiously enough, a political interest for us in the fact that both of them are arguments against the passing of restrictive legislation toward the mining companies formed in England to exploit Spanish-American mines. The Congressional Library in Washington, D. C. has copies of these.

² It is interesting to gather some of the criticisms which *Vivian Grey* received. *William Cullen Bryant* said: "The work is rather a series of sketches than a regularly built story. The hero has no mistress but politics, and no adventures but political ones. He is constantly before us displaying various abilities in a variety of ways. The other prominent characters are fools or knaves, and all are more or less forced and unnatural. Their aggregate makes a showy picture, which dazzles, but does not satisfy. The style of writing is dashing and careless, occasionally rising into lively extravagance, and at times sinking into mawkish sentimentality. The morality of the book is loose. The work is in fact little more than a picture of the vices and follies of the great, with one active spirit in the midst of them, making those vices and follies the stepping-stones to his ambition." — United States Review and Literary Gazette, December, 1826. Vol. I., no. 3, pp. 231-2.

Monypenny quotes from Morley's *Life of Gladstone*, II, p. 499. "In Mr. Gladstone's diary for March 20, 1874, we find this entry: 'Finished *Vivian Grey*. The first quarter extremely clever, the rest trash.'"

Edmund Gosse says: "As the opening work of a literary career, it promises well; the impertinent young gentleman dashed off to Parnassus at a gallop . . . It is a sort of social fairy tale, where every one has exquisite beauty, limitless wealth, and exalted rank, where the impossible and the hyperbolic are the only homely virtues . . . It was a bold bid for personal distinction, which the author easily perceived already to be 'the only passport to the society of the great in England.'" — *The Novels of Benjamin Disraeli*, in "Transactions of the Royal Society of Literature of the United Kingdom," Vol. XXXVI, 1918.

³ In the preface to the later editions of *Vivian Grey*, from 1854 on, Disraeli says: "Books written by boys, which pretend to give a picture of the manners and to deal in knowledge of human nature, must necessarily be founded on affectation. They can be, at best, but the results of imagination, acting upon knowledge not acquired by experience. Of such circumstances exaggeration is a necessary consequence, and false taste accompanies exaggeration . . . Such productions should be exempt from criticism, and should be looked upon as a kind of literary lusus."

⁴ For a key to the originals of the characters in the novel the one most to be relied upon is that given in the Empire Edition of Disraeli's collected works, published by Dunne of London, in 1904–1905 (see *supra*).

⁵ It ought to be said that Monypenny (op. cit.) discusses *Vivian Grey* mainly to show what autobiographical material the work contains of its author at the age of twenty-one.

⁶ Published in May, 1832, by Colburn, London, anonymously in the original edition.

⁷ This diary is part of the collection of the private papers of Disraeli to which access for the first time has been given to Disraeli's official biographers. I am indebted therefore for the quotation to *Monypenny*, volume I, pp. 181–182.

⁸ Of contemporary opinion there is Heine's: "Modern English letters have given us no offspring equal to *Contarini Fleming*. Cast in our Teutonic mould, it is nevertheless one of the most original works ever written: profound, poignant, pathetic; its subject the most interesting, if not the noblest, imaginable — the development of a poet; truly psychological; passion and mockery; Gothic richness, the fantasy of the Saracens, and yet over all a classic, even a death-like, repose."

Beckford, the author of *Vathek*, wrote to Disraeli, who had sent him a copy of the novel soon after its publication, a letter which Disraeli quotes to his sister under date of May 26, 1832: "Beckford . . . (his) answer is short but very courteous. It commences with four exclamations. 'How wildly original! How full of intense thought! How awakening! How delightful!'"

In our own time its reception has been no less sympathetic. Sir Leslie Stephen believes this one of the finest of novels. "*Contarini Fleming* is the perfection of English prose." *Hours in a Library*, II, p. 139. Mr. Edmund Gosse says "This beautiful romance is by far the best of Disraeli's early books."

⁹ See Smiles. *A Brief Biography of Benj. Disraeli*, II., p. 338.

¹⁰ Horace B. Samuel: "The Psychology of Benjamin Disraeli," in *Modernities*. N. Y. Dutton & Co. 1914.

¹¹ Cf. Disraeli's Preface to the Collected Edition of the Novels, pub-

lished in 1870. For *Contarini Fleming* he repeats what he had said about it in the preface to the 1845 edition: "In *Contarini* I would show the development and formation of poetic character."

[12] Published by Colburn, London, in 1830.

[13] In the *General Preface to the Novels* written by Disraeli in 1870, in which he passes all his early work in review, no mention is made of this work. And even before its publication Disraeli writes to his sister Sarah: "I don't care a jot about *The Young Duke*. I never staked any fame on it; it may take its chance." (Letters written in 1830, 1831, edited by Ralph Disraeli, and published in 1887 in a *Collection of Disraeli's Letters.* Harper & Bros. Cf. pp. 62–64).

[14] Book II, chapter 7; Book III, chapter 8; Book III, chapter 18; Book V, chapter 6.

[15] Contributed to Colburn's *The New Monthly,* of which Bulwer-Lytton was the editor, in 1833. *The Infernal Marriage* was contributed to the same magazine in the following year.

[16] In *A History of Nineteenth Century Literature,* p. 161.

[17] In his *Lord Beaconsfield,* page 26.

[18] Disraeli wrote *Henrietta Temple* in 1836. This is a pure love-story, and nothing more. In the following year, 1837, he published *Venetia,* in which the lives of Byron and of Shelley, under disguised names, are reflected. In both of these there is a complete absence of any political motive. The only other novel of this period is *The Wondrous Tale of Alroy,* (1833), in which the ideal ambition of David Alroy, a sort of twelfth century Judas Maccabaeus, who fights for his people and then returns their old land to them, is realized, and then he is himself destroyed. Except that this last-mentioned work shows Disraeli's interest in Jewish history (an interest which becomes political in *Coningsby* and in *Tancred*), it has no other importance for us.

CHAPTER III

DISRAELI'S POLITICAL PHILOSOPHY—TORY DEMOCRACY

[1] For a full understanding of Disraeli's Tory Philosophy, the reader must study not alone Disraeli's novels, but also the following of his works: *A Vindication of the English Constitution,* Saunders and Otley, London, 1835; *Lord George Bentinck: A Political Biography,* Colburn and Co. (588 pages) London, 1852; *The Collected Speeches and Addresses of Benjamin Disraeli, the Earl of Beaconsfield.* Edited by T. E. Kebbel. 2 vols. London, Longmans, Green and Co., 1882.

Since the main intention of this Study is to be of purely literary character, and is not to be either an examination into History or Politics, it is not within our province to analyze all the material of English history and of English politics, gathered from a period extending over the days of the first Stuarts to the 40's of the nineteenth century, which Disraeli liberally scatters throughout the trilogy, and out of which he adduces a theory that he weaves into the texture of the novels. Nor will it be necessary for us to understand these conceptions, involving as they do some ten reigns of English political life, since they but serve Disraeli the cumulative purpose of rooting firmly into the Past those convictions and opinions which, as a statesman in Victorian England, he held in his own day — guiding his policies as a statesman, and his pen as a writer. The convictions and the opinions which distinguish him as a man of public affairs *among his contemporaries*, and which he states in his novels, are our main concern.

[2] Cf. *Tancred*, Part II, Chapter 9, on "The revelations of Chaos," and the *Speech at Oxford* in 1864: "I, my Lord, am on the side of the angels."

[3] Chapter V.

[4] Chapter VI.

[5] Part I, Chapter 3.

[6] Book IV, Chapter 14.

[7] Volume II, pp. 298–9.

[8] For Disraeli's ideas upon the English Nobility see: *Coningsby*, Part III, chapter 5; IV, 4. *Sybil*. I, 3; II, 1, 2, 7, 11, 12; III, 2, 8; IV, 5; VI, 2. *Tancred*, I, 2.

[9] For the Middle Classes, see, in particular, *Coningsby*, Part I, chap. 9; II, 7; IV, 2, 3, 4; V, 3; VI, 3; VII, 4, 8; VIII, 2; IX, 6.

[10] For the Working and Industrial Classes, see *Sybil*, Book II, chapters 3, 5, 8, 10, 12, 13, 16; III, 1, 2, 3, 4, 5, 6, 7, 8, 9; IV, 5, 8; V, 1, 2, 3; VI, 5, 6, 7, 12, 13.

[11] For the Church, see *Tancred*, Book III, chapter 1; IV, 7; and *Sybil*, Book II, Ch. 11, 12, 14. Also *Coningsby*, Preface written for the 5th edition of 1849.

CHAPTER IV
Disraeli Masters the Art

[1] *Op. cit.* Vol. II, pp. 220–1.

[2] The full title was *Coningsby; or, The New Generation*. Published in May, 1844, by Colburn & Co., London.

[3] The original of Lord Monmouth was the Marquis of Hertfordshire, the notorious roué and friend of George IV. Thackeray immortalized him as the Marquis of Steyne in *Vanity Fair*. Disraeli's is, by all odds, the more perfect satire.

[4] *Coningsby*, last paragraph of the novel.

"*Coningsby* is the best political novel in any language," is the opinion of Kebbel. Cf. *The Life of Lord Beaconsfield*, in the Statesmen Series published in London, 1888. For "Coningsby" see page 40 *et seq.* Mr. T. E. Kebbel was an intimate of Disraeli's and his books upon him are valuable.

[5] Published in 1845 by Colburn and Co., London.

[6] See in particular the figure of St. Lys (book II, chapters 11, 12, 14). He carries out in this volume, but in a broader fashion, the ideas first presented by Eustace Lyle in *Coningsby*. This religious aspect of the Tory political philosophy, begun in *Coningsby*, and broadened in *Sybil*, gains its full sweep in the novel *Tancred*.

[7] The evidence that Disraeli was profoundly stirred by the conditions of the working people in "the hungry forties," that he was determined for their welfare to exhibit their dreadful difficulties to the world, is definitely and completely proved by the great care with which he went about to gain accurate information. The evidence of this is now complete, and ought to settle forever the taunt of insincerity that was often in the past hurled against him. Mr. Edmund Gosse, in his address made on Disraeli in 1918 (see page 337 above) says: "The late Duke of Rutland, that illustrious and venerable friend who alone survived in 1904 to bear witness to the sentiments of Young England, told me that he accompanied Disraeli on the journey which led to the composition of *Sybil*, and that he never, in long years of intimacy, saw him so profoundly moved as he was at the aspect of the miserable dwellings of the hand-loom workers."

The publishers of *Sybil* said in their Advertisement of the book, in 1845, "He thinks it therefore due to himself to state that the descriptions, generally, are written from his own observation; but while he hopes he has alleged nothing which is not true, he has found the absolute necessity of suppressing much that is genuine. For so little do we know of our own country, that the air of improbability which the whole truth would inevitably throw over these pages, might deter some from their perusal."

Kebbel points out in his *Lord Beaconsfield*, chapter III, how, accompanied by Smythe and Manners, Disraeli travelled as far north as Yorkshire, visited the factories, studied the work being done by the various charitable and other ameliorating agencies, etc. And that he spoke to his companions of the need of somebody's "writing these facts up," so that the world might know about them. It must be obvious, of course, that as a member of Parliament, he would have been familiar with the Parliamentary *Blue Books* of the time, as well as with the writings of the Chartists, and would have known many of their leaders.

[8] See Book IV, chapter 15.

[9] In chapter 8 of the work. "Lord Beaconsfield as a Man of Letters," is the chapter title.

[10] Lord Iddleseigh, (Sir Stafford Northcote, first Earl of Iddleseigh), in his *Lord Beaconsfield's Novels*. The Monthly Review (John Murray, publisher, London) November, 1903. pp. 87–102.

[11] Sir Leslie Stephen: "*Mr. Disraeli's Novels*," in *Hours in a Library*, second series.

[12] In his *Lord Beaconsfield: A Study*. Chapter 15.

[13] In *The Right Honourable Benjamin Disraeli. A literary and political biography*. London, George Bentley, publisher. 1854. By Thomas Macknight.

[14] Lord Morley's *Life of Cobden*, page 297, volume I. "The author of *Sybil* seems to have apprehended the real magnitude, and even the nature, of the social crisis. Mr. Disraeli's brooding imaginativeness of conception gave him a view of the extent of the social revolution as a whole, which was wider, if it did not go deeper, than that of any other contemporary observer."

[15] James Russell Lowell: *op. cit.* pp. 220, 223.

[16] *The Nineteenth Century*, volume 45. pp. 245 ff.

[17] "In considering the Tory scheme, the author recognized in the Church the most powerful agent in the previous development of England, and the most efficient means of that renovation of the national spirit at which he aimed. The Church is a sacred corporation for the promulgation and maintenance in Europe of certain Asian principles, which, although local in their birth, are of Divine origin, and of universal and eternal application.

In asserting the paramount character of the ecclesiastical polity and the majesty of the theocratic principle, it became necessary to ascend to the origin of the Christian Church, and to meet, in a spirit worthy of a critical and a comparatively enlightened age, the position of the descendants of that race who were the founders of Christianity. The modern Jews had long laboured under the odium and stigma of mediaeval malevolence. In the dark ages, when history was unknown, the passions of societies, undisturbed by traditionary experience, were strong, and their convictions, unmitigated by criticism, were necessarily fanatical. The Jews were looked upon in the middle ages as an accursed race, — the enemies of God and man, — the especial foes of Christianity. No one in those days paused to reflect that Christianity was founded by the Jews; that its Divine Author, in his human capacity, was a descendant of King David; that his doctrines avowedly were the completion, not the change, of Judaism; that the Apostles and the Evangelists, whose names men daily invoked, and whose volumes they embraced with reverence, were all Jews; that the infallible throne of Rome itself was established by a Jew; and that a Jew was the founder of the Christian Churches of Asia.

The European nations, relatively speaking, were then only recently converted to a belief in Moses and in Christ, and, as it were, still ashamed of the wild deities whom they had deserted, they thought they atoned for their past idolatry by wreaking vengeance on a race to whom, and to whom alone, they were indebted for the Gospel they adored.

In vindicating the sovereign right of the Church of Christ to be the perpetual regenerator of man, the writer thought the time had arrived when some attempt should be made to do justice to the race which had founded Christianity." — *Preface* to *Coningsby* (the fifth edition, 1849).

[18] See George Saintsbury: *The English Novel*. Dutton & Co., N. Y. 1913. pp. 215–216.

[19] See *A History of Nineteenth Century Literature*. 1896. pp. 160–161.

CHAPTER V 347

[20] Brandes says, in chapter XVII of his *Lord Beaconsfield: A Study*, of the religious views set forth by Disraeli in this novel: "Those who have a lively recollection of the enlightened views of the leading statesmen of the 18th century, and of their liberal way of treating of the scholastic problems here treated of in so narrow a spirit, cannot fail to regret the retrograde step; but when it is considered that Disraeli was speaking to England before the year 1848, and that his Liberal opponent, Gladstone, still in his most liberal phase ("Juventus Mundi" 1869), showed an entirely different bias on theological topics, and seriously thought he had found the Christian Trinity among the Homeric Gods, even in Poseidon's trident, we see Disraeli's doctrines of atonement and predestination in another light, and perceive that, within the prescribed limits, for a Tory, he is almost an advocate of religious Radicalism."

[21] For Disraeli's ideas about Judaism and the Jewish race see, besides the novel *Tancred*, the places in *Coningsby* already mentioned, and in *Sybil*. Also the following: The General Preface to the Novels, 1870; Disraeli's speeches on the Jewish Disabilities Bill, in the House of Commons, December 1847; also in the Commons in 1849; the Preface to the fifth edition of *Coningsby*, 1849; *Lord George Bentinck: A Political Biography* (1851), Chapters X, XXIV; *Correspondence with his sister* — 1832–1852. Cf. also, *Sybil:* chapter 12, part II (St. Lys's ideas); *Tancred:* Part II, 11; III, 4; IV, 10; IV, 15; IV, 4; and *Alroy*.

Monypenny says, in chapter 3 of the third volume of his biography, p. 61, "Disraeli's teaching is that those elements of it (modern civilization) which have their origin in a wider spread and a better comprehension of the great truths of the Old and New Testament are more vital to the greatness of a nation than those which spring from the literature of Greece, the Empire of Rome, the advance of science, and the development of invention. This, after all," Monypenny concludes, "is very much the teaching of Matthew Arnold, that the Hebrew sense of conduct is far the most important thing for man, as conduct embraces three parts of life."

[22] See various references in volumes 1 and 2 of the *Monypenny and Buckle* biography for the relations between the two men.

[23] See *One Hundred Cartoons from Mr. Punch*, published in London, 1878, mainly of Disraeli.

CHAPTER V
The Prime Minister's Contribution

[1] *Op. cit.*, pp. 61 *et seq.*

[2] The success of the book may be best summed up in the following paragraph from Mr. Buckle (V., 167). "With the appearance in November (following the outbreak of the Franco-German war in 1870) of a collected edition of Disraeli's novels, at 6s. a volume, having *Lothair* as the first volume, the '*Lothair* mania,' as Longman wrote, broke out again

'with all its virulence. Twice we have printed 5,000 copies, and now we have another 5,000 = 15,000, at press!' The book was translated into every European language, and the demand in Germany so far exceeded expectation that Baron Tauchnitz, the publisher, as Longman noted, 'doubled, *more suo*, his tribute money.' In America the sale was even greater than in England. Messrs. Appleton began by printing 25,000 copies, which were sold out in three days; and in July the demand was still a thousand copies a day. By October 80,000 copies had been sold there. Disraeli proudly claimed, in the General Preface which he wrote for the collected edition, that the book 'had been more extensively read both by the people of the United Kingdom and the United States than any work that had appeared for the last half-century.'"

³ I choose for illustration the words from a few typical criticisms of this sort:

(1) "Do not look in his (Disraeli's) books for any sincerity, any experience, any startling view, any political philosophy of experience. Be content with finding a certain vivacious wit, a sort of *brio* and 'go,' thanks to which the reader gets to the end of the volumes without too much trouble. If the metal has not the resonance that one might wish for, we are obliged to confess that the tinsel is very prettily worked and does not fail to produce a certain effect of dazzling." From *Essays in English Literature* by Edmond Scherer. Translated by Professor Saintsbury. Scribners Sons, 1891. *See the essay on* "Endymion," *pp. 236 and following.*

(2) "It is after all disappointing that the noble author after half a century of intimate knowledge of English politics, so thoroughly acquainted as he must have been with the hidden machinery of that complex matter, should not, in this his last work, give us some philosophy, either of history or of political changes . . . or of the secret of success in public life." *The Dublin Review*, volume 36, pp. 145 and following — the article on "Endymion."

(3) The last is from Julia Ward Howe who reviewed the novel in 1881 in an article entitled "English Society and 'Endymion,'" which appeared in the first volume of *The Critic* (New York), pages 30–31. "But Disraeli does not describe these excellent people (i.e. Sydney Smith, Monckton Milnes, Landseer, the Duchess of Sutherland and her brilliant daughters, Lady Blessington, the Sheridan sisters, and the Hon. Mrs. Norton who was pre-eminent in beauty and talent among the brilliant society which existed in Disraeli's early manhood). His story is like a game of chess, in which lord and lady, prelate, commoner, and man of letters are but the pieces which his skill manoeuvres on the chess board. It is a devil's game, too, in which victory rests with ambition, freighted with talent, and guided by cool judgement. . . . Heaven forbid that we should look to the England of Lord Beaconsfield for our standard of morals and manners!"

⁴ The full significance of these years may be measured by the interesting fact that of six large volumes which constitute the Monypenny and Buckle

definitive biography of Disraeli (*supra*) one full third of that work, or something close to twelve hundred quarto pages, are devoted to the years 1868 to 1881.

[5] For my summary of facts here given I am sketching an outline of the two volumes mentioned in the preceding note.

[6] Of his two predecessors, Peel had led the Conservatives in the House of Commons for 18 years and had seen it twice broken from under him; Russell led the Liberals in the Commons for 17 years and then resigned.

[7] November 25, 1875. See Monypenny and Buckle, volume 5, p. 449. Lady Bradford and her sister, Lady Chesterfield, were two of Disraeli's confidantes with whom he carried on a voluminous correspondence in his last years, after the death of his wife. The relationship between him and them forms one of the most romantic episodes in the life of an English statesman. See vols. 5 and 6.

[8] I have in mind, for one instance, Sir Gilbert Parker's play *Disraeli* which George Arliss has presented with much success in recent years in both England and America. The play embodies a few graphic incidents in Disraeli's life occurring during this period. The dramatist has, of course, taken some liberties with the actual facts which he attempts to present.

[9] Volume VI. pp. 642–643 (I quote from the fragment which Monypenny left, and which Mr. Buckle has published).

[10] Volume VI. pp. 545–546.

[11] See *The Shooting Niagara, and After?*

[12] Monypenny and Buckle, vol. VI, page 357, discuss the attacks upon Disraeli for his part in the Congress of Berlin.

[13] Letter from Disraeli to Lady Bradford discussing Gladstone. *Ibid*, VI, 180.

[14] "The greatest thing in the Disraeli biography," said the *Times* (London), upon the completion of Mr. Buckle's work, "is due to the fact that the kindness of his Majesty, the King, has now allowed for the first time the publication of these letters."

[15] Volume V, pp. 245–249.

[16] "I would inscribe this work to one whose noble spirit and gentle nature ever prompt her to sympathize with the suffering; to one whose sweet voice has often encouraged, and whose taste and judgement have ever guided, its pages; the most severe of critics, but — a perfect Wife!"

[17] James Anthony Froude: *Lord Beaconsfield — a Biography*. London, 1891.

[18] Volume III, chapter 13.

[19] So numerous were these letters between Disraeli and his sister that the earliest of them, those of the 30's, while Disraeli was abroad and was then just beginning his political life, were published in one volume in 1885, and again in 1887. The first volume of the Buckle biography contains many of them.

[20] See Buckle, vol. I, page 81.
[21] Herbert Woodfield Paul: *A Modern History of England*, in 5 vols. Macmillan, 1904–1906. See vol. II, page 318.
[22] Volume VI, pp. 554, 557.
[23] Edmond Scherer: *Essays in English Literature*, tr. Saintsbury. Pages 236 ff.
[24] *Endymion*, chapter XXIV.
[25] Volume VI, 556–557.
[26] *Endymion*, chapter LXVI.
[27] Chapter XXXVIII.
[28] Chapter XXXVIII.
[29] Chapter III.
[30] Chapter LII.
[31] Chapter LXXI.
[32] Vol. VI, p. 564.
[33] The character is best revealed in chapters XL, XLI, XLIV, LV, and in LXXXVI in which his conspiracies succeed and he gains his throne.
[34] Chapter LX.
[35] Chapter LXXXIV.
[36] Chapter XXXVI.
[37] Chapter XLII.
[38] For the means of interpreting the characters of the novel I have compared the 'Key' given in the 'Empire Edition' of Disraeli's collected works published by Dunne (*op. cit.*) and edited by Edmund Gosse, with a work of R. W. Howes: "Key to the Characters in Disraeli's novels" (Collier's, N. Y., 1907) which purports to be based upon identifications made by Lord Rowton, Disraeli's secretary. These have been checked with Buckle's list, VI, 562, 564.

CHAPTER VI

THE LITERARY SIGNIFICANCE OF BENJAMIN DISRAELI

[1] The following is the first half of a letter which Disraeli sent to Queen Victoria, upon the completion of the business — a transaction carried out with great secrecy, and without even the knowledge or the sanction of Parliament. Disraeli took the chance that after the *coup* had been made the House of Commons would reimburse the Rothschilds for the £4,000,000 purchase price which they had advanced to the Prime Minister.

"2, Whitehall Gardens, Nov. 24, 1875. Mr. Disraeli with his humble duty to your Majesty:

It is just settled: you have it, Madam! The French Government has been out-generaled. They tried too much, offering loans at an usurious rate, and with conditions, which would have virtually given them the government of Egypt.

The Khedive, in despair and disgust, offered your Majesty's Government to purchase his shares outright. He never would listen to such a proposition before.

Four millions sterling! and almost immediately. There was only one firm that could do it — Rothschilds. They behaved admirably; advanced the money at a low rate, and the entire interest of the Khedive is now yours, Madam. ...."
Quoted in Monypenny and Buckle, vol. 5, pages 448–449.

[2] *Contarini Fleming*, part III, chapt. 8.

[3] *Coningsby*, part IV, chapt. 13.

[4] Brandes: *Lord Beaconsfield — a Study*. Tr. G. Sturge. London, 1880. Page 14.

[5] Bryce: "Lord Beaconsfield" in *Studies in Contemporary Biography*.

[6] G. G. Butler: Lectures delivered at the University of Pennsylvania in 1913, and published by Murray, London, in 1914. The four were gathered under the title: *The Tory Tradition*. Cf. page 69.

[7] In 1837 Disraeli published *Venetia, or the Poet's Daughter*. This is a love-story only, in which the leading male characters are Cadurcis (Lord Byron) and Marmion Herbert (Shelley). One side of the influence of Byron upon Disraeli is transcendently displayed here, for the work is in reality a memorial to Lord Byron. For the influence of Shelley upon this novel there has been an interesting investigation made by Richard Garnett, which leaves nothing more to be said upon the subject. It consists of an address delivered before the Shelley Society in England, October 12, 1887, and is entitled *Shelley and Lord Beaconsfield*. It has been reprinted in Mr. Garnett's "Essays of an Ex-Librarian," London, 1901.

[8] This criticism is quoted by Dr. F. C. Brewster, in his volume entitled *Disraeli in Outline* and I was not more successful than Monypenny and Buckle were in finding the reference in Heine's works. (Cf. *op. cit.*, vol. I, page 192). That Heine undoubtedly made the criticism is proved by Disraeli's own reference to it in the General Preface to his Novels, published in 1870, where he speaks of the German writer's praise of his *Contarini Fleming* in the following words: "I have seen a criticism on it by Heine, of which any writer might be justly proud."

[9] Page 46.

[10] William E. Henley: *Views and Reviews*, vol. I. Essay on Disraeli, pp. 23–37.

[11] Lord John Manners: *"England's Trust and other Poems"* (London, 1841) III, page 16.

[12] *Ibid.*, pp. 95–97.

[13] Monypenny and Buckle, vol. II, page 195.

[14] *Ibid.*, chapters 11 and 12.

[15] Louis Cazamian: *Le Roman Social en Angleterre*, page 167.

[16] These quoted phrases summing up something of the place of Dickens are from Professor W. L. Cross's admirable history of *The Development of the English Novel* (Macmillan, 1906), chapter V.

[17] Renan: *Histoire des Langues Semitiques*, i, 9, 11. The idea is interestingly enforced by Carlyle in his *Life in London*, ii, 480. "The Jews," he says, "have shown no trace of humor in any period of their history."

[18] Carlyle: *The Shooting Niagara: and After.*

[19] Froude: *Life of Beaconsfield*, pp. 252–253.

[20] The letters together with a full discussion of the whole episode are best presented in Sir William Fraser's *Disraeli and his Day*, page 352; and in Monypenny and Buckle's Biography, vol. V, pp. 356–358. The entire episode is one of the most picturesque in the history of English literature, and would have delighted the author of "The Curiosities of Literature" for reasons other than family affection. It marked, of course, a splendid act on Disraeli's part.

[21] Carlyle, discussing the receipt of the Prime Minister's generous offer, remarked to his friend, Sir William Fraser, "The letter of Disraeli was flattering, generous, and magnanimous; his overlooking all that I have said and done against him was great."

Sir William Fraser: *Disraeli and His Day*, page 494.

[22] The quoted phrases describing Carlyle are Professor Saintsbury's from his essay on "Carlyle" in *The History of Nineteenth Century Literature*," page 297.

[23] The entire series of the articles is reprinted in *Whigs and Whiggism: Political Writings* by *Benjamin Disraeli*, edited with an Introduction by William Hutcheon. The Macmillan Company, New York, 1914. Cf. pp. 408–430 for text.

[24] *Coningsby*, part IV, chapter 13, closing paragraphs.

[25] Cf. *Coningsby*, part III, chapter 1.

[26] Cf. *Tancred*, book II, chapts. 10, 11, and the close of chapt. 16.

[27] Cf. *Sybil*, part III, chapter 9.

[28] See *Lothair*, chapter LXXVII for Paraclete's teachings. For his complete influence, the two succeeding chapters need also to be mentioned.

[29] Cf. *Contarini Fleming*, part I, chapters 13, 14, 22.

[30] Cf. *Vivian Grey*, volume II. Part VI, chapter 4 and many of the subsequent chapters are of importance in this connection.

[31] The quoted phrases are from Froude in his description of Carlyle's philosophy.

[32] Cf. *Chartism*, book IV, chapters 6, 7, 8. *Past and Present*, book III, chapter 3. See, also, *Shooting Niagara: and After* for Carlyle's faith in a rejuvenated aristocracy.

[33] Though obvious enough in all of Disraeli's novels beginning with *Coningsby* and ending with *Endymion*, the satirical pieces entitled *Popanilla*, *Ixion in Heaven*, and *The Infernal Marriage*, are to be especially noted. See for a discussion of these *supra.*, pp. 41–43.

[34] Cf. Carlyle in *Past and Present*, particularly book II. Compare with the teachings of this work the opinions of 'Egremont,' particularly at the closing chapters of the novel, *Sybil*, where Disraeli shows his character to

have been properly educated by his preceding experiences, the results of which he gives to Sybil: book IV, chapter 15. Note also, the picture of the model patron in 'Trafford' (in *Sybil*) and the nobleman 'St. Lys' (book II, chapters 11, 12, 14) — the ideal manner in which, according to his creator, he manages his vast estates and his peasantry. In *Coningsby* there is 'Eustace Lyle,' who carries on the same ideal tradition as 'St. Lys.' Of the estate of Henry Sydney at Beaumanoir, which Disraeli depicts as presenting the ideal relationship which should exist between lord and peasantry, he says: "The moral influence of residence furnishes some of the most interesting traits of our national manners. The presence of this power was very apparent throughout the district that surrounded Beaumanoir. The ladies of that house were deeply sensible of the responsibility of their position: thoroughly comprehending their duties, they fulfilled them without affectation, with earnestness, and with that effect which springs from a knowledge of the subject. The consequences were visible in the tone of the peasantry being superior to that which we too often witness. *The ancient feudal feeling which lingers in these sequestered haunts is an instrument which, when skilfully wielded, may be productive of vast social benefit. The Duke understood this well; and his family had imbibed all his views, and seconded them.*" — *Coningsby*, Book III, chapter 5.

[35] Cf. *Coningsby*, book IV, chapter 13.

[36] Cf., particularly, the severe attack in *A Defense of the English Constitution*, page 88, and in *Sybil*. Here Carlyle's famous phrase: "Cash-nexus the sole link between man and man" is also alluded to in the description of the model patron of labor, Trafford. "He (Trafford) felt that between them (employer and employed) there should be other ties than the payment and the receipt of wages." Book III, chapter 8, pp. 208–209, *Sybil*.

[37] Cf. *Past and Present*, book III, chapter 2, p. 126. "Our life is not a mutual helpfulness; but rather, cloaked under due laws of war named 'fair competition,' and so forth, it is a mutual hostility."

[38] *Coningsby*, book III, chapter I.

[39] Chapter VIII, pp. 165–166.

[40] Cf. *Past and Present*: book III, chapter 1, p. 118. "There is no religion: there is no God; man has lost his soul, and vainly seeks antiseptic salt."

[41] Cf. *Tancred*, parts III, chapt. 1; IV, chapt. 7; and *Coningsby*, preface to the 5th ed. of 1849.

[42] Cf. in particular *Chartism*. And, for one example, book IV, chapter 3, p. 229. "Our little isle is grown too narrow for us; but the world is wide enough yet for another six thousand years. England's sure markets will be among new colonies of Englishmen in all quarters of the Globe."

[43] Monypenny and Buckle, volume V, chapter 10.

[44] *Coningsby*, New York ed. page 373.

CHAPTER VII
ANTHONY TROLLOPE

[1] Cf. *Lord Palmerston*, English Political Leaders Series, London, 1882.

[2] Cf. *An Autobiography*, in 2 vols. Wm. Black & Sons, Edinburgh and London, 1883. *Phineas Finn* was completed in 1867.

[3] The work first appeared in *St. Paul's Magazine*, serially, from 1867 to 1869. It was then published by the magazine owners, Virtue & Co., in a 2 vol. ed.

[4] T. H. S. Escott: *Anthony Trollope* — his public services, private friends, and literary originals. London, John Lane Co., 1913.

[5] Cf. vol. IV, chapter 8 "The Prime Minister's Political Creed." I present it here as a consistent body of doctrine — as Trollope intended it to be — and avoid mentioning the interruptions of an eager disciple that are made by the author merely to break up a chapter of long reflections so that it might be readable.

[6] I am quoting here the prevailing opinion of Mr. Escott's (cf. *supra*) work, which goes so far as to say that in Thackeray you have "the man in whom Trollope saw his literary and personal ideal" (p. 131). It is to be remembered, too, that Trollope was the one chosen, in 1876, to write the *Life of Thackeray* for John Morley's "English Men of Letters Series," a work which Trollope completed three years after Thackeray's death, for it was published by Macmillan in 1879.

[7] Trollope shows this same revolt again in *The Duke's Children*, where the older son of the duke, one-time Prime Minister, breaks the traditions of his noble house by marrying an American girl, while his sister marries a commoner.

[8] A judgement given by Hawthorne in a public letter which is discussed in Hawthorne's *American Note Books* (Houghton Mifflin Co.), page 8, vol. I.

[9] See *Phineas Finn*, vol. I, chapter 10.

[10] *Phineas Finn*, vol. I, chapter 14.

[11] *The Prime Minister*, vol. I, chapter 11.

[12] *The Prime Minister*, vol. II, chapter 5.

[13] *Phineas Redux*, vol. I, chapter 22.

[14] *The Prime Minister*, vol. III, chapter 9.

[15] *Ralph the Heir*, vol. II, chapters 1 ff.

[16] *Phineas Redux*, vol. I, chapter 22.

[17] *Phineas Finn*, vol. II, chapter 19.

[18] *Phineas Finn*, vol. I, chapter 18 entitled "Mr. Turnbull."

[19] *Phineas Redux*, vol. III, chapter 26. ˙

[20] *Phineas Redux*, vol. II, chapter 6.

CHAPTER VIII
George Eliot

[1] Chapter XXX.
[2] For this historical fact I am indebted to Monypenny and Buckle, volume IV, chapter 14.
[3] George Eliot's diary, last half of volume II. In *Life and Letters of George Eliot*, ed. by Cross, Merrill and Baker, N. Y. 3 vols.
[4] Printed in Blackwood's Magazine, January 1868. Cf. pp. 1–11, volume CIII.
[5] Chapter VII.
[6] Chapter XVII.
[7] Chapter XXX–XXXIII.
[8] Chapter XXXI.

CHAPTER IX
George Meredith

[1] *Beauchamp's Career* by George Meredith. First published in book form in 1876.
[2] Cf. the poem entitled "Foresight and Patience" (National Review, 1894).
[3] Chapter IV.
[4] Chapter II.
[5] Chapter XXXVII.
[6] Chapter LV.
[7] *The Comic Spirit in Meredith* by Joseph Warren Beach. Longmans, Green & Co., New York, 1911. Cf. chapter on "Diversions," number X.
[8] Cf. his article in *Time* (London) for October, 1886.
[9] W. C. Brownell: *Victorian Prose Writers*, Chas. Scribners Sons, 1909. Cf. the chapter on "Meredith," and in particular, pp. 240–241.
[10] J. A. Hammerton: *George Meredith in Anecdote and Criticism*, Grant Richards, London, 1909. Cf. page 217.

CHAPTER X
Mrs. Humphry Ward

[1] *The New Fiction and Other Essays*, Hurst & Blackett, London. Page 49.
[2] Published in the American edition by Harper and Bros., N. Y. 2 vols. 1918.
[3] *Op. cit.* volume II, page 168.

CHAPTER XI
Mr. H. G. Wells

[1] American edition by Duffield & Company, N. Y., from the English edition first published in 1910.

[2] Cf. Professor C. D. Hazen's *Modern European History*, Henry Holt Co., 1917, pp. 478 *et seq.*

APPENDIX

An OUTLINE FOR A COURSE OF STUDY ON THE POLITICAL
AND THE SOCIAL NOVEL

PART 1. BOOKS AND WRITERS
PART 2. THE SOURCE OF THE POLITICAL NOVEL

PART 1. BOOKS AND WRITERS

(The following writers and their works are suggested as forming suitable material for a course in *Nineteenth Century Literature*, in which the social and the political life of England and of America is seen through the medium of prose fiction. The aim has been merely to suggest the names of those works which were undoubtedly written with a conscious purpose in mind. Some, therefore, of the standard writers and most of the well-known novels of the 19th century which reflect the social life of the time are not even mentioned. These will be found discussed in any good history).

(Dates mark the year of publication)

I. ENGLAND

William Godwin. *Caleb Williams* (indictment of penal methods and of man-made laws) 1794

Mrs. Amelia Opie. *Adeline Mowbray* (false educational systems) 1804

Maria Edgeworth. *Castle Rackrent; The Absentee; Patronage* 1800–1814 (education, Ireland, etc.)

ROBERT PLUMER WARD. *De Vere, or the Man of Independence* (*infra.* pp. 363–365) 1827

Lady Morgan. *Florence Macarthy* (Irish Nationalism) 1819

Bulwer-Lytton. *Paul Clifford* (English penal institutions) 1830

Harriet Martineau. *Illustrations of Political Economy*, 9 vols. 1832–1840

Mrs. Frances Trollope. *Michael Armstrong* (slavery of factory children) 1840

BENJAMIN DISRAELI. The earlier novels; the trilogy; the novels of the later years. (See above, chapts. II, III, IV, V, VI)

Charles Kingsley. *Yeast, a Problem* (the agricultural poor) 1848. *Alton Locke, Tailor and Poet* (wrongs of the working class) 1850

Mrs. Elizabeth C. Gaskell. *Mary Barton* (factory life in Manchester) 1848. *North and South* (scenes in manufacturing towns) 1855

Charlotte Brontë. *Shirley* (employees vs. introduction of new machinery) 1849

Charles Dickens. *Hard Times* (false political economy) 1854. *Little Dorritt* (debtor punishment) 1856–1857

ANTHONY TROLLOPE. The Parliamentary Series (*supra*. chapt. VII)

Charles Reade. *Put Yourself in His Place* (jealousy and prejudice of trade-unions) 1870

GEORGE ELIOT. *Felix Holt* (See above, chapt. VIII)

GEORGE MEREDITH. *Beauchamp's Career* (See above, chapt. IX)

MRS. HUMPHRY WARD. *Marcella; Sir George Tressady* (*supra*. chapt. X)

MR. H. G. WELLS. *The New Machiavelli* (See above, chapt. XI)

II. AMERICA

Albion Tourgée. *Bricks without Straw; A Fool's Errand* (political status of the South). *The Invisible Empire* (Ku Klux activities)

Edgar Lee Masters. *Children of the Market Place* (politics of the Lincoln-Douglas period)

WINSTON CHURCHILL. *The Crisis* (fierce political movements of the Civil War). *Mr. Crewe's Career; Coniston* (*supra*. chapt. XIII)

John Hay. *The Breadwinners* (old economic order against demands of labor)

John Hume Ferguson (Wyllis Niles, *pseud*.). *Five Hundred Majority or the Days of Tammany*

Edward Bellamy. *Looking Backward* (Principles of the Nationalist Party)

HENRY ADAMS. *Democracy* (See above, chapt. XII)

Francis Marion Crawford. *An American Politician*

James L. Ford. *Hot Corn Ike* (the Boss in New York and Coney Island)

Frances Hodgson Burnett. *Through One Administration* (woman used for base political ends)

W. O. Stoddard. *Crowded Out of Crowfield* (Cleveland's early life)

PAUL LEICESTER FORD. *The Honorable Peter Stirling* (See above, chapt. XIV)

Hamlin Garland. *A Spoil of Office* (Western politics)

Ellen Glasgow. *The Voice of the People; One Man in His Time* (Virginia politics)

Thomas Nelson Page. *John Marvel, Assistant*

Brand Whitlock. *The 13th Ward* (the professional politician); *Her Infinite Variety* (women in politics)

Jerome K. Jerome. *All Roads lead to Calvary*

Frank Norris. *The Octopus* (railroads and wheat); *The Pit* (wheat speculation in Chicago)

Upton Sinclair. *The Jungle* (Chicago stockyards); *King Coal*

Jack London. *The Iron Heel* (Socialism)

PART 2. THE SOURCE OF THE POLITICAL NOVEL

(AN OUTLINE OF THE NOVEL WITH A PURPOSE)

A heritage which resolves itself into a tradition is, in art as in human life, rooted in many persons and in various precedents and works.

Daniel Defoe, in the early decades of the eighteenth century, expressed at once the didactic purpose, the strong moral emphasis, which is so peculiar in marking the tone and form of much of the literature of his generation. In *Robinson Crusoe* (1719), the first realistic novel of our language, we have the first purpose-novel. Living on an island, out of the pale of man's law, the hero never forgets that he is responsible to a God above for his manifold blessings, he is always aware that he cannot escape from his own conscience, and he attains the full dignity of manhood only after he has beaten Friday at his theological sophistries, and converted him to a belief in an Omnipotent God. In *Moll Flanders* (1722) Defoe sets forth his completely didactic purpose in the *Preface* to his work. As we follow the history of this extraordinary creature we are not only introduced to the miseries and the misfortunes which beset youth in a great metropolitan centre (to be treated later in an industrial world by both Dickens and Disraeli), but we watch the infinite misery of a sinner who, after arriving at Newgate, gets no satisfaction from repentance when she knows that it has come after the power of sinning further has already been removed from her. An analogous character in a psychological sense portrayed in later nineteenth century was Paula Tanqueray, whose infinite misery Pinero showed as coming upon her after she was made aware that repentance had come too late, so that— as a result of modern convention — she saw no release except through self-destruction. Moll, a decidedly simpler character and infinitely more depraved, tells us at the close of her story, however, that both she and her husband, after having 'served their sentences' and learned their lessons, resolved "to spend the remainder of our years in sincere penitence for the wicked lives we have lived."

The moral fervor of these works, and their didactic purpose, clothes itself in other means but serves an end no less significant in Richardson and in Fielding. (For *Tom Jones*, see the dedication — ". . . simple endeavor has been to recommend Goodness and Innocence. . . .") In the preface of *Roderick Random* (1748) Smollett says: "I have attempted to represent modest merit struggling with every difficulty to which a friendless orphan is exposed, from his own want of experience, as well as from the selfishness, envy, malice, and base indifference of mankind." In painting the misfortunes of his character, and the abuses of society which these reveal, the author devotes a considerable number of his chapters to expose the evils that then existed in the English navy. (See chapts. 24, 26–30, 34, 35). Abuses of a different sort such as Charles Reade exposed almost a century later in *It's Never Too Late to Mend* appear in *The Vicar of Wakefield* of 1766. If Goldsmith borrows much Richardsonian sentiment wherewith to fortify his 18th century lessons of fortitude and prudential morality, the graphic portion of the work which teaches the world what untold misery is heaped upon the debtors who must live in English jails is the peculiar product of his own experiences. (See chapts. 26-27). From a disciple we turn to the master. The four-square moralist of the eighteenth century opens *The History of Rasselas* with the following: "Ye who listen with credulity to the whispers of fancy, and pursue with eagerness the phantoms of hope; who expect that age will perform the promises of youth, and that the deficiencies of the present day will be supplied by the morrow; attend to the history of Rasselas, prince of Abissinia." And concluding his novel which treats of the vanity of human wishes Samuel Johnson lets the Princess say that of all sublunary things Knowledge was the best; so she prepares to found a college of learned women where there might be reared for the next age models of prudence and patterns of piety. From Samuel Johnson it is but a short step to pure pedagogy. In *The Fool of Quality* (1766) Henry Brooke, amid a diversity of interest, still manages to set up a pattern of virtue in the young earl of Moreland — product of unsophisticated morality and of an unfettered and natural education. (See chapt. 11, and the Preface). Twenty years after came a natural child born of the last-named work. In Thomas Day's *Sandford and Merton* (1783-1789) a thoroughly spoiled and youthful aristocrat named Merton receives a remarkable education from an honest youth of the common people named Sandford. Though a child of Henry Brooke's pedagogical fiction, in order of time *Sandford and Merton* shows more direct inspiration from Rousseau's *Émile*.

The influence of Rousseau and of the teachings of the French Revolution fell potently upon the English revolutionist William Godwin. His preface to *Things as they are; or the Adventures of Caleb Williams* (1794) prepares us for "a general review of the modes of domestic and unrecorded despotism by which man becomes the destroyer of man." In this polemical work the author shows off 'the corruptions of the aristocrat,' 'the ingrained cowardices of an overgoverned mankind,' the rottenness of the English penal methods, and the absurdities of law made by society when contrasted with the natural virtues of uncorrupted man. This work, by which Godwin popularized his essay on *Political Justice*, was deliberately intended as a vehicle for propaganda; as a means for preaching a sermon engagingly upon public matters. It was the most perfect thesis-novel in the language. The connecting link between this thesis-novel and the political novels of Disraeli, is to be found later in Robert Plumer Ward's *De Vere, or the Man of Independence*.

Just as William Godwin is said to have put the substance of the ideas he held in common with his devoted friend, Thomas Holcroft, into his *Political Justice*, Holcroft on his side set forth his own political creed in the preceding year in his *Anna St. Ives* (1792). To the lives and theories of both Godwin and Mary Wollstonecraft we may note two immediate contemporary reactions in *novels with a purpose*. Charles Lloyd in *Edmund Oliver* (1798) tells us that he has written his novel to counteract that generalizing spirit, that indefinite benevolence of certain 'modern philosophers,' and aims his book in particular against Godwin, and his ideas on marriage. Of a different sort was *Adeline Mowbray* (1804), wherein Mrs. Amelia Opie paints the practical results of an educational system which ignores the cumulative experience of ages by its effect upon a daughter who is taught by her lover and her mother to believe in 'free love.' In Godwin's Circle stands Shelley, whose address to the Irish Nation flung from the balcony of a house in Dublin reminds us of the attempt of writers at the turn of the century to cry out in the name of that people. First of these was Maria Edgeworth to whose novels about Ireland Walter Scott paid so gracious and gallant a tribute when he said, in 1829, that to these he owed the inspiration to do for his own country what they had done for Ireland. In *Castle Rackrent* (1800), in *The Absentee* (1812), and in *Patronage* (1814) we may see what the father of Maria Edgeworth meant in this preface: "It has been my daughter's aim to promote, by all her writings, the progress of education from the cradle to the grave." In the purely nationalistic Irish story entitled *Florence Macarthy* (1819) Lady Morgan sketches 'the brilliant aspect of a people struggling with adversity, and by delineation of national virtues, to excite sympathy, and to awaken justice.' It is interesting to note that one of the group of political adventurers painted in this work, Con Crawley, was the caricature of the John Wilson Croker whom both Disraeli and Thackeray used later, the first-named writer converting him into the inimitable Rigby of *Coningsby*.

In 1827 appeared *De Vere*. This contribution of Robert Plumer Ward, as has already been pointed out, marks in the most complete manner the transition from the thesis-novel to the political novels of Disraeli. The author, himself a man of some political experience, tells us, in the opening pages of his work, what his purpose was in writing it. He would show how the passions of Ambition and of Independence, — among the greatest of those which govern mankind — once they seize upon their victim, if they are not tempered by Conscience and guided by Reason, breed monsters! When a man seeks idolatry for himself, and grasps at place and power at the price of character, he will thrust aside all the recognized principles of law and honor, and, in his determination to gain his ends, will sacrifice the tenderest of human relations — the devotion of friends and the love of his wife and his children. Ward would inveigh against the sin of Hypocrisy, which is the besetting sin of the age: hypocrisy in society, in private life, but most of all in public affairs. He proposes to show how the passions level all distinctions of rank, and that true happiness and the greatest contentment may often lie as much in the quiet by-ways of life as in the great Courts and Houses of Parliament. I have said that this novel relates itself to Godwin's *Caleb Williams*, — that it is essentially a novel with a purpose. There is this difference, however, between the two thesis-novels, a difference great enough to tie Ward closely to Disraeli's early work: whereas Godwin's book is a diatribe against society in general, and the English aristocracy in particular, Plumer Ward chooses to be analytic, and to focus his attention upon the human heart and mind when under the influence of two great passions. The first of these is 'the pride of Independence.' This, he explains to us in the preface of the work, is "to bear up the hero under all his reverses, and is the main cause of much of the action." The second is Ambition. He would show to what lengths this passion may drive a man.

Now, where Ward employs politics in his novel, he does so merely to provide the proper *scenery* for setting off 'the pride of Independence' and the passion of Ambition in action. It is never for him, what it became in Disraeli's great political novels, the raw material of life. Ward's aim is to present a detached, philosophic romance, partly against a political back-ground. When other 'spheres and aspects' can serve to illus-trate his sermon, he employs them generously. Thus, almost the entire third volume of the novel deals with matters not at all political. There is still another distinction between this work and those of the political *genre*. The political novelist generally, and Disraeli in particular, aims to show political life in *action:* the hero aways 'gets into the fight,' and is either successful in attaining his political goal, or else is broken upon the wheel of political fortune. Ward's hero is actually an on-looker, a disciple to others, a philosopher musing upon the for-tunes of those who are active participants in the game. Having a purpose so objective as he does, Ward thinks it profitable enough to make so much of characters in his story who act only the Sir Oracles to De Vere: thus the men like Flowerdale, Harclai, and Dr. Herbert, preach long sermons upon their own past experiences, or upon the characters of others who had been at one time in the public service, but do not themselves engage in action before us.

But all this was quite enough for Benjamin Disraeli. His swiftly active mind was ready to seize upon any means at hand which might further his own ambitions. That he was thoroughly familiar with the works of Plumer Ward before any of his novels following *Vivian Grey* were published, is perfectly clear. The Disraeli family had rented Plumer Ward's residence, Hyde House near Amersham, in 1825, the year that Ward's *Tremaine* appeared. In that house Disraeli wrote his *Vivian Grey* in 1826. Mrs. Austen, whom Monypenny, Disraeli's biographer, calls Disraeli's Egeria, was the wife of Plumer Ward's solicitor, and was in Ward's confidence no less than her husband was, who had negotiated for the publication of Ward's earlier novel. These fortuitous circumstances only serve to show the more certainly wherein Ward's *De Vere* became the ultimate inspiration for the development of Disraeli's political novels.

But let us resume the narrative which traces the thesis-novel to the middle of the century.

The moral deterioration of a youth of brilliant parts due to prevalent social conditions is what we follow in a work that shows, on the one side a strong influence of Godwin's revolutionary doctrines, and which on the other must itself have exerted an influence upon Benjamin Disraeli when he produced *Sybil* in 1845. For the year 1830, Bulwer-Lytton's *Paul Clifford* was a powerful novel. Its hero is a robber whose fortunes we follow from the time that his mother dies, betrayed by her husband — a man who eventually rises in the law to the dignity of Chief Baron, — to Paul's own full manhood where he is obliged, because of an unjust punishment meted out to him for a theft he never committed in his early youth, to practice, for self-preservation and for revenge upon the Society which unjustly put him in prison, the teachings that had been forced upon him in the House of Correction. Bulwer frankly avows his main purpose in writing the novel. (See, especially, chapt. 35). It was to draw attention to two errors in the English penal institutions: the habit of corrupting the boy by the very punishment that ought to redeem him, and then hanging the man, at the first occasion, as the easiest way of getting rid of the blunders originally made. In the drawing the author makes of the father of the youth Clifford, Sir William Brandon, and of the selfish aristocrat Lord Mauleverer, we are furnished the expression of the author's second purpose in writing the novel. This was, namely, to show that there is nothing essentially different between vulgar vice and fashionable vice, — that the slang of one circle is but an easy paraphrase to the cant of the other. (See chapts. 18, 31, 33, 34, 35). The injustice of human law, satire upon the smug complacency of the Bishops of the Church toward the many social evils that should be corrected, and the sympathy which the author would draw from us for the poor and the unfortunate in humanity who have been made so by the selfishness of the wealthy, make this book an immediate part of the Victorian literature devoted to Social Reform. Two years after the publication of this work the first Reform Act was passed, and within the decade there opened those flood-gates of sentiment which had been provoked by the pauperism induced by the Poor Laws, the economic hardships which brought on the Chartist Rebellion, the grinding poverty and ignorance which came in the train of the opening of the great manufacturing centres; and lesser evils, foreign as well as domestic, which made the literature of the next twenty years virile with its conscious mission to startle a world of thinking men and women into activity. The torch was to be fed from now on with mightier fuel, and was to be kept trimmed by many hands of various persons. Since we are for the moment still following the course of the *novel with a purpose* it will be well to dispose of its subsequent history in a brief resumé.

In Mrs. Frances Trollope's *Michael Armstrong* (1840) we have the prototype of Disraeli's factory boy, Devilsdust, created five years later. In the pictures which are here presented of the Lancashire mills and the Deep Valley 'prentice prison house we watch the slavery of the children, stunted, ignorant, infected with loathsome disease, and we stand by the death-bed of Sir Matthew Dowling, with a belief that the ghosts of several hundred little ones of whose death he was the cause hover around him and haunt him. *Alton Locke* takes up a similar theme in 1845-50, when Kingsley paints the miseries of the workingmen, and the consumptive and rickety children and the miserable dwellings. The main purpose of all in writing this work was — as he told the Cambridge Undergraduates in 1861, — "to express what I knew were the feelings of clever workingmen looking upon the superior educational advantages of our class." With a work of this sort the doctrines of Christian Socialism which Kingsley sponsored were well launched. How far the problem of social welfare is a church problem brings us to his *Yeast* (1848) and asks a question which Disraeli answered in his own fashion in *Sybil*. By the side of Kingsley stands Mrs. Gaskell. If Disraeli finds a political solution for bridging the gap between the Two Nations, viz., the rich and the poor, *Mary Barton* (1848) goes directly to Christ and Christianity for its solution. The destitution of the manufacturing districts, especially those of Manchester, the woes of the workingmen to whom "machines is the ruin of poor folk," the loneliness of the uneducated masses, and the dangers of the murder of their own children, by misunderstood employees, which men like Harry Carson's father are apt to face — all these things can be removed, asserts Mrs. Gaskell, by making the spirit of

Christ the motivating force and the regulating law between the two classes. The same note of Christian intervention as a solution of the problems between employer and employed appears in *North and South* (1855). Another woman novelist, Charlotte Bronté, paints in *Shirley* (1849) the tragedy that comes about in the lives of the handworkers at the looms when machinery takes their work from them, and shows at the same time the difficulties of the manufacturers who have to meet the new problems which the march of a new industrial age brings. Charles Dickens, in *Hard Times* (1854) reflects (a fact already pointed out), in his portraits of Gradgrind and Bounderby, the evidences of a false political economy which can permit such men as these are to own the mill hands; by his own realistic methods, he arouses our sympathy for the mill workers. In a later work, *Little Dorritt* (1855-1857), his purpose is to show how a debtor's prison unfits men for remaining normal social beings after their discharge. He thus broadens out in Victorian literature an idea launched earlier by Goldsmith in *The Vicar of Wakefield*.

INDEX

Judas Maccabaeus, 144
Julius Caesar, 4, 16.

Kebbel, T. E., 77, 143
Keferinis, Prime Minister to Astarte, 87
Khedive of Egypt, 143, 146
Kingsley, Charles, 29, 159, 160
Kipling, Rudyard, 2, 3

Lady Beaumaris, 131, 133
Lady Bertie and Bellair, 82, 181
Lady Bertram, 115–116, 120
Lady Blessington, 122
Lady Bradford, 122
Lady Chesterfield, 120, 122
Lady Constance Rawleigh, 82
Lady Corisande, 102
Lady Firebrace, 76, 181
Lady Gaverstock, 182
Lady Glencora Palliser, 199, 200
Lady Hampshire, 83
Lady Holland, 141
Lady Jersey, 141
Lady Laura Standish, 197, 198, 199, 205, 209
Lady Mable Grex, 212
Lady Marney, 76
Lady Montford, (Berengaria, Queen of Society), 130, 131, 132, 137, 139
Lady of Bethany, 84
Lady St. Julians, 76
Lancashire, 127
Land League, 100
Leander, Chef, 181
Leonore, 326 ff.
Lewis, Mrs. Wyndham, 46
Liberals, 98
Life of Lord Palmerston, 186
Lightfoot Lee, Mrs., 290 ff.
Literary Significance of Benjamin Disraeli, The, chapt. VI, pp. 143–184
Liverpool, Earl of, 69
London Times articles of Disraeli, 165–167

Longman, the publisher, 20
Lopez, a young adventurer, 203, 204, 211
Lord Beaumaris, 133
Lord Chiltern, 207
Lord Dunbeg, 293
Lord Eskdale, 82
Lord Fitzheron, 72
Lord Walter Frewen, 80–81
Lord Grey, 68
Lord Marney, 72, 75
Lord Maxwell, 255, 257
Lord Milford, 72
Lord Monmouth, 64, 65, 69
Lord Montford, 127, 130–131, 142
Lord Palmet, 241, 248
Lord Pomeroy, 134
Lord Roehampton, 128, 131, 136, 141
Lord St. Aldegonde, 106, 181
Lord Silverbridge, 211, 216
Lord Skye, 293
Lothair, 97–109 (main discussion), 146, 168, 182, 208
Lowell, James Russell, 2, 28, 80, 317
Lucretius, quoted, 22
Lyle, Eustace, 62, 63, 157

Mabie, Hamilton Wright, 308
Macaulay, Thomas B., 64, 224
Macdonald, Alexander, 175
Machiavelli, Niccolo, 275
MacKnight, Thos., *The Right Honorable Benjamin Disraeli*, 78, 95
Madame Goesler, 195, 205–206, 216
Madre Natura in Italy, 105
Magog Wrath, 69
Manchester, 71, 136, 173
Manchester School, 49
Manners, Lord John, 156–157
Marcella, by Mrs. Humphry Ward, 257–259, 260, 264
Mary Anne, 121
Mary Anne associations of France, 104, 105
Maximus, Sir, 230

Working Class in Tory Democracy, 59

Writer's Recollections, A, by Mrs. Humphry Ward, 256, 264

Yeast, 160
Young Duke, The, 40–41
Young England, 56, 61, 63, 74, 88, 98, 145, 152, 155–158 (in relation to Disraeli), 178, 282

Young Germany, 155
Young Italy, 145, 155
Young Syria, 89

Zanoni, 63
Zenobia, 133, 141